CORRUPTION: THE ENEMY WITHIN

Corruption: The Enemy Within

Edited by

Barry Rider

Institute of Advanced Legal Studies
University of London

KLUWER LAW
INTERNATIONAL

THE HAGUE · LONDON · BOSTON

Published by Kluwer Law International
P.O. Box 85889
2508 CN The Hague, The Netherlands

Sold and distributed in the USA and Canada by
Kluwer Law International
675 Massachusetts Avenue
Cambridge, MA 02139, USA

Sold and distributed in all other countries by
Kluwer Law International
Distribution Centre
P.O. Box 322
3300 AH Dordrecht, The Netherlands

A C.I.P. Catalogue record for this book is available from the Library of Congress

Printed on acid-free paper

Cover design: Robert Vulkers

ISBN 90 411 0712 6

© 1997 Kluwer Law International

Kluwer Law International incorporates the publishing programmes of Graham & Trotman Ltd, Kluwer Law and Taxation Publishers and Martinus Nijhoff Publishers

Table of Contents

Director of the Counselling Centre, Director of Placement, Assistant to the Vice President for Student Development.

Raymond KENDALL has been Secretary General of the ICPO-Interpol (whose headquarters are located in Lyons, France) since 1985 and is currently serving his third five-year term of office. Before being elected Secretary General he previously served at Interpol Headquarters as Head of Police Division (1976–1985) and prior to that as Head of the Drugs Sub-Division (1971–1975). Raymond Kendall also served as Deputy Assistant Commissioner (CID), mostly in the Special Branch of the Metropolitan Police at New Scotland Yard (1962–1986). He graduated from Exeter College, University of Oxford with a modern languages honours degree and has a Master of Arts. He has been awarded the Queen's Police Medal for Distinguished Police Service and similar distinctions from other countries such as Chile, Spain, Peru, Russia and France where he has recently been appointed a Chevalier de la Légion d'Honneur.

Professor Michael LEVI is Professor of Criminology at the Univeristy of Wales, Cardiff. Most of his research and writings have been on the prevention and criminal processoing of white-collar and organized crime – including money laundering and asset confiscation – and in 1997, he was appointed by the Council of Europe as their scientific expert on a new major initiative on organized crime. Professor Levi obtained a M.A. from the University of Oxford, a Diploma in Criminology from the Institute of Criminology, University of Cambridge and Ph.D from the University of Southampton. He has directed a number of research programmes and has been a consultant to various inter-governmental organizations. He has written widely on criminology, particularly in regard to the control of white collar crime and money laundering.

Ms Robin MACKENZIE teaches Banking and Finance and Intellectual Property Law at the University of Kent at Canterbury. She publishes in both areas from the perspective of economic crime and risk management. She has previously taught in Scotland and New Zealand, and is a member of the Kent Criminal Justice Centre. She is a graduate from the University of Canterbury (New Zealand) and Otago University Law School (New Zealand). She is a member of the editorial board of *Feminist Legal Studies*.

George J. MOSCARINO is a Cleveland partner and trial attorney for the international law firm of Jones, Day, Reavis & Pogue. He is Chairman of the Corporate Criminal Investigations Section of the Firm's Litigation Group. His criminal defence and white-collar practice involves complex criminal litigation and government and grand jury investigations. His practice is international in scope and he has been frequently involved in matters in Europe, Asia, and the USA. Mr Moscarino has represented national and international banks in criminal and civil bank secrecy matters, and currently represents First American Bank in litigation matters related to the BCCI and Manuel Noriega scandals. Mr Moscarino is a Fellow of the American College of Trial Lawyers, a former Assistant Attorney General and Assistant County Prosecutor, Ohio and has been listed in the Criminal Litigation Section of 'The Best Lawyers in America'.

Denis OSBOURNE is an advisor on governance and development, and training, and an Associate of the Institute for Development Policy and Management at the University of Manchester. In the last five years he has undertaken consultancies on governance in twenty-eight countries in four continents, and studied initiatives to combat corruption. Dr Osbourne served in Malawi as the British High Commissioner from 1987 to 1990, and in the Overseas Development Administration (now the Department for International Development) from 1972. From 1957 to 1972 he lectured in universities in Britain and Africa, being Professor of Physics in the University of Dar es Salaam from 1966 to 1971 and Dean of Science. He is a Companion of the Order of St Michael and St George (CMG) and a Fellow of the Institute of Physics.

Wilmer 'Buddy' PARKER recently accepted an appointment as Partner to the Atlanta-based international law firm Kilpatrick Stockton LLP to head its Criminal Defence and Special Matters Group. Prior to this appointment, Mr Parker was in government service first as a Trial Attorney in the Department of Justice, Washington D.C. and later as an Assistant US Attorney in Atlanta where he headed the Organized Crime Drug Enforcement Task Forces for the south-eastern United States. Mr Parker is one of the pioneers of money laundering prosecutions and while in government service received on five separate occasions national awards for his trial advocacy skills. A specialist in racketeering cases involving corruption, Mr Parker received his B.S. in Commerce, Masters of Business Administration and Juris Doctorates from the University of Alabama and his LLM (Taxation) from Emory University. He is a member of the bars of Georgia, Florida and Alabama.

Marvin G. PICKHOLZ received his A.B., L.L.B. and L.L.M. from New York University. He is a partner of Hoffman Pollok & Pickholz LLP in New York City. He has served in various positions with the Securities and Exchange Commission's Division of Enforcement and its New York Regional Office; the last of these positions was as Assistant Director of the Division of Enforcement. He serves on the editorial advisory boards of several publications including the *Securities Regulation Law Journal*, the *RICO Law Reporter*, and the *Journal of Financial Crime*. He is the author of numerous articles on the federal securities laws, white collar crime, the Foreign Corrupt Practices Act and authored the treatise *Securities Crimes*, part of the Clark Boardman Callaghan Securities Law Series.

Professor Barry A.K. RIDER is a Professor of Law at the University of London and Director of the Institute of Advanced Legal Studies. He is also a Fellow and former Dean of Jesus College, University of Cambridge. Professor Rider has taken doctorates in Law from both the University of London and the University of Cambridge and has been awarded an LL.D from The Dickinson School of Law in the USA. He is a also a member of the English Bar. Professor Rider was head of the Commonwealth Commercial Crime Unit from 1981 to 1989 and has served as an advisor to a number of governmental agencies on the prevention and control of economic crime and corruption. He is Executive Director of The Centre for Documentation on Organized and Economic Crime, Cambridge and has been the Director of the annual International Symposium on Economic Crime in Cambridge since its inception fifteen years ago.

Henry H. ROSSBACHER is a member of the Bars of both New York and California as well as numerous federal courts, including the Supreme Court of the United States. He has practised law for over 25 years. Included in his experience are seven years as Assistant United States Attorney and Senior Litigation Counsel for the Department of Justice in Los Angeles and two years as Adjunct Professor of Law at the UCLA School of Law. He also served as Deputy General Counsel of the New York State Special Commission on Attica. Mr Rossbacher is a graduate of the Wharton School of Finance and Commerce of the University of Pennsylvania and of the University of Virginia Law School. At present, he heads a law firm in Los Angeles with a wide litigation and appellate practice while also acting as Advisory Counsel to the Office of Independent Counsel re Secretary of Agriculture. He sits on the Civil RICO Subcommittee of the Antitrust Committee and the White Collar Crime Committee of the American Bar Association.

Professor Brice DE RUYVER is Professor of Criminal Law at the University of Ghent and Director of the Research Group Drug Policy, Criminal Policy, International Crime of the University of Ghent. Professor De Ruyver has taken doctorate in Criminology from the University of Ghent. In addition to his research and advise to a number of governmental agencies, he has served as an expert for the Parliamentary Enquiry Commission on Human Trafficking in 1993 and has acted since 1996 as expert for the Parliamentary Enquiry Commission on the investigation into the *Dutroux and Co* Case.

Professor Ernesto U. SAVONA is professor of Criminology and Director of the TRANSCRIME research group on transnational crime, at the Faculty of Law, University of Trento. He took his law degree from the University of Palermo and conducted post graduate research at the University of Rome. He was elected, in June 1996, a member of the Criminological and Scientific Council of the Council of Europe, and is responsible for the 'Octopus' project – promoted by the European Union and the Council of Europe, on organized crime and corruption in Eastern European countries. For three years (1990–1994) he was project director at the National Institute of Justice, Research Centre of the US Department of Justice, Washington D.C., on organized crime and international money laundering. He has been visiting professor at a number of universities including Yale Law School, Berkeley, Montreal and Oxford. He has published a large number of papers and books on the relationship between organizational crime and criminal justice systems and other issues in criminology. He is a frequent speaker at international conferences.

Dr. Ibrahim SHIHATA is Senior Vice President and General Counsel of the World Bank and Secretary-General of the International Centre for Settlement of Investment Disputes (Washington DC). He is Chairman of the Board of the International Development Law Institute (Rome), a member of the Institut de Droit International (Geneva), and a member of the boards of a number of international development and international law institutes and associations. An Egyptian national, with a law degree and two diplomas from Cairo University and a Doctorate in Juridical Science from Harvard, Mr Shihata was the first Director-General of the OPEC Fund for International Development, Executive Director of the International Fund for Agricultural Development, past Legal Advisor of the Kuwait Fund for Arab Economic Development, and a member of the Faculty of Law of Ain Shams University, Cairo, and of the Egyptian Conseil d'Etat. He has published extensively on international law, foreign investment and international development issues. Mr Shihata received honorary doctor or laws degrees from the University of Dundee, United Kingdom, and the University of Paris I (Panthéon-Sorbonne), France.

Michael R. SHUMAKER is an associate in the Litigation Section of Jones, Day, Reavis & Pogue's Litigation Group in Washington, D.C. His practice deals with corporate litigation and investigations and related proceedings including civil, administrative and criminal litigation, and he has considerable experience in national and international bank secrecy matters. Mr Shumaker is admitted to practice law in both Pennsylvania and the District of Columbia. He is a graduate of Lafayette College and the University of Notre Dame.

Susan TAYLOR is a Branch Crown Prosecutor in Central Casework, Crown Prosecution Service. She is a graduate of Leeds University and a member of the English Bar. She is joint author of *Confiscation and the Proceeds of Crime* published by Sweet and Maxwell and a former member of the Home Office Working Group on Confiscation.

by design unlikely to be over-effective. In the area of economic abuse, there is not a seamless web of moral principle. Much depends on the time and place! Having said this, however, it is right and proper that those aspects of the problem of, for example, corruption, which are inimical to us all, are identified and dealt with on the broadest possible basis. It is our hope that the Fourteenth International Symposium on Corruption – the enemy within – went some way towards doing this, and it is also our hope that this volume will take the march, if not the crusade, a little further.

Putting together a work of this nature necessitates the support of a number of people. Obviously we wish to acknowledge the help of those whose papers have been included, but even more so the generosity of those who contributed excellent papers to the Symposium and who have exhibited understanding in accepting that we cannot carry them in this volume. Of course, many have been published separately, not least in the *Journal of Financial Crime*, which is the official journal of the Symposium. It is also necessary to acknowledge the help of those who organized the Fourteenth Symposium, those who spoke and, of course, those who attended as delegates. The present work does attempt to reflect, in the selection of papers – many of which were subsequently revised –, the contribution of all those who participated in the programme. The contribution of the Symposium Chairman, Mr. Saul Froomkin QC, the Chairman of CIDOEC, his Co-Chairman Mr. T.M. Ashe QC, the Honorary General Counsel of CIDOEC, the convenors, Ms. Chizu Nakajima, of the City University Business School, Mr. Michael Ricks, Director of Information, CIDOEC; Mr. Mads Andenas, of Kings College, University of London, Mr. Tarrant Green, of the IALS, Dr. George Gilligan, of the Department of Criminology of the University of Middlesex, Mrs. Anita Bishop, of the IALS and Mrs. Ruth Easthope of Jesus College, Cambridge, must also be acknowledged. Last, but certainly in no way least, I must acknowledge the support that we have received in Cambridge from the organizing institutions of the annual symposium over so many years. The preparation of this book, like the annual symposium, teaches us something about the fight against economic crime, and in particular corruption – you cannot do it on your own!

I. The Nature of the Problem

DENIS OSBORNE

1. Corruption as Counter-culture: Attitudes to Bribery in Local and Global Society*

INTRODUCTION

1. The purpose of this paper is to examine the basis for seeking cooperation between people of different nations and cultures in fighting corruption.

2. Such cooperation is important to protect existing cultures and for development, trade and global security, but there are several obstacles. Political leaders in some countries argue that allegations about corruption are based on misunderstanding, and resent them as attempts at external interference, especially when they are made by investors or representatives of governments or agencies that give aid. Western business people speak of adapting their behaviour to local custom, which they believe to include generous gifts or bribes, and there are complaints that in so doing they introduce corruption on a previously unimagined scale. Nongovernmental organizations cause disquiet if they appear accountable only to their own constituencies, or have a hidden agenda, or if they are interfering or judgmental or over-concerned to win recognition for their own role in fighting corruption. Postmodern thinkers argue for local diversity, and against meta-narratives. All these make it hard to seek universally accepted ideas or to agree on global standards of behaviour.

3. In this paper we shall focus on bribery as one aspect of corruption. We shall consider how bribes are viewed in major cultural traditions, followed

* I wish to thank the British Government's Overseas Development Administration (now the Department for International Development) for supporting a study of Development, Aid and Better Government between November 1990 and September 1992, and several Governments and Donor Agencies for contracts more recently. I am grateful for lessons learned from participants when I directed seminars on preventing fraud and corruption for RIPA International in London in 1995 and 1996, and helped at seminars on this theme during 1995 in Ghana, Russia and Nicaragua; and from participants at the Fourteenth International Symposium on Economic Crime, Cambridge, Britain, 1996. The views expressed are personal and do not represent the people or organizations whose help I acknowledge.

Barry A.K. Rider (ed.), Corruption: The Enemy Within, 9–34
© *Kluwer Law International. Printed in the Netherlands.*

by descriptions of corruption in various countries and the idioms used in contemporary society. The purpose of this is to establish links between local customs and business practice in a global economy. The study leading to this paper is part of a broader programme aimed at helping governments improve the quality of their governance and thus benefit all their citizens.

4.   People pay bribes to get things done. They want the recipient to show them a favour, perhaps awarding a contract unfairly or waiving a fine they ought to pay. Or they may want the recipient to act more quickly. Bribes may take many forms, from cash to sexual favours to honorary degrees. Not all bribes are illegal, but in nearly all countries it is against the law for public servants to receive or ask for bribes. In many countries it is also against the law to pay or offer bribes to public servants.

5.   Definitions have been considered in detail by Theobald,[1] Werlin,[2] and other writers but those preferred for this paper are relatively simple. A *bribe* is a reward to pervert the judgement or corrupt the conduct.[3] Bribery is one form of *corruption*, a loss of purity and purpose, a social decomposition.[4] Where employees will not do what they ought to do without payment of a bribe the act is *extortion*, taking forcefully and unlawfully money or things of value that are not their due. Intimidation and protection rackets are extreme forms of extortion. Bribery may be associated with *fraud*, understood as criminal deception, false representation to obtain unjust advantage. Some see these and all definitions as necessarily culture-loaded.

6.   There are several classifications for bribes and corruption, using the apparent causes, consequences, or context as a basis for that classification. A distinction is made between *bureaucratic corruption* (officials taking bribes) and *political corruption* – which includes politicians taking bribes to award contracts, paying bribes to influence elections, and using their position to provide patronage. The organization Transparency International deals with *grand corruption*, which George Moody-Stuart[5] describes as 'the misuse of public power by heads of state, ministers and top officials for private, pecuniary profit'.

---

[1] R. Theobald, *Corruption, Development and Underdevelopment*, Durham, USA, Duke University Press, (1990).

[2] Herbert H. Werlin, 'Revisiting Corruption: With a New Definition', *International Review of Administrative Sciences* 60 (1994), 547–558.

[3] Johnson's *Dictionary* (1535), quoted in *The Shorter Oxford English Dictionary*, Oxford, The Clarendon Press (1973).

[4] This and subsequent definitions based on *The Shorter Oxford English Dictionary, op. cit.*

[5] George Moody-Stuart, *Grand Corruption in Third World Development*, Oxford, WorldView Publishing, 1997, p. 2.

ATTITUDES TO BRIBERY IN DIFFERENT TRADITIONS
AND SOME WORDS FROM THE PAST

7.   In most cultures ethics are related closely to religion, to founding figures and leaders and to sacred texts. An examination of religious writings suggests that there are many common features in the traditional ethics of different societies. Thus murder is thought wrong, though views differ on whether one may kill in war or for self-defence or as capital punishment. Theft is forbidden, though there are different views about rights of ownership, for example over titles to land.

8.   Explicit references to bribery in the writings central to several religions are given in Boxes 1 and 2, with sources noted in the Annex. These words have influenced cultures, motivated people and within their different contexts been taken as 'givens' for philosophical discourse and political decision. I suggest they show four broad areas of convergence:
   – that *bribery is wrong*, giving a rule-based ethic for those who believe;
   – that *this is not thought self-evident*, as for murder or theft, but a conclusion derived from the consequences – 'bribery is wrong because...';
   – that *pragmatic arguments* are needed, therefore, to show why bribery is wrong; and
   – that *arguments based on care* are stated most strongly – bribery is wrong because its effects are unjust and unfair.
It follows that there is a basis for cooperation to prevent and reduce bribery between people from different religious traditions and cultures, and with people who may reject those traditions but accept arguments based on pragmatism and care. There is an uncanny familiarity about some past references to corruption and its consequences: we might imagine we were reading to-day's newspaper.

9.   *Moses* (Box 1A) was advised to appoint as officials and judges those who hated dishonest gain. Moses gave instructions later against accepting bribes because a bribe 'blinds the eyes' and leads to injustice. Under its early constitution, Israel was ruled for several hundred years by judges who had a political as well as a judicial role. When Judge *Samuel* was old he made his sons judges over Israel, but they took bribes and twisted justice. In consequence, the people demanded a king rather than judges to rule them. 3,000 years ago public discontent and anger about bribery and its consequences led to a change of government and a change of constitution. Something similar happened in Italy after 1990.

10.   The *Laws of Manu* (Box 1B) have an uncertain date, possibly from around 600 CE. They form one of the principal parts of Hindu tradition. The

penalties match contemporary calls for the seizure of property gained from drug deals, etc.

Box 1: Attitudes to Bribery in Different Traditions

A. The Hebrew Scriptures

Advice to Moses, 1,400 CE
Look for able men ... who fear God, are trustworthy, and hate dishonest gain; set ... them as officers over thousands. Let them sit as judges.

The Law of Moses, 1,400 CE
You must not distort justice; you must not show partiality; and you must not accept bribes for a bribe blinds the eyes of the wise and subverts the cause of those who are in the right.

About Samuel's sons, 1050 CE
His sons ... turned aside after gain; they took bribes and perverted justice.

B. Hindu Writings

Laws of Manu, about 600 CE
(in written form probably later)
Men who are appointed by the king to protect his subjects generally become hypocrites who take the property of others, and he must protect those subjects from them.

The king should banish and confiscate all the property of those evil-minded men who take the money from parties to lawsuits.

C. Confucian

Confucius, about 500 CE
was warned that an emphasis on virtue would make officials too benevolent and hence corrupt.

Hsiao Ching, 145 CE
(parts of an Imperial edict)
Anyone arresting or informing on a person guilty of bribery would be given the bribe received by the accused.

Some officials ... make a business of presents and bribes.

Wang an Shih, about 1050 CE
attributed corruption to bad men and bad laws...

and referred to a multitude of minute and harassing prohibitions.

D. The Teachings of Buddha

about 585 CE
If an important minister neglects his duties, works for his own profit or accepts bribes, it will cause a rapid decay of public morals. People will cheat one another ... take advantage of the poor, and there will be no justice for anyone.

... only flatterers will find government positions, and they will enrich themselves with no thought for the sufferings of the people.

Unjust officials are the thieves of people's happiness ... they defraud both ruler and people and are the cause of the nation's troubles.

11. For *Confucius* (Box 1C), care and kindness were primary virtues, especially care for one's family. Confucius was warned that too much emphasis on virtue would make officials corrupt because they would favour their families. As officials, it was necessary for them to be impartial. In the same Confucian tradition, *Hsiao Ching* issued an edict that anyone informing on a person guilty of bribery would be given the bribe received by the accused. This was matched in Tanzania in 1989, where the police were told that if they were offered bribes they should take them and hand them over, and that when the offender was convicted they would be given the bribe money as a reward. (It was an incentive that cost the state nothing.) *Wang an Shih* thought that in order to cure corruption it would be necessary to change both the people's motives and a nation's laws. And he saw people demoralized and the law brought into disrepute by a multitude of minute and harassing prohibitions.

12. *Buddha* (Box 1D) recognized that a corrupt leadership would have consequences that would pervade the whole society and lead to exploitation of the poor and injustice for all. Bribery and corruption do not only lead to unfair decisions, they lead to the wrong people getting the top jobs, as Buddha knew when saying that only flatterers would find government positions. Many leaders fall because they lose touch with the people. They are told what they want to hear rather than what they need to know, by officials offering flattery or driven by cowardice or by desire for their own corrupt advantage. Buddha's pragmatic argument that unjust officials are thieves of people's happiness and the cause of a nation's troubles is relevant today.

13. *Plato*'s prohibition on public servants taking presents (Box 2E) has a disconcerting twist at the end, with the requirement that those convicted shall 'die without ceremony'. One must, however, respect the caution shown by Plato that such action should depend on their being properly convicted.

14. For *Jesus Christ* (Box 2F), in a small colony of the Roman Empire, one prevalent form of corruption was fraudulent tax collection for personal gain. We are not told what Jesus said about this when he went as a guest to the home of Zacchaeus. Nor are we told whether Zacchaeus had the funds to pay back fourfold the amounts by which he had defrauded people, nor whether he kept his promise. But Jesus used Zacchaeus' words to define his own mission as bringing restoration and hope to people in need. In some societies where corrupt practice has become entrenched, it is impossible to exclude from public life all who have offended. Restoration may be more important than punishment. An amnesty may be difficult but necessary.

Box 2: Attitudes to Bribery in Different Traditions

E. Ancient Greece

Plato's 'Laws', about 300 CE
The servants of the nations are to render their service without taking any presents ...
The disobedient shall, if convicted, die without ceremony.

F. Christian

Jesus said to tax collectors
Collect no more than the amount prescribed for you.

And to soldiers
Do not extort money from anyone ... be satisfied with your wages.

Zacchaeus, a chief tax collector, said to Jesus after inviting him home
If I have defrauded anyone ... I will pay back four times as much...

and Jesus replied
Today salvation has come to this house ... For the Son of Man came to seek out and to save the lost.

G. Islamic

The Qur'an, compiled about 600 CE
And eat up not one another's property unjustly ... nor give bribery to the rulers (judges before presenting your cases) that you may knowingly eat up a part of the property of others sinfully.

The sayings of the Prophet
Allah curses the giver of bribes and the receiver of bribes
and the person who paves the way for both parties.

The Fatwa Alamagiri
(a present to influence a judge is unlawful, but) if a present be made to a judge from a sense of fear, it is lawful to give it, but unlawful to accept it.

H. Western

Queen Elizabeth I, 1588, when appointing Sir William Cecil to be a senior official
This judgement I have of you, that you will not be corrupted by any manner of gift,
and that without respect to my private will, you will give me that counsel that you think best.

15. In *The Qur'an* (Box 2G) there is a specific prohibition against paying bribes, with bribery considered unjust because the motive is to devour another person's wealth. That occurs when a bribe is given in order to win contracts unfairly against the competition. One saying attributed to the Prophet warns that Allah curses those who pay bribes and those who receive them, and any negotiator, fixer or go-between. Another *haddith*, a saying by the Prophet,

challenges governors to recognize as bribes any gifts they would not have received if they had stayed at home but which are given to them because of their position. The *Fatwa Alamagiri* (an opinion by a religious leader) indicates that a person, for example a judge, who extorts presents or money does wrong, but that one is allowed to pay a bribe when driven by fear. In accord with Islamic principles, this should be understood to apply to situations of 'emergency'. One lesson for our contemporary society is the need to formulate carefully laws that deal with extortion as well as bribery.

16.   That *Queen Elizabeth the First* (Box 2H) was aware of her need for impartial counsel or advice is much to her credit. She saw that advice would be distorted if her official favoured someone who had given a bribe, or if he feared her displeasure when it was necessary to tell her something unpleasant. She wanted to avoid the situation – described by Buddha – where only flatterers won government posts. Her desire for incorruptible and courageous staff is shared by many leaders today. If they are to govern well, Presidents and ministers need to know what they may not like to hear.

17.   However, there are many claims that some traditions provide a precedent for bribery. Two examples are given in Box 3. Does gift-giving to chiefs or other leaders in village societies justify offering gifts today in business transactions? Do traditions of personal or group or ethnic loyalty – leading to a morality based on personal obligations rather than loyalty to a code – make it normal to exchange personal favours which outsiders may see as bribes?

18.   *Gifts to local elders and chiefs* (Box 3J) are common to many parts of the world. Some writers blame patterns of bribery in contemporary society on traditional village society, at least in part. Leys[6] suggests that 'The open gift of a chicken is replaced by a more furtive gift of a pound note... in which the precise nature of the rule-infringement is partially concealed by continuity with older custom'. (Leys qualifies this later, in some measure.) Accounts from several regions support the view based on the author's experience in Ghana. Klitgaard[7] recognizes that claims that African traditions of gift-giving lead to bribery are challenged by Africans. Referring to gifts in the traditional administration in Viet Nam, Alatas[8] argues that these were not corrupt because (and I summarize) (1) the scale was specified, (2) the transaction was not secret, (3) the rights of the public were not violated and (4) the revenue was for a function of government rather than for private gain. Gifts in village

---

[6] Colin Leys, 'What is the Problem about Corruption?', *Journal of Modern African Studies*, Vol. III, no. 2 (1965), 225, quoted by Alatas.

[7] Robert Klitgaard, *Controlling Corruption*, Berkeley, Univ. of California Press (1988), 63.

[8] Syed Hussein Alatas, *The Problem of Corruption*, Singapore, Time Books International (1986), 13.

communities are not secret and set a precedent for taxation rather than bribery. Similarly the 'dash' or tip in some cultures is often sought openly and then not to be equated with the secret inducement of a bribe.

19. Group loyalty (Box 3K) is specially noticeable in traditional communities. Such communities are mostly of small size, with their members knowing personally the people with whom they do business. Klitgaard[9] quotes Greenberg[10] as saying that 'Mexicans treat one another as persons with the result that formalized codes of behaviour carry little weight'. Sivalingam and Yong Siew Peng[11] found for part of Malaysia that any reluctance to use 'bureaucratic power to fulfil traditional, kin and social obligations may be interpreted as a mark of disrespect to royalty, friends and relatives'. Khassawneh[12] claims that 95 per cent of 240 Jordanian civil servants interviewed said 'relatives expect to be treated better than clients' (but would that be surprising, anywhere?). Bista[13] blames slow development in Nepal, in part, on caste loyalties setting a pattern for working relations based on a circle of close contacts. Lucian and Mary Pye[14] argue that the concept of power in Asia is personal and paternalistic in contrast to a supposed institutional bias in the West. Hyden[15] describes the impact of an 'economy of affection' on management and organization in Africa, with economic decisions based on personal considerations as much as on 'value for money', perhaps expressed better by saying that the effects on social relationships are given a high value. These problems are widely shared and it may be naive to think them more important in some cultures than in others. 'Old Boy Networks' in Britain based on family, school or profession and their influence on appointments and the award of contracts are described at length by Heald.[16] The challenge everywhere is to internalize rules that protect impartiality while giving value to personal relationships and social cohesion.

---

[9] Robert Klitgaard, *op. cit.*, 62.

[10] Martin Harvey Greenberg, *Bureaucracy and Development*, Lexington, Mass., D.C. Heath (1970), 70, as quoted by Klitgaard.

[11] G. Sivalingam and Yong Siew Peng, 'The System of Political and Administrative Corruption in a West Malaysian State', *Philippine Journal of Public Adminstration* 3 (1991), 246–286.

[12] Anis S. Khassawneh, 'A Sociological Approach to the Study of Bureaucratic Corruption in Developing Countries', *META Studies in Development* (Turkey), no. 3–4 (1989), 127–146.

[13] D. Bista, *Fatalism and Development*, Hyderabad and Calcutta, Orient Longman (1991).

[14] Lucian W. Pye and Mary F. Pye, *Asian Power and Politics, the Cultural Dimensions of Authority*, Cambridge, Mass., The Belknap Press of Harvard University Press (1985).

[15] Goran Hyden, *No Shortcuts to Progress: African Development Management in Perspective*, Heinemann Educational Books (1983).

[16] Tim Heald, *Old Boy Networks: Who We Know and How We Use Them*, London, Hodden and Stoughton (1983).

Box 3: Attitudes to Bribery in Different Traditions

J. Gifts in Village Tradition: A Personal Experience

I had to see the Chief. I was seeking permission for a geophysics experiment in Northern Ghana for which we needed to dig four holes in the ground, a hundred metres or so apart, place copper tubes in them, and connect them with wires to record small electric currents thought to image properties in the ionosphere. My local adviser and interpreter insisted I gave the Chief a bottle of whisky. I took it with reluctance, hiding it carefully in a brown paper bag. We sat on benches outside the Chief's hut with the people of the village gathered round. I paid my respects and explained my request as best I could. My adviser whispered, 'Give him the whisky'. 'Now', I asked, 'with all these people here?' 'Yes.' I tried to pass it unobtrusively in its paper bag but my adviser protested: it had to come out of the bag and be given so that all could see. There was a murmur of appreciation from the people, and very happy smiles on the faces of the Chief's counsellors who sat nearby.

On reflection I recognized that the transaction was the equivalent of a licence fee in a pre-literate society that kept no accounts. It differed from bribes in three ways. It was done so that all could see, not in secret. It was a benefit the Chief would share with his colleagues who were involved in the decision. It was modest in scale and did not make one person or group so wealthy as to be the envy of others. Village customs can be corrupted, but they provide no valid precedent or justification for bribery in the city.

K. Group Loyalty: A Personal Experience

One of our funds was fully spent although my calculations showed this should not be so. A check revealed six payments of exactly the same amount, for the same contract. I was in a foreign country and we found that a locally employed accountant had developed a system to present invoices and have cheques signed that he would then cash for himself. He had escaped discovery for six years. He had grown rich and had many friends. He repaid some money he had taken, but sadly after more losses were discovered he committed suicide.

His fellow nationals on our staff thought his misdeeds had been reported by their most senior local colleague and were intensely angry with him. Group loyalty was felt more strongly than their obligation to protect institutional funds. I boasted that I had detected the fraud, and helped rebuild relationships when I said at his funeral that I had liked and admired our accountant and appreciated his efforts to make good the losses, and that at the end all of us will need forgiveness. But I learnt the moral strength of personal loyalty within a group, possibly exacerbated because group members thought of themselves as 'poor' nationals dealing with expatriates from a rich former colonial power.

20. The hope of some religious leaders and social reformers that changes of belief or structure would eradicate corruption have led to disillusion. Some thought that changed structures and the doctrine that private property is theft would bring a socialist 'new man', seeing human perfectibility as the antidote to corruption. Such ideas appeared to gain credibility from a lessening of corruption in some countries, but any reduction appears to have been temporary. Lo[17] reports 63 per cent of those interviewed in a 1988 survey of 10,000 workers in the People's Republic of China as listing official corruption as China's most serious social problem, and refers to Womack[18] as identifying cadre corruption and privilege as probably the single most prominent issue causing the confrontation in 1989. He quotes Li Peng[19] reporting to the National People's Congress, 'The struggle against corruption is a crucial issue between the party and the people' and urging leaders to exercise self-discipline and educate their offspring.

21. Plays and novels also indicate what people in different societies consider right or wrong. One example is given in Box 4. Readers may think of examples more relevant to their own culture.

Box 4: Bribery in Literature

William Shakespeare 1564–1616, *Henry VI*, Part Two

The Queen complains (Act 1, Scene 3 lines 49, 50)
What! shall King Henry be a pupil still
Under the surly Gloucester's governance?

she challenges the Duke of Gloucester (Act 1, Scene 3 lines 138–140)
Thy sale of offices and towns in France
If they were known, as the suspect is great,
Would make thee quickly hop without thy head.

The Duke of York accuses him (Act 3, Scene 1 lines 104–106)
'Tis thought my Lord,
that you took bribes of France,
And, being protector, stay'd the soldiers' pay;
By means whereof his highness hath lost France.

and the Duke of Gloucester denies (Act 3, Scene 1 lines 107–109)
I never robb'd the soldiers of their pay
Nor ever had one penny bribe from France.

Shakespeare, in *Henry VI* Part Two, writes about the Queen's annoyance that the Duke of Gloucester rules England as governor for her son, King Henry. She threatens to expose the Duke's suspicious business practices,

---

[17] Jack Man Keung Lo, *Bureaucratic Corruption in China During the Reform Era: Current Issues and Future Directions*, Department of Management, Hong Kong Polytechnic University, private distribution (1996).
[18] B. Womack, *Contemporary Chinese Politics in Historical Perspective*, Cambridge, Cambridge University Press (1991).
[19] Li Peng, The political report presented by the Premier in the first meeting of the eighth National People's Congress, 23 March 1993.

adding the macabre warning that if they were known, he would be beheaded. Later, the Duke of York alleges that the Duke of Gloucester took bribes, and that because he defrauded the soldiers of their pay, battles were lost in consequence. Bribery in defence transactions is a major concern today. Many defence budgets are large, and secrecy surrounding the specification of equipment and costs makes audit and accountability difficult.

DESCRIPTIONS OF BRIBERY IN SOCIETIES IN TRANSITION: SOME WORDS FROM THE ACADEMICS

22. Several writers attribute corruption to ways in which national administrations differ from a modern ideal, especially in rapidly changing or developing countries, and use keywords and phrases for different patterns of corruption.

Although new words have been invented to describe different patterns of bribery, they help to identify common themes. From the examples given below, it becomes clear that bribery is thought to be made more likely by:
 – *monopoly power*, wielded by the state or others;
 – *over-regulation*;
 – *discontent* with rewards at levels considered unfair;
 – *strong kinship ties*; and
 – *rapid change*.

The consequences of bribery are seen as political, social and economic. Bribes help a ruling elite retain power by providing funds for patronage, but in the longer term bribes fuel pressures for political change from public anger at the unfair advantages given to some and the damage done to others. The economic damage caused by bribery is argued by many but disputed by some. It is claimed that low levels of corruption have promoted economic growth in Malaysia and Singapore, for example, but that allegedly higher levels of corruption in Indonesia, Japan and South Korea have not stunted short-term economic growth there and in other countries. The economic argument against bribery is not only that it inhibits growth in the longer term but that the economic benefits brought by bribes are perceived to be unfair. Bribes damage the economy because they are socially damaging and politically destabilizing.

23. Weber[20] saw modern bureaucracies, with their impartiality and fairness and their legal and rational delegations of responsibility, as a contrast to the

---

[20] Max Weber in *Economy and Society*, G. Roth and L. Wittech (eds.), Berkeley, University of California Press (1978), Vol. 1, 228–234, also Vol. 2, 1070–1110. Weber also describes Sultanism, where authority is more discretionary and less tied by tradition, so that the ruler or officials do not distinguish between personal and public property (Vol. 1, 232).

patterns of traditional authority. He described one of these, *patrimonialism*, as a ruler having 'an administrative and a military force which are purely personal instruments of the master' but with the ruler's decisions constrained by tradition. Dia,[21] following Klitgaard, gives an 'equation' of *Patrimony = Monopoly of Power + Discretion – Accountability – Transparency.*

24. Medard[22] writes of *neo-patrimonialism*, in which the state is undermined by a failure to distinguish between the position and the holder, and between public and private. Where the emphasis is on the monopoly power of the state to reallocate rights at a price, the behaviour of officials is often described as *rent-seeking*. Leff,[23] Nye[24] and others claimed that bribery brings economic benefits by creating a market in place of an inefficient monopoly. Alam[25] argued that any benefits may be short term, because there are incentives for officials to create damaging shortages and delays to maximize their gains. The benefits would result normally from corruption ameliorating poor government, with its excessive regulation and unchecked monopoly power. Klitgaard quotes a claim by Huntington[26] that 'In terms of economic growth the only worse thing than a society with a rigid, overcentralized dishonest bureaucracy is one with a rigid overcentralized honest bureaucracy'. Social cohesion and political stability are at stake as well as economic growth. It is better to improve government than hope that corruption will reduce its awfulness.

25. Clapham[27] points out that there is a role reversal when the clients provide a service that the patron-state needs and can get in no other way,

[21] Mamadou Dia, 'A Governance Approach to Civil Service Reform in Sub-Saharan Africa', Washington DC, The World Bank, Technical Paper No. 225, October 1993.

[22] J.-F. Medard, 'The Underdeveloped State in Tropical Africa: Political Clientelism or Neo-Patrimonialism?' in C. Clapham (ed.), *Private Patronage and Public Power*, London, Frances Pinter (1982), 162–192.

[23] N.H. Leff, 'Economic Development Through Bureaucratic Corruption', in Arnold J. Hiedenheimer (ed.), *Political Corruption: Readings in Contemporary Analysis*, New York, Holt Reinhart and Winston (1970), 510–520.

[24] J.S. Nye, 'Corruption and Political Development: A Cost-Benefit Analysis', in Arnold J. Hiedenheimer (ed.), *Political Corruption: Readings in Contemporary Analysis*, New York, Holt Reinhart and Winston (1970), 564–578.

[25] M.S. Alam, 'Some Economic Costs of Corruption in LDCs, *Journal of Development Studies* 27, no. 1 (1990), 88–97.

[26] Samuel Huntington, 'Modernization and Development', in Moday U. Ekpo (ed.), *Bureaucratic Corruption in Sub-Saharan Africa: Towards a Search for Causes and Consequences*, Washington DC, University Press of America (1979), as quoted by Klitgaard, *op. cit.*, 34.

[27] C. Clapham, 'Clientelism and the State' in C. Clapham (ed.), *Private Patronage and Public Power*, London, Frances Pinter (1982), 1–35.

describing this as *clientelism*. Khan[28] makes a clear distinction between patrimonial systems and clientelist patterns where groups of clients have the power to demand preferential prices for the support the state requires. Joseph[29] writes about *prebendalism*, meaning the practice of granting government offices to provide a direct source of income to the holder. This requires the unique control of access to resources by one group. *Mercantilism*, the system of monopoly trading rights granted by states to individuals in 16th and 17th Century Europe, is claimed by De Soto[30] to describe recent patterns in Peru. De Soto observes that mercantilism collapsed in France, Spain and Russia through violence, but through peaceful process in Britain. In Peru it has been associated with excessive bureaucracy and collapsed through 'informal' entities acquiring land and setting up business. Initially they acted outside the law but later took over mercantile business activity and were legitimized.

26. De Soto also describes the alarming effects of excessive bureaucracy, claiming that between 1947 and about 1987 the Peruvian state produced 27,000 laws and administrative decisions annually. He found the costs of compliance by making a case study of negotiations to set up a small factory.[31] Osborne[32] described countries with excessive regulations and permits as *permitsive* societies, in contrast to the 'permissive societies' spoken of in 1960s Europe. The anthropologist Paul Stirling[33] tells of contrasting responses when visiting villages in Turkey. In some villages people talked freely. In others people asked first, 'Who gave you permission?'. Stirling claims this illustrates different traditions in small-scale village society. In some societies the authorities decide what people may do; they give permits. In other societies the authorities focus on what people may not do; they make prohibitions to protect others. Both patterns are needed in modern society, but where the emphasis is on people doing only what is expressly permitted, there is a greater loss of freedom than in societies where the emphasis is on a limited range of prohibitions.

---

[28] Myshtaq Khan, 'A Typology of Corrupt Transactions in Developing Countries', *IDS Bulletin* 27, 2 (1996), 12–21.

[29] R.A. Joseph, *Democracy and Prebendal Politics in Nigeria*, Cambridge, Cambridge University Press (1987).

[30] Hernando De Soto, *The Other Path: The Invisible Revolution in the Third World*, translated by June Abbott, London, I.B. Tauris (1989).

[31] To set up a small garment factory, in 1983, it required 289 days of work to negotiate and fulfil the eleven requirements of different parts of government, and the unavoidable payment of two bribes out of ten requested, for a total cash cost equal to 332 times a normal low monthly wage (De Soto, *op. cit.*, 133–135).

[32] Denis G. Osborne, 'Action for Better Government: A Role for Donors', *IDS Bulletin*, 24 (1993), 67–73.

[33] Paul Stirling, University of Kent at Canterbury, private communication.

27. Hyden – quoted already, *see* note 15 – refers to an *economy of affection*, stressing the personal or relational character of transactions. Dia[34] reports a study of 'African cultural traits' that include a self-interest that is weaker than group loyalty, and a regard for riches as something to be shared and socially visible (leading sometimes to conspicuous consumption). But such characteristics are not limited to Africa and are found elsewhere when people experience rapid change from traditional ways of life and when uncertainty about the future brings pressures to 'live for the present'.

28. I argue that there is also a *culture of disaffection* or *resentment*, where officials resent the authority of colonial rule or dictatorial government. Officials are then less committed to obey the rules and regulations of the state and more open to bribes. Similar disaffection may be caused by fears of down-sizing and redundancy. Disaffection is caused by rates of pay that are thought unfair when compared with rates for similar work elsewhere, or the rewards for an organization's top executives from high salaries, share options or bribes. When pay is thought unfair, employees think it fair to cheat – and to take bribes. More recently Harriss-White and White[35] have argued that liberalization (as well as excessive regulation) may help corruption flourish. Sidel[36] uses *bossism* as yet another word to describe the problem, arguing that democracy and decentralization may bring conditions where local bosses thrive and gain a monopolistic control over resources.

29. Rapid change makes people uncertain about the future and more prone to value short-term gains. Where there is little continuity in relationships with work colleagues or customers, there is less obligation to maintain a reputation or give value for money. Morality is a long-term commitment. When there are changes the controls are often weak, giving a lower risk of detection, conviction and punishment. It is, therefore, reasonable to expect that countries undergoing rapid change – including developing countries and the transitional economies – will be fertile ground for corruption. However, there exists no reliable measure of corruption and, therefore, no fair comparison of the incidence of corruption in different countries. Tables grading countries as more or less corrupt may reflect the prejudices of the groups of people providing the data and risk offering a corrupt assessment of corruption.

---

[34] Mamadou Dia, 'Development and Cultural Values in Sub-Saharan Africa', *Finance and Development*, December 1991, 10–13.

[35] Barbara Harriss-White and Gordon White, 'Editorial Introduction: Corruption, Liberalization and Democracy', *IDS Bulletin*, 27, 2 (1996), 1–5.

[36] John T. Sidel, 'Siam and its Twin? Democratization and Bossism in Contemporary Thailand and the Philippines', *IDS Bulletin*, 27, 2 (1996), 56–63.

30. Corruption spreads. Although it is difficult to measure the scale of bribery, there is general recognition that bribery escalates unless efforts are taken to prevent it. Where bribery has become entrenched as a normal pattern of business, the sequence and the causes appear often as suggested in Box 5. If bribery that is a matter of individual choice goes unchecked, it leads to extortion that *has* to be paid to get jobs done. When corruption becomes systemic it brings new behavioural norms that differ from the former culture of the organization or the nation. Systemic corruption is not necessarily systematic, it is a condition where the disease affects the whole body rather than causing only a local infection. (Features of systemic corruption are described well in *The TI Source Book*.[37]) But systemic corruption is less benign than it may appear. Corruption is itself a major cause of escalating corruption, creating increased opportunity for further corruption as bribes reduce the risks of detection and conviction. The sight of people who get rich corruptly stimulates greed, giving incentives to others to maximize their profits. The public anger at corrupt riches brings political unrest.

Box 5: The Growth of Corruption: An Epidemiology of Bribes

Greed causes 'occasional corruption'
Payment of bribes a matter of individual choice – a few pay bribes
Those bidding for contracts seek unfair advantage over competitors
– an abuse of power and money by the private sector
Those awarding contracts take advantage of their monopoly
– an abuse of position and trust by employees, officials or politicians

Opportunity leads to 'systemic corruption'
Payment of bribes socially acceptable – many pay bribes
Those taking and paying bribes escape punishment
Structures weak, society in rapid change; or political patronage

Need, and 'sustainable corruption'
Payment of bribes unavoidable but level sustainable for a time
– 'everybody does it'
To win contracts, get licences etc., people need to pay bribes
Officials poorly paid, extra income from bribes needed to maintain standard of living

More greed leads to 'destructive corruption'
Escalating bribes cause social instability
Officials seek bigger bribes (often to fund own businesses), cause delays and shortages to raise prices
Politicians distort policies for personal gain, development slows
Government revenues fall because bribery leads to tax evasion
Public anger leads to political unrest

---

[37] Jeremy Pope (ed.), *National Integrity Systems, The TI Source Book*, Berlin, Transparency International (1996), 40 and 41.

ATTITUDES TO BRIBERY TODAY:
WORDS OF THE PEOPLE AND THE MEDIA

31. The changing idiom in everyday speech and the media to describe corrupt behaviour indicates culture and culture-shifts. An examination of contemporary international slang about corruption shows, I suggest, three main characteristics:
- *anger* against its unfairness;
- *admiration* for those who make themselves rich (who are perceived as 'clever'); and
- *disillusion* about the ability to reduce or prevent corruption, and mistrust of those who promise to do something about it.

Thus allegations about corruption have become an election issue in many countries, but seeming proof of corrupt behaviour does not always lose votes.

32. A number of words have been in fashion in recent years.
- *Sleaze* became a popular word to describe corruption in *Britain*. Its original definition (as thin or flimsy material) progressed through meaning shoddy or untidy to mean now inappropriate behaviour. As described in The Times:[38]

  'Sleaze is an ideal insult for one politician to hurl at another. The word conjures up something sordid and disreputable, political mud that is intended to stick, and often does. [It is] used to cover everything from the sexual peccadilloes of back-benchers, via the business activities of peers and the son of a former Prime Minister ... to payments to MPs for asking parliamentary questions.'

  Subsequently sleaze received international recognition on the front cover of *Time* where an article by Church[39] described attacks on governmental corruption worldwide.
- *Les affaires* describe corrupt business alliances with a hint of inappropriate romance which led, in *France*, to several ministers losing office.
- *Tagentopoli* – bribe city – is shorthand in *Italy* for investigations into corruption and the system of corruption itself. The role of the prosecutors and the downfall of prime ministers have been widely reported.[40]

---

[38] *The Times*, London, 21 October 1994.

[39] George J. Church, 'War Against Sleaze', *Time*, 6 May 1996, 38–44.

[40] See, for example, Robert Graham, 'Pride of a Nation Damaged by Tagenti', London, *Financial Times Survey*, 'Italy', 30 June 1993, 9; *The Economist*, London, 27 November 1993, 47; Michael Sheridan, 'One Hundred Days of Chaos', *The Independent*, London, 15 August 1994, 17; Gherardo Colombo, 'The "Clean Hands" Investigations in Italy' in Duc V. Trang (ed.), *Corruption and Democracy*, Budapest, Institute for Constitutional and Legislative Policy (1994), 153, 154.

- *Black mist* is the term used to describe the uncertainties caused by political corruption in *Japan*. Some claim this contrasts with widespread respect for the integrity of officials and blame long periods of rule by one political party.
- *419* is the number for the clause in the Legal Code in *Nigeria* about Advance Fee Fraud, a form of false representation designed to secure a payment into an overseas bank in the expectation of a share in great, but often admittedly ill-gotten, benefits. It has become symbolic for any form of bribery or more general corruption.
- *Air supply* was a term used in *Uganda* to describe payment for goods or services not supplied. The government paid – with its people's money – and got nothing, air. Bribes did not just increase the price, they ensured that no goods would be delivered because the delivery would not be checked.
- *19.99* is the dollar cash limit in the *United States* for a free lunch that may be accepted from a contractor or potential contractor by an American official. By contrast with allegations of corruption affecting big business in the United States, the concept is trivial. However, it illustrates the possibility that these catchwords may humanize and normalize corrupt practice and make it more acceptable. (Similarly, sleaze sounds less hurtful than theft of the people's money.)

33. Because the United States economy is large and American business influential, it is worth considering ways in which American practice affects other countries. The United States Foreign Corrupt Practices Act (1977) makes it an offence for an American citizen to pay bribes in a foreign country. It was adopted in response to public outrage about massive bribery payments for defence contracts and others, and is explained well by Noonan.[41] Such extraterritoriality in the application of national laws is much debated. It has been widely accepted for terrorism, drug handling and money laundering. The OECD, the Organization for Economic Cooperation and Development, debated in 1996 the usefulness of having other countries adopt something similar to the United States' Foreign Corrupt Practices Act. Since then, several governments have expressed concern about pressure from the United States to ban trade with Cuba or Iran. Extraterritoriality may be out of favour for a time, especially for trade matters, though there seems to be a growing global consensus that it should be applied against child abuse. We shall consider later reasons for seeking global cooperation against bribery.

34. In contemporary United States culture there are pressures for political correctness. Writers point out the need for accountability and whistle-

---

[41] John T. Noonan, Jr., *Bribes*, New York & London, Macmillan (1984), 668–674.

blowing. Glazer and Glazer[42] describe its essential role in exposing corruption in the New York City Police, where their claim that 'corruption thrived because of loyalty' suggests an 'economy of affection'. However, Garment[43] asks about the costs to society of a culture of mistrust, quoting one senior American official estimating that 30–40 per cent of working time was spent 'on issues involving the rules and procedures designed to prevent and deal with corruption and scandal'. There are deep social costs from persistent suspicion.

35. The acknowledged practice in the United States of rewarding contributions to party funds by appointments and contracts after election would be considered corrupt in many other countries.

36. Political corruption has been a major issue in Britain, leading the government to establish a committee under Lord Nolan to investigate public concerns about corruption. In its first report in May 1995, the committee gave 'Seven Principles of Public Life'[44] that it had found the British public expected their elected representatives and public servants to observe. These are, with my summary of the explanations:
- selflessness – decide in the public interest, not for personal gain;
- integrity – accept no obligations to others that might affect official duties;
- objectivity – make appointments of staff, place contracts, etc., on merit;
- accountability – give account (ultimately to the public), submit to scrutiny;
- openness – give reasons for decisions, restrict information only when that is in the wider public interest;
- honesty – declare private interests, resolve any conflicts to protect the public interest; and
- leadership – promote principles by leadership and example.

These contemporary expectations of the British public have been fostered by media exposure of 'misbehaviour'.

BRIBES AS A THREAT FOR THE FUTURE

37. Bribes, in most cultures in all countries, are recognized as corrupting and unfair. This has been shown by an examination of traditional writings, academic analyses and contemporary jargon. There is wide recognition that

---

[42] Mynon Peretz Glazer and Penina Migdal Glazer, *Whistle Blowers: Exposing Corruption in Government and Industry*, Harper Collins, Basic Books (1989), 54.

[43] Suzanne Garment, *Scandal : The Culture of Mistrust in American Politics*, New York, Dell (Anchor Books Edition) (1992), 297.

[44] First Report of the Committee on Standards in Public Life, London, HMSO, 1995.

corruption is ultimately destructive. The boundaries are uncertain: whether tips are socially acceptable and how large a tip may be before it is deemed to be a bribe, or whether it is corrupt for contributions to a political party to be rewarded by appointment to public office. There are different definitions of corruption in different jurisdictions. However, bribery for personal gain is condemned in all. Moreover, whenever there is secrecy about a gift there will be suspicion that it is a bribe. If people are content that their actions should be transparent, that readiness to accept transparency is a proof of cultural acceptability.

38. In deciding what efforts are likely to be cost effective in preventing and reducing bribery, it is necessary to look in more detail at the damage done by bribes. Following Alfiler,[45] we may categorize public sector bribery as affecting a government's revenue collection, or its expenditure, or its enforcement of regulations. These categories may be extended to cover the ways in which corruption destroys different aspects of culture.

39. *Bribes undermine governments.*
  - Bribes reduce income. Bribes to tax collectors, customs officers, etc, reduce government revenues. One estimate put the losses at up to 50 per cent. The loss to government is much greater than the gains of corrupt officials: a Customs officer may be paid $100 to waive $2,000 duty or not inspect goods at all.
  - Bribes increase costs. Companies load their prices to cover the cost of any bribes they pay. More than that, bribes destroy competition and reduce supervision. When companies are under no pressure to give 'value for money', their profits can soar. Bribes on telecommunications projects and power stations in Italy were estimated at 2 or 3 per cent of the total value but inflated bids and lax supervision raised the actual costs of projects 'between 15 and 20 per cent more than was necessary'. One municipal construction tender in Milan in June 1993 was reportedly 50 per cent below the rate prevailing before the widespread exposure of corruption there starting in February 1992.[46]
  - Bribes distort policy. Choices and priorities are determined by personal gain rather than national advantage.

---

[45] Concepcion P. Alfiler, 'The Process of Bureaucratic Corruption in Asia: Emerging Patterns', in Ledivinia V. Carino (ed.), *Bureaucratic Corruption in Asia: Causes, Consequences and Controls*, Quezon City, JMC Press Inc., and Manila, College of Administration, University of the Philippines (1986), 16–68.

[46] Robert Graham, 'Pride of a Nation damaged by Tagenti', London, *Financial Times Survey*, 'Italy', 30 June 1993, 9.

40. Bribes subvert company cultures.
- Bribes corrupt people. Those who pay bribes are corrupted as well as those who receive them. Corrupt employees may cause companies to fail.
- Bribes breed disloyalty. Those who pay bribes to win contracts have little incentive to refuse bribes when placing contracts for the company.
- Bribes reduce competitiveness. The receipt of bribes by employees may distort company policies, and lose it value for money in buying goods and services.
- Bribes damage non-profit nongovernmental organizations too. They reduce their effectiveness, distort their policies and pervert their cultures.

41. Bribes destabilize society as a whole.
- Bribes divert resources. Those who take bribes raise their 'rents' when they can, and though at first they may invest their gains locally, fear of public anger, or of a change of government bringing prosecution and confiscation, leads them to invest their money abroad.
- Bribes create inequalities. A corrupt system is unfair. The poor suffer most (and with little to lose may risk violence in giving vent to their anger). In some countries discontent is greatest – or most vocal – among the middle class, who see all the benefits being taken by a small rich elite, forming a closed group, while their salaries are low.
- Bribes reduce productivity. Because they bring unfair rewards, bribes demotivate people. There is little reason to work well to give value for money, if bribes rather than production are the main source of reward.

42. Bribes threaten global security.
- Bribes make controls ineffective, bringing great and wide-ranging risks, because bribes to inspectors make it possible to avoid compliance with regulations, and bribes to the police and judiciary make it possible to escape the penalties.
- The risks include drug production and trafficking, havens for terrorists, uncontrolled financial flows and environmental disaster through unregulated pollution or unmonitored research. A much-respected Russian physicist linked the nuclear disaster at Chernobyl to corruption and patronage in appointing experts and managers.[47] That disaster was significant for the way it led to cooperation between cold-war protagonists in the interests of global security. Such cooperation is needed not only after disasters but also to prevent them.

---

[47] Sergei P. Kapitza, 'Lessons of Chernobyl', *Foreign Affairs* 72, no. 3 (1993), 7–11.

43. Bribes anywhere threaten everybody everywhere. Bribes destroy cultures at all levels. What has long been perceived as unfair and damaging at the local level now brings risks of global disasters that are unfair to all. There are pressures to cherish and protect cultural diversity, both from within different cultures and from postmodern thinkers. But in order to protect local diversity it is necessary to have a universal respect for local and group rights, and a reciprocal responsibility not to put at risk the rights of others.

A CALL TO ACTION

44. There is a need to identify, promote and act on a global consensus against bribery. In the pursuit of global protection against bribery and its effects there are several issues that need to be resolved.

45. Cooperation is needed across national boundaries in investigations, in applying extraterritorial legislation and for extradition. There is a need to share information, but also to protect the confidentiality of investigations in progress. That argues against a centralized control system that would put at risk access to information by those suspected of corruption, and argues for informal networks and exchanges. But cooperation requires agreement on what constitutes a crime.

46. Definition is less difficult than some make it seem. The quest is not for an all-embracing definition of corruption, but for working legal definitions of bribery that may be used in cross-border police cooperation and in providing evidence for extradition or the application of acts such as the United States Foreign Corrupt Practices Act. If it is easier at first to omit payments to political parties, so be it, though it is important to include all bribes paid to evade regulations, including bribes to the police to prevent charges being brought and bribes during the judicial process.

47. The law can be applied more effectively if the illegal act is any gift where one party is involved in enforcing regulations, or checking delivery or performance, or receiving payments for state or employer, or authorizing contracts, without the need to prove a corrupt intention. Under Britain's Prevention of Corruption Act 1916 (Section 2) any gift to a government employee by anyone seeking a contract 'shall be deemed to have been paid or given and received corruptly... unless the contrary is proved'. Some speak of this as a 'presumption of guilt'. It is, rather, a definition of the guilty act to include anything that might reasonably give rise to suspicion of corruption. Then what has to be proved is only whether a gift was offered, paid, requested or received, not whether this influenced a decision or was intended to do so.

48. Proportion is needed. How big does a gift need to be for it to be deemed corrupt? Feedback from international groups in seminars shows a remarkable consensus on what participants say it would be right for public servants to receive from someone with whom they did business, based on the lists in Box 6. If small gifts are allowed it becomes necessary to specify values above which any gift must be declared by the recipient, and surrendered if orders are given for that to be done. It is necessary to educate people to recognize how differences of degree become differences of kind. There is a fundamental difference between accepting a cup of coffee and receiving a large payment into an offshore bank account, even if there is something arbitrary about where we draw the line between them. Such lines need to be drawn and their positions made known.

Box 6: Drawing Lines...

As officials working for a government, where should we 'draw the line' about the gifts we may receive from contractors or potential contractors for goods or services?

Things for myself
- calendar for the new year
- book
- tie or scarf
- bottle of wine or whisky
- watch
- TV set and video
- car
- house

Entertainment
- a cup of coffee
- lunch
- dinner in the evening for me and my partner
- theatre or opera tickets
- a week-end away
- an overseas holiday

Family needs
- book for our son
- help with school fees for our daughter
- fares and expenses for daughter or son to study abroad

49. Tips have been forbidden in several Socialist countries. There is a case for forbidding tips for monopoly suppliers, and an experience with tips in Hong Kong some years ago is salutary. Poor families often lived at the top of high-rise blocks without elevators (lifts). They appreciated the postman's effort when he climbed the stairs to bring a letter or parcel and gave a small tip. This became customary, and some families that could not afford to pay a tip, or refused to do so, found their mail was no longer brought to them but left at the bottom of the stairs from where much was stolen. It was the postman's duty to deliver the mail to the address. The poorest families would dread the arrival of a postman if they had no funds left with which to pay the tip that had become a fee for future service.

50. Disclosure rules hamper the work of the police, making it difficult sometimes for them to record and analyse their suspicions. But their suspects may hold funds in secret bank accounts. It is necessary to challenge the supporters of individual human rights about the need for more secrecy for the police and less privacy over personal bank accounts. In many ways this is a conflict between group rights and benefits and the rights of the individual. Modern technology makes it easy to send money as well as information anywhere in the world, so that requirements for disclosure of bank assets need to be applied globally to all reputable banks if they are to be effective. The need to divulge bank assets is recognized for money associated with terrorism and drugs. It is necessary to use this against corruption as well. At the national level, a requirement that officials and political leaders shall declare their assets and explain their lifestyle is a useful check on corruption. Moreover, if corrupt gains cannot be enjoyed because the fast car or the extra house will cause suspicion, the motive to take bribes is reduced. But to be more fully effective, this needs to be linked with international disclosure of holdings.

51. Consensus is elusive. The adversarial character of many democracies gives cause for concern. In fighting corruption, there is an opportunity for consensus within a country, but in practice much of the effort goes into an opposition group alleging that government ministers are wrong (or corrupt) and government supporters alleging the same against the opposition. Nongovernmental groups, the media and officials need help to cooperate in building a national and global consensus.

52. Motivation is essential. It is said frequently that effective action against corruption depends on the political will and has to be top-down. This is a half-truth and a counsel of despair where people are not convinced about the integrity of their leaders. In the longer term politicians respond to public pressures to win support or through fear of losing office or property or life. Action has to be 'bottom up' to initiate and sustain action from the top down. As in many military operations, the most important part of the battle is that to win people's hearts and minds. It may be necessary to expose corrupted cultures in parts of society. There is need for a pluralistic approach to fight corruption, which may include:
- national and international seminars to increase awareness of the issues;
- training that is aimed at improving policies, management, institutions and investigatory techniques;

- support for the media and its freedom, with sufficient accountability to reduce the risk of reporters, publishers or owners being muzzled by bribes;
- improving legislation and investigation, and promoting fast and fair process in the courts;
- introducing codes of conduct and performance pledges or charters, with customers told what to expect and using that transparency to hold officials accountable for their behaviour; and
- pressures from investors and donors.

53. Global security depends on effective action by governments against the breach of regulations that bribery brings. This affects supplies of arms and drugs, flows of information and finance, protection of the environment and safety, including safeguards against the uncertain effects of novel experimentation. Patterns of bribery and corruption *anywhere* bring the threat that regulation will fail, endangering people *everywhere*. Locally and globally, bribery militates against people's cultures and values. We need to see corruption as counter-culture.

SUMMARY

The aim in this paper is to identify shared concerns and promote cooperation between people of different cultures in fighting corruption. Cooperation has been made difficult by arguments that allegations of corruption are culturally unacceptable and contrary to a post-modern welcome for local differences. Cooperation is frustrated when foreign business people claim that offers of large bribes accord with local culture.

Explicit references to bribery in the Hebrew Scriptures, the Laws of Manu, Buddha, Confucius, Plato, Jesus Christ and the Qur'an show that for many traditions bribery is wrong. This is not considered self-evident (as for murder) but it is argued that bribes are unfair and damaging to society. Alleged precedents for bribery in village traditions about gifts are refuted, however it is recognized that group loyalties make it necessary to seek patterns of impartiality that retain social cohesion.

In transitional societies, where modern administration conflicts with established patterns, corruption is described or partially explained with labels such as patrimonialism or rent-seeking behaviour. Different writers find corruption fostered by monopoly power (by the state or client groups), over-regulation, discontent with rewards that are thought unfair, personal obligations such as kinship, and rapid change (as in many developing countries and transitional economies). Corruption escalates from occasional (individual choice) through systemic ('everybody does it') to compulsory extortion, which becomes destructive when excessive levels of corrupt wealth provoke anger that leads to social unrest.

Our contemporary idiom uses 'sleaze', the Italian *tangentopoli* and other words to express public concern. There is a danger that such words make bribery seem more acceptable and mask the damage it can do. Bribes undermine governments, subvert company cultures, destabilize society and – because bribery enables people to evade compliance with regulations – put global security at risk from drugs, uncontrolled financial flows and environmental disaster. Corruption anywhere threatens everybody everywhere.

That global threat makes cooperation against bribery essential. The political will for leaders to initiate action 'top-down' needs to be generated and sustained by 'bottom up' pressures from civil society, and further motivated by international cooperation. We should seek a global consensus against corruption, recognizing its threat to both local cultures and global security.

ANNEX: REFERENCES FOR QUOTATIONS IN BOXES 1 AND 2

A) *Advice to Moses*, from his father-in-law; 1,400, perhaps nearer 1,290 CE
    Exodus Chapter 18, verses 21, 22
    Law of Moses, given when appointing officials and judges
    Deuteronomy Chapter 16, verse 19
    About Samuel's sons: 1 Samuel Chapter 8, verses 3–5, quotations here and in
    section 5 taken from the Holy Bible, New Revised Standard Version, New
    York, Oxford, Oxford University Press, 1989, some shortened by paraphrase.

B) *Buddha, The Teaching of Buddha*, Tokyo, Bukkyo Dendo Kyokai, 630th
    revised edition, 1990, pages 468, 470.

C) *Confucius*, as described in Syed Hussein Alatas, *Corruption: Its Nature,
    Causes and Function*, Aldershot, Hong Kong (etc.), Avebury, 1990, page 54
    Hsiao Ching, Syed Hussein Alatas, *op. cit.*, page 44 – quoting Pan Ku, *The
    History of the Former Han Dynasty*, Vol. 1, translated Homer M. Dubs,
    Baltimore, Waverly press, 1938, page 306
    Wang an Shih, quoted by Syed Hussein Alatas, *op. cit.*, pages 72–74.

D) *Laws of Manu*, Chapter 7, sections 123, 124, translated by Wendy Doniger and
    Brian K. Smith, London, Penguin Classics, 1991, page 14 (I am indebted to
    Syed Hussein Alatas, *op. cit.*, page 14, for locating this reference).

E) *Plato, The Laws*, ed. Edith Hamilton and Huntington Cairns, New York,
    Pantheon, 1961, book 12, sec. d.

F) *Jesus Christ*, to tax collectors, Luke chapter 3, verses 12, 13; to soldiers, Luke
    chapter 3, verse 14; with Zacchaeus, Luke chapter 19, verses 1–10.

G) *The Qur'an*, Al-Baqara (The Cow), Sura II, 188, 189, from *The Noble Qur'an
    summarized by Dr Muhammad Taqi-ud-Din Al-Hilali and Dr Muhammad
    Muhsin Khan, based on text given by Muhammad Zafrulla Khan*; *see also*, for
    example, the *Qur'an*, London, Curzon Press, 2nd edition 1975, page 30
    The Sayings, quoted in promotional video from the Anti-Corruption Agency,
    Kuala Lumpur, Malaysia, based on Hadis Riwayat Thauban, as narrated by
    Ahmad and Hakim; Ref Al-Fathu Kabir, Juzu 3, Jalalul Sayuti, Beirut,
    Lebanon
    The Fatwa Alamagiri, T.P. Hughes, *Dictionary of Islam*, Lahore, Premier
    Book House, 1966, pages 43, 44, attributed by Hughes to Hamilton's Hidayah,
    Vol. 3, page 332. (The teacher Jawi required the situation to be one of
    emergency.)

H) *Queen Elizabeth the First*, recorded by Peter Hennessy, in C. Campbell and
    B.G. Peters (eds.), *Organizing Governance and Governing Organizations*,
    Pittsburgh, University of Pittsburgh Press, 1980, page 185.

MICHAEL LEVI

2. The Crime of Corruption

Before the 1990s, many in the West saw corruption as a problem limited to underdeveloped countries with fledgling political institutions, or else at least as being something more typical of Mediterranean, Asian or other similar cultures. However, political scandals in most Western European countries mean that there is now no escaping its systematic presence in developed democracies. Why should this be happening, what is being done about it, and what are likely to be the limits of the current wave of anti-corruption campaigns?

The *modus operandi* of occult financing of political parties normally requires the use of bribes, kickbacks and other forms of payoffs, tax evasion, fraud, undeclared slush funds, and planned bankruptcies. In some European countries, this in turn relies, to an extent perhaps unimaginable in Britain with its different bureaucratic traditions, on the massive production and acceptance of false invoices. So it is fruitful to examine links between political financing, fraud, and money laundering. Indeed, it is arguable that one can relate the resistance in some countries to all crime laundering legislation to their concerns about the effects that this might have on their campaign financing and risk of incrimination, *especially if they were to lose power or lose control of the criminal prosecution system.*

However, our understanding of corruption can also be enriched by using concepts found in the wider literature of criminology, such as labelling theory. Even if corrupt agreements are often in breach of the criminal law, we must still ask whether corruption is deviant or simply normal in some social groups or some countries. More exactly, why should some countries prohibit what is a widespread practice of their elites? In Japan, 9 of the 15 Prime Minsters who held office in the period 1955–1993 were involved in corruption scandals. At least half its members of Parliament, it is estimated, could only have obtained their seats through the aid of illegal financing.[1] At the height of the Italian *Tangentopoli* (kickback city) investigations, a

---

[1] J.-M. Bouissou, 'La corruzione in Giappone: un sistema di redistribuzione?', in D. Della Porta and Y. Meny, *Corruzione e Democrazia*, Naples, Liguori (1995), 157–183.

Barry A.K. Rider (ed.), Corruption: The Enemy Within, 35–47
© *Kluwer Law International. Printed in the Netherlands.*

third of the deputies were under investigation for various offences.[2] Are Western observers justified in labelling as 'corruption' the traditional giving of presents of appreciation to leaders and administrators (whether in Africa, Pakistan or Japan)?[3] In the more heavyweight and commonly agreed sense of corruption as massive embezzlement, we note that many of those who have come to power through anti-corruption campaigns in the last generation in Africa, South America, Asia, Mexico and the Philippines have themselves in turn been accused of corruption. Were their original allegations of corruption nothing more that a tactical device to obtain power, or did their exposure to political realities change their initial high ideals?

The questions posed in and by political science are central to understanding the context and meaning of political corruption. Corruption and the response to it reveal the relative power of the executive, parliament and the parties, and also illuminate the role of the criminal investigators, the judiciary and the fourth estate (the media). The attack on corruption (as that against other forms of white-collar crime or 'crimes of the powerful') can be seen as an attempt to re-legitimate the rulers and/or specific political actors or criminal justice agencies. Both corruption and anti-corruption, however, can serve to undermine, or extend, the legitimacy of politicians, parties and the state. Other questions take us further afield. The reduction of corruption is often used as a rationale for a shift from a state to a market economy. Yet, unless one makes it tautological, actual market economies seem quite prone to corruption, as the ideology shifts from one of public service to self-interest maximization: privatization, in other words, is not the answer to corruption except in so far as it may shift some personnel out of range of corruption legislation because they are no longer public officials. Likewise, the relationship between corruption and democracy is a very complex one: democracy is often viewed as the answer to corruption, but it can also be increased by it, as there is greater competition for the spoils of government, and hurt by it, as countries use local corruption cliques as an excuse to centralize or re-centralize power – France being a good example.

As may be seen in Italy, for some politicians it can be a positive client-gaining asset to display the capacity to survive successive attempts to put a stop to their illegal activities, as they profit from collusion of those involved in their projects as well as from a court system which permits a number of appeals before definitive judgment is given and allows the regular awarding of amnesties. As in the study of white-collar crime,[4] to study corruption is an attempt to follow a moving target – the way that certain transactions

---

[2] D. Nelken, 'White Collar Crime', in M. Maguire, R. Morgan and R. Reiner (eds.), *The Oxford Handbook of Criminology*, OUP (1994), 355–393.

[3] It is often assumed the traditional implies consensual, but what local people actually feel about their leaders' receipt of substantial gifts is seldom researched. Ethnic tensions being what they are, we would predict that group membership would affect tolerance levels.

[4] *See*, e.g., *supra*, note 2.

move in and out of acceptable behaviour as the boundaries of what is legitimate are softened, reaffirmed or redrawn: this is the classic stuff of labelling theory. Where those involved in corruption are political figures who embody the authority of the state, however, the implications are enormous for the legitimacy of the state.[5] Where corruption creates its own normative patterns, anti-corruption campaigns may even function as a lawless force destroying existing order.

IS POLITICAL CORRUPTION GROWING?

Public opinion polls show an increasing perception of corruption and the media increasingly report such stories,[6] as do those of the growth of fraud, including computer fraud.[7] But given low visibility of the behaviour and modest enforcement, it is easy to produce an artificial control wave which may not correspond to any underlying behavioural change. Notwithstanding these severe empirical difficulties, it is widely assumed that the 1980s was a period of particularly rampant corruption in continental Europe, especially within – though by no means restricted to – the Socialist parties in countries such as France, Italy and Spain. The proud slogan of the Spanish socialist party, '100 years of honesty', found itself capped by their opponents' reply 'and not a day more'.[8] This rendered them open to accusations from political opponents. Thus in Spain, we see a right-wing media-inspired campaign to undermine a nominally Socialist party and the Prime Minister Felipe Gonzalez, by associating them, *prima facie* plausibly, (i) with 'noble cause corruption' – that is, the use of secret intelligence service funds to finance assassinations of supporters of the Basque separatist group ETA in France and Spain, and extortion of party 'donations' from the business sector (the *Filesa* case), and (ii) with personal corruption as a symbol of 'the state we are in' (unlike the good old Franco-ist days!).[9] Indeed, it is the need for campaign finance and the ability of the political victor to grant or

---

[5] Corruption may unambiguously harm for economic development, where the Head of State simply embezzles a large proportion of GDP and state assets, as appears to have been the case in countries as diverse as the Philippines and Zaire.

[6] *See*, e.g., Siebel 1995:109, and Ruggiero in this volume.

[7] *See* M. Levi and A. Pithouse, *Victims of White-Collar Crime: the Social and Media Construction of Corporate Fraud* (in press).

[8] P. Heywood, 'Dalla dittatura alla democrazia: le mutevoli forme della corruzione in Spagna', in D. Della Porta and Y. Meny (eds.), *Corruzione e Democrazia*, Naples, Liguori (1995), 87–107.

[9] Spanish financial scandals include the brother of the former Deputy Prime Minister (who resigned to reduce political damage), and the politically appointed former head of the Guardia Civil, Luis Roldan, who was extradited back to Spain and who, as we write, awaits trial for allegedly embezzling funds for his personal use from the same covert intelligence 'pot' allegedly used to pay mercenaries for the assassinations.

deny favours, such as development permits and public sector contracts, that provide a heady mix capable of corrupting all but the most disciplined.[10] The succession of dramatic corruption scandals in Japan followed by 'business as usual' demonstrates this unholy alliance very powerfully.

Distress about the present is often associated with 'Golden Age-ist' distortions of the past: scandal-ridden Spain under the Socialists succeeded a period under Franco where corruption was the glue that bound together the fascistic economy. Much the same was true of the later stages of Russian Communism. Whereas the 1980s saw leading politicians in Germany surviving accusations of large-scale corruption and mendacity, political scandals in the reunited Germany now erupt over the small change of irregularities in their employment of domestics or use of their credit cards. While this has been explained as hysteria or as a safety valve to express deeper worries over the costs of German unification (*see* Siebel, 1995), the reduction in tolerance levels was common to many other European countries. Does this simply reflect the resentment of the old guard at the invasion of their privileges by the *nouveaux riches*,[11] or might it also reflect the coming of age of the less pro-Establishment 'children of the 60s' as consumers of media censures,[12] or even the loss of interest in broader ideologies and their substitution by anti-corruption sentiments as part of 'the politics of envy'? Geo-political changes are important to the revelation of pre-existing corruption: the collapse of the Soviet Union and world communism enabled the Americans to withdraw their support for the *status quo* in Italy, Pakistan and (after the Gulf War was over) Abu Dhabi, thereby undermining both the long-term Christian Democrat/Mafia alliance in Italy and the Bank of Credit and Commerce International (BCCI).

The deterioration in political and administrative service which results from the privileged access offered to their clients leads others to seek their own privileged routes, and so the cycle of corruption spirals. In the same way, a cycle of mutual dependence between politicians and organized criminals can develop, which breaks only when important persons withdraw from the exchanges. But those engaged in corrupt agreements tend to overreach themselves and bring about the collapse of these exchanges (i) through ever-increasing competition amongst those seeking clients, (ii) through the eventual fight back by those excluded, and (iii) above all, once investigations get started, because of the scramble – in the classic Prisoner's Dilemma logic – to be the first to confess once they know or believe that

---

[10] Once people have discretionary control over such non-transparent funds, it is easy for them to divert a portion for their own use: this was alleged of Colonel (and almost Senator) Oliver North in relation to the secret funds used to supply the Contras during the Reagan Presidency.

[11] *See* the comments on insider dealing of M. Clark, *Business Crimes*, (1990), 162.

[12] C. Sumner, *The Sociology of Deviance: an Obituary*, Milton Keynes, Open University Press (1993?).

trust in mutual silence has been broken. The term *pentiti* is amusing, in the light of the absence of remorse of most people in Italy and the US desperately seeking plea bargains for reduced sentences: penitence has little or nothing to do with it, but the penitentiary has!

We know that scandals and moral panics about particular social problems often have a built-in lifespan or natural history before they are succeeded and displaced by new concerns: here, corruption and most white-collar crimes have a built-in disadvantage not just because – collapsed buildings resulting from corrupt economies in construction excepted – they are visually less dramatic, but also because investigations and trials tend to take so long to develop that the media becomes bored.[13] However, there are inconsistencies in the evidence: some argue that criminalization campaigns come to a halt when they aim too high,[14] but this cannot account for the Italian case.

THE POLITICS OF CORRUPTION

Accusations reflect wider ideological positions – while the right connects corruption with wastefulness of left wing administrations, it is itself accused of using its political base to line the pockets of business elites. At the same time, the political significance of the source of such denunciations (as an index of battles between the central and local powers, or between 'old money' and emerging 'enterprise capital') tells us much about the progress of power struggles. Many accused of corruption respond that their accusers – whether judges, prosecutors or government agencies – have a hidden political agenda. One response is that 'they would say that, wouldn't they?', but the search for the interests behind anti-corruption campaigns and their limits can tell us a great deal about who can mobilize the public interest and may enable us to understand why levels of corruption (or campaigns against it) get out of control. Where there is a strong and unambiguous response, there may well be special motives. Thus, the demonization of BCCI, and Islamic banking in general, used the evidence of fraud, drugs money laundering, and involvement with Libya to deflect people from focusing on the way the bank had been used by *Western* intelligence agencies to launder the money to help with illicit overseas operations and arms trafficking.

---

[13] *See* the analysis of the media in white-collar crime cases in M. Levi and A. Pithouse, *Victims of White-Collar Crime: The Social and Media Construction of Corporate Fraud* (in press).

[14] E. Currie in Black and Mileski (eds.), *The Social Organization of Law*.

COMPARING CORRUPTION

There is much to be gained in examining corruption and control in a comparative perspective. At the level of basic description, this extends our opportunities for seeing who is involved in corruption, the wider causes, which groups act to expose or conceal corruption, and the cultural peculiarities of the role of law, ethics and the judges, prosecutors, police and other agencies, as well as the media. Corruption is often itself a transnational crime: as with many other examples of white-collar crime, the businesspeople and politicians involved at the highest level typically use other countries to hold or launder their slush funds or payoffs. The search for common factors has thrown up a number of causes (or concomitants) of corruption. Some of these causes are seen as common to only some countries, such as the need of Socialist parties without an existing solid financial base in France, Spain and Italy to obtain new sources of funds. Other features are more universal: the way that regulation opens up the opportunity for massive bribes to gain favour or avoid disfavour.

However, comparison should not be confined to seeking out what there is in common, but should also be used to understand the many relevant differences in political and legal cultures. Why do some countries rely mainly on the criminal law and others on self-regulation? Did campaigns start from above, from below, from part of the state apparatus aimed at other parts, from some political groups or individuals aimed at opponents? What divergences are there between countries in the way they conceive of checks and balances, of public and private, or of 'the rule of law'? For example, the rule of law in Britain is linked to the role of parliament as overseen by the judges, whereas in Italy it is seen to depend on an active judiciary, and in Germany, it is associated mainly with the integrity of the administration.

How anti-corruption campaigns form part of the cycle of corruption, and the responses to such campaigns, vary by culture. Thus, if such campaigns are part of normal politics in some countries of Africa, Asia and South America, they may have different significance in Italy and the UK, where, for different reasons, campaigns against corruption are more exceptional. In Italy, the recent *Tangentopoli* investigations constituted something of a watershed between the first and second republic, as corruption took on the role of symbolizing all that was wrong with the previous political system and its institutional arrangements. In Britain there continues to be a reluctance to draw the sharp line between business and political life, which creates suspicion of a blurring between public and private interest: this is reinforced by a deep cultural complacency that the British Establishment is trustworthy and would not allow their public roles to be influenced by private interests.

Even countries with similar legal and political arrangements can have intriguing differences in their definitions of where private interest interferes with public performance.[15] There are important but less acknowledged differences between countries in their toleration of open political lobbying by businesspeople: here, it is Britain and America which are perhaps more tolerant. On the other hand, we could contrast the way politicians and businessmen work out their hidden exchanges in different countries: in Britain, France and the US, successful politicians move out of politics into the business world, but they seldom do so in Italy, though businesspeople sometimes move into politics. Furthermore, there are interesting differences in the recent roles of judges and the media in anti-corruption campaigns. Why has the media played a larger part in exposing corruption in some countries, such as Britain and, especially, the US, whereas in others, such as Italy, it has been left to the judges, and while at the same time, in France, the media has often leaked material to the judges, in the hope that they will do something and enable the press to write about it without being sued for libel?

How can one account for the British tendency to deal with corruption as an all-party problem, at least prior to 1994, when the Labour opposition decided it could fruitfully link 'sleaze' with the Conservative 'greed' ethos? Does the existence of multi-party systems encourage more competition over corruption allegations than in basically two-party states? In one-party states, such allegations tend to be buried with their makers. There is need for a balance between looking for wider generalizations about corruption, and explaining it in terms of the specific historical context and culture in which it occurs;[16] but here, as elsewhere in comparative social science, a synthesis is not always easy to achieve.

THE CONTROL OF SCANDAL AND CONTROL BY SCANDAL

There are many opposites that cause corruption: if the alleged wider causes of corruption include the weakness of political parties, or their excessive power; the lack of a historically strong executive, or too strong a centralized executive; centrally owned economic units, or privatization; and loyalty to local groups, or absence of sentiments of loyalty, then it is unlikely that any solutions brought forward to specific scandals will overcome these underlying problems. It is a common assumption that corruption arises from allowing administrators too great discretion, and a common remedy proposed is to cut back on this. But it is illusory to believe that all demands can be processed at the same time, so there must always be scope for 'speed money' as well as specific favours. Absent 'proof', who is to decide whether

[15] E. Halevy-Etzioni, 'Comparing Semi-Corruption Among Parliamentarians in Britain and Australia', in E. Oyen (ed.), *Comparative Methodology*, London, Sage (1990), 113–133.

[16] P. Sztompka, 'Conceptual Frameworks in Comparative Inquiry : Divergent or Convergent', in M. Albrow and E. King (eds.), *Globalization, Knowledge and Society*, London, Sage (1990).

the particular form that such prioritization takes is the result of corruption or merely different valuation?

What solutions have been offered to the problem of political corruption? Law may often be part of the problem of corruption. Too many laws, excessive formalism, and vexatious procedures help create corruption – by forcing people to get round them – and weaken attempts to control it. Law may encourage corruption by setting artificially low limits to political expenses, but as the case of Israel shows, even a generous limit will be insufficient to combat the pressure of political competition, where the gains from access to power and the possibility of rewriting the law normally far outweigh the legal penalties or the loss of legitimacy; and new laws may merely displace competition elsewhere.

Law diffuses responsibility; investigations and punishment over-dramatize; and the need to distinguish between the legal and illegal creates artificial dichotomies between behaviour. Legal campaigns block predictability, and law can express an over-ambitious ideal of the relationship between citizens and the state. Unanticipated side effects occur, as when laws blocking corruption slow down the award of public works, allowing organized criminals the opportunity to buy up building firms which are short of cash. The implementation of law always remains culture-dependent: the American enthusiasm for whistleblowing, and the financial rewards for it, has not at all been matched in Britain, where political elites regard it as encouraging sneaking, and whistleblowers are easily marginalized as mentally ill. No senior American politicians, though, have fallen foul of the legislation, which has benefited the Federal government through revelations of cheating by such as defence contractors.

The enforcement of laws involving corruption and white-collar crime, often enacted on a tide of popular resentment in harness with a need for political elites to re-legitimate the state, often involves major intrusions into civil liberties, which may have broader social consequences. Precisely because there are seldom any complainants, even where the corrupt extort money from businesspeople or the public, corruption may be seen as an opportunity for policing agencies to develop proactive strategies: but this gives powerful elites the opportunity to target selectively their political opponents, or those who refuse to pay bribes/make political 'donations' to the 'right' party for 'Sting' operations or intensive tax reviews, while leaving 'friendly' parties alone.[17]

In short, high-level corruption – and those economic crimes involving business elites that do not involve corruption – raise a variety of problems for the normal functioning of policing and prosecution agencies. Issues of evaluating discretion are intriguing. What would a fair distribution of investigation of high and low level corruption look like? How do we ensure

---

[17] *See*, e.g., A. Block, *Masters of Paradise*, (1990).

that the interests of powerful groups do not buy themselves either generally low priority in being regulated/policed/prosecuted or the ability to interfere with particular decisions? It is these power inequalities, which benefit also corruption *Mafiosi*, and benefitted those 1930s American professional criminals with access to 'the fix' in the political machine described by Sutherland,[18] that give a difficult twist to the accountability debate. For the lack of transparency in the decision-making of investigators, prosecutors, and judges means that distinguishing evidential caution from socio-political bias is very difficult.[19]

In some countries of continental Europe, law can *potentially* deal with corruption, but reliance is placed on collusive non-enforcement. By contrast, in common law countries, as explained by Riesman,[20] one may witness *lex imperfecta*, that is, law that is deliberately designed to be imperfect. While not taking the view that all apparent inadequacies are 'designed in', we consider that there are four ways in which corruption prosecutions can be undermined. The first – the *substantive law* route – is either not to criminalize it at all or to do so in such a way that only crude exchanges of money for favours, either 'doing good' or 'not doing harm', are caught. The second – the *procedural law* route – is to make it difficult to mount covert strategies such as 'Sting' operations which make prosecutions of elite persons easier.[21] As the example of Berlusconi's attempts to call a halt to *Tangentopoli* shows, elite self-interest can be disguised as generalized concern for defendants' rights, though few were fooled in that particular case. The third – the *resourcing* route – is to provide so few *general* resources for corruption and white-collar crime investigations in the specialist squads that normally deal with such matters, that there is unlikely to be any *practical* possibility of prosecuting or even seriously investigating allegations involving corporate or political elites. Moreover, even if investigators and/or prosecutors were to contemplate such far-reaching inquiries, they would appreciate that this might have long-term negative effects not only on their own personal futures but upon future funding and political support for their agency's objectives.[22] The final – *political control* – route refers to the

---

[18]   E. Sutherland, *The Professional Thief*, (1937).

[19]   Those of a post-modern disposition may not see the issue as relevant, since assessing the plausibility of different accounts has no inherent meaning. There are, of course, biasses built into law itself, particularly in relation to chains of responsibility in organizational contexts.

[20]   D. Riesman, *Folded Lies*, (1979).

[21]   *See* C. Fijnaut and G. Marx (eds.), *Undercover: Police Surveillance in Comparative Perspective*, (1995); M. Levi, *The Investigation, Prosecution and Trial of Serious Fraud*, (1993); and G. Marx, *Undercover: Police Surveillance in America*, (1987).

[22]   Quite apart from any political interference and careerism, organizational practices – for example, a focus on minimizing investigative costs and risks of acquittal – may lessen the chances of prestigious figures being prosecuted in complex organizational corruption cases, since they may not touch the money directly. Unless they get careless – as does happen – senior figures are normally harder to connect.

ability of elites to frustrate investigations that threaten them and their allies or, alternatively, to press prosecutions against their political opponents.[23] There are major cultural differences in the degrees of actual and perceived political independence and managerial accountability – both *de facto* and *de jure* – afforded to criminal investigators and prosecutors in different countries.

This analysis of the third and fourth routes to non-prosecution of corruption should be situated within the routines of criminal investigation and prosecution. Here, we note that in many countries – including not only Britain but also many of its former colonies – powers to investigate corruption and economic crime exceed normal powers, for it is often argued that the proper detection and investigation of such crimes needs the power to compel answers and documentary evidence from witnesses and even suspects. In several British colonies and former colonies – such as Hong Kong and Malaysia – there is legislation requiring civil servants who wish to avoid conviction for corruption to rebut allegations – once the facts are *prima facie* proven – that they have been living 'in a manner inconsistent with their legitimate income'. Investigative powers in England and Wales are inconsistent, for if a case is dealt with by the police and Crown Prosecution Service – by statute, the consent of the Director of Public Prosecutions is required to prosecute corruption offences – suspects are not required to answer questions, and confidential documents can be obtained only after a judicial order under Schedule 1 of the Police and Criminal Evidence Act 1984; whereas if the *same* matter – for example, corruption among brokers in the North Sea oil industry[24] – is dealt with as a serious fraud, much greater and less judicially supervised powers can be brought into play. Likewise, if there are tax or company offences under investigation, the power regimes may vary enormously.

In continental Europe, career investigating magistrates who are not specialists in economic crime or corruption do the greater part of the criminal investigations but, with the exception of Italy, corruption has not been felt to be so serious a political issue as to require a special body with extraordinary powers. But in England and Wales, it is only in exceptional cases, and at the instigation of the police, who are reluctant to spend huge resources on a case without any assurance that it will be prosecuted along the lines that they are investigating, that prosecutors have any direct input into a corruption case before a suspect is charged.

---

[23] It should not be thought that this is solely the prerogative of Third World nations – *see* White in this volume. President Nixon made considerable use both of the FBI and the Internal Revenue Service in this regard: *see* A. Block, *Masters of Paradise*, (1990).

[24] *See* J. Andvig, 'Corruption in the North Sea Oil Industry: Issues and Assessments', *Crime, Law and Social Change*, 23(4), 289–313. The UK Serious Fraud Office, rather than the police, successfully dealt with one major case of this kind.

How do we reduce the risk of political interference in the decision to prosecute? In principle, by analogy with the Victim's Charter, one form of accountability might be to require the prosecution agency to give challengeable reasons for *non*-prosecution: yet this does not happen. If an Australian Royal Commission, a US Senate, or an external UK Department of Trade and Industry inspection is authorized and published, there is some evidence for outsiders to set against the decision not to prosecute, though they might have to form their own judgments about what evidence would be legally admissible. Otherwise, the media is the principal potential source of investigative accounts and critique. But in the UK and, in different ways elsewhere, the media is enormously inhibited by libel laws, editorial and owner conservatism, and – in some cases – journalistic laziness. Except where undercover operatives can film politicians receiving bribes or where victims are obviously hurt, corruption often lacks the visual impact needed for television.

Is it possible to circumvent central control over prosecutions for corruption? In England, it is assumed that there is no need for any more independent public official to investigate or prosecute, and a private prosecution would be able to take place only for frauds such as falsification of accounts rather than for corruption offences *per se*. In the US, as the lengthy Iran-Contra investigation showed, the appointment of Special Prosecutors and Independent Counsel[25] to supervise highly sensitive political investigations does not fully resolve the twin difficulties of demonstrating independence and mounting prosecutions in a timely way.[26] As Williams puts it:

> The decision [of Congress] to grant immunity to North and Poindexter dealt what proved to be fatal blows not only to the North and Poindexter prosecutions but also the Independent Counsel's entire prosecution strategy. Thus, the political needs of Congress blocked the Independent Counsel's efforts to prosecute key players in the scandal and created technical obstacles which made prosecutions most unlikely.[27]

---

[25] A 1983 Amendment to the Ethics in Government Act 1978 PL 95–521 replaced the post of special prosecutor with that of 'independent counsel'. The former are appointed by and may be removed by the Attorney General – in the US, as in England, a political appointment. The latter are appointed by a division of the US Federal Court of Appeals following a request by the Attorney General: Attorneys General have no formal say in who is appointed, and cannot fire them, as they did Archibald Cox during the Watergate investigation when he showed too great enthusiasm for following the leads upwards to the White House.

[26] The Walsh Final Reports into Iran-Contra were published only in January 1994, some seven years after his appointment: *see* R. Williams, 'The Last Word on the Iran-Contra Affair?', *Crime, Law and Social Change*, 23 (1995) 367–385.

[27] *Supra*, note 26, at 379.

In August 1994, the Special Prosecutor appointed on a bipartisan basis to investigate Presidential involvement in the 'Whitewater' loans scandal was replaced by a judicially nominated Independent Counsel, partly because the original one was considered insufficiently active in his approach to suit the needs of the Republican Congress. That case still rumbles on.

In the US, parallel legal structures sometimes make it possible for corruption-related prosecutions to occur when they are resisted at their 'normal' level: one of the clearest illustrations was the prosecution of BCCI by Robert Morgenthau, District Attorney for New York County, while the US Department of Justice prevaricated, allegedly because of the CIA's active involvement in espionage and money laundering through the bank. BCCI is a highly politicized case, spawning inter-agency conflicts at an international as well as national level, not only between the West and Abu Dhabi and Pakistan, but also between the UK and the US as, to the outrage of some Americans, the UK Serious Fraud Office has arrested (and the courts have later imprisoned) some key witnesses who have assisted New York County prosecutors in their actions against other BCCI personnel and in their attempts to recover assets for the US courts and, it is intended, for BCCI creditors. Doubtless, this was highly convenient for those American and Arab figures whose corrupt alliances might have received considerable exposure, had the prosecutions in England not discredited (and incapacitated in jail) these witnesses. But no one was prosecuted for corruption in any of the myriad BCCI cases: BCCI has been treated as a case of fraud and money laundering – as organized rather than white-collar crime.

The important issues of accountability raised by serious fraud and corruption prosecutions are unlike most faced in other arenas, and arise principally because of the combination of (a) lack of transparency of decision-taking (at case acceptance, investigative resource-allocation, use of search and interview powers, and prosecution decision levels), with (b) the political (with a small or a large 'p') ramifications of particular cases. As far as we know, adult high status persons are seldom involved in any property crimes other than fraud or corruption. These political ramifications include party political donations from businesspeople – on which the heavily-indebted British Conservative party became highly dependent during the 1980s and 1990s to finance its campaigns and its Headquarters – who sought favours such as well-photographed dinners with the Prime Minister. They also include broader conceptions of public interest which are difficult to unpack, such as the dilemma between 'showing that we are sorting out crime in the suites' and 'not undermining the confidence of the public in business (or politicians)', whose balance shifts considerably over time and between countries.

Though – especially where there is a jury trial or an independent judiciary – neither government nor state has direct control over convictions, extra resources can always be found for those cases that involve people whom 'the system' is determined to 'get': despite the fact that most of the key defendants had been charged in the US or Abu Dhabi, or were unavailable in Pakistan, Parliament voted the Serious Fraud Office millions of pounds extra to deal with BCCI; and the otherwise short-staffed Merseyside police had 33 officers working full-time on the investigation of corruption allegations against the influential former left-wing Liverpool councillor Derek Hatton. (He was acquitted of all charges of corruption and subsequent theft trials.) These areas of indirect influence occur because even where there is no direct political control over crime investigation (as there is in many Third World countries), bureaucracies need the support of politicians, including the Attorney General, for resources, and are inclined to please them. In polities where power is more centralized and investigation and judicial agencies less autonomous, Pandora's box can remain even more tightly shut against those allegations of elite fraud and corruption that threaten the hegemony of those who enjoy current power. In countries such as Britain, the tendency is to play down the extent of corruption and to suppress scandal for fear of rocking the boat. Whilst in some other countries, control by scandal may do little more than substitute one set of political actors for another, to be followed by a further set of scandals. In short, the politics of corruption in some countries is played out by attempting to suppress scandal, while in others, scandal campaigns form part of the routines involved in the circulation of elites.

MARK FINDLAY

3. Corruption in Small States: Case Studies in Compromise

INTRODUCTION

Both the particular contexts of socio-economic development, and the unique post-colonial/post independence agendas of small states in the Pacific, present predictable invitations for the creation of corruption relationships. The two case studies discussed in this paper provide scenarios common to this region, wherein customary structures of power and influence converge on modern commercial institutions and instruments to produce corrupt consequences. However, the contextual analysis of these as corruption, from a developed or global perspective, is neither straightforward nor uncontested, and the challenge inherent in their regulation is problematic. The integration of such relationships within deeply rooted and accepted customary authority structures qualifies their description as corrupt, and tends towards a process of reinterpretation and denial which prevents the effective intervention of regulation and control processes. The integration of these relationships within otherwise legitimate structures of economic development and promotion makes their perpetuation likely, and even their exposure largely inconsequential in conventional control or sanctioning terms.

This paper will explore some of the issues which tend to confuse corruption and compromise control. Initially, the connections between corruption and the early stages of economic development are commented upon. Political imperatives which generate and rely on what in other contexts would be determined as corruption relationships are analyzed in case study situations of modern commerce. Characteristics of customary obligation are seen to counter and confuse claims of corruption. The processes through which such claims are made themselves reveal interesting conflicts between custom and constitutional legality. Even the conventional economic regulators, such as bank boards and law enforcement institutions – including the police and commercial crime investigators, are involved in the perpetuation of these relationships. These contradictory relationships, at least in conventional commercial and political contexts, are analyzed.

Finally, the globalization both of economic development paradigms and associated corruption scenarios are indicated as having a potentially signifi-

Barry A.K. Rider (ed.), Corruption: The Enemy Within, 49–61
© *Kluwer Law International. Printed in the Netherlands.*

cant impact on corruption in small states. The contextual understanding of corruption in these states therefore should not remain bound to custom or local politics. As international finance impinges on the economic strategies and commitments of small states, international discourse on corruption and regulation agendas can influence the way small states redefine traditional relationships and obligations.

CORRUPTION AND ECONOMIC DEVELOPMENT

If crime is identified as one of the behavioural or culturally negative consequences of development, then conventionally it is either the pace or personalities of change which are held responsible. In so doing, the international advocates of development are able to deflect the 'blame' for any crime/development correlation away from the necessary contextual features of development and onto corrupt bureaucrats, lazy politicians or uncommitted communities.

In small Pacific states there seem to be common imperatives behind contexts of development and relationships of crime. Often similar forms of relationships also exist as strong structural features of customary social organization and obligation. For instance, the 'big man' in Melanesian village governance is the principal in provincial or national politics, and a beneficiary in the corrupt rewards of economic development. The complex and concrete loyalties of chiefly politics in Polynesian society are consistent from the village council to the national parliament and the corporate boardroom. As such, they conceal corruption in government commerce, countering such labels and arguments for its control.

Global juxtapositions of corruption as 'bad' and development as 'good' fail to appreciate or reconcile their commonality in particular cultural contexts, such as those which prevail in the politics of small Pacific states. International interests in selective socio-economic development often share a similar terrain with the selective criminalization of corruption in development.

The context of cultures in developmental transition are contexts of marginalization and crime, as well as modernization and wealth creation. Why, then, from a global perspective, are the problems of development and crime represented by control agencies, at least in a paradoxical discourse?

In small Pacific states, the contextual interaction and interdependence between:
 – customary social structures and modes of development;
 – development and corruption; and
 – corruption and customary social structures
are issues which are strangely absent from both criminology and development studies. In addition, the resilience of both local and globalized misrepresentations of the consequences of development, in terms of custom

and corruption, merit explanation. Looking at both economic development and corruption as integral to markets and enterprise where customary structures prevail is a useful predicate to further analysis of corruption in small states.

ENTERPRISE, MARKET MODELS AND CORRUPTION

The principal motivation for commercial enterprise, legitimate or otherwise, is profit. Profit through enterprise is realized under specific market conditions. A market is a framework of commercial relationships, and corruption can form just one such relationship.

Certain forms of criminal enterprise develop and flourish under specific market conditions (for example, illicit drug trafficking requires organized business arrangements which can operate within highly regulated, monopolistic market relationships). Criminal enterprise relies on market conditions which may be regulated so as to diminish the viability of the enterprise for certain participants.

Such regulation, however, differs from that influencing legitimate business enterprise (for example, the profits of criminal enterprise, while not available for taxation, may be confiscated on identification). While the regulation of criminal enterprise is largely set apart from that which influences legitimate commerce, the consequences of both forms of regulation may be similar (for example, contraction in market players; increased market risk; increased governmental participation in the market; pressures for deregulation).

Traditionally, criminal enterprise is controlled through the criminal sanction. While directed against individuals and behaviour, the criminal sanction and more particularly law enforcement practices may also influence market conditions (for example, the selective prohibition of drugs determines issues of distribution, product purity, and 'street price', in an atmosphere of absolute or inelastic demand).

Where criminal sanctions do not result in the total prohibition of a criminal enterprise, then such sanctions will add to the market regulation of those criminal enterprises which remain (for example, where the law generally prohibits trade in a particular drug, but law enforcement concentrates on the lower end of the distribution chain, small-time drug dealers are squeezed out of the market to the benefit of the better organized and capital-resourced traders).

Globalized efforts at controlling criminal enterprise generally fail to recognize their consequent effect on market regulation, and specifically on opportunities for criminal enterprise. Controlling criminal enterprise involves the effective closure of profit opportunities from some, while in particular supply and demand environments it may mean an expansion and diversification of market share for others. For instance, police activity against street prostitution may make the more unobtrusive environment of the brothel more attractive to the client and to law enforcement policy makers.

Market regulation may create new opportunities for profitable enterprise. The regulation of any enterprise (and the control of crime in particular) through adjusting market conditions can generate new criminal opportunities (for example, through the development of specialized policing institutions and methods directed against lucrative drug trafficking, the invitation to corrupt conduct within police organizations becomes focused; the potency of the corruption relationships which arise may alter the market situation of drug trafficking, wherein the law enforcers themselves may move into the chain of supply).

While crime control may act as a market regulator for corrupt relationships, its effectiveness and that of any market regulator will depend on the overall structure of the market. In small Pacific states no market structure can operate without the influence (and recognition of the influence) of customary obligation. Structures of such obligation determine market parameters and the boundaries of profitability, legitimate or otherwise. Therefore it is hardly surprising that the nature of most commercial enterprise here, and the form of its regulation, will be essentially predetermined by structures of customary obligation. If commercial relationships become corrupt within enterprise, then these relationships will also evidence the influence of custom.

Corruption as a commercial phenomenon goes beyond markets which centre on crime. Wherever profit opportunities exist under regulated conditions which favour restricted access to profit opportunities, and where the accountability of regulators is limited or highly conditional, then criminal enterprise, because of its structure, will have a competitive edge over legitimate business, because it is also not bound by the legitimate regulations of the market. Effective control strategies need to neutralize the relationships and conditions which make corruption and criminal enterprise commercially viable.

Further, the market/opportunity context in small Pacific states will be a custom-centred context, despite the refinement of the politics of development and modernization. As both government and private sector enterprise in small Pacific states recognize structures and personalities of customary obligation, and where status and profitability within enterprise relies on custom, then corruption may be supported by or provide a support to custom, so as to produce a commercial 'edge'. Structures of customary obligation, in turn, will insulate the commercial enterprise and its participants from the slur of corruption or attempts at its control.

Corruption is a relationship of power and influence existing within and taking its form from specific environments of opportunity. In small Pacific states, opportunity in so many situations is predetermined by custom, status and obligation. Opportunity is further designated by the aspirations for power relationships, and structures and processes at work towards their regulation.

Opportunities for corruption, and market opportunities advanced through corrupt relationships, are essentially dependent on the market context of illicit enterprise. Police corruption, for instance, usually takes the form of bribing individual officers with money or favours in order that the enforcement activities of these police might favour a particular criminal enterprise. Because the exercise of police discretion is often on a 'one-to-one' level (and often it is away from public view), the benefits resulting from the bribery of individual officers may be considerable. Such contexts are defined by frameworks of regulation, and corruption control mechanisms are important within these (Findlay, 1993).

Relationships of corruption provide important market conditions for the profitability of criminal enterprise. Effective crime control directed against corruption should attack the relationship (bribery), the participants in the relationship (personalities and corporations), the structures of the relationship (secrecy, discretion and authority), and the profit produced through the relationship.

Commercial enterprise in small developing states often forges and relies on corrupt relationships within the mechanisms which regulate the market. These mechanisms include government and the agencies of criminal justice. In order to attack this connection between commercial enterprise and corruption, it is essential to engage and change the dimensions of the market so that a corrupt relationship is no longer a profitable commercial choice. Profit structures need to be undermined and in order to achieve this, the nature and form of market regulation must move away from monopolistic supply and inelastic demand situations.

In the case studies which follow, the complexity of this invocation becomes apparent. As the characteristics of certain markets are shaped by both traditional and newly emergent commercial custom, regulation and control strategies built on respect for custom find it difficult, if not impossible, to protect the requirements of legitimate commerce against corruption fostered and redefined through custom.

Case 1: The Failure of the National Bank of Fiji
– Reinterpreting Corruption

In July 1995, *The Review*, the principal business magazine in Fiji, ran a series of feature articles under the title 'The Chaos at the NBF'. This was the first major exposé of what many in the commercial community in Fiji had suspected for months, if not years: that due to incompetence and shady dealing, the government-owned bank was insolvent. The article commented on a World Bank expert who had reviewed the state of the bank two months previously. When referring to the completely inadequate management information systems operated by the NBF, he had quipped: 'It would be like driving at high speed on a highway in a car without a dashboard and a steering wheel'. The bank had no real idea of the state of loan provisioning, bad debts and cash flow. With a paid-up capital of $15 million and $450 million in deposits, the bank had $300 million out in loans, of which up to $120 million had been assessed as nonrecoverable. In particular, $40 million in loans had been granted to bank employees or were extended to companies in which employees had an interest. For instance, a loan out of the Rotuman branch of the bank (which had around $5 million in loan accounts outstanding and only a little over $150,000 invested in savings) for around $2 million was held by a company in which the bank's chief executive officer of the NBF was a director.

It would not be fair to say that all these staff loans were corrupted. However, ample evidence of the disadvantageous term of these loans from the bank's perspective brought into question the motivations of branch managers and loans officers.[1] Their incompetence in the exercise of considerable discretion seemed to be beyond what might be explained away in terms of loose bank practice. The repayment of loans from overdrawn current accounts, the absence of requirements that loans be insured or the issuance of further loans to cover these premiums, were the types of practices which led the bank, in October 1995, to create a new code on self-dealing. It also meant that staff were sacked, demoted or repositioned as part of the bank's restructuring.

The mess at the bank has also been put down to undue political interference. Such an allegation is not surprising, when one considers the circumstances surrounding the appointment of the recently-removed chief manager of the NBF. During his 1987 military coup, the present Prime Minister of Fiji, Major General Rabuka, appointed a branch manager of the bank to head the NBF. Apparently, on 2 December 1987, the coup leader's appointee entered NBF headquarters with a group of soldiers to announce that he had been installed as the chief manager. The expatriate incumbent was turned out. The new appointment was one of which even the then Minister for Finance had no knowledge.

The Review (July 1995, p. 21) quoted NBF 'insiders' as agreeing that the mess was partly due to a 'higher level of political consideration in lending'. While no clear evidence has emerged that there was direct political pressure to approve loans, 'sometimes you got the message', admitted the former deputy manager of the NBF. When asked about nepotism and political interference in the bank's dealings, a previous chairman of the NBF board

---

[1] For instance, a staff member was given a loan that required monthly repayments of $692. His monthly salary with the bank was $700. When he could not meet his repayments, a loan review was carried out. The outcome was his consideration for a pay-rise – *see The Review* (July 1995), 22.

stated, 'there are always these factors coming into any decision situations and you play it as you see it at the time' (*The Review*, July 1995, p. 28).

A further complication when considering the relationship between politics and the NBF is the corporate aim for the NBF to advance the national interest, which surfaced after the coup. Of this, the present Finance Minister has said: 'Government cannot expect the NBF to be viable by asking it to pursue national objectives. I do not know who actually defined the NBF's goal as to act in the national interest. Definitely, we do not want this to mean losing money' (*The Review*, July 1995, p. 22). The present chairman of the bank board, however, agrees that one of the bank's functions is to pursue the national interest. When asked to what extent, he conceded: 'it depends on how one defines national interest' (*The Review*, July 1975, p. 32).

This issue of national interest seems to have taken on a clearly partial interpretation since the coup. The chief manager following the takeover developed the bank to favour indigenous Fijians and Rotumans. The NBF acted more like a development bank for many Fijian enterprises, and continued to prop them up as their commercial fortunes faltered. A significant number of these were connected to prominent Fijian politicians, past and present, and leading chiefs. When it comes to the review and pursuit of defaulted loans, the response of the bank and the government continues to be one of discrimination. Firms with indigenous Fijian interests at their heart have largely been spared, while Indo-Fijian enterprises like the Baijapi supermarket chain have recently been forced to the wall. In the case of prominent individual defaulters, the normal civil claims have largely been ignored. When pressed, the Minister of Finance made the shocking revelation that the NBF debacle 'could even lead to some people being declared bankrupt' (*The Review*, July 1995, p. 23).

Regarding the national interests of taxpayers who, after all, are the real shareholders in a state bank such as this, these are compromised on two fronts. Initially the public and investors have seen bank profits squandered through the NBF subsidizing (with taxpayers' funds) the operations of some borrowers who should have folded. Further, the government may now be called upon to invest over $100 million as part of a rescue package for the bank over the next two years. The money is to be found through skimming-off from otherwise profitable government enterprises, or through their sale.

The regulation scenario is another tale of political interference and prevarication. Conventional market regulators, such as the Auditor General, the bank board, and the Reserve Bank, have each been criticized as tardy in their oversight and early intervention. The government has resisted repeated calls for a public inquiry into the NBF, despite a recent opinion poll which revealed that over two-thirds of respondents favoured this outcome. The police have investigated, but their report appears to have stalled at the Office of the Director of Public Prosecutions. One year after the commencement of their investigation, the Police Commissioner felt constrained to hold a press conference, and against the background of concern over the cost of the investigation, to indicate that charges against the chief manager had to await the processing of other convictions of other employees. The recent demise of a serious fraud bill has been linked to the interests of those in parliament with an interest in the NBF. The Reserve Bank is investigating, but the Minister for Finance has said that its report will not be made public.

One year after the original *Review* exposé, the *Fiji Times* newspaper published what it claimed was a full list of loan accounts in default with the bank. Amongst the names were the present and past presidents of Fiji, and many prominent members of the SVT, the ruling political party. In letters to the editor which followed, some correspondents decried the disgrace that these people, who had given so much to their country, should be exposed to such public scrutiny. The inference was that this slice of the national pie was small and legitimate recompense for high public office.

Below the list in the *Fiji Times* was a court report on an NBF employee who was being prosecuted for fraud in the form of dealings which in so many other contexts had either been ignored or justified in terms of the bank's 'national interest' practice. As I write, the government is in the process of negotiating redundancies with NBF staff in order to save the bank, and its branches are closed due to national industrial action.

Case 2: Bank Guarantees from Vanuatu
– Disclosing and Decoding Corruption

Early in July 1996, the Ombudsman of Vanuatu published a report in which she described a 'scam' that the report alleged 'could lead to the bankruptcy of the Republic of Vanuatu'.[2] The Ombudsman had been investigating this matter for several months prior to the publication of her report, and despite the preliminary nature of her findings, the absence of confirmation of many of the crucial facts on which her conclusions relied, and the existence of contemporaneous and ongoing criminal proceedings against a principal player in the scam, she felt compelled 'to try and cut through the complexities of international finance and leave the maze of legal technicalities to be unravelled by the appropriate authorities' (the Report, p. 1).

It is useful to understand the relationship between the Ombudsman and the politically powerful in Vanuatu. During the two years of her office, the Ombudsman has publicly criticized Prime Ministers and Ministers, and has been taken to court on a number of occasions in efforts to contain her public

---

[2] Republic of Vanuatu Office of the Ombudsman, *Public Report: The Provision of Bank Guarantees Given in the Sum of US$ 100,000,000 in Breach of the Leadership Code and Section 14 of the Ombudsman Act and Related Matters Thereto, on the Prime Minister, the Minister of Finance, the Governor of the Reserve Bank of the Republic of Vanuatu and the First Secretary to the Minister of Finance* (hereafter referred to as the Report), 3.

reporting function. In her words, 'since the appointment of the Ombudsman it has become increasingly obvious that many – indeed most – of our officials and office-holders have very little idea of two things – firstly the realistic demands of the job they have been allocated, and secondly, the moral and ethical standards by which the public is entitled to be served' (the Report, p. 2). More than this, her office and investigations are dogged by 'many obstructions' and 'hostility'. Regularly, 'promises of cooperation are made, only to be followed by unwillingness to be open with the truth' (the Report, p. 2).

However, with almost religious zeal, the Ombudsman in Vanuatu has interpreted her responsibilities as being to protect the people from their governments. But such protection is deemed to implicate the people in the vigilance essential for their own protection. 'If the people of Vanuatu really wish the office of the Ombudsman to be an effective one, they themselves will need to ascertain where truth and justice are being served, and to be vigilant in ensuring that offenders are effectively dealt with. It is easy to become bored by official reports and legal technicalities, but the prosperity and future of the country depends in the long run on the quality of leadership which the people select'. Almost as if anticipating the criticism which was to be levelled against her by those named in her report, the Ombudsman continued: 'It is commonplace for the Ombudsman to get accused of personal bias, or political partisanship, or colonialist mentality, etc., when conducting investigations. The public should have no difficulty in knowing why these personal charges are made by those being investigated' (the Report, p. 3).

The present investigation centres on a fraudulent financial scheme which was disturbingly similar to that which recently bankrupted the Cook Islands. Simply, it involved the issuing of bank guarantees by government officials which were then to be transacted by a financial adviser through secondary markets with major world banks. It was alleged by the promoters of the scheme that vast profits would be realized with little or no financial risk. Of this inducement, the Report observed: 'It appears that the country's leaders were duped into believing that a visiting group of so-called "promoters" or "investment managers" were able to secure vast profits for Vanuatu ... for whatever reasons – whether ignorance or greed or both – our leaders at the highest level went along with this incredible plot, even to the extent of issuing some of these foreign adventurers with Vanuatu Diplomatic Passports, in order to make their dubious transaction more credible. As a result, there are at this very moment official Vanuatu "I.O.U.'s" circulating in unknown hands among the international community, amounting to more than twice the total foreign reserves of the Vanuatu people' (the Report, p. 1).

The Ombudsman ranged her criticism of the Finance Ministry and the Reserve Bank from 'pitiful ignorance' to 'criminal neglect'. On the strength of the Report, there seems little doubt that the four officials who signed and issued the bank guarantees were acting beyond their authority and even against the law. The action had been examined by the Attorney General and the

Governor of the Reserve Bank. The Attorney General advised that the transactions were illegal. The Governor of the Reserve Bank took the view that the 'trading programme', in respect of which the bank guarantees had been issued, was a scam and could lead to the bankruptcy of the Republic of Vanuatu. This did not, however, stop the Governor from co-signing the guarantees.

The financier who promoted the scheme, a discharged bankrupt with questionable financial credentials in Australia, initially sold the idea to the Minister of Finance. The Minister had the guarantees drafted and directed them to be signed by the Prime Minister, the Governor of the Reserve Bank, and the First Secretary of his Ministry. Along the way, he became a co-director of a company, 'New Resources Group Vanuatu Ltd.', through which the guarantees would pass during one stage of their transaction, and profits were to result and be paid to the company. Another director was the Australian financier, and shareholders were designated as the national and a provincial government of Vanuatu, and two shelf trust companies with false addresses. The Minister also issued to the promoter a Power of Attorney to transact for the government.[3]

Some conflict of recall emerged between the Prime Minster and the Governor of the Reserve Bank regarding their authorization of the bank guarantees. The Prime Minister indicated to the Ombudsman that when the bank guarantees were presented to him by the Finance Minister for his signature, he refused until the Governor of the Reserve Bank had signed and thus indicated his approval. Once this was done, the Prime Minister signed. The Governor of the Reserve Bank contradicted this view, saying that his signature only came after the others had signed. Of this, the Ombudsman has commented: '[the signatories] must all be taken as having been purposeful in the actions by them, given that the documents involve the largest sum of money ever committed by Vanuatu. Not one of them can deny liability by saying that they signed because the others did and thus assumed that the proper procedures had been gone through. To do so would be an abrogation of responsibility and of their high office' (the Report, p. 19).

Neither the Minister for Finance nor the Prime Minister presented information on the scheme to their Council of Ministers, nor to Parliament as a whole, which both law and convention require.[4] The Prime Minister later argued that Parliament is often asked to approve and authorize loan arrangements or other financial dealings retrospectively, and that this would be just such

---

[3] The Ombudsman sought from the Minister information on this Power of Attorney, but he refused to answer her questions or to answer a summons to appear and respond.

[4] For instance, Section 13 of the *Public Finance Act* requires that such guarantees be authorized by Parliament. In addition, the Ombudsman reports that terms of the *Reserve Bank Act* and the *Economic and Social Development Act* have been breached. There was no consideration or authorization by the Board of the Reserve Bank for the Bank to jointly issue the guarantees. The Attorney General advised that the guarantees were void *ab initio* because of the failure to comply with the domestic laws of the Republic.

an instance. The Ombudsman did not agree that this was a common practice amongst other Commonwealth countries, and reiterated that the legislation of Vanuatu does not permit such a retrospective authorization.

Besides the criticisms about breaches of the Leadership Code and the laws of Vanuatu, the Ombudsman suggested that the actions of these top officials have brought Vanuatu's international financial standing into disrepute. She considered this to be particularly serious when put against the country's efforts to establish itself as an attractive and legitimate financial centre. 'Vanuatu will now be regarded as a money laundering centre by its involvement in this scam through the participation of the Prime Minister and the Minister of Finance' (the Report, p. 17). Aligned with these concerns was the belief that global financial agencies which significantly support the Vanuatu budget reserves would lose confidence; 'The Prime Minister and Minister of Finance have brought Vanuatu into international disrepute and thereby forever damaged its hitherto good financial reputation in general and with the International Monetary Fund, the World Bank, the Asian Development Bank, and all the donors to Vanuatu' (the Report, p. 20).

The Ombudsman's Report recommended that for his part in the scam, the Minister of Finance be dismissed from his ministerial function. The Prime Minister should be reprimanded by the President and dealt with by Parliament. The Governor of the Reserve Bank and the First Secretary of Finance should be dismissed from office.

The Minister of Finance greeted the report with derision, alleging that the Ombudsman was partial, biased and ill-informed. He denied that his actions were illegal or improper, and expressed confidence in the legitimacy of the financial dealings. He chose not to answer in detail any of the Report's allegations. The Prime Minister held a press conference at which he attacked the factual accuracy of the Report and denied that Vanuatu and its financial reserves had been put at risk. He stopped short of further endorsing the scheme, or expressing confidence in any of its participants.

The Australian financier has since been arrested, charged and initially remanded in Vanuatu. He is at present on bail in Port Vila.

The Minister of Finance was demoted to a lesser ministry, and has indicated that when Parliament reconvenes, he will withdraw his support from the coalition government. No doubt this will lead to a change of government, but in Melanesian politics this does not necessarily mean the fall of the Prime Minister.

CORRUPTION AND CONTROL IN CONTEXT

The Fiji and Vanuatu examples establish:

  a) that the identification and confirmation of certain commercial relationships as corrupt, or otherwise, is culturally relative;

b) that politics and commerce are inextricably linked in small Pacific states;
c) that politics and commerce are influenced and shaped by pre-existing custom obligations;
d) that the custom obligation may create opportunities for corrupt relationships to flourish;
e) that the bonds of custom obligation which underpin political and commercial relationships in small Pacific states may also stand in the way of regulating and controlling corruption;
f) that despite (and even in spite of) custom obligation, the public, politicians and the commercial community are sensitized to the dangers of corruption through its potential to undermine national credibility, which is essential to economic development; and
g) that economic development within unchallenged contexts of custom obligation can stimulate corrupt along with commercially viable relationships.

These realizations have important implications for corruption regulation and its impact.

Identifying and Labelling Corrupt Relationships

Attempts to regulate corruption are unlikely to come to much where either the definitions of corruption or their application to persons and relationships are contested within environments of powerful, competing obligation. The localized and prevailing nature of these environments are crucial to the question of making labels stick. Despite the significance of universal labels and labelling agencies external to these environments of obligation, the likelihood that they will be rejected or reinterpreted remains high where the labels challenge the personalities and connections crucial to environments of obligation.

Relevance of Regulation Agencies

In small Pacific states, conventional law enforcement and regulatory agencies are not removed from the structures and influence of custom obligation. In some instances, they are relied upon to endorse and protect such obligation. Therefore it is simplistic and suspect to assume that these agencies can effectively enforce corruption regulation policies arrived at and sponsored outside the structures of custom.

Specialist investigation agencies, such as the Ombudsman, possess a greater likelihood for success in this regard, not only because they appear more focused in their exploration of corruption, but also because the structures of their institution are less influenced by, and less likely to reflect, the structures of customary obligation.

Reliance on Commercial Viability Rather than Public Morality as a Measure of the Consequences of Corruption

In small Pacific states, challenges to corruption based on public morality seem generally unpersuasive. Competing interpretations of public morality and national interest take the steam out of arguments tending to reflect on codes of conduct or objective and model moralities in high office.

However, where forms of corruption are represented as blatant self-interest, such that tends to endanger the wealth of the nation, the potency of corruption as a trigger for regulation and control is enhanced and enlarged. Claims that conditions and institutions which promote socio-economic development on a national scale are also adversely effected by the corruption of the few and the powerful certainly engenders more effective political concern than relying on purely local perspectives of national interest.

In order to implicate the community in corruption regulation in small Pacific states, the cost must be shown to outweigh any reflex recourse to customary obligation.

Globalizing the Context of Corruption Relationships

If corruption remains conceived and controlled within the context of small Pacific states, then the reactionary influence of customary obligation will prevail as disproportionate to all other national interest and social cost issues. Considerations of corruption need to be projected beyond the influence of customary obligation into settings where the national identity of the state relies on globalized interpretations and definitions. In such an expanded context, the involvement and influence of international commercial, development and regulatory agencies need to be orchestrated against the reinterpretive power of customary obligation and authority.

II. Organized Crime and Corruption

MARGARET E. BEARE

4. Corruption and Organized Crime: A Means to an End

Nothing in this paper is intended to diminish the importance and seriousness of the issues relating to corruption. Nationally as well as internationally, every jurisdiction has serious and distinct problems relating to gaining and maintaining a 'corruption-free' environment. My intention is only to suggest that we may wish to apply some of the lessons we have learned from the decades of rhetoric concerning 'organized crime' to the concept of 'corruption'. In retrospect, after much debate, we have come to realize that organized crime rhetoric may serve public officials in ways unrelated to issues of criminal justice and control. Politicians, the media and law enforcement take positions and win resources and/or support based not only on the size of a particular threat to the society but also on the nature of the threat. While the threat may be real, the portrayal of the threat distorts the image and uses up some of the scarce resources.

In Canada, we are at present undergoing various exercises to attempt to understand more fully the nature of organized crime and corruption.[1] This may seem to be a little naive and untimely, given the large amount that has been proclaimed and written about organized crime internationally. Perhaps most profound in terms of the influence upon Canada, has been the literature and legislation from the United States. However, empirical and critical analysis has often been overshadowed by rhetoric. Little has been accomplished by making this criminal activity too all encompassing, too omnipotent, or too 'distinct' from anything we have learned about other forms of crime and criminal operations.

---

[1] The government is at present reviewing the need for legislation that would criminalize membership in organized crime groups. The new Centre for the Study of Organized Crime and Corruption (Osgoode Hall Law School, York University, Toronto) is an attempt to bring an academic focus to issues related to transnational crime.

Barry A.K. Rider (ed.), Corruption: The Enemy Within, 65–76
© *Kluwer Law International. Printed in the Netherlands.*

LESSONS FROM ORGANIZED CRIME

With organized crime, we have had to 'walk backwards' to appreciate that there are concrete processes and definable issues that could be studied and specifically addressed with policy and legislation. Without a clear under-standing of the complexities of the processes that make up organized crime, efforts aimed at reduction/elimination will have little impact. Organized crime itself is not any one thing. From a law enforcement perspective, you have not one 'concept', but several. I have argued[2] that organized crime ought to be responded to as a 'process' rather than as some uniform criminal activity. The processes can then be dissected, understood and responded to appropriately.

During the 1960s and 1970s, we created a monolithic monstrosity out of the concept of organized crime, which we are only now attempting to dismantle. The accusation of some critics has been that the focus on Mafia-like operations diverted attention away from other organized crime groups and away from the reasons why the criminal activity existed.[3] Others have argued that there was a 'preferred' political and law enforcement view that created:

- a public image of organized crime that resulted in increasing resources to fight the threat;
- a justification for the fact that law enforcement actions were having little impact on the criminal activity due to its size, scope and imperviousness; and
- an 'alien' conspiracy notion that separated organized crime from 'normal' society and therefore distanced organized crime from the corruption and collusion of public officials and law enforcement.[4]

What must be emphasized and re-emphasized is that 'something' con-sidered to be of value is provided by organized criminals – either in the form of goods, services, protection, assistance through an unwieldy system, and/or job security. Therefore, even though organized criminals violate moral codes, notions of democratic rule and fair competition, in addition to violating the law, organized crime becomes in a very real way an integrated part of the economic and social fabric. Hence, there is little threat of it being eliminated.

---

[2] Margaret Beare, *Criminal Conspiracies: Organized Crime in Canada*, Canada, Nelson (1996).

[3] Joseph L. Albini, 'Donald Cressey's Contribution to the Study of Organized Crime: An Evaluation', in *Crime and Delinquency* 34, no. 3 (July 1988); D. Cressey, *Theft of the Nation: The Structure and Operations of Organized Crime in America*, New York, Harper and Row (1969); C. Rogovin and Frederick Martens, 'The Evil that Men Do', *Journal of Contemporary Criminal Justice* (Feb. 1992), 62–79.

[4] *Supra*, note 2, at 29.

To say that there is a functionalistic explanation for organized crime does not mean that 'countries would be worse off without the corruption and/or fraud'.[5] The point is only that customers appear and markets are created because of the gap that is filled by the illicit market. Robert Merton's observation regarding the manifest and latent functions of the political machines in the United States during the early 1900s can be applied directly to our understanding of organized crime and corruption.[6]

One has, as Merton states, a plethora of explanations as to why the phenomenon is not eliminated by law enforcement or by government (such as problems of training, resources, motivation, nature of the offences, etc.), but more compelling and relevant are the basic latent functions that the activity is fulfilling. Merton discusses (i) the 'structural context' that makes it difficult for essential needs to be addressed by strictly legitimate structures and (ii) the 'subgroups' whose distinctive needs are left unsatisfied. As a consequence

... the functional deficiencies of the official structure generate an alternative (unofficial) structure to fulfil existing needs somewhat more effectively.[7]

Political machines in the United States operated between legitimate society and the less legitimate world of vice, rackets and crime, and acted as a facilitator for both – with only slightly different rules for either side. As the machines lost their positions of control in American politics, and in countries that never developed a clear machine structure, corrupt officials and organized crime took over this role. The interface between the legitimate and illegitimate operations could be argued to be a key role of organized crime networks[8] and this interface is facilitated by corruption.

One important dimension in which the processes employed by different organized criminals vary is in their ability to garner support and assistance via corruption. The dilemma is that the ability to corrupt is dependent on how integrated the individual or group is into the 'legitimate' society. If they have secured positions of influence and power and therefore have entwined themselves into the power structure through either the economic sphere, political alignments, or the enforcement/criminal justice field, their activities are more easily defined as legitimate.

---

[5] L.W.J.C. Huberts, 'Expert Views on Public Corruption Around the Globe', *PSPA Publications*, Department of Political Science and Public Administration, Amsterdam, Vrije Universiteit (1996), 23.

[6] Robert Merton, *On Theoretical Sociology*, New York, Free Press (1967), 125.

[7] *Supra*, note 6, at 127.

[8] A. Block and W.J. Chamliss, *Organizing Crime*, New York, Elsevier (1981); G. Potter, *Criminal Organizations: Vice, Racketeering and Politics in an American City*, Prospect Heights, Ill., Waveland Press Inc. (1994).

With this integration comes invisibility, in that decisions taken, policies passed and agreements signed are not defined as corruption but rather as 'normal' operations of business or enterprise. Therefore, the greater the ability to corrupt, the greater the ability to remain invisible, or to be seen to be legitimate – unless the entire system is blatantly corrupt and has redefined payoffs and the like as publicly recognized business procedures.

The ability to corrupt enables one to buy protection from enforcement, eliminate competition and therefore build up the 'empire' of the organized crime group. Some organized crime groups lack this level of integration and sophistication. They do not have corruption as an option and use violence instead. Acts of violence that so distress the police, politicians and public may indicate an unsophisticated organized crime group, that may, however, gain greater integration and be transformed into one with the 'clout' sufficient to employ corruption. With growth comes an increasing need to corrupt.

CORRUPTION AS A REQUIREMENT FOR ORGANIZED CRIME

There is not full agreement as to how essential it is for organized crime to be able to corrupt officials – some prosecutors and investigators see the corruption as critical and others see it as exaggerated.[9] Whether or not corruption is essential, Peter Reuter is correct in arguing that a corrupt political authority at the local level can be a 'uniquely powerful instrument for organized crime'.[10] The corrupt political machines that controlled cities like Chicago attest to this advantage.

Aside from the corruptibility of individual political officials, there is an even greater consequence when political systems choose to collude with organized crime in order to stay in power, eliminate opposition, or fund raise through the involvement in illegal commodities, that is, drugs. As Lupscha states:

> The use of criminal gangs by political machines to harass the opposition was a commonplace of our (U.S.) urban history. But politics in the United States is not unique in this.[11]

---

[9] W.J. Chambliss, *On the Take: From Paltry Crooks to Presidents*, Bloomington, Indiana Univ. Press (1978); J. Landesco, *Organized Crime in Chicago*, Chicago, Univ. of Chicago Press; H. Edelhertz and T. D. Overcast, *The Business of Organized Crime: An Assessment of Organized Crime Business-Type Activities and Their Implications for Law Enforcement*, California, Palmer Press (1993), 128.

[10] Peter Reuter, *Disorganized Crime: The Economics of the Invisible Hand*, Cambridge, Mass., MIT Press (1983).

[11] P. Lupscha, 'Organized Crime: Rational Choice Not Ethnic Group Behaviour: A Macro Perspective', *Law Enforcement Intelligence Analysis Digest*, published by the International Association of Law Enforcement Intelligence Analysts, Washington, (Winter 1988), 1–8.

He provides the following examples:
- Chiang Kai Shek and the Kuomintang used the organized crime Triads of Shanghai as enforcers to massacre party members in 1927.
- The French government used the Corsican organized crime groups of Marseilles as informal security agents against both French communists and right-wing military terrorists.
- The US military occupation forces and Army intelligence (G-2) in Japan made similar tacit agreements with Japanese organized crime, the Yakuza, and helped establish their primacy in postwar Japan.
- Cuban and Vietnamese organized crime groups trace their histories to US military failures, such as the Bay of Pigs and South Vietnamese Air Force.
- Organized crime triad societies in China rooted their beginnings in patriotic resistance to the Manchus.
- Italian organized crime groups began as opposition to foreign occupations.
- Corsican crime originated as nationalistic opposition to the French.

The foundations for Miami's emergence as an international crime centre were laid in the 1930s and 1940s, when gangsters like Lansky and Traffi-cante settle there, but it was not until after the CIA organized hundreds of trained killers in the early 1960s that Miami began to fulfil its promise of notoriety. Protected by their CIA ties and frustrated in their political ambitions, these agents turned to the drug trade for a living.[12]

Likewise, the corruption of governments also operates against interna-tional efforts to create standards of uniform practice. As Nadelmann states:

Among all the obstacles to the long-term harmonization of criminal justice systems, governmental corruption represents the most resilient.[13]

Second only to collusion between governments and organized crime, corrupt relations between criminals and the 'control' mechanisms may be used to fuel the criminal enterprises. Control agencies may facilitate the activity, while ironically most dispute settlement activity that usually falls to these agencies is carried out inside the criminal organizations via the use of violence, intimidation and extortion. The control forces therefore provide the important service of granting the 'permission' to operate.

As Edelhertz suggests, perhaps the best way to see the role of 'corruption' is in relation to the ability of organized crime to exercise a wide range of power. There may be strict corruption in exchange for kickbacks or the power at the disposal of the criminal group may allow those individuals to gain control over a public process and in that way corrupt the system:

---

[12] Lernoux, (1986), 107–108.
[13] Ethan A. Nadelmann, *Cops Across Borders: The Internationalization of U.S. Criminal Law Enforcement*, Pennsylvania, Pennsylvania State Univ. Press (1993), 311.

The capacity to corrupt public processes provides significant regulatory advantages in terms of protecting an organized crime enterprise or operation as it moves into a new sphere of illegal activities, and to a large extent also can be used to protect existing markets from non-organized crime competitors.[14]

INTERNATIONAL RESPONSE TO ORGANIZED CRIME

The international community, through cooperative operations such as the Financial Action Task Force (FATF) has encouraged nations internationally to re-examine aspects of the organized crime regulation and control processes via the study of the individual processes essential to organized crime operations, such as money laundering. This exercise – accomplished in a manner respectful of sovereignty issues – has advanced our knowledge and served to remove some of the stereotyping and mystique from organized crime.

Aside from general guidelines, codes of conduct, model legislation and recommendations for regulatory scrutiny, international efforts against organized crime have tended to recognize that organized crime must be studied within the environments (host and home) where it is operating. This criminal activity is socially created via the creation of illegitimate markets; its growth or shrinkage is related in part to the perceptions and reality of risk factors, and it is dependent on the presence or absence of a demand. International collaborative pressure has been chosen rather than blacklisting and ranking systems.

APPLICATION OF LESSONS TO THE CONCEPT OF CORRUPTION

Unlike this recent collaborative approach to strengthening the international community against organized crime, the increasing focus on the concept of 'corruption' is taking a form more reminiscent of the 1960s' focus on organized crime. The notion appears to be that corruption is 'out there' and can be eliminated by drawing up charts illustrating who is the most guilty.

One must critically evaluate those movements that become 'crusades'. The narrow international focus on business-related corruption is driven too blatantly by the commercial/financial interests of the West, at the expense of the less-developed nations. For example, in 1977 the US passed their Foreign and Corrupt Practices Act (FCPA), prohibiting businesses from paying bribes or under-the-counter fees to obtain contracts. They argue that

---

[14] H. Edelhertz and T.D. Overcast, *The Business of Organized Crime: An Assessment of Organized Crime Business-Type Activities and Their Implications for Law Enforcement*, California, Palmer Press (1993), 129.

this has cost them over 100 foreign contracts, worth $45 billion, to overseas rivals.[15] The message is clear – if we cannot benefit from corruption as we define it, then no one should.

The difficulty arises that corruption is not 'alien', but very much entwined into the fabric of societies, and like a chameleon, it takes very different forms, depending on its environment. When the international community focuses on specific aspects of corruption, those are the aspects that will be identified, and targeted as being corruption. The societally approved of, or at least socially ignored, forms of corruption will be missed in the debate.

During the last few years, under the guise of public education, a number of international conferences and surveys[16] have publicly ranked countries, based on perceptions of international respondents, as to the reputation for corruption in each country. For example, Transparency International (TI) is a private organization that is attempting to eliminate corruption in international business transactions. TI completed several surveys concerning the extent of corruption in different countries. The much-reproduced '1995 TI Corruption Index' claims to assess to what extent corruption had an impact on commercial activities in various countries.

Likewise, Leo Huberts[17] surveyed international conference attenders on public corruption and ethics in the public service.[18] Huberts comments that comparative research of the sort he was doing was not popular with scholars. While he attributes this to the sensitive nature of the data, it could have to do with the nature and diversity of 'corruption'.[19]

These surveys may accurately be measuring accurate perceptions of the most unsophisticated forms of corruption, that is, the demands for money by low-level public officials and the payoffs in exchange for contracts. Perhaps this is the full extent of what is expected and claimed by the surveys. The

---

[15] *Toronto Star*, 13 July 1996.

[16] For example, a series of conferences were convened by the Hong Kong Independent Commission Against Corruption (1983 in Washington, DC; 1985 New York City; 1987 Hong Kong; 1989 Sydney, Australia; 1992 Amsterdam, the Netherlands; 1993 Cancun, Mexico; 1995 Beijing, China); Transparency International survey of how international business perceived the levels of corruption in 41 countries (1995); survey undertaken by Huberts (1996) of attenders at corruption conferences and members of the Research Committee on Political Finance and Political Corruption of the International Political Science Association.

[17] L.W.J.C. Huberts, 'Expert Views on Public Corruption Around the Globe', *PSPA Publications*, Department of Political Science and Public Administration, Amsterdam, Vrije Universiteit (1996).

[18] In the various accounts of these survey results, the authors forget that they are not dealing with hard comparative measurements of corruption but rather with the perception of individuals regarding corruption levels.

[19] Huberts (*supra*, note 17) defines corruption as being the 'behaviour of public functionaries when they act (or do not act) as a result of the personal rewards offered to them by interested outside private actors'. He differentiates this from public fraud where the actor is involved in crime for private gain without the involvement of outside.

problem arises that, at the most sophisticated, integrated level, the ability to corrupt enables one to control the definitions of what is or is not defined as corruption. As Stier and Richards state:

> In its most advance form organized crime is so thoroughly integrated into the economic, political and social institutions of legitimate society that it may no longer be recognizable as a criminal enterprise. Such integration represents the most serious potential for social harm that can be caused by racketeers. However, the criminal justice system is least effective in dealing with organized crime when it reaches this level of maturity.[20]

The organized crime activity and/or actions of corrupt officials reach deep into the particular society and broaden to become international. The threat posed by the final stage is not the illicit commodities themselves, or even corrupt business practices or extortion demands, but rather the reliance by legitimate business or political regimes on the ability and willingness of the corrupted process to provide their services. At this point societies' institutions have themselves become corrupted.

Citing examples is difficult, due to the very fact that the activity has successfully avoided being classified as 'corrupt'. However, a controversial Canadian example relates to the activities of the tobacco industry. For several years prior to 1994, the tobacco manufacturers in Canada were the corporate entity which knowingly exported to the United States close to 90 per cent more cigarettes than the foreign market could absorb. It is estimated that from 80–95 per cent[21] of all exports to the US were re-entering Canada. The remaining small percentage (between 5–20 per cent) was being consumed by Canadian tourists or non-residents. This excessive exportation supplied the commodity for the criminal smuggling activity.

Just as in drug trafficking, in the cigarette smuggling industry there are suppliers, importers and a distribution network. One must ask at what point the tobacco corporations become responsible for the illegal activities that were perpetuated with their products. Canadian tobacco manufacturers exported 1.8 billion cigarettes in April 1993 – more than four times the figure from April 1992.[22] During the first four months of 1993, exports had increased over 300 per cent from the equivalent rates during the first four months of 1992.[23] Given that the foreign market had not increased by this margin, or likely at all during the year, the resulting excessive exported amount of tobacco

[20] Stier, Edwin H., and Peter Richards, 'Strategic Decision-making in Organized Crime Control: The Need for a Broadened Perspective', in *Major Issues in Organized Crime Control*, National Institute of Justice, Washington, D.C., Symposium Proceedings (1987), 65.

[21] Estimates from law enforcement and from the Non-Smokers' Rights Association.

[22] Customs Intelligence Reports and Statistics Canada, figures released in May 1993.

[23] Linquist, Avey, Macdonald, Baskerville, *Contraband Tobacco Estimates* (1993), released March.

could be argued to be intended for smuggling back into Canada for profit to the smugglers – and, of course, the initial sale for the tobacco company.

The act of exporting excessive tobacco products outside Canada could be interpreted as a significant facilitator of the tax avoidance, criminal violence, and wasted enforcement resources. The emphasis has not, however, been on attempting to hold the tobacco corporations accountable for a complicity in the growth of an organized crime enterprise around their products. Less powerful, less legitimate players in the smuggling scenario were targeted as the renegades, racketeers or plain, ordinary criminals.[24] In her study of tax evasion and tax avoidance, Doreen McBarnet states:

> To suggest then that the key to staying on the right side of the line is 'not what you do but the way that you do it', is not to imply simply a distinction in style, a matter of cleverness or moral choice, but to under-line the significance of opportunity and resources. Manipulating the law to escape control yet remain legitimate is an option more readily available to large corporations and 'high net worth' individuals than to the mass of the population.[25]

The tobacco corporations argue that their sales for export are indisputably lawful – and likely are, as we at present accept the dynamics of the cigarette issue. By exporting to the foreign jurisdiction, tobacco corporations were avoiding selling their cigarettes with tax applied, knowing that others would commit the crime of tax evasion by smuggling the same commodity back into Canada. This may be a legal evasion on the part of the corporations; however, it is tax avoidance deserving of serious ethical and criminal scrutiny.[26]

---

[24] David Friedrichs encourages the reader to acknowledge the importance of the perception of respectability or legitimacy in discussions regarding white-collar crimes or corporate crimes, and in the case of cigarette smuggling, we must ask whether the corporate 'suppliers' would be seen as culpable if they were less powerful. *See* David Friedrichs, 'White-Collar Crime and the Definitional Quagmire: A Provisional Solution', *Journal of Human Justice*, Vol. 3, No. 2 (Spring 1992), 18.

[25] Doreen McBarnet, 'Legitimate Rackets: Tax Evasion, Tax Avoidance, and the Boundaries of Legality', *Journal of Human Justice*, Vol. 3, No. 2 (Spring 1992), 56–74.

[26] This reminds one of the role of the North American tobacco industry abroad. Stan Sesser documents the deliberate and aggressive foreign strategies that the United States tobacco manufacturers are using to introduce American cigarettes to all age, sex and economic groups in Asia. Evidence presented by Sesser illustrates the North American tobacco industries' willing-ness to advertise to a market that can only afford to buy on the black markets and therefore they encourage a global network of cigarette smuggling; they employ children as the sellers – and in some areas they are the market – of the American cigarettes. They propagate a belief, as expressed by Joaquin Ortega, head of the National Tobacco Administration in the Philippines, that smoking only affects a person 'if he's genetically disposed'. *See* Stan Sesser, 'Opium War redux: Pushing American Cigarettes in Asia', *The New Yorker*, 13 September 1993, 78–89.

Power relations should not be ignored – either within any society or across nations. The Huberts survey indicates that there is an inverse relationship between 'a country's wealth and its public corruption and fraud'.[27] The reality is, of course, that while the corruption may occur in those countries, the corrupt payments are often being made by multinational corporations from 'clean' countries. A second issue relates to how serious corruption, as defined by the international surveys, is regarded in the different countries.

Different countries do not regard the presence of corruption equally seriously. Two-thirds of the respondents from the lower income countries indicated that corruption and fraud were rarely isolated from other forms of public misconduct, such as mismanagement, waste, and power abuse. The majority of respondents stated that, while corruption and fraud were serious, there were more serious social and political problems.[28]

The reason for this may be obvious. The focus of much of the international work against corruption is on the impact that corruption is having (or perceived to be having) on commercial/corporate life. As business becomes global in scope, companies wish to be able to operate as inexpensively and rationally as possible throughout the world.[29] Systems of graft and bribes are unpredictable, unreliable and costly. This may seem relatively unimportant if your society is poor, violent and politically unstable – in addition to having a high amount of corruption and fraud.

Culture appears also to help to determine how a society will regard corruption. Ernesto Savona[30] describes a system of corruption in Italy that operates on a delicate balance. Forms of corruption in that culture are defined quite favourably – that is, to be 'sly' (*furbo*) implies that the person was able to take advantage of opportunities others might miss – as long as the corruption remains within certain limits. He argues that criminal law and prosecutions became successful only when the corruption in Italy exceeded a physiological limit of a modern state. A focus on corruption allowed the country to discredit the reputations of the old and powerful political class and facilitated a shift towards a new political system. Corruption became the lever for change – however, as Savona states:

[27] *Supra*, note 17, at 33.

[28] *Supra*, note 17, at 17.

[29] Robert Galvin, Chairman of Motorola Inc., predicts that world populations will be the market for many corporations. The US population is approximately 300 million (5% of world total). Motorola does close to 70% of its business outside the US market. Motorola is attempting to change this to 95% – the same proportion as the rest of world and US population split. *Financial Post*, 18 May 1966, 22.

[30] Ernesto U. Savona, *Beyond Criminal Law in Devising Anti-Corruption Policies: Lessons from the Italian Experience*, Research Group on Transnational Crime, Italy, University of Trento School of Law (1995), 31.

... it cannot be said that corruption will end. The major risk is that new corrupters will enter the corruption market having learnt the lesson of the Italian case. And, by thus becoming more sophisticated, they will be able to minimize the law enforcement risk.

In Latin America, critics point out that some of the most corrupt politicians are the ones speaking out the loudest against corruption. As the news-weekly *Noticias* in Argentine said:

> Everyone accuses and everyone is accused. If everyone is corrupt, no one is.[31]

This is similar to the situation described by Savona in Italy. He quotes the adage: 'The more we are guilty the less we are perceived' – each defendant enlarges the circle by introducing others to the prosecutors.

The stated purpose of Transparency International is to 'curb the increasingly rampant corruption stunting the development of poor countries'. Depending on the nature of the corruption, in some jurisdictions the level of corruption may result from a more prosperous era rather than the reverse. Likewise, any sudden political or economic shift – such as into free-markets, democratic systems – may result in a temporary state of heightened corruption and instability. The corruption may not be to blame for this chaos, but in fact may be reflective of it. The development may be stunted by low salaries, environmental destruction, and the flight of capital out of these nations into the developed nations.

Some of these conditions that fingers are busy pointing at in the 'worst' countries may be directly or indirectly caused by the interference and global policies of countries perceived to be relatively corruption-free. The test for any country is the moment when profitable international trade becomes threatened by pressure to take governmental stands against violent and corrupt regimes.

While reducing corruption, however it is defined, is a valuable activity, some strategies may have less positive results. There may be unanticipated consequences from labelling nations as corruption- and fraud-prone. We speak of the self-fulfilling prophecy, when initially incorrect situations are acted upon as if they were true and they become true as a consequence. Receiving a high-corruption ranking on the TI and the Huberts surveys informs the world that certain practices will be tolerated within those countries. This may in fact serve to encourage and normalize the various corrupt payments.

Corruption can be used by individuals in numerous sectors of any society – governments, law enforcement, corporations, and the public – via their

---

[31] *The Wall Street Journal*, 1 July 1996.

support of illicit commodities. One does not corruption-proof a jurisdiction. Rather it is a constant struggle to gain and maintain a culture of intolerance to corruption. A change of personnel or a change of the environment (economic, political or social) may jeopardize this culture.

BRICE DE RUYVER AND TOM VAN DER BEKEN

5. Corruption and Organized Crime

There is no doubt that corruption and organized crime are closely connected. But the question whether corruption is intrinsic to organized crime gives rise to interesting discussions. This was illustrated during the recent Dutch Parliamentary Enquiry Committee concerning Investigation Methods, known as the Van Traa Commission. During this enquiry, which revealed the serious problems which the Dutch authorities had with the use of special investigation techniques, several discussions about the definition of organized crime were held. Here we will focus only on what was said about corruption and organized crime.

The definition of organized crime that was finally accepted refers to 'corruption' as an essential element of organized crime. The definition says that there is organized crime when – among other requirements – the group is *'capable of covering up their crimes in a relatively effective way, particularly by demonstrating their willingness to use physical violence or to rule out persons by means of corruption'* (our translation).[1] The willingness of groups to use violence or corruption is thus considered as an essential element of organized crime.[2] Van Duyne[3] criticized this proposi-

---

[1] The original Dutch version is '... in staat zijn deze misdaden op een betrekkelijk effectieve wijze af te schermen, in het bijzonder door de bereidheid te tonen fysiek geweld te gebruiken of personen door corruptie uit te schakelen.' *See Inzake Opsporing. Enquête-commissie opsporingsmethoden (About Investigation. Enquiry Commission on Investigation Methods)*, Amsterdam, Sdu Uitgevers, 1996, 25.

[2] H.G. van de Bunt, 'De Definitie van Georganiseerde Criminaliteit' (The Definition of Organized Crime) in F. Bovenkerk (ed.), *De Georganiseerde Misdaad in Nederland. Het Criminologisch Onderzoek voor de Parlementaire Enquêtecommissie Opsporingsmethoden in Discussie* (Organized Crime in the Netherlands. The Criminological Research for the Parliamentary Enquiry Commission on Investigation Methods in Discussion), Deventer, Gouda Quint (1996), 33.

[3] P.C. Van Duyne, 'Definitie en Kompaswerking' (Definition and Compass), in F. Bovenkerk (ed.), *De Georganiseerde Misdaad in Nederland. Het Criminologisch Onderzoek voor de Parlementaire Enquêtecommissie Opsporingsmethoden in Discussie* (Organized Crime in the Netherlands. The Criminological Research for the Parliamentary Enquiry Commission on Investigation Methods in Discussion), Deventer, Gouda Quint (1996), 54–55.

Barry A.K. Rider (ed.), Corruption: The Enemy Within, 77–84
© *Kluwer Law International. Printed in the Netherlands.*

tion by emphasizing that violence and corruption are only tools used by organized crime and in no way essential to its activities. It is possible that the structure of a criminal organization does not require any form of violence or corruption at all. In that case, the willingness to use these tools remains uncertain. A second objection of Van Duyne to the definition is the use of the word 'corruption'. Corruption refers to a criminal law concept that is probably too narrow to grasp the activities of criminal organizations which take place in the grey zone between illegality and what is allowed. For that reason, terms such as 'fading of forms' and 'corruptive behaviour' are also used besides 'corruption'. These three terms are gradations of the same concept, but only corruption is a criminal offence. The terms also differ with regard to the question of proof. Delivering the proof of corruption will be much harder than proving 'fading of norms' or 'corruptive behaviour'.[4] That is why the definition used by the German Bundes-kriminalamt can be suggested as a possible alternative. The BKA does not refer to 'corruption' but uses the word '*Einflussnahme*' – which can be translated as 'manipulation' or 'influencing' – of politics, the media, the civil service, justice and industry. Next to this, the BKA-definition indicates 'manipulation' or 'influencing' only as a possible tool for organized crime and not as an essential element.[5]

In this paper we will try to overcome the differences between those two definitions by analyzing some aspects of the specific relationship between organized crime and corruption and by giving three examples.

THE RELATIONSHIP

The starting-point for the analysis is the difference between the so-called 'underworld' and 'upperworld'. Although we realize that this artificial distinction between a world of illegal activities and a world of legal industry can be criticized, we believe that it provides very good grounds for discussion. One of the main advantages of this premise is that it makes it

---

[4] B. De Ruyver, 'Tussen Wet en Werkelijkheid. Bespiegelingen over Tuchthandhaving en Rechtshandhaving' (Between Law and Reality. Reflections on the Upholding of Discipline and Law), in F. De Mot, (ed.), *Politie en Gezag* (Police and Authority), Brussels, Politeia (1995), 96–97.

[5] The entire definition is: 'Organisierte Kriminalität ist die von Gewinn- oder Machtstreben bestimmte planmässige Begehung von Straftaten, die einzeln oder in ihrer Gesamtheid von erheblicher Bedeutung sind, wenn mehr als zwei Beteiligte auf längere oder unbestimmte Dauer arbeitsteilig a. unter Verwendung gewerblicher oder Geschäftlicher Structuren, b. under Anwendung von Gwalt oder anderer zur Einschüchterung geeigneter Mittel, oder c. unter Einflussnahme auf Politik, Medien, öffentliche Verwaltung, Justiz und Wirtschaft zusammen-wirken.', as quoted by P.C. Van Duyne, *Het Spook en de Dreiging van de Georganiseerde Misdaad* (The Phantom and the Threat of Organized Crime), The Hague, Sdu (1995), 10.

possible to discern certain gradations in the relations between organized crime and the 'upperworld'.

Firstly, it is possible that no real relationship between organized crime and the 'upperworld' exists. This is the case when organized crime stays completely underground and even tries to avoid contact with the 'upperworld'. An example of such an organization is that of a Turkish heroin trader in the Netherlands. His organization, which deals with illegal goods, can operate with very limited contacts with the 'upperworld'. Besides a coffee-shop, he has no specific ties with the legal world. And since he does not need business contacts with the 'upperworld' officials for his trade, corruption is not a necessary instrument for his organization.[6] But this type of organization can only flourish in relatively closed communities with their own standards and norms. The evolution of police investigation and the growing attention to the proceeds of crime, make it difficult for such complete organizations to survive.

Van de Bunt[7] sees three further relationships of organized crime with the 'upperworld'. The first relationship he calls *parasitical*. In this kind of relationship there are contacts between organized crime and the upper world, but not on a wide scale. Organized crime makes use of the 'upperworld' in a unilateral way. When needed, the 'upperworld' is contacted and, if necessary and opportune, corrupted in order to secure the illegal activities. The 'upperworld' does not benefit from this relationship, since the profits only go to the criminal organization; for example, the EC-fraud organization bribing EC or customs officials.

The second kind of relationship is called *symbiotic* and is more complex. This relationship is based on the mutual interests of the criminal organization and the 'upperworld'. Symbiosis becomes important when criminal organizations need permanent contacts with the 'upperworld'. These contacts are more intense when the 'upperworld' benefits more from their crimes. This is the case for sectors of the 'upperworld' which can draw enormous advantages out of their relations with the criminal world. We refer to bankers, accountants, inspectors and lawyers. This is also the case when criminal organizations give better answers to existing needs than the legal world can. We refer to cheap and flexible labour, to waste-processing and to prostitution. In this close connection between organized crime and the 'upperworld', corruption becomes more important and more complex. Corruption, however, is not the link between 'underworld' and 'upperworld', but the mutual benefit of both worlds. 'Underworld' and 'upperworld'

---

[6] Van Duyne, *op. cit.*, 20.

[7] H.G. Van de Bunt, 'De verlokkingen van de georganiseerde misdaad' (The Temptation of Organized Crime), in A.W.M. Van der Heiden (ed.), *Criminele Inlichtingen. De Rol van de Inlichtingendiensten bij de Aanpak van de Georganiseerde Misdaad* (Criminal Information. The Role of Intelligence Services in the Approach Towards Organized Crime, The Hague, Vuga (1993), 13.

cooperate because they both have interests in doing so. And since the relations between the partners are close, corruption becomes more subtle and far more difficult to prove.

The third and last kind of relationship between organized crime and the 'upperworld' is called *implantation*. In this situation, the criminal organization has left the underground – at least in part – and takes a full place in the 'upperworld'. Sound and legal business is taken over by organized crime and operates as an efficient cover-up for illegal activities. It is the logical outcome for the criminal entrepreneur in the legal economy and fits into a strategy that aims at a position from which society as a whole can be influenced. And that is when organized crime becomes a real part of the 'upperworld' and participates fully in all legal activities. In such a situation, corruption is always there. But we are not dealing with a one-way corruptive relationship, but with a very complex mixture of interests. At that point it becomes nearly impossible to prove corruption as a criminal offence. The mere presence of an implanted criminal organization is often enough to influence the business. The fact that, for example, a criminal organization made huge and legal investments in real estate in a certain area, can influence the authorities competent for town and country planning. The suspicion that real estate has been obtained by illegal funds cannot play a determining role, since this cannot be proved in court. At that dangerous stage, organized crime has become a part of the 'upperworld' and its corruptive activities affect all sections of society. Goldstock described this situation thus:

> While bribery by an individual seeking private gain can, depending upon the nature of the act performed in return for the bribe, cause widespread public harm, the effect of widespread corruption by organized criminal organizations is more insidious. It can affect the costs of utility rates, public transportation and construction. It can encourage criminal activity through ineffective law enforcement. When it is pervasive, it can affect the public's belief in the integrity of the government.[8]

A well-determined prevention strategy, based on the transparency of the decision-making structures within the law enforcement services and public services, and function-rotation in those structures, is essential to combat this phenomenon. On the reactive side, we should admit that the traditional instruments of criminal law and criminal investigation cannot deal with this type of corruption and organized crime alone[9] and that new and other tools

---

[8] R. Goldstock, *Organized Crime and Corruption*, Fifth International Anti-Corruption Conference, Amsterdam, 1992, 1.

[9] E.U. Savona, 'Beyond Criminal Law in Devising Anticorruption Policies', *European Journal on Criminal Policy and Research* (1995), 34.

are needed to succeed in disentangling this mixture of interests.[10] With regard to the investigations, specific corruption intelligence-work and the use of special investigation techniques are necessary. On the law enforcement side, it should be possible to focus more on the search, seizure and confiscation of the proceeds of crime, since the crime of corruption itself will be very hard to prove.[11]

LEGITIMATE CRIMES

The next step to take is a small one, but brings us into a different world. We leave the 'underworld' and go to the respected and legal organizations. The importance of crimes of the members of these *bona fide* organizations, which are called *organizational* crimes,[12] cannot be underestimated. Although these crimes are not committed by the traditional 'underworld' criminal, it is a fact that most crimes with regard to taxes and environment are committed by members of legal organizations. In order to cover up these crimes, corruption is very often used. The difference between this organizational crime and the implanted form of organized crime is often very hard to make, since they are both situated in the grey zone between what is legal and what is not.[13] Both forms of crime are related to legal goods and anchored in the legal world. That is why they are so difficult to deal with. We know that corruption or corruptive behaviour is necessary in this kind of business, but it is so subtle that it evokes disapproval rather than prosecution.

So we see that with regard to organized crime, the concept of 'corruption' cannot be understood in a very strict way. The more contacts the organization gets in the 'upperworld', the more corruption is necessary, but the more its appearance turns away from the criminal law definition of corruption. If we take the strict definition of corruption, there is no clear link between corruption and organized crime, because there is no doubt that many forms of official corruption are unrelated to organized crime and that crime syndicates are sometimes able to operate without corruption.[14] But

[10] L. Huberts, 'Western Europe and Public Corruption: Expert Views on Attention, Extent and Strategies', *European Journal on Criminal Policy and Research* (1995), 18.

[11] H. Berkmoes, *Witwassen, Georganiseerde Criminaliteit, Corruptie. Democratie op de Helling?* (Money laundering, Organized Crime, Corruption. Democracy in Danger?), Brussels, Politeia (1995), 93–105.

[12] H.G. Van de Bunt, *Organisatiecriminaliteit* (Organizational Crime), Arnhem, Gouda Quint (1992), 48 p.

[13] N. Passas and D. Nelken, 'The Thin Line Between Legitimate and Criminal Enterprises: Subsidy Frauds in the European Community', *Crime, Law and Social Change* (1993), 223–243.

[14] J.A. Gardiner, *Defining Corruption*, Fifth International Anti-Corruption Conference, Amsterdam 9 March 1992, 5.

if we use the BKA-term *Einflussnahme*, we see that organized crime that has extended its contacts and activities to the 'upperworld' always needs to influence the legal decision-making processes in order to continue its business. In that respect, corruption can be considered as an essential element of organized crime.

I will give three examples to illustrate the gradations made in the different relationships between organized crime and corruption.

The first example concerns the trade of illegal goods and refers to the trade in human beings in Belgium. When, in September 1992, a journalist published a revealing book[15] about the degrading situation of the women from the Philippines who were victims of a network of trade in human beings, Belgium really became aware of the phenomenon. Since public opinion and even the Belgian King were filled with indignation, the Belgian Parliament installed a Parliamentary Enquiry Commission to investigate the scope and causes of trafficking in human beings and to formulate recommendations for an effective approach towards the phenomenon. As an expert for this Belgian Parliamentary Enquiry Commission, we had the privilege, together with Professor Fijnaut, of studying the subject for one and a half years.[16] Eventually, it all came down to a simple question of supply and demand. The 'traders in women' appeared to be persons already occupied in the prostitution sector who took advantage of some new developments. On the one hand, Asian women were in great demand in the prostitution sector, and on the other hand, there was – and still is – a substantial supply of men and women attracted to the Western world, hoping to find a better future. Under false pretences, the traders lured the women to Belgium and the Netherlands, deprived them of their visas and official documents, kept them as prisoners and forced them into prostitution.

It is remarkable that these activities could go on for such a long time without substantial reaction from the law enforcement authorities, especially since the offenders, who were in many cases just ordinary pimps, did not operate in well-structured organizations, meeting the criteria of organized crime.[17] Their predominant position in 'trading in women' was not acquired by special, sophisticated crime or organization, but by the permissiveness towards prostitution in politics, and by the police and the judiciary. Police services have seen the prostitution milieu as a source of information

---

[15] C. De Stoop, *Ze zijn zo lief, meneer* (They are so Sweet, Sir), Antwerp, Kritak (1992), 288 p.

[16] B. De Ruyver, *Prostitutie en Vrouwenhandel in Gent: Een Fenomeenanalyse* (Prostitution and Trade in Women in Ghent: An Analysis of the Phenomenon), Universiteit van Gent, Onderzoeksgroep Drugbeleid, Strafrechtelijk Beleid, Internationale Criminaliteit, 107 p.

[17] This does not mean that there are no links to organized crime. *See* for the relationship between criminal gangs and organized crime, P. Arlacchi, 'Organized Crime and Criminal Gangs' in S. Flood (ed.), *Illicit Drugs and Organized Crime. Issues for a Unified Europe*, Illinois, Office of International Criminal Justice (1991), 13–21.

and have turned a blind eye to the various illegal activities. In our study we found more of this 'fading of norms' than we found real corruption. Corruption appeared only to be used with regard to the policemen competent for the direct control. But 'corruptive behaviour' and 'fading of norms' were omnipresent and infected the whole structure.

The second example refers to the development of the mafia in Italy.[18] We see that after the Second World War, the mafia left its autarkic rural position and started to participate in legal economic activities as well. As entrepreneurs with allies in local and central authorities, they soon became influential and flourished in the Italian clientelism of that time.[19] The mafia entrepreneurs achieved enormous economical and political influence. These relations were important to assure money laundering operations and to avoid or withdraw criminal prosecution. In the early 1990s, the Italian Parliament recognized that the mafia had integrated not only into politics, but also into industry, private practice and public authorities.[20] As revealed in the later *mani puliti* or *tangentopoli* campaign of the Italian judges,[21] corruption was everywhere. The distinction between the traditional criminal and the respectable member of society became vague, since they all were involved.

The third example deals with the thin line between the implanted form of organized crime and organizational crime. On the one hand, many criminal organizations use legal industry to cover their illegal activities or to launder their money; some industries, such as the hotel and catering industry and diamond sector, offer excellent opportunities. On the other hand, legal corporations seem prepared to commit offences to maintain or improve their market position. In some industries, corruption and corruptive behaviour are used frequently, which explains the exorbitant commissions that go with the signing of some contracts. In the weapon and aviation business, these practices are common property, which was illustrated when, at the beginning of 1995, the *Agusta* scandal[22] – called after the Italian aviation company that sold helicopters to the Belgian army – broke. What started as a sidetrack in the investigation of the murder of a Minister of State in 1991, led to a story of party financing. Finally, the case caused the resignation of the Secretary-General of NATO and four ministers in function. Until today, no legal proof of criminal corruption has been found, but there is no doubt about the existence of corruptive behaviour, since it is certain that two

---

[18] F. De Pauw, *De Firma Mafia* (The Mafia Firm), Leuven, Davidfonds (1993), 123 p. and M. Leijendekker, *De Italiaanse Revolutie* (The Italian Revolution), Amsterdam, Meulenhoff (1994), 256 p.

[19] J. Walston, *The Mafia and Clientelism. Roads to Rome in Post-War Calabria*, London and New York, Routledge, 265 p.

[20] E.U. Savona, *l.c.*, 33.

[21] D. Nelken, 'The Judges and Political Corruption in Italy', *Journal of Law and Society*, No. 1, March 1996, 95–112.

[22] R. Van Cauwelaert, *De Agusta-Crash*, Groot-Bijgaarden, Globe (1995), 229 p.

aviation companies paid hundreds of millions of Belgian francs to Belgian political parties which had a central position in the decision-making process with regard to two major army acquisitions. At the time the money was paid, party financing was still allowed in Belgium, but it raises important questions about the danger of corruption in a political democracy. Now a new law on election expenses and party financing makes such practices illegal.

CONCLUSION

Thus we see that corruption, as criminal behaviour, is not always necessary for criminal structures. But the parasitical and sometimes symbiotic or implanted relationship between criminal organizations and the 'upperworld' reveal the presence of corruptive behaviour that is difficult to trace and prove. For that reason, other measures to combat the phenomenon, such as the creation of an anti-corruption apparatus and an external control mechanism, are necessary.[23]

---

[23] B. De Ruyver and C. Fijnaut, 'De Restauratie van het Recht van Onderzoek? Tevreden Experten over de Parlementaire Onderzoekscommissie Mensenhandel' (The Restauration of the Right to Investigate? Satisfied Experts about the Parliamentary Enquiry Commission on Human Trafficking), *Panopticon* (1994), 101–111.

III. Corruption in Public and Financial Life

WILMER PARKER III

6. Every Person Has a Price?

INTRODUCTION

Does every person have a price? Or, rather, should it be said that every person has a price? 'Corruption', the act or result of corrupting or of being corrupt relates to a person who is marked by immorality and perversion; depraved, venal; dishonest.[1] Corruption may attach to any person, regardless of whether he or she is involved in a public or non-public endeavour.

What kind of society do we want? K.A. Westurberg, a Swedish teacher and founder of the Hassela Nordic Network, an organization established, *inter alia*, to counteract legalization of drugs, to educate the public about organized crime, money laundering and other serious crime, and to inform the public about the links among drugs, money, power and corruption, stated at a recent conference, '... that for one to survive in, or close to, the corridors of power often means that one cannot follow his conscience'.[2]

Power may be found in government, business, religion, and academia; indeed, in every pillar supporting the foundation of a civilized society. Often power attaches to those with the greatest access to wealth. The temptation to be corrupt arises in order for one to be and remain powerful. After all, the likelihood of one's illicit conduct being detected is minimal, with even less prospect of being investigated – much less prosecuted.

In an article by Raymond Bonner, entitled 'The Worldly Business of Bribes: Quiet Battle Is Joined', *New York Times*, 2 July 1996, the reader is informed that a Mr. Peter Eigen of Berlin, Germany, has 'started a non-governmental organization to combat corruption ... called Transparency International ... [whose] goal ... is to rid society of corruption'. It is noted that 'moral opprobrium toward bribery is nothing new. It goes back some 4,000 years, with prohibitions found on Babylonian tablets', John T. Noonan writes in *Bribes*, a 839–page moral, historical and legal tome on the subject (Macmillan, 1984).

---

[1] *American Heritage Dictionary*, 2nd College ed. (1984).
[2] Hassela Nordic Network International Conference, 10–13 June 1996, Hassela, Sweden.

Barry A.K. Rider (ed.), Corruption: The Enemy Within, 87–103
© *Kluwer Law International. Printed in the Netherlands.*

The article further states that, 'unlike Amnesty International and Human Rights Watch, which have discovered that their effectiveness in combating abuses comes through issuing reports criticizing governments, Transparency International practices "quiet diplomacy"'. The article identified a corruption index which reflected that New Zealand and Denmark were the least corrupt countries, with Nigeria, Pakistan and Kenya being the most corrupt.

It was asserted that Transparency International's hardest task involved European governments and businesses. For example, in Germany it is stated that it is against the law for a company to bribe a German civil servant, but it is not against the law for a German company to bribe a government official in a foreign country. Further, '... in Germany, Greece, Luxembourg and Belgium, foreign-paid bribes are fully tax-deductible. In other countries – France, for example – a bribe is a legal business expense, but only part of it can be deducted ...'. What message is sent by such public policies? Are there any ethical constraints when one conducts business or is one's conduct to be judged solely against the black letter of the law?

A recent example of non-criminal corruption may be found in the publication in the United States of a highly successful novel, *Primary Colors*. This book, a veiled attempt at fiction depicting the 1992 Presidential Campaign of Bill Clinton, was published with the author being described as 'anonymous'. For months, journalists and the public opined as to who was the author. One journalist, Joe Klein, a writer for *Newsweek* magazine and a commentator for CBS News, consistently denied to one and all that he was the author. By mid-July 1996, Klein's deceit had been discovered. In an editorial of the *New York Times*, entitled 'The Color of Mendacity', Friday, 19 July 1996, the following paragraph appeared:

> One of the artistic models for Mr. Klein's book was *All the King's Men*, by Robert Penn Warren. But we have to wonder if Mr. Klein really mastered the theme of the book, which has to do with the insidious nature of corruption. Mr. Klein wants his colleagues to view his actions as a diverting and highly profitable whimsy. But he has held a prominent role in his generation of political journalists. For that reason, people interested in preserving the core values of serious journalism have to view his actions and words as corrupt and – if they become an example to others – corrupting.

It is unquestionable that often we mortals are corrupted through our own vices: greed, sex, gluttony, etc. As a global economy is ever more the reality, it might be argued that corrupt behaviour in business and government may have a greater adverse impact on society – at least as it affects larger populations. For example, in the multi-billion dollar drug trade, it is estimated that at least $3 billion a year of drug proceeds are successfully laundered through US businesses, on behalf of the Cali, Colombian cocaine drug lords.[3] Those businesses knowingly involved in this insidious activity are, competitively speaking, at an advantage when compared to their law-abiding competitors, since the illicit businesses have access to untaxed and unregulated capital (drug proceeds) to supplement their cash flow. While one may not traditionally think that money laundering is an act of corruption, one should recall that the *sine qua non* to money laundering is to 'clean' the 'dirty' money by making it appear to have the smell of lawful proceeds of commerce rather than the stench of criminality.

FREDERIC WILLIAM TOKARS – A CASE STUDY OF CORRUPTION

Drug Trafficking and Money Laundering

A recent Atlanta criminal prosecution, *United States of America* v. *Frederic W. Tokars, et al.*, Cr. No. 1:93–CR–359 (N.D.Ga.), provides an anecdotal account of corruption by a person believed by many to be a law-abiding pillar of the community. Frederic W. Tokars, an attorney and part-time judge, was in April 1994 convicted of acts of racketeering (RICO), including drug money laundering, drug trafficking and murder-for-hire in the contract killing of his wife, who threatened to disclose to the authorities her husband's illegal conduct. The following edited passages are written in the style presented to the United States Court of Appeals for the Eleventh Judicial Circuit, an intermediate court directly under the jurisdiction of the Supreme Court of the United States, in support of Mr. Tokars' conviction.

RICO Enterprise Created

Julius Cline was murdered on 25 July 1992. Cline and Jessie Ferguson had started selling cocaine in Detroit, Michigan in 1983. They moved to Atlanta, Georgia, where in July 1985 they met James Mason. In 1986, Mason discussed with Ferguson a proposal to open a nightclub. Ferguson and Cline invested $75,000 from the sale of cocaine into the club. Mason was the club's manager and obtained its liquor licence. Ferguson testified that 'Julius and I got into a little trouble up in Detroit, so we knew we couldn't get a liquor licence'. (The 'little trouble' involved a gun fight which left one dead and the authorities seeking Ferguson's arrest for murder.)

According to Ferguson, Cline's principal source of cocaine was 'Andrew', who sold it to Cline in Miami, Florida. Andre Willis testified that in 1987 he met Cline in an Atlanta nightclub, where they discussed the cocaine 'business'. Willis began obtaining cocaine from Cline and continued to do

---

[3] Clifford Krauss and Douglas Frantz, 'Cali Drug Cartel Using U.S. Business To Launder Cash', *New York Times*, 30 October 1995.

so until Cline's death. Willis sold the cocaine in Atlanta and elsewhere. By 1992, according to Willis, Cline was also obtaining cocaine from Al Brown, 'a guy from Detroit who was part-owner of 'Diamonds and Pearls' [a nightclub in Atlanta]'.

Willis and Cline received and sold approximately twenty kilograms of cocaine a week. Willis took instructions from Cline, delivered cocaine for Cline, received hundred of thousands of dollars in cash in payment for cocaine, and stored the cash in Atlanta. Willis testified that, in 1992, Cline described his relationship with Mason, saying 'that James was just a front for the nightclubs because Mitch [Ferguson] and himself had a criminal record, and they could not get any liquor license in their name, so James Mason would be the front for all the nightclubs'.

Willis and Cline discussed the entertainment business: 'He [Cline} owned it, but it was in James Manson's name'. According to Willis, Cline owned several clubs: 'VIP', 'Traxx', 'The Parrot' and 'Zazu's', as well as 'Park Place Beauty Salon'. Ferguson testified that in addition to the initial $75,000 investment in 'VIP', he and Cline invested $60,000 in cocaine proceeds into 'Traxx', a gay club. Cline also told Ferguson that he invested '$40,000 to $60,000' into 'The Parrot', a jazz club; $50,000 into 'Dominique's Club 21', and monies into 'Zazu's', a comedy club.

Tokars Solicits Business

Marvin Baynard, a drug dealer, testified that he met with Frederic W. Tokars, an attorney, in late 1986 to discuss Tokars defending Dexter Askew, a 'drug runner' who had been charged with possession of cocaine which Baynard had provided. Baynard told Tokars that he sold ¼ – ½ kilo of cocaine per week. Baynard grossed $5,000 – $10,000 per week. Tokars requested a $10,000 'retainer fee', and said he could help Baynard get incorporated so Baynard could 'try to legitimatize myself'.

Tokars incorporated a business which Baynard used with Alex Yancey, a 'personal friend' of Baynard's, who associated with Baynard in the cocaine business. Yancey confirmed that he delivered cocaine for Baynard as did Dexter Askew. Baynard testified that he sold cocaine from 1986 until 1989. When his original source of cocaine died, starting in 1987, he obtained his cocaine from Julius Cline.

Baynard testified that often Tokars discussed 'offshore banks'. Baynard described Tokars as having 'some elaborate little blue book; right, that would tell how you can set up your own bank offshore for $15,000 to set it up. So, if you want to buy a house or a car, you pay $15,000, set it up and the rest of the money – say you want to buy a house for $100,000. You give him $15,000, and then you pay the rest of the money in, give that to him, and he sends it offshore, and you bring it in through your own bank. He described it as a way of setting up your own bank'. Baynard did not believe it, saying it was 'one of them lawyer tricks'.

Baynard testified that he knew that he could not invest his drug money into property, so he basically 'enjoyed life with it as far as going out to nightclubs, traveling, ...'. He kept his cash in his bedroom. Based on Tokars' advice, he kept his cocaine in another apartment in a different name. Tokars claimed that as long as the drugs were found in a place not in Baynard's name, Tokars could get Baynard 'out of it' if there were a 'bust' by the police.

Yancey was present with Baynard when Tokars discussed offshore banking. Yancey recalled Tokars stating that he was opening an offshore bank account and taking investments of $10,000, for which the investor would receive 'loan documentation which would legitimize you making expensive purchases, you know, cars, property, or whatever'. Yancey confirmed that Baynard discussed with Tokars that Baynard's money was derived from selling drugs. Yancey heard Tokars advise Baynard to use a business as a means of 'working his money in'.

Tokars Solicits Money Laundering Customers
Murray Silver testified that he first met Tokars 'when he [Tokars] was an Assistant District Attorney in the Fulton Country District Attorney's Office'. From July 1986 until October 1989, Tokars shared office space with Silver. Silver related an incident with Tokars regarding a multi-page document entitled 'Tax Havens and Offshore Investment Opportunities'.

Based on a secretary's complaint, Silver approached Tokars and inquired as to why the secretary had been required to work overtime. Tokars said that he was preparing a speech regarding money laundering and gave Silver the booklet. According to Silver, Tokars asked him to read the document, indicating that it would give Silver good ideas, saying, 'you might want to do this'. Silver said, 'Do what?'; Tokars responded: 'Utilize some of your clients you have. You are representing some drug dealers'. Silver acknowledged that he was, but that most of the drug dealers he represented were 'street level'. Tokars said that what he was trying to do was to 'get individuals to invest at least $10,000, and that if I [Silver] could refer some of my clients to him [Tokars], that he would appreciate it'. Silver testified that the type of clients Tokars wanted Silver to refer to him were drug dealers.

Silver related that Tokars discussed how drug dealers 'come across a lot of cash, and ... that most of the ones he knew were stupid, that they really did not know what to do with the money after they made it, with the exception of buying big cars and gold necklaces'. Silver discussed with Tokars whether or not he had any concerns with the IRS. Tokars stated that 'he was not concerned about the IRS for the simple reason he was not going to leave a paper trail'. '[W]ithout that trail, he [Tokars] said they cannot follow me. They can't find me, and they can't find the money'. Silver asked Tokars whether or not the document referred to 'money laundering', to which Tokars responded: 'Yes'.

Later Tokars invited Silver into his office. Tokars closed the door and showed Silver a briefcase, claiming it contained $150,000 in cash from a client who was going through a 'nasty divorce'. Tokars informed Silver that he was taking the money offshore to hold for safekeeping so that his client could avoid paying the money to the wife and making payments to IRS. Some days later, Tokars confirmed to Silver that he had taken the money to the Bahamas, indicating that he had an offshore bank in the Bahamas.

In an article entitled, 'How Lawyers Help Drug Dealers Launder Money', published on 12 February 1990, Tokars publicly admitted his in-depth knowledge of drug money laundering. During the trial, Tokars admitted learning about the drug business when he was a prosecutor.

Tokars and 'The Parrot'

Mark McDougall, also known as Rocky, testified that in January 1990, he and an acquaintance, Billy Carter, discussed investing in a nightclub. According to McDougall, Carter informed him 'about these guys that run clubs [who] were very successful ... that "Dominique's" was one of the clubs they run, ... and ... this other club was down on Luckie Street ... a gay club [Traxx], but it was very successful'. In February 1990, Carter introduced McDougall to Mason at the 'gay club'. Mason offered McDougall cocaine and McDougall snorted it.

McDougall testified that he and Zane Carroll discussed with Tokars the proposed investment in 'The Parrot', a nightclub. Tokars told McDougall that the club would be 'a good money maker, a good investment'. McDougall understood that he and Carroll would own 51% of the club; Mason and Cline, the remaining 49%. However, as McDougall was a convicted felon, a liquor licence could not be obtained if his name was involved, thus Carter's name would be used.

At Tokars' request, McDougall delivered $30,000 in currency to Tokars at Tokars' law office. Present were Tokars, Carter, Mason and Cline. Tokars and Carter informed McDougall that 'Julius, the tall, skinny one' was 'the silent partner' and 'the money man for James Mason'.

As time passed, McDougall did not believe that he and Carroll were getting a fair return on their investment. McDougall visited Tokars and then went to the club, complaining to Cline. McDougall and Cline exchanged angry words; McDougall accused Cline of 'ripping' him off and pulled a gun. Carter grabbed McDougall, calmed him down and got him out of the club. McDougall claimed that except for a few small payments, he and Carroll never received any return on their investment, which was never refunded.

Tokars and 'Deion's Club 21'
In September 1990, Tokars incorporated Atlanta Entertainment Management Inc., listing Mason, Cline, and Willie Harris as its directors. Tokars testified at trial that Mason approached him about creating the corporation; Mason identified Cline and Harris as being co-owners of the club.

The grand opening of 'Deion's' was noted in Tokars' 1990 calendar as October 2. Carl Tatum was an employee. Tatum met Mason in 1989. From mid to late 1989, until the trial, Tatum talked with Mason, 'sometimes several times a week'. Tatum testified that he discussed with Mason that fact that Cline was a cocaine dealer, and that Mason knew Cline dealt in cocaine. According to Tatum, Mason described his relationship with Cline as being that of a 'business partner, more or less looking out for Julius' interest financially'.

Harris Enters the Enterprise
In 1988, Willie Harris began selling cocaine for Cline, acting as a 'middle-man', brokering transactions with other customers. Harris received cash for the cocaine and gave the money, less his percentage, to Cline. He recalled that on one particular day he received 'between a quarter of a million and half a million dollars, something like that'. He put the cash in a safe located 'at Julius' apartment'. Harris testified that Cline claimed the cocaine was coming from Miami and California.

Harris testified that on one occasion, at the request of Cline, he delivered cocaine to Mason. On a weekend when Cline was in Detroit, Mason called. When Harris returned the call, Mason indicated that he needed 'to get a quarter key for some lady in his complex'. Harris called Cline to see if it would be all right to deliver the cocaine to Mason, and he did. After delivering the cocaine, Harris heard from Mason that the cocaine was intended for a woman in Mason's residential complex.

Harris' Arrest – Tokars' Advice
On 25 June 1991, Harris was arrested on cocaine charges. While in custody, Harris was visited by Tokars who indicated that Mason had paid $5,000 to Tokars to help Harris. Later, Tokars appeared on behalf of Harris, filing affidavits by Mason and Cline at Harris' bond hearing. Each affidavit stated that neither affiant knew Harris to sell, distribute, possess or consume illegal drugs. Harris stated that, at the time the affidavits were filed, he had already delivered the cocaine to Mason and had been conducting, on behalf of Cline, a substantial cocaine business. Harris at first was denied bond, but later received one. Having obtained a bond, Harris visited Tokars' law office. Harris testified that Tokars opined that Harris would be found guilty and receive a substantial sentence. Harris agreed. The discussion then turned to

whom Harris could assist the government in arresting. Specifically, Tokars asked if Harris would set up Cline.

According to Harris, Tokars said, '[H]ey, you're cool with Julius. Could you do Julius?' Harris testified that he had never admitted to Tokars 'about doing any business with Julius', and declined Tokars' request. Harris claimed that he just was not going to 'do it to him [Cline]'. Tokars responded, '[Y]eah because if you do Julius, it will roll down and get James because everybody knows James doesn't have any money, and he gets his money from Julius'. Harris asserted that 'we know James basically got his money from Julius and [Ferguson]'. Harris said that Cline's drug money was behind all the clubs. After getting out on bond, Harris returned to 'Deion's', where he was informed by Mason that the club had lost business during Harris' incarceration. A welcome-back party was given and business picked up, but Harris felt 'animosity' and left the club within a couple of weeks. Later on, Harris and Mason 'got together to do "Diamonds and Pearls"'.

Mason, Tokars, and 'Diamonds and Pearls'
Harris testified he and Mason discussed opening a new club. Mason claimed that he had spoken with Al Brown, a drug dealer, and was going to get money from Brown to open the club. Harris said that Mason worked out the arrangements to lease the club and get money from Brown. Mason told Harris that he obtained $50,000 from Al Brown to use in purchasing the club. John Vara testified that he, through his corporation, JDV, sold the leasehold rights to 'Diamonds and Pearls' for $250,000. Mason's attorney was Tokars. Vara recalled one meeting at Tokars' office in November 1991, where the sale was closed. The closing agreement reflected that $50,000 was the down payment, with $200,000 financed. Vara stated that before the closing he already had received cash payments from Mason. Vara was introduced by Mason to Brown, who Mason identified as part of management. Mason and Tokars used Atlanta House Clubs, Inc. as the purchaser of the lease.

Tokars introduces Lawrence to Mason
Eddie Lawrence was introduced by Tokars to Mason at 'Diamonds and Pearls' in the spring of 1992. In addition to Mason, Lawrence, through Tokars, met Julius Cline, Andre Willis, and Willie Harris. According to Lawrence, Tokars said that Cline was a drug dealer. Tokars previously had informed Lawrence that Mason was a 'client' for whom Tokars laundered drug money. Tokars claimed, and Mason agreed, that half a million dollars in drug money was used to renovate 'Diamonds and Pearls'. Later, on a separate occasion, Lawrence, Mason, Tokars and another cocaine dealer discussed using Mason, Lawrence and Tokars' services to launder drug money.

Cline Receives Cocaine from Brown – 'The Phoenix Club'
By 1992, Cline started receiving cocaine from Al Brown. Cline, at the time, was renovating 'Traxx' with the intention of changing it from a gay club to a 'hip-hop' club. Willis testified that Cline expressed anger about Mason because of Mason losing 'The Parrot' over a civil lawsuit, and Cline having 'had all his money tied up into "The Parrot"'.

Willis testified that Cline asked Willis to invest $150,000 into the renovation of 'Traxx', which was to be renamed 'The Phoenix'. Willis made investments from cocaine sales. Cline advised Willis that he 'had a white friend that was an attorney and judge that was advising him on how to invest his money in the right way'. Cline indicated that this person was helping him with the nightclubs. Before 'The Phoenix' opened, Cline was killed.

Brown's Arrest
On 5 August 1992, in Amarillo, Texas, a car with 115 kilograms of cocaine destined for Atlanta was stopped. Thereafter, DEA airlifted the car to Atlanta, with its driver, who agreed to cooperate. Following an intermediary's arrest, the cocaine was delivered to Anthony Brown, also known as Al Brown, who was arrested. Brown's car was searched. Among items seized were business cards identifying Brown and Mason as being associated with 'Peachtree Entertainment', weekly reports of 'Diamonds and Pearls', two digital beepers, and $49,700 in cash. After Brown's arrest, DEA served grand jury subpoenas seeking to identify assets purchased by Brown with cocaine proceeds. Two search warrants were executed at Brown's residence. During the first, agents found a money counting machine, a bulletproof vest, digital beepers and records. The second search resulted in the seizure of expensive clothes.

On 11 August 1992, Brown was represented by Tokars at a bond hearing. Afterwards, Assistant US Attorney Janis Gordon discussed with Tokars the government's desire to have Brown cooperate. Also, as AUSA Gordon had been made aware that 'Diamonds and Pearls' had been incorporated by Tokars, she indicated to Tokars that he might have a conflict, 'because if the government decided or attempted to seize the nightclub, he may end up having to be a witness'.

Atlanta House Clubs, 'Diamonds and Pearls', and Al Brown
Tokars incorporated Diamonds, Inc. and Diamonds and Pearls, Inc. on 8 January 1992. Each corporation identified Mason as the sole director and shareholder. On 16 August 1991, Tokars had incorporated Peachtree Entertainment Group, Inc., identifying Mason and Brown as directors.

After Brown's arrest, AUSA Gordon supervised the grand jury's investigation of Brown's drug trafficking activities, focusing on whether he had purchased assets with drug proceeds – more particularly, whether he had invested drug proceeds into 'Diamonds and Pearls' and whether he had an ownership in the club. To that end, Mason was subpoenaed to produce all records of the club.

Prior to serving the subpoena, DEA and IRS agents interviewed Mason, informing him that they were investigating Brown's interest in the club. Mason told the agents that he was the 100% owner of Atlanta Club Houses, Inc., which owned the club. Mason said Brown had a job as 'doorman' and as a handyman for the club. Mason delivered the subpoena to Tokars who referred Mason to another attorney. Later, AUSA Gordon contacted Tokars who indicated that he had been fired by Brown.

Sara Tokars Gets the 'Goods'
On 19 September 1992, at a political reception, Tokars talked about his wife, Sara, stating that she had recently been in his office working on his books. Tokars testified at trial that Sara learned facts 'because we lived together, and you know, we talked about things'.

Sarah Suttler, a neighbour of Sara Tokars, testified that Sara Tokars often discussed divorcing her husband but expressed fear that her husband would keep custody of the boys. However, in 'September or early October of '92', Mrs. Suttler said she found Mrs. Tokars 'to be very elated'. Sara Tokars professed to Mrs. Suttler, 'I can divorce Fred now because I have the goods on him ... I have found papers of income tax evasion'. Mrs. Suttler testified that Sara Tokars exclaimed that 'she was turning them [the goods] over to the proper authorities and now she could divorce him and take her boys'.

Murder of Sara Ambrusko Tokars

Tokars Meets Lawrence
In 1991, Eddie Lawrence employed Alex Yancey in the construction business. Lawrence knew Yancey as a cocaine dealer. Yancey asked Lawrence for $10,000 to purchase cocaine, which Yancey and Lawrence planned to resell. Lawrence advanced the money, but Yancey's plan failed. Yancey then embarked on a scheme to produce counterfeit money as a means of repaying Lawrence and profiting for himself.

As Yancey, Lawrence, and other engaged in counterfeiting activities through the fall and winter of 1991, the United States Secret Service began investigating. According to Lawrence, he and Yancey passed counterfeit money by going to nightclubs, buying drugs and then reselling the drugs for legitimate money. By December, Yancey and Lawrence became aware of the Secret Service's investigation.

In January 1992, Yancey introduced Lawrence to Tokars; the two sought legal advice. At the meeting, Yancey and Lawrence informed Tokars of their counterfeiting activities and the investigation. Tokars asked for counterfeit money, indicating he could distribute it in the Bahamas. They declined. Lawrence hired Tokars, but Yancey fled, avoiding arrest until December 1993.

After meeting Tokars, Lawrence was confronted by the Secret Service, and he denied his involvement in the counterfeiting scheme. Later, Lawrence informed Tokars of the contact. Tokars advised Lawrence to cooperate. Lawrence and Tokars went to the Secret Service's office, where the Secret Service requested permission to polygraph Lawrence. Tokars consented. Lawrence failed the test. Tokars was told that Lawrence was deceptive.

Tokars and Lawrence Become Partners
Lawrence testified that after the test, he and Tokars went in business 'to launder drug money'. 'Well, obviously he knew I was involved in criminal activities, and he was a lawyer. He wanted to launder drug money. I know a lot of drug dealers after having been one myself, and from that point we determined that we could set up business'. Lawrence testified that over time they discussed different types of drug money laundering activities. Tokars claimed that Lawrence's construction business, Lawrence Industries, could be used as a 'front' as a 'reason for me having cash money'.

Tokars discussed offshore banks and how he used them to launder money. Tokars said, 'if you are going to be serious in business, it is to your advantage to have a corporation'. To that end, Lawrence detailed corporations which Tokars incorporated on his and Lawrence's behalf to assist in 'laundering drug money'. Lawrence's role was to solicit drug dealers by going to nightclubs. Tokars advanced over $75,000 to Lawrence to purchase equipment and other materials to operate.

Murder Scheme
Lawrence testified that in late July or early August 1992, Tokars 'asked me if I would kill somebody'. Around 'mid-September', Tokars discussed killing his wife, stating that his wife 'was going to divorce him, you know, take everything he had'. Later, Lawrence was told that Tokars' wife wanted the house and his money. Lawrence advised: 'Let her have it', saying to Tokars that he 'could always get that back'. According to Lawrence, Tokars stated, 'he worked too hard, he went to school at night and she never did anything. All she ever did was spend his money, and that he wasn't going to give it to her. He would kill her first'. A fifth discussion of murder raised the subject of Tokars' children. Lawrence testified Tokars said, 'They will be alright. They will get over it. They are young. They will get over it'. Lawrence testified that Tokars just wanted 'it done' and that 'she was putting pressure on him and he wanted to kill her, that was what he wanted to do, he wanted her dead'.

Tokars first indicated that he wanted his wife killed in his office, as 'he had a lot of influence in the City of Atlanta, and could cover it up', but Lawrence did not agree. Tokars next discussed murdering his wife at home, because 'nobody would really suspect anything when there is a burglary', and offered to pay Lawrence $25,000 after the murder, together with a portion of the life insurance proceeds.

Tokars continued to exert pressure on Lawrence to kill Sara Tokars, which increased to the point that Tokars was threatening to destroy Lawrence's 'business' if the murder did not occur. Lawrence claimed that Tokars 'didn't care who did it'. Lawrence approached Curtis Rower, a 'hit man', offering Rower $5,000 for the murder. Rower agreed to the murder contract.

On the Monday or Tuesday prior to Thanksgiving 1992, Lawrence met Tokars to discuss the murder. Tokars informed Lawrence that his wife would be going to Florida and that 'when she came back, he wanted her killed'. Tokars said he was going to be in Alabama meeting with 'some guy that was in jail ... and that would be his alibi ...'.

Dr. John Ambrusko, the father of Sara Tokars, testified that his daughter and two grandchildren arrived on Tuesday before Thanksgiving 1992, having driven to Bradenton, Florida, from Marietta, Georgia. Mr. Tokars arrived the same day by flying from Atlanta to Tampa. On Saturday, Tokars returned home. Tokars contacted Lawrence and arranged to meet at Tokars' office the following day.

On 29 November, Lawrence met Tokars around 1.00 p.m. at Tokars' law office, where they 'discussed the murder ...'. Tokars informed Lawrence that he had just called the Ambrusko's and confirmed his wife was on her way back, and that she should arrive around 8.00 or 9.00 o'clock'. Tokars left for Montgomery, Alabama.

Dr. Ambrusko testified that, just as his daughter and grandchildren were returning to Atlanta, he 'went in and answered the phone, and it was Fred, calling on the phone'. Tokars inquired as to whether Sara had left, and Dr. Ambrusko informed him that 'they just pulled out of the driveway, and they were on their way home'. Dr. Ambrusko stated that it was about a nine-hour drive, and Sara's custom was to call him as soon as she arrived home. He never talked with his daughter again.

Tokars arrived in Montgomery and checked into a hotel. Around 6.13 p.m., he called his answering service, leaving the message, 'If emergency, Fred can be reached at area code 205 264–2231, room 109 until 11.30 a.m.'. Stipulated testimony identified a litany of telephone calls on 29 November 1992, involving telephones associated with Tokars, Lawrence, Ambrusko and the Montgomery hotel.

Around 7.00 p.m., Lawrence 'picked up Curtis Rower', who had a sawed-off shotgun, and drove to Tokars' residence. Lawrence left Rower at the residence, instructing Rower to kill a white female about 40 years of age. Lawrence drove to a neighbouring subdivision to wait. Two hours later,

Lawrence saw Sara Tokars' white 4–Runner driving off the road. Rower, carrying the gun, exited the vehicle and ran toward Lawrence. They returned to Atlanta where Lawrence took Rower to buy cocaine.

In prior testimony introduced at trial, Rower said he was offered $5,000 to kill Lawrence's 'wife'. Rower indicated Lawrence instructed him that the murder had to be done in the house and should look like a burglary. Rower stated that after the woman came to the house, 'I made her get back in the car and leave, and told her to take me to Atlanta'. Rower testified that they pulled over, stopped, and that he saw Lawrence approaching. Rower claimed Lawrence 'reached and grabbed' the gun, which 'went off'.

A police officer arrived at the crime scene. Located in the driver's seat was a body of a woman with long blond hair, slumped with her head resting against the steering wheel. Stipulated testimony indicated that Sara A. Tokars died from a gunshot wound to the head, that the estimated distance from the gun to the head was approximately one foot, and the injury was homicide.

Wilbert Humphries, a money launderer, was in custody in Montgomery in November 1992. Tokars was his attorney. On the Sunday after Thanksgiving, Humphries was surprised to receive a visit from Tokars. At the jail, Tokars asked Humphries to sign some papers. Humphries attempted to talk with Tokars about the case, but Tokars 'talked to me very brief like he was in a hurry or something'. The face-to-face meeting lasted about ten minutes.

'If Anything Should Happen'
On hearing the news of Sara Tokars' death, the family began arriving in Atlanta. On Monday, a cousin of Sara's contacted Sara's sister, Christine Ambrusko, seeking to find 'the papers I had had Sara xerox'. She went to Ms. Ambrusko's residence, found the documents, returned to her house, xeroxed them, and delivered a copy to the police. The records Sara Tokars copied reflected 'offshore bank accounts' in the Bahamas and a Class B licensed bank issued by Montserrat, a Leeward Island of the Lesser Antilles. Christine Ambrusko testified that Sara Tokars had delivered to her the documents, 'about the summer of 1989'. The two discussed the documents which appeared to identify bank accounts located 'offshore in some islands'.

Ms. Ambrusko testified that Sara Tokars asked her to keep the documents in a safe place and instructed her 'that if anything should happen to her [Sara Tokars], that I should take them to the police'. In 1989, at the time the documents were delivered to Ms. Ambrusko, Sara Tokars 'wanted to divorce Fred, but she was concerned that he would take the kids away from her, her two children'. Ms. Ambrusko stated that Sara Tokars 'was very scared and intimidated'.

Reaction of Tokars

On learning of the death of his wife, Tokars 'appeared to be quite hysteric-al'. He was returned to Atlanta by his brother. Tokars was first interviewed by the police the next day.

Gretchen Ambrusko Schaeffer testified when she first saw Tokars after the murder 'he seemed very anxious, and he was making loud noises, kind of moaning and saying, "I'm so afraid" and "I'm scared" in a loud tone of voice, very nervous appearing'. Schaeffer recalled a time when she and Tokars' mother talked with Tokars about assisting the police. Schaeffer testified that Tokars said, 'Gretchen, I don't want to talk to the police right now. I'm trying to stall talking to them hoping that they will find the person who killed Sara, because I'm afraid if I talk to them now, they are going to look into my business dealings, and I have gotten some money from some criminal people and some drug people that I was supposed to put into some sort of escrow account and declare on my income tax ... If they look into that, I'm afraid I could go to jail for tax evasion'. Schaeffer told Tokars that if he knew something, he had to tell the police.

6 December 1992, Interview

On 6 December, Tokars, with counsel, was interviewed by the police. He acknowledged that he was in Atlanta on 29 November, before he travelled to Montgomery. He said his wife 'always talked about my clients and stuff like as not being, you know, good clients that I have'. When asked as to whether he had received any threats, Tokars stated: 'the type of business that I had, and I guess I'm sort of ashamed to say it, but they were all scumbags, and, uh, they had done bad things, and, yeah, they would say things to me, but it wasn't like – I used to just sort of thing, you know, they're just saying them'. The police requested that he describe 'these people', and Tokars began by describing a cocaine dealer who had committed murder. When questioned as to whether there was anyone else about whom he was concerned, Tokars discussed Mason.

Tokars stated that he had represented James Mason for 'about four years'. He said that in the last three months, one close business partner, Julius Cline, had been murdered; that another business partner, Al Brown, had been arrested and jailed; that Al Brown's brother Darryl Hill, was murdered; that Mason's business was that of being a nightclub owner; that Mason and Cline were partners in owning 'The Parrot' club; that Mason owned a club called 'Diamonds and Pearls'; that he assisted Mason in incorporating 'The Parrot' club; and that he had represented Mason in a number of civil suits, 'everything, liquor licenses'.

Tokars described the history of his relationship with his wife, including his knowledge that she had previously hired an attorney, seeking a divorce. He acknowledged that his wife was 'concerned that I was like representing bad people, and running around and drinking ...'. He also stated that Sara

Tokars 'had started to just work in [his] office'. Tokars was asked 'do you have any idea who may have wanted to kill Sara?' His response was: 'I just can't even imagine it. I just can't even imagine it'. Eddie Lawrence's name was never mentioned. Later that evening, pursuant to Tokars' consent, police and federal agents searched Tokars' residence. Tokars' calendars for 1988, 1989 and 1990 were seized.

Lawrence was arrested on 12 December 1992, for writing bad cheques. He was questioned about the murder of Sara Tokars. He lied. Lawrence was released only later to be arrested on a different bad cheque charge. While in custody, Lawrence was visited by a private investigator of Tokars who questioned Lawrence about the murder.

20 December 1992, Interview
On 20 December, Tokars was re-interviewed by the police. When confronted that during the prior interview he never mentioned Lawrence, Tokars responded by noting he had discussed their corporations, claiming that 'everything that I've done with Eddie Lawrence is a matter of public record'. He described Lawrence as a 'business partner'. Tokars admitted that Lawrence had bad business practices. Tokars again discussed Mason, describing Mason as 'an on-going, regular client of mine'. Tokars acknowledged that he met Lawrence in connection with the Secret Service's investigation of Yancey. At the conclusion of the interview, Tokars was asked: 'Is there anything else that you can tell us that might help us find who killed Sara Tokars?' He responded, 'It's sort of an open-ended question. I mean I've agonized, I've thought about it, and, ah, you can be assured that if I think of anything, that we will definitely provide it to you'.

Arrests of Lawrence and Rower
On 23 December, Lawrence and Rower were arrested for the murder of Sara Tokars. Following the arrest, a police officer called Tokars at Dr. Ambrusko's home and informed Tokars of Lawrence's arrest; Tokars responded 'okay'. Tokars made no other response. Dr. Ambrusko described Tokars as having no reaction to the information. Following the call, Ambrusko asked Tokars to inform the family about Lawrence. Tokars claimed that he did not believe that Lawrence was involved. He further refused to discuss the matter.

Neal Wilcox testified to having a conversation with Tokars later in the evening. According to Wilcox, Tokars 'kept repeating to me that he was worried about the police making a deal'. Tokars claimed that the police 'were using these guys to get him, and he was worried about the police making a deal for their testimony against [him]'. Wilcox acknowledged that there was tremendous media scrutiny of Tokars, who was being portrayed as a co-conspirator.

The next morning, the family expected Tokars to go to Busch Gardens, an amusement part. Tokars provided an excuse for not attending. As time passed without any communication from Tokars, family members became concerned. Dr. Ambrusko went to Tokars' hotel room where he found him unconscious. Police found a suicide note. Tokars lived to be tried, convicted and sentenced to life without parole.

CONCLUSION

During the trial, Tokars' attorneys presented their client as a pillar of the society, a respected attorney, a family man, and a political supporter of respected elected officials. The government argued that he was 'a wolf in sheep's clothing'. A man who had carefully cultivated an outward appearance of goodness, but who underneath was evil and corrupt. Government counsel in rebuttal closing argument suggested to the jury that an analogy of Tokars' conduct may be found in the poetic masterpiece, the *Inferno*, of Dante Alighieri, one of the greatest poets of all time. The *Inferno*, written over 750 years ago, describes a journey into Hell.

As the poets travelled through Hell's gates, thereby abandoning all hope, they visited many levels. In the Sixth Bolgia they came upon the Hypocrites. At first, they observed each hypocrite wearing robes brilliantly gilded on the outside and shaped like a monk's habit. Dante described the hypocrites' outward appearance as shining brightly, passing for holiness. But, underneath the gilded robes, each hypocrite carried the terrible weight of his deceit which his soul must bear throughout all eternity as he continued to walk in a circle. It was suggested to the jury that, while Frederic Tokars' outward appearance was of goodness, underneath he carried the weight of deceit and the responsibility of causing the death of the mother of his then five- and seven-year-old sons. The reason for her death, it was argued, was simply to prevent her from disclosing to the authorities his criminal activities as a drug money launderer. Frederic W. Tokars lived a life of hypocrisy, a life of corruption.

Does everyone have a price? Are we all at some level subject to being corrupt? Not all corrupt conduct may be motivated by greed and avarice. Pride, envy and conceit may motivate one to engage in corrupt behaviour. Do we all have some price, some temptation, some event or series of events which might prompt us to engage in corrupt behaviour? Possibly. Whether or not such is a component of the human condition we do not know; but what we do know is that we all have the ability to make decisions which govern our future.

We must be vigilant in guarding against putting ourselves in positions where temptations to engage in corrupt actions may be too great for our wills to withstand. The debate of whether or not every person has a price should be secondary to the realization that every person will at some point in their life and at some level hear the seductive, siren song of the corrupt temptress summoning us to, in Dante's words, enter past the gates of Hell, thereby abandoning all hope. Should we follow that path, then we have become corrupt, living the life of the lie and deceit, not only with others but also with ourselves.

ERNESTO U. SAVONA AND LAURA MEZZANOTTE

7. Double Standards in Public Life: The Case of International Corruption

INTRODUCTION

There is a common belief that international corruption flows in one direction only. According to this widespread conviction, international corruption is mainly caused by Western countries' enterprises supposedly paying officials in the Third World in order to do business in their countries, where things are corrupt anyway and where they cannot do business otherwise. All this with the implicit excuse that this corruption will in no way contaminate commercial and institutional links within Western countries. Nothing could be more false.

This paper attempts to prove that international corruption does take place within the industrialized countries and that for reasons ethical and functional to international competition, it has to be effectively fought on the same level as national corruption.

The excuse for the 'double track' theory between international and national corruption is that one tends to consider the corruption of foreign officials as something extra in commercial competition that, after all, favours the economic interests of the country by helping the export business or in general the business deals of national enterprises abroad. This is the reason why some European states even allow the deduction from taxes of bribes paid to foreign officials under the heading of 'commission to inter-mediaries', while at the same time they are seriously combatting corruption within their own countries.

The different standards of behaviour imposed by the legislation of the two markets seem to be based on the non-verified assumption that there is no link between the two phenomena and that therefore it is possible to turn off the taps of corruption on the inside while leaving them to run freely outwards.

Consider the fact that a bribe paid to an official or politician in a foreign country offers very little power or none at all that might create 'social alarm'; when the objects of bribery are foreign persons, the public immediately tends to assume that it is the others who are corrupt, that this corruption does not concern them. Even more so, since on a practical level the

Barry A.K. Rider (ed.), Corruption: The Enemy Within, 105–111
© *Kluwer Law International. Printed in the Netherlands.*

further costs to the corrupting enterprise (such as the transfer of the corruption money) will be added to the price to be paid by foreign taxpayers/consumers. The inquiries of Italian magistrates have, in fact, revealed that multinational concerns in Italy have also adopted the practice of corruption.

> Being accustomed to operating in the most varied social and institutional contexts, many multinational concerns are likely to regard a request for bribery as a simple 'environmental' factor, a further cost to be calculated in the investment. The distance that exists between this kind of enterprise and the social and institutional context in which the bribery is paid consents an almost total objectivation of the underhand exchange ascribed to local factors in front of which the enterprises claim to be completely powerless.

This legal standing, which allows for fiscal deduction of bribes, offers public opinion and enterprises legal support. Basically, it is the others who are corrupt and we are 'out of it', honest and clean. This, however, is an assumption that is quickly proved wrong when we look closely at some of the salient cases of international corruption between countries of the European Union that have come to light in recent years.

CASE STUDIES

According to the OECD, international corruption involves the 'direct and indirect offer or provision of any undue pecuniary or other advantage to or for a foreign political official, in violation of the official's legal duties, in order to obtain or retain business'.

This definition perfectly describes the most clamorous international intra-European corruption case that took place in recent years: the so-called 'Agusta' affair in Belgium, which involved, among others, the ex-Secretary-General of NATO, Willy Claes, who was forced to resign because of the scandal.

Although, as yet, there exists no legal truth concerning this – or many other – cases, it is certain that 51 million Belgian francs were paid by the Italian helicopter producing company, Agusta, to the Franco-Belgian and Flemish socialist parties, in order to obtain an order for 46 military helicopters from the Belgian Government.

The proofs came from the ex-treasurer of the Flemish Socialist Party, Étienne Mange, who declared during the inquiry that he also received 60 million Belgian francs from the French company Dassault, in order to obtain the contract for anti-radar equipment to be installed on F-16 aeroplanes belonging to the Belgian military air force. Following this statement, the

Belgian court issued an international order to arrest Serge Dassault, ex-owner of the company.

Neither the Italian nor the French courts have, however, been able to prosecute the corruptors for the payment of these bribes, even though the Agusta affair in the end turned out to be much more complex than a straightforward corruption case, and resulted in the judges of the two countries collaborating on two fronts, including the murder case of André Cools, President of the Flemish Socialist Party, who was involved in the scandal and murdered on his doorstep by an unknown killer.

Even more important is the privatization case of the Greek cement company Aget-Heracles. In this case, the then Prime Minister himself, Constantin Mitsotakis, was accused of having taken a bribe of US $22,5 million from the Italian agro-alimentary firm Ferruzzi, in order to smooth the way to the sale of the company for a total of US $225 million.

The scandal burst during investigations by the Italian magistrates of 'Clean Hands', when they were looking for elements of corruption in Italy in which the Ferruzzi firm was involved. In the course of inquiries, officials of the company Calcestruzzi (a company controlled by the Ferruzzi group) admitted having paid bribes for the acquisition of Aget-Heracles and that part of the bribe paid in Greece had again been redirected towards Italian political parties.

Other examples of the capillary networks of corruption that thrive undisturbed within the European Union are the bribes that were paid to Spanish officials and probably also to politicians during construction work connected with Expo '92 in Seville. In that case, two big European enterprises, the German company Siemens, and the French company Alsthom, fought over the contract for the modernization of the railway network. The battle was fought on two levels: the political level (with exchange of favours between France and Spain concerning the question of Basque terrorism) as well as the monetary one. Large sums were paid by both companies to some consultancy firms, which then turned out to be closely linked to the Spanish Socialist Party (then in power). The firms were, in the end, revealed to be nothing more than front companies, lacking all necessary structure to carry out the works which they had billed to the two multinational concerns.

A final – and perhaps the most classical – example of international corruption concerns the arms market, by its nature a highly obscure area. This market accepts in almost legal terms – or, at least, known and accepted terms – commission paid to intermediaries which favour the sales of the goods. French law even tries to regulate the matter by assigning to the Defence Ministry the task of keeping tabs on and supervising 'foreign commerce expenditures', as they are prudishly called. In 1994, the total sum of these payments in France was around 10 billion French francs.

This mechanism, however, is not sufficient to keep control of such a slippery situation. According to the statement of a former French judge, 'the contracts [of armaments] generate commission in favour of French intermediaries who then return these sums to political entities or business speculators'.

At this stage some further points need to be considered. Firstly, monies paid by enterprises as 'commission to intermediaries' are difficult to trace and control. It is unlikely that documentary proofs exist, except for simple bank transfers, of how companies pay in bribes to foreign officials. This is where the first danger crops up: bribes paid abroad could become channels for creating illegal (black) funds. It is possible that only part of the money officially paid by companies goes to officials and that part of it is hidden in foreign accounts by the companies themselves, thus creating illegal funds which can then also be used to pay bribes within national territory.

Second, a corruption agreement can include a sub-agreement, according to which part of the paid bribe money is returned to the country of origin of the corrupting company in the shape of bribes for internal corruption. The Greek case is a good example, but aspects of other recent negotiations are also questionable, especially when big business deals, furthered by corruption, require political approval not only in the country of destination but also in the country of origin.

INTERNATIONAL COOPERATION

At an intermediate stage between international corruption and internal corruption, we have corruption that is tied to development aid. The intermediate position exists because normally a development aid project includes, explicitly or implicitly, a massive intervention to carry out the aid on behalf of companies from the donating country.

Two situations can arise: either a case of internal corruption, in the real sense, which has the national enterprises competing for the aid contract by means of bribes to national politicians, or a case of international corruption, in which politicians of the donating country ask local enterprises of the receiving country to pay bribes in order to obtain the contracts. What distinguishes these situations from the two archetypes is the fact that in both cases the contracts are carried out outside the national territory, a characteristic that makes control by the competent organs much more difficult.

In this case, too, Italy is an important example. Many international cooperation projects, carried out mainly in the eighties, have been deeply affected by corruption. 'It was above all the humanitarian nature of the financing which made them interesting [from a point of view of corruption], scantily controlled, easily manipulated and in any case far removed from public opinion, which rarely demanded accounts of how the money had been employed.' The circumstances of the Italian international cooperation will be subject to investigation, but the work of the investigating magistrates has been made unduly difficult by the fact that the actual appearance of the contracts (of the foreign state territory, always a non-Western country) has greatly diminished the possibility of checking the keeping and transparency of the accounts.

Another example comes from the United Kingdom. The case of the Pergau dam in Malaysia, financed by development aid from the British Overseas Development Agency, has raised serious questions, both about the size and the utility of the project (which does not seem to correspond to the main aims of the ODA) and about it having probably been tied to an agreement between the British and Malayan Governments. According to this agreement, vast financial help had been approved in exchange for British military equipment being bought by the Malayan Government.

Anxiety about the political opportunism of such an exchange has opened the door to a more thorough inquiry about the case. As a result of the inquiry, John Toye, consultant to the Minister for Overseas Development, Lynda Chalker, has declared that

> [t]he scope of an NAO audit does not extend to the activities of the recipient government subsequent to the transfer of aid. It, therefore, does not have anything to say about the propriety or otherwise of those activities, or any repercussions which they may have at the UK end. British political parties are not obliged by law to disclose the sources of the foreign donations which they receive. Until political parties are legally required to disclose the sources of foreign donations, or they volunteer to do so, there can be no assurance that part of the proceeds of any financial improprieties occurring in connection with aid projects does not find its way back into the British political system, thus closing the loop of collusion.

The NAO, therefore, pointed out a loophole in the control network which could theoretically allow a circular movement of uncontrolled money from Britain to the receiving country and back again. Whether or not this actually happened in the case of the Pergau dam is, relatively, of little importance. What matters is the existence of a real opportunity for corrupt exchanges made acceptable by the absence of laws.

CONCLUSIONS

British legislation is not alone in having considerable loopholes in this area. Almost all European countries are unprotected in the face of such eventualities. International corruption is not sanctioned by European legislation; among the industrialized countries, only the US has – many years ago – adopted appropriate norms.

The Foreign Corrupt Practices Act, passed in its first phase in 1977 by Congress, makes the corruption of foreign officials on behalf of American enterprises a similar crime to that of corruption taking place on national territory. American enterprises have, from the start, protested against this harsh law and there have even been attempts to abolish or at least to soften it. American business enterprises have always made lively protests against American lawmakers, arguing in this case that the restriction has made it impossible for US enterprises to compete in a large number of Third World markets.

This objection is based on fact. Whoever has experience with Third World countries is well aware how few American companies manage to obtain contracts in those areas, whereas European enterprises succeed in getting all the big business, especially in the field of know-how and technology for huge public (mainly state) works, a sector in which the underdeveloped countries are not competent.

The topic is complex and needs to be further researched. The aim of this paper is to formulate some essential points for thought.

Most European states are running a big risk by adopting different standards of morality for internal and international corruption (the legal positions range from silence to open legitimization). On the one hand, they are determined to combat corruption within the national frontier, but they are also running the risk of having their efforts thwarted, if they do not take measures to combat international corruption. The trend towards globalization of the economy makes the movement of capital increasingly easy, whereas it is increasingly difficult to follow its track along the international money trails.

Therefore, if international corruption is not adequately dealt with, its perpetrators will finds the means to continue operating. Even if national corruption could be stopped, international corruption would remain an open field, in which only those enterprises which are big enough to operate in the international markets can draw profit. What makes the battle even more arduous is that the very size of these enterprises is such that they can put pressure on those in political power.

The Italian case has clearly shown how the general feeling that corruption is widespread can activate further corruption. The judges of 'Clean Hands' declared themselves that the turning point in their inquiries and sanctions of corrupt practices came only at the moment when public opinion became conscious of the unlawfulness of corrupt behaviour.

In this sense, if the law allows or does not punish certain practices, it is unlikely that public opinion will turn against them. It is, therefore, the norms that have to indicate the illegality of certain behaviour. We do not want to moralize here, but only want to follow the simple reasoning of where the opportunity lies.

The deduction from our earlier reasoning is that international corruption is an open door for national corruption. Even if we succeed in stopping the infection caused by corruption within single states, sooner or later (in times of recession or political instability, or even when democratic tension drops) it will again pick up force, because the virus will return through the international channel. This process will be speeded up by the increasing globalization of the economy. A half-won battle is not a victory.

In order to win the battle, it is indispensable that decisions against corruption should be global, and they should be taken by all countries. Consider, for instance, the case of transnational concerns, where the phenomenon of loss of citizenship of money and enterprise makes them slowly slip out from under state sovereignty. Just as production lines are nowadays (fairly easily) transferred from one country to another, in order to find situations and laws facilitating low or even very low production costs, enterprises can do the same if the battle against corruption is conducted in a haphazard way. They can and will transfer their interests if it is worth their while.

When drawing up laws against international corruption, states must keep this possibility in mind. Once again the example comes from the US. The Foreign Corrupt Practices Act does not limit its sanctions to international corruption carried out by American enterprises; it also extends them to companies generated by or affiliated to American enterprises, even when they fall under the jurisdiction of another country. American law punishes the mother country for what the daughters do, making it responsible for all actions. This is certainly a hard line, but it has the merit of attacking the problem at the roots. Not a single loophole must be left open if the battle is to be won.

THOMAS C. BAXTER, JR.

8. Breaking the Billion Dollar Barrier: Learning the Lessons of BNL, Daiwa, Barings and BCCI

My topic is 'Corruption in Banking' and I will focus on four specific cases that I have known during my career with the Federal Reserve: the cases of the Banco Nazionale de Lavoro (BNL), the Daiwa Bank, Barings Bank and the Bank of Credit and Commerce International (BCCI). My involvement in each one of these cases was as a bank supervisor.

These four cases are famous, or perhaps infamous, because with respect to each one, an official was able to cause a loss in excess of $1 billion through unauthorized, fraudulent or otherwise unlawful conduct. Of course, it is no surprise that unlawful conduct happens within banks. The legendary American bank robber, Willie Sutton, explained it best with the observation 'that's where the money is'. The reason that the BNL, Daiwa, Barings, and BCCI cases are exceptional is not the solitary fact that bad acts occurred in a banking house, but for two other reasons. These reasons concern the magnitude of the loss suffered by the houses – more than a billion dollars – and the fact that no government entity saw these losses until they reached their gargantuan proportions.

We study these cases to learn the lessons of our experience, so that we might detect other such losses at a much earlier point and act decisively before they can break through this incredible billion dollar barrier. In undertaking such a study, it is useful to adopt a competitive analogy, because in a very broad sense what we have is a competition between right and wrong. On the government side, we deploy our bank supervisory force to see that banking organizations operate safely and soundly and in compliance with law. On the malefactor's side, they must operate in shadows and must be sufficiently manipulative to avoid being detected by us. We are their adversary and we are in competition; we want to observe their conduct and they want to conceal it.

Because the competitive analogy is useful, it is worth applying it to assess the performance of the bank supervisors in each of these four cases. Consider for a moment what it takes to be a world-class competitor, for example, in the Olympic games. World-class runners who compete capitalize on their strengths, recognize their weaknesses and train to compensate for them, and pay close attention to the external factors (temperature, wind speed and humidity, for example) that affect performance.

In assessing the performance of bank supervisors in these four cases, I will not dwell on who won and who lost. That is not to suggest that the competition has no consequence. It is clear who gets blamed when these episodes occur. Being a bank supervisor today is very much like being the watchdog stationed at a warehouse full of valuables. When that warehouse gets robbed, no one is going to congratulate the watchdog for all the felons he has foiled. There is no doubt that the successes in the watchdog's past are irrelevant and probably unknown to his master, and we know that, once the warehouse is robbed, the watchdog gets a whipping.

In analysing each of these cases from a competitive perspective, I believe that there are some things we bank supervisors did extraordinarily well, and I will discuss them first. Then, I will discuss what I perceive to be weaknesses exhibited through our performance in these cases. These are the things which detract from our capability to detect fraud at an earlier point and stop it before losses become extraordinary. These are also things that we can correct with training and resolution. Finally, I discuss the external factors that influenced the competition. We need to pay closer attention to these external factors if we expect to win in world-class competition. And, make no mistake, there will be another competition and we will win.

CAPITALIZING ON OUR STRENGTHS

When situations like BNL, Daiwa, Barings and BCCI occur, the bank supervisor feels the switch. This is because we are perceived as sleepy watchdogs, who were not up on our hind legs barking and biting. What no one seems to understand is that we are not now, nor have we ever been, watchdogs in the sense that it was our job to catch all of the fraudsters within a banking organization. Loss prevention and detection is the job of the bank's internal controls, and they are administered by the audit and compliance departments. Our mission is different.

Controlling Systemic Risk

One of our jobs is to prevent and control systemic risk to the banking system, and this is one reason why we seek to assure that the participants in the system are conducting themselves in a safe and sound manner. Banking supervisors in the United States and around the world perform incredibly well in controlling systemic risk arising from major fraud, *once* that fraud has been identified. We also work exceptionally well together in containing the effects of detected fraud, to avoid any major disruption in the financial markets.

Consider the BCCI case. On 4 July 1991, the Bank of Credit and Commerce International had $23 billion in assets and was conducting business in 72 nations. On the following day, BCCI disappeared from the financial world's radar screen without causing so much as a blip in the financial markets. This extraordinary accomplishment of making a significant and far-flung banking organization disappear was the product of careful planning and close coordination among a host of bank supervisory authorities around the world – and it all occurred in absolute secrecy. There were no leaks, and more importantly, there was no shock to the banking system or systemic consequences.

Barings is also an illustration of this strength. On Thursday, 23 February 1995, Nick Leeson packed up and fled Singapore, leaving behind a billion dollar hole in Barings' balance sheet. Yet, by Monday morning, largely because of the work of the Bank of England with the support of certain other supervisors, Barings too had passed into oblivion without any systemic consequences.

Punishing the Perpetrator

Another objective for banking supervisors with enforcement power is to punish those bankers who have committed unsafe and unsound practices, or who have committed violations of law. Those of us who have this power have, in my view, shown strength and good judgement in its exercise. I should also say that we have shown wisdom in cooperating with prosecutorial authorities to see that justice is done, despite the extraordinary view of at least one US law professor that such cooperation is unethical. Let us quickly review the cast of characters and their respective fates:
  – Swaleh Naqvi, BCCI's former chief executive officer – currently a resident of the Federal prison in Allenwood, Pennsylvania.
  – Christopher Drogoul, BNL's former branch manager – serving a three-year prison sentence in the United States.
  – Toshihide Iguchi, Daiwa's former officer – convicted of various offences and awaiting sentencing in the United States.
  – Nick Leeson, Barings' 'rogue trader' – serving a six-year prison sentence in Singapore.

In conjunction with these criminal actions, a panoply of parallel civil enforcement actions has also been taken. While time will not permit a complete inventory, consider the US governmental response with respect to Daiwa. The US banking supervisors terminated Daiwa's activities in the United States, in careful coordination with the prosecutorial authorities who, following a criminal conviction, obtained a $340 million fine. In the case of BCCI, consider the situation of Ghaith Pharaon, one of BCCI's principal shareholders. Pharaon became a fugitive from justice in the United States, deciding not to face multiple federal and state indictments relating to his business and affairs with BCCI. But his fugitive status did not preclude a civil enforcement action by the Federal Reserve. An administrative law judge earlier this year issued a decision imposing a $37 million civil money penalty against Pharaon, which is now on appeal to the Federal Reserve Board.

These strong and aggressive actions are important because of their deterrent effect. They send a simple message to those in the financial community who are in a position to commit fraud: if you do it, you may run but you cannot hide; we will catch you and punish you, using all reasonable means. Over time, I believe that our message will become clear to those who are considering such conduct, and that they will be deterred by the prospect of punishment.

RECOGNIZING OUR WEAKNESSES

Like world-class runners, banking supervisors know that we do some things well. With our strong actions in Daiwa, BCCI, Barings and BNL, we communicated to all the world that we have no tolerance for fraud. But, like world-class runners, banking supervisors know there are some things that we need to do better if we are to win. These four cases, where we performed well *once* fraudulent conduct was identified, also reveal that we are not quite as good at uncovering the scheme before it reaches the point where it collapses from its own weight. At a minimum, banking supervisors know we can improve our performance, and we are working to do just that.

We learned about Daiwa when Iguchi confessed. We learned about BNL when one of the employees working under Drogoul approached the FBI. We learned about Barings when Leeson fled Singapore. And with BCCI, we closed the stable door after the horses had bolted. No knowledgeable person could refute the charge that the banking supervisors should have seen these problems at an earlier point. There are several training objectives that will allow us to perform better next time.

Internal Controls

Earlier, I made the point that it is not the banking supervisor's job to immunize the bank from all fraud. It is not, and we could not if we tried. Furthermore, establishing a goal of 'no fraud' would be an impossible objective. A marathon runner might set a goal of running four-minute miles, but he could not finish a full 26 miles at that pace.

It is much more productive to set realistic goals and work to achieve them. In that vein, a realistic goal is to assure that our banks are operating in a safe and sound condition, which means they must have sound internal controls. The strength of a bank's internal controls is its best defence against fraud. In each of the four cases, there was an internal control breakdown that enabled the fraud. In each of the four cases, the banking supervisors demonstrated weakness in either not identifying the internal control problem early, or in not acting to remedy a control problem that was detected.

One of the most significant internal controls relates to separation of function, and a failure to separate certain functions played a part in every one of our four cases. Separation of function is a fraud deterrent because it requires the fraudster to act in concert with someone else. Fraudsters do not want to expand the circle of knowledgeable individuals; they want to stay in the shadows where detection is unlikely. Let us review how a failure to separate function played a part in each of the four cases.

With respect to Daiwa, Iguchi should not have been involved in both trading and the back office where those trades were recorded. This is an elementary internal control principle for trading operations, and its break-down enabled Iguchi to sell customer securities to fund his betting the bank's assets in trading run riot.

With respect to Barings, Leeson had charge of both the trading floor and the back office in Singapore. Everyone there reported to him. Because he controlled effectively the entire Singaporean operation of Barings, he was able to make trades far in excess of his limits on the floor, and then see they were entered into Barings' trading system.

With respect to BNL, Drogoul operated BNL's agency in Atlanta with no less authority than Leeson operated Barings in Singapore. In fact, Drogoul was so powerful in Atlanta that he could operate a billion-dollar 'bank within a bank'. He caused BNL to extend billions of dollars in credit and then funded all of these credits with Federal Fund purchases. His hands were all over the Atlanta operation, from the letter of credit desk to the wire transfer room.

With respect to BCCI, the fraud was much more complex but the breakdown in the separation of function is again a contributing cause. Naqvi was able to make loans on behalf of BCCI, which should surprise no one, given his position as acting chief executive officer; but he made loans to some companies that he controlled through a power of attorney. According-ly, he was able to deploy loan proceeds in whatever way he needed to, including – but not limited to – covering a secret hole in BCCI's balance sheet. When the auditors became suspicious of a particular credit, all Naqvi needed to do was cause BCCI to make a 'new' loan to a shell company he controlled, and then wire the loan proceeds circuitously through several locations until the funds came back into BCCI and discharged the suspect credit.

In all four cases, Iguchi, Leeson, Drogoul and Naqvi had powers far broader than any one of them should have had. Iguchi should not have been able to sell off securities of Daiwa's customers while he traded the bank's own portfolio. Leeson should not have had control of Barings' back office staff in Singapore. Given that Drogoul was situated in a small outpost of a very large banking organization, it is understandable that he had significant power but, in banking as in politics, there is truth in the notion that absolute power corrupts absolutely. Naqvi should not have been able to make loans to customers which he effectively controlled through powers of attorney. The risks that were run in all four cases were the very risks that materialized, although the individual motivations may have differed significantly from one case to another.

The Will to Act Decisively

In every one of the four cases, there were warning signs. Instead of reacting to these signs with lightning, the banking supervisors' thunder turned out to be insufficient. The lesson here is knowing when to strike, when to rumble.

Take Daiwa first. The banking supervisors knew that Daiwa had prevaricated about the movement of a trading operation. The banking supervisors had also identified and counselled the organization about a failure to separate Iguchi's functions. But the bank supervisors' words fell on deaf ears. In retrospect, it is clear that we should have acted more decisively.

Next, consider Barings. From Leeson's book, *Rogue Trader*, it would appear that the Singaporean authorities were focused on his behaviour at a point when the overall loss was significantly smaller than the amount realized on 23 February 1995. Their reaction was to respond to Barings with a letter requesting an explanation, which management bucked down to Leeson himself. Here, again, the supervisory response consisted of words and not more affirmative action. I also understand from my British colleagues that the words of the Singaporean authorities did not reach British ears because of Singaporean secrecy laws, a subject which I will address later.

Last, let us focus on BCCI. For years before 5 July 1991 – the date of BCCI's closure – rumours circulated about the organization's financial health. The supervisors responded with a wealth of words, but a dearth of decisive action. I think that Lord Justice Bingham put it well in his BCCI Inquiry Report, where he gave the following prescient advice:

> The overriding need is to ensure that the supervisors' attention is drawn to and concentrated on the suspect banks, that the judgement they exercise truly is informed and that appreciation of a problem is *reinforced by willingness, where appropriate, to take decisive action.*

I say 'prescient' because Judge Bingham's suggestion foreshadowed the Barings situation. Given that, supervisors should listen attentively to the sound of Justice Bingham's clarion.

Think Small

There is a widespread misperception that each of these cases resulted from such type of precipitous action taken by a malefactor at a single moment in time. This is not accurate. Each of the four cases started out small, and grew gradually over time. While each of the malefactors had his own discrete motives, all of them were, in a perverse way, trained by circumstances. Initially, they engaged in some type of fraudulent conduct to cover a loss that was small. Over time, they used the same basic technique to cover the loss as it grew. Eventually, they found themselves covering enormous losses, which broke through the billion dollar barrier. In each case, fraud crept – it did not sprint.

Leeson's troubles at Barings began with a simple trading error. In the summer of 1992, a clerk had accidentally sold rather than bought 20,000 futures contracts on the SIMEX, generating a loss of about 20,000 pounds. Afraid of losing his new position of authority in Singapore and jeopardizing his bonus, Leeson decided not to report the loss but to trade out of it. Leeson believe that if he admitted the loss, the clerk would be fired; he, too, might lose a position that he had worked very hard to obtain. He was 25 years old, and had just been appointed head of Barings' operations in Singapore. He had worked his way up within Barings, having started out in the 'back office'. And he was not about to go back down the way he had come up.

Instead, he opened an 'error account', where he booked the clerk's mistake, and tried to trade out of the loss he had hidden. He tried again and again. By August 1994, the losses Leeson was hiding had grown from 20,000 to 80 million pounds. In one day, after the earthquake in Kobe, Japan, Leeson lost another 50 million pounds. On Monday, 6 February 1995, Leeson had a particularly good day; he made 15 million pounds. Unfortunately, by that point, his losses had grown to more than 200 million pounds. In the next three weeks, he tripled these losses to 600 million pounds.

Leeson is not an anomaly; Iguchi's story at Daiwa is remarkably similar. He incurred a $50,000 trading loss in 1983. Rather than report the loss, which would have affected his performance rating and bonus, he tried to trade his way out to it. Over a period of time, his losses grew from that small amount. In 1995, when Iguchi's fraud was 12 years old, the losses had reached $1.1 billion. Between 1983 and 1995, Iguchi had entered into some 30,000 unauthorized trades.

Our failure to appreciate that these cases start small is a weakness, but it is a weakness that training may overcome. In explaining how, it is important to identify two different problems. The first is what I would characterize as a tendency not to become concerned about a perceived trifle. This aspect of human nature dovetails with the generalized tendency of the bank supervisor to deliberate rather than to decide, largely due to a fear that decisive action might later appear to be capricious or improvident. Take Leeson's first act, covering up a clerk's 20,000 pound error with a false entry. If it had been seen by a bank supervisor at the time, what are the chances that stern and decisive action would have been taken? Do you think it is likely that some type of enforcement action would have been brought against Leeson or his employer? We need to learn to accept the principle that not all trifles are created equal. There are some forms of conduct that need to be taken as serious, not because of the insignificant financial consequences we see in their wake, but because of what might be lurking in the seas across the bow.

My second point relates to the form of enforcement action for this kind of conduct. In the United States, it is possible to bring a criminal action against a trader who takes an unauthorized position and then makes false entries in the books of a bank to conceal the position. But try to convince a jury to convict such a person. In the absence of personal gain to the trader, most jurors will apply everyday experience to this kind of case and perform a kind of rough justice. They will view the trader as violating a work rule of his employer and then not being truthful about it to avoid getting sacked. They will not regard such conduct as criminal, most probably because many of them have massaged facts in answering a boss's query. Given the small probability of a conviction, my prosecutor colleagues are understandably unenthused about prosecuting such cases.

Because of this, the Federal Reserve has made these cases a civil enforcement priority. These civil enforcement actions are tried by an administrative judge, rather than a jury, and do not carry with them the stigma of a criminal conviction. What these actions can accomplish is the functional equivalent to debarment for a lawyer – we can obtain an order that removes an individual engaging in this conduct from the banking industry. In bringing cases like this, our object is to remove people with this penchant from the banking business. Our theory is, if such individuals are willing to do this on a small scale, then they are willing to continue this when small losses get larger. Like an addicted gambler, the trader facing ever-increasing losses is always just one good trade away from redemption. A civil enforcement action will get such traders out of the banking organization, similar to efforts to keep the addicted gambler away from the gaming table. We have also accumulated a telling trove of anecdotal evidence, which shows traders afflicted with this characteristic committing their misconduct in one financial institution, getting sacked, and then moving and repeating their behaviour in successive organizations.

These civil enforcement initiatives are important because they break the cycle. I suggest that those jurisdictions not having civil enforcement mechanisms consider developing them. I also will leave this topic with a question that may be troubling in those jurisdictions which lack such mechanisms. Where do you think the people who are removed from the US banking business go to ply their trade?

Adapting to a Change in Culture

In the last twenty years, there has been a profound change in the banking business and its culture. Last month, at the American Bar Association's Annual Meeting, one of the speakers asked members of the audience to identify themselves as banking or securities lawyers. Some of the audience were visibly uncertain as to their identity; my sense was that the uncertainly was the product of a convergence of the industries. My prediction is that the convergence of the banking and securities industries will continue and that, by the turn of the century, the distinction between them will be absent.

There was a time when the culture of the banking industry was very different from the culture of the securities industry. In the banking industry, there were 'counterparties' with which you traded and which provided you with a source of profit. In the banking industry, deals were done over scotch at the country club. In the securities industry, trading strategy was formulated over beer in a noisy bar. While some of these generalizations will hold true, there is little doubt that the banking and securities industries have come together. With that homogenization has come a change in the culture of the banking business. In many banks nowadays, the culture of the trader has replaced the culture of the service provider.

Many now-senior bank supervisors spent their formative years in the banking industry's more halcyon days, when the job was more genteel. Conduct could be made conforming with a raised eyebrow during a meeting. Today, a raised eyebrow by a bank supervisor will often be viewed as an invitation to be poked in the eye.

In my view, the natural evolution of the business of banking into trading has brought with it a cultural change. It is a change that is inevitable because it is a natural byproduct of economic forces. While we might fondly recall an easier past, as supervisors we are only fooling ourselves if we believe that the pendulum will swing backward; it will not. Consequently, we must recognize that the techniques that worked in the past might not work in this different world, where some bankers treat their clientele as counterparties to be exploited for profit. In this new world, if profit is indeed king, it should come as no surprise that people raised in this new world will cut corners to achieve the profit objective.

In the United States, our brothers and sisters in the securities regulation business have earned a reputation for using adversarial techniques to enforce the securities laws. More importantly, and the recent Sumitomo experience notwithstanding, they have been effective in their efforts. If adversarial techniques work to foster compliance in the securities industry, and if the banking business is becoming more like the securities business, then perhaps we banking supervisors ought to borrow some of our colleagues' tools. I think that is one of the lessons taught in these four cases, and if you study our response to the more recent of them, you will see that it is a lesson the supervisors are learning.

At the same time, a bank supervisor should not apply the adversarial techniques of the securities industry to all problem institutions. The informal methods of the bank supervisor have their own especial merit, and have been demonstrably effective and far more efficient than adversarial methods. In many instances, the old way remains the better way. Perhaps what we banking supervisors need to do is to narrowly tailor our methods to suit the problem that confronts us, and be continually mindful of the culture of the institution that we are supervising.

Trust

Many people do not appreciate that, in the United States, the supervisory process is an iterative process between the bank and the supervisor. You will see this most clearly in our bank examination, where personnel within our employ will visit a banking organization for a full scope examination, or alternatively, for a special targeted examination directed towards a particular problem. Whatever the type of examination, the best examiner is an inquisitive person who will engage the examined in a dialogue of free inquiry. Questions will receive answers, and the answers will lead to more questions. When the examiner is satisfied, conclusions will be reached and set forth in a document, usually an examination report.

In reaching their conclusions, the examiners will principally rely upon the representations of the examined. They do this not because they are gullible people, but because of the nature of our process. The process of bank examination is *not* an adversarial process where alleged facts can be put through truth-testing techniques like cross-examination, nor is the examiner's report fairly analogous to a jury's findings of fact following trial. We rely on representations from a bank's officials as to how the bank actually operates. And we rely on the bank's management to tell us about problems and managerial challenges. If we did not so rely, a bank examination would necessarily consume an infinite amount of time and an infinite amount of resources. We would need independently to verify every statement that comes to us from a bank official, turning the process into a *Jarndyce* v. *Jarndyce* proceeding without end. Instead, the supervisory process depends to a large degree on candour. Bankers need to understand that we will tolerate no gamesmanship here; the condition of their institutions must be presented in a truthful manner.

As the customer service culture changes to the culture of the trader, it is important for those with the new culture to recognize that we might not appreciate the difference between a salesman's puffery and a deliberate lie. For them, this is a difference in degree; for us, this is the difference between right and wrong. It is sometimes said that a person must turn square corners when dealing with the government. When dealing with a US bank supervisor, truth-telling is so important that the corners turned should be at perfect

90 degree angles. It is not so much that we supervisors are moralistic people (although we are). The reason for the premium on square dealing is that our process depends on it. Consequently, we reserve our most serious penalty – our 'death penalty' if you will – for the institution we can no longer trust. When we can no longer trust an institution, we can no longer effectively supervise it and the relationship simply must end in a divorce. And you all know, given the balance of power, when the divorce comes who will continue to live in the house!

BEING AWARE OF EXTERNAL FACTORS

To be a winner in a world-class competition, it is not enough to capitalize on strengths and to train to compensate for weaknesses. A true winner pays close attention to environmental conditions, and runs the race with a close eye on those conditions. The same principle holds true for bank supervisors, and in our four cases, there were environmental conditions that contributed to cause a breakthrough of the billion dollar barrier.

Technology

I am going to give you a hot tip about two items that were absolutely necessary to perpetrate each of my four billion dollar booms. Without the telephone and the computer, they would not have happened. These technological marvels enable business and commerce to move faster and faster. Without them, it would be impossible to trade across time zones and to control accounts in multiple jurisdictions. These devices – perhaps more than anything else – have rendered national frontiers an historical anachronism and have forever changed what 'location' means in the English language.

While it would be a grave error to ignore the role that technology plays in these cases, it would be equally unwise to conclude that technology causes situations like these. In the middle ages, scientists believed in the 'spontaneous generation' of life. Given the right conditions, life would naturally spring forth. As proof of this theory, one enterprising young scientist put a handful of grain wrapped in an old flannel shirt in the corner of a barn. He left it there for a week. When he returned, there was a family of mice living in the shirt. He concluded that these mice had been spontaneously generated by the conditions he created.

We know the young scientist employed faulty logic. However, we also know that, given the right environmental conditions, some things are likely to happen. Technology in a banking organization is much like the flannel-wrapped grain our scientist left in the barn. It is an environmental condition that might aid the fraudster, because it increases the speed and complexity

124   *Thomas C. Baxter, Jr.*

of the transactions that are conducted, making it more difficult for all of us to see what is happening. Nevertheless, it would be foolish to suggest that all banking organizations forego reliance on sophisticated technology to run their business. They cannot and should not.

It follows from this, that if we are not going to eliminate technology, then we have to get better at using it and knowing how our competition is using it. That is my simple point.

Cross-Border Information-Sharing

An understanding of how technology is used by malefactors underscores the need for effective information-sharing across borders. From his offices on the fourth floor of Leadenhall Street, in the City of London, Naqvi controlled BCCI offices in Grand Cayman and Luxembourg. At Barings, Nick Leeson gambled away Barings' capital in Singapore, receiving daily infusions by wire from Barings' head office in London. At BNL, Chris Drogoul, and obscure officer of a Georgia agency of an Italian Bank, made loans from this Atlanta office to instrumentalities of the Iraqi government, funding them with daily purchases of dollars in the Federal Funds market. At Daiwa, Iguchi, a Japanese expatriate working in Daiwa's New York branch, essentially looted the custodial securities of Daiwa's customers and used the proceeds to support his speculative dealings.

In each one of these cases, the malefactor was in a 'host' country but he caused a balance sheet injury in the 'home' country. In the cases of BCCI and Barings, legal restrictions fettered the ability of host supervisors to share supervisory information with the home supervisor. In case of BCCI, the secrecy laws of the Cayman Islands, Luxembourg and Switzerland precluded the sharing of customer-specific information with a 'foreign' governmental entity. Similarly, in the Barings case, the secrecy laws of Singapore precluded the SIMEX from sharing suspicious information about Barings' trading activity in Singapore with the home supervisor.

One can hardly blame a domestic supervisor from acting in compliance with domestic law. That would be unfair and wrong. Having said that, that we should blame ourselves for not acting to repeal laws that no longer make any sense. In a world where commercial activities cross borders in an electronic instant, secrecy laws that proceed on the false assumption that commercial activity is localized within a particular territory make no sense whatsoever. What such laws do is encourage a balkanization of information among the supervisors, and cause all of them to see only part of a larger picture. We simply cannot allow ourselves to be blinded in this way. To go back to the world-class runner analogy, someone may be the fastest athlete in the world, but if blindfolded, that runner will never win a single race.

Individual Motivation

Of all the environmental factors, this one is the toughest. Oversimplification would suggest that in each of the four cases, the motivation was money. The problem is that that is inaccurate. Of all four cases, I am best acquainted with BCCI. In connection with the Federal Reserve's enforcement initiatives, I spent a substantial amount to time with Swaleh Naqvi, who was my witness for two weeks in the Pharaon proceeding mentioned earlier. I do not believe Naqvi was motivated by money. I might also startle my reader with the revelation that I do not believe Naqvi is a 'bad' man, although I will readily agree that he has done 'bad' things. I certainly would not place him in the category of individuals who I encountered early on in my legal career; members of organized crime who would kill a person for money. Naqvi is not of that kind. He would tell you that he engaged in fraud to save his bank, a bank that he believed was serving *his* world. Naqvi's world was the lesser developed world; Naqvi believed then (and now) that its people were not well served by the institutions of the West. I wonder sometimes if things would be different if we had a better appreciation of the man. If we had known that Naqvi was totally dedicated to the bank he believed in, and would do absolutely anything to save it, would our supervision have been closer and more careful?

I have no idea what motivated Chris Drogoul. His enigmatic personality led the media to speculate whether he is a genius who stashed away millions or a lunatic who was drunk with power. As far as I know, no one has suggested that he did it only for money, although there exists some evidence that money was a contributing factor.

With respect to Iguchi and Leeson, money is a much more plausible explanation for their motivation. And in their respective institutions, one sees salary structures that may well be an incentive for fraud. Individuals are compensated based upon the profit that they earn. When awarding bonuses, managers rarely evaluated the subjective risks that a trader has taken, to determine the trader's compensation. Rather, managers tend to rely on the objective measure of success – whether the trader has made money, and if so, how much. In this regard, I have never heard of anyone getting a handsome bonus because they executed a brilliantly-conceived trading strategy that, given unexpected market events, lost their employer millions of dollars. But it is unfortunately probable that a total gamble, or even an unauthorized position, that turns into a handsome profit for the bank will result in a bounty to the trader. In a nutshell, our institutions tend to reward behaviour that they should be sanctioning.

In reading Leeson's book, one can see how important his bonus was to him and how it influenced Leeson's trading behaviour. I believe that we have to search our own souls on this, and question whether we are instigating the very conduct that we later punish so vigorously. Institutions and governmental organizations need to send a very clear message that excessive risk-taking merits sanction *regardless* of whether that risk-taking is profitable.

So far, I have dealt with money, one of the positive incentives that can motivate people. But there is also fear. Fear of being prosecuted and going to jail is, of course, the essence of deterrence. It is self-evident that, in each of the four cases, our malefactors may have been afraid but they were not deterred. I do not know why. But I do believe that, with the prosecution of each malefactor, we reinforce a message. I take it as an act of faith that eventually we will effectively communicate our message and our message must be simple and straightforward: if you engage in this behaviour, we will catch you and you will pay.

Funding

The advice that all seasoned fraud investigators appreciate is that when you are investigating fraud, you must follow the money. This is easier said than done, but it is a basic principle that continues to prove itself. Consider a subtle variation on that old tried-and-true theme. In order to perpetrate a fraud nowadays – the objective of which is to get money – the malefactor must have access to money.

Leeson was amassing huge positions in Singapore and he needed to meet margin calls. To meet those calls, he solicited head office funding and he got it. Without that funding, his trading activity would have been impossible, and he acknowledges this in his book. Drogoul was in the very same situation. He was causing BNL to make massive credit extensions 'off the books'. But like any garden-variety loan, the off-the-books loans still needed to be funded. To do this, Drogoul made massive purchases of Federal Funds. Without the Federal Funds purchases, Drogoul could not have operated his 'bank within a bank'. With respect to Iguchi, we might say he got his money the 'old-fashioned way'. He stole it. Entrusted with a large cache of customer securities, Iguchi simply reached into a figurative 'cookie-jar' and sold off the contents. But the proceeds that he received from these sales were his unique source of funding, and they enabled him to engage in his own speculative trading. Finally, there is Naqvi. Naqvi struggled desperately to keep BCCI afloat until 'extraordinary profits' could be generated to replenish BCCI's lost capital. He thought that these extraordinary profits could come from investments in private corporations made through nominee owners, who were fronting for BCCI. For example, BCCI invested in an oil company, a grain company, and a bank in the United States. To make these nominee investments, BCCI needed money and that money was obtained by originating loans in the names of its frontmen. The loan proceeds were used to buy securities in a permutation on a familiar theme – here, BCCI sought to invest its way out of a loss position.

The funding in these cases is fascinating, because it may well be the point of structural weakness in the architecture of modern fraud schemes. The people who were providing Leeson with funding from Barings' head office were best situated to detect his fraud; they just did not question him. Similarly, with respect to Drogoul, one wonders what the sellers of Federal Funds really thought about Drogoul. Why did an Atlanta agency of an Italian bank need all those dollars?

In the United States, we require banking organizations to file with us 'suspicious activity reports'. We have found these reports to be extremely useful investigative tools, both in providing us with leads and informing us of new matters warranting our attention. Nevertheless, I have the sense that the banking community does not recognize the potential here, because I sense that many institutions do not report activity that, in their heart of hearts, they believe to be suspicious. And, of course, there is a very substantial grey area where suspicious activity is in the eye of the beholder.

Reporting suspicious activity may also cross one of those facts of commercial life. When a 'rogue trader' is out engaging in trades that cause large losses, someone on the other side of the rogue's trades is realizing large gains. The expectations that a 'counterparty', who has its figurative hands on the udders of the proverbial 'cash cow', will report such incredible largesse to the government may be fanciful. I suspect we will see these reports only when banking organizations realize that, at some future point when it is their organization that is being milked, a right-minded person will act responsibly and file a suspicious activity report. All too often, the near-term interest causes people to be short-sighted, and we do not receive as many suspicious activity reports as we should.

Audit

Bank supervisors have placed great reliance on the internal and external auditors. In my view, bank supervisors cannot rely on the audit function to do the job of bank supervision, any more than a world-class runner can rely on the wind to win a race. In all four cases, the audit function failed to detect gargantuan fraud.

In some of the cases, the auditor did not detect the fraud because he was not even looking. In the case of Daiwa, for example, the external auditor did not ever visit the New York branch, notwithstanding the fact that it was about $ 10 billion in asset size. Logic would suggest that we require such audits, but the logic works only if we conclude that an audit would have made a difference; I am unsure. In BCCI, for example, there were external audits of Cayman and Luxembourg, but they did not detect the fraud. Why should we believe that the Daiwa would be different? In BNL there were audits, but they did not detect the activity of Chris Drogoul.

This is particularly troubling, given all the funds sloshing around these institutions to support the trading activities of our malefactors. Furthermore, bank secrecy laws did not interpose a barrier between the auditor and the organization's books and records, and did not blind the auditor's eyes like they do the bank supervisors'. Perhaps auditors have not focused on funding because the auditing profession has not learned the lessons of the experience of these cases. Perhaps auditors need to spend more time in the wire transfer room and less time in the boardroom. Until that change occurs, however, bank supervisors cannot rely on auditors to prevent the occurrence of situations like these.

CONCLUSION

To borrow a metaphor from my President, we are on the last lap of the race into the 21st century. Our competitors are those who would penetrate and corrupt our banking organizations, and cause the problems that are evidenced in the four cases discussed. In a very real sense, they are racing us. I know that we will win this race for the following reasons.

Firstly, we will capitalize on our considerable strengths, and continue to control systemic risks and punish those who abuse our institutions or violate our laws.

Second, we will also train hard to overcome our weaknesses. We will continue to focus our efforts on sound internal controls. And when we are hesitant about taking action, we shall err on the side of action rather than passivity. In our consideration of individual cases, we will embrace the principle that any unauthorized action or fraudulent conduct must be addressed, no matter how small the financial consequence, because these are the seeds out of which mature frauds grow. We will also turn our attention away from a more genteel past and accept the fact that the culture of the banking business has changed. We will used the tools proven to be effective in a trading culture against those in our industry who have that culture. Finally, we will continue to insist on candour, and drive home the point by reserving our most potent weaponry for those who abuse our trust.

Third, we know that to win, we must pay close attention to environmental conditions. We will. We will make technology an ally rather than an enemy, and we will use it to our advantage. We will exchange information with each other, not to invade individual privacy, but to protect collectively the organizations that we care so much about. We will be attentive to what motivates individuals, and will seek to educate our organizations so that profit will not be the only factor affecting compensation. In addition, we will counter the positive incentive of great profit with the deterrent effect of meaningful enforcement action. Finally, we should resolve to pay much closer attention to funding, and work with our colleagues in the auditing community to develop audit tools that will stop the fraudsters by cutting off their source of supply.

In running this race, we must be prepared for setbacks. There will be times when we will be behind, and the race may seem unwinnable. But we cannot despair or lose confidence. We will also have bad training days, days when we do not feel like getting out of bed and running 10 miles or biking 100 miles or swimming 10,000 yards. But we cannot stop training, and every single day we need to remember the competition. This is hard, because we must accept the reality that, like the warehouse watchdog, when the race is over no one is going to place a gold medal around our necks. Instead, we will train for the same reasons that have motivated men and women throughout history. We will train because we are professionals, because we are on the side of right, and because we want to provide a safer economic system for ourselves and our children.

JAMES F. GILSINAN, JAMES E. FISHER, WILLIAM B. GILLESPIE,
ELLEN F. HARSHMAN, FRED C. YEAGER

9. From Regulation to Deregulation to Re-regulation: Rhetorical Quicksand and the Construction of Blame in the US Savings and Loan Crisis

OVERVIEW

On 22 June 1990, Germania Bank, a 100–year-old United States savings institution which served nearly 50,000 households in the St. Louis metropolitan area, was closed by federal regulators. As a result, scores of jobs disappeared, capital noteholders (primarily older retired persons) lost $10 million, one institutional noteholder lost $5.8 million, bank directors lost $5 million in personal stock investment, and by one estimate, US taxpayers lost $50 million via government insured deposits. Bank officers were charged with fraud and convicted. This is an analysis of the competing accounts of the events that overtook Germania Bank and indeed, the entire savings and loan (S&L) industry in the United States.[1] It explores the rhetorical tools used to convince various constituencies of the sources of corruption and culpability.

INTRODUCTION

The fields of public administration and policy analysis, ironically, are among the last of the social sciences to examine the potential impact of postmodern theory on their disciplines. This state of affairs is ironic because the very stuff of the disciplines, that which they seek to explain, is the result of rhetoric, persuasion, and symbolic manipulation. The affinity between postmodernism and the policy sciences can be captured by one of the key assumptions of the anti-positivist perspective as explained by Danziger (1995): '[T]he "motor" by which science moves is not verification or falsification, but persuasion'. This of course implies, as Danziger notes, that the ancient sophists were correct in their assessment of what is necessary for successful government policy. In both private and public affairs, it is the

---

[1] Savings and Loan Associations in the United States were established by law in 1932. These depository institutions traditionally accepted time and savings deposits from consumers and made residential mortgage loans.

Barry A.K. Rider (ed.), Corruption: The Enemy Within, 131–147
© *Kluwer Law International. Printed in the Netherlands.*

ability to persuade others of the 'truth' of the matter that is the essential ingredient of a successful outcome.

This insight is particularly relevant for those engaged in the study of economic crime. The organizational actions that lead to corporate and governmental corruption are recognized *after* the fact as deviant. To quote Ermann and Lundman (1996):

> [N]o organizational action is intrinsically deviant. Instead, organizational actions are deviant only to the extent that they are perceived, reported, accepted, treated, and defined as deviant (p. 25).

Ermann and Lundman go on to suggest a three factor model for understanding how corporations structure their rhetorical arsenals to defend against charges of corporate deviance. First, before any charges of corruption are made, organizations seek to build a climate of trust and goodwill. If they are successful, even the idea of company malfeasance fails to develop. Second, if an accusation of wrongdoing is made, the organization or individuals targeted offer alternative accounts. Finally, various audiences judge the accounts and become the final arbiters in deciding which stories are 'true'.

The importance of rhetoric and persuasion in this process is obvious. Less clear are those elements that make for a successful account. John W. Kingdon (1984) provides a framework for analyzing the policy process. Specifically, he is concerned with how items become the focus for governmental action. While his model was originally designed to elucidate both agenda setting and the development of policy options, we argue in this paper that it can also be used to understand the dynamics of how certain accounts of problematic economic activity become definitive.

According to Kingdon, the policy process can be considered as having three streams. The first stream he terms the problem stream. It consists of potentially troublesome situations that have not yet been recognized as a problem for the public policy agenda. Numerous factors aid in the recognition of situations as problems. Among those cited by Kingdon are a change in indicators, focusing events or crises, the values of those observing a situation, and the placement of the situation in a particular category.

The second stream, the policy stream, consists of technical or scientific advances in knowledge that can provide new or alternative solutions. While this stream can yield a very large number of ideas for ameliorating a problem, only a relatively few options, according to Kingdon, survive to become viable alternatives. Among the characteristics of these options are technical feasibility, value acceptability, constraint recognition, and familiarity. This last item deserves additional comment. In brief, a new idea is welcome if it is not too new or too radical. Thus, policy options that represent a recombination of previously tried interventions are often acceptable because they are new but familiar.

The third stream is termed the political stream. This consists of those events that influence the courses of action government takes. Factors such as elections, changes in the dominant governing party, or a particular shift in the public mode changes the potential for what government will or can do.

When the three streams come together, they create for a time a window of opportunity to make policy – a formal, institutionalized, coordinated, longer-term government response to an issue. Policy entrepreneurs seize the initiative by attempting to bring together policy alternatives with nascent problems and current political events.

Adding a postmodern frame to Kingdon's model suggests that such entrepreneurs – legislators, private sector lobbyists, government agency representatives, and/or citizen coalitions – attempt to persuade others of the 'truth' of the problem and their solution to it. If they successfully control the rhetoric that constructs both the problem definition and the strategies of amelioration, the resultant government action legitimates their beliefs about the world and their place within it. Thus the stakes in this game are high indeed. They are psychic as well as material, since not only resources but the definition of oneself and one's ability to 'make sense' are potentially at issue.

This paper attempts to extend both the Kingdon model and that of Ermann and Lundman by examining certain accounts of the savings and loan crisis in the United States to determine those rhetorical elements that led to 'successful' sense-making of the event. Specifically, the paper examines the demise of a particular savings and loan institution, Germania Bank of St. Louis. Debates about the cause and effect of government policy in either exacerbating or alleviating the situation were plentiful. What may make this case unique is the extensive record of accounts attempting to explain, justify, and literally 'make sense' of what occurred. Thus, there are not only newspaper accounts of the situation as it developed over more than a decade, but extensive trial transcripts, and even published documents by one of those accused and eventually found guilty of criminal activity. This last source of information is particularly useful, since it represents an account by one of those who came to be seen as the culprit. His construction of events is, of course, diametrically opposed to what became the 'accepted' story of the scandal. Thus, an opportunity is available to examine the different rhetorical constructions surrounding the savings and loan debacle and to perhaps ascertain those elements that led to the 'successful' emergence of a particular account, in this instance, an account of corporate deviance and economic crime.

Following this introduction, three distinct perspectives of the savings and loan crisis are presented: a macro-analytic perspective, a legal perspective dealing specifically with Germania Bank and accusations of criminal wrongdoing, and a personal account representing the viewpoint of a Germania Bank officer subsequently convicted of fraud. These accounts are then analyzed to determine what made for successful rhetoric in each of the policy streams. The paper concludes with a brief commentary on how rhetorical processes both have shaped and continue to shape our understanding of economic corruption and culpability.

THREE ACCOUNTS

Macro-Analytic Perspective

Financial depositories, even in good times, are thinly capitalized institutions; thus relatively small changes in the value of their assets can result in comparatively large percentage changes in their net worth (White 1991). In the 1980s and 1990s, efforts to chart a path of economic recovery for the thrifts had to reckon with the considerable erosion of net worth throughout the industry. This lack of a capital cushion, either to absorb future losses or to temper risky decisions, confounded or otherwise complicated certain policies intended to restore the thrift industry.

For example, a major policy initiative in the early 1980s permitted deregulation of both asset and liability powers of the thrifts. At the same time, however, net worth standards were lowered and accounting rules were changed to allow thrifts to report higher net worths than standard accounting principles allowed. (This switch was from generally accepted accounting principles, commonly known as GAAP, to regulatory accounting principles or RAP.) Diminished net worth coupled with new opportunities and capabilities for expansion set the stage for rapid growth in the S&L industry. In the case of Germania Bank, we find that the bank experienced rapid growth in this period. Deposits doubled between 1980 and 1985 and commercial loans, previously not a part of Germania's (or any thrift's) loan portfolio, grew to approximately $150 million between 1982 and 1985.

By the end of 1985, the thrift industry had increased by over 50 per cent in a period of three years (White 1991). Much of this growth was in assets that represented loans and investments that historically S&Ls had not made and with which they were largely inexperienced. Not surprisingly, many of these assets declined in value. These and other losses imbedded in S&L balance sheets became increasingly evident after 1985. Changes in the economic environment that in particular adversely affected real estate investments forced a public recognition and reckoning with the precarious state of thrifts. One aspect was a reappraisal of the relatively unchecked growth of many S&Ls, especially those involving new and nontraditional assets. At Germania Bank, new ownership and new management that took charge in 1986 was engaged in such a reappraisal. In an effort to control the damage that had been done to Germania's net worth, primarily by low quality commercial loans, management developed a strategy that called for a halt to such lending and a push to bolster regulatory capital.

Interesting parallels to Germania's situation are found in the public policy and political arenas at this time. As White (1991) explains:

> By late 1986, with tighter safety-and-soundness regulations and an expanded (and expanding) regulatory field force, the Bank Board now had a firmer regulatory grip on the industry. Rapid growth was less common, and closer scrutiny of thrifts' investments and action was more likely ... Thrifts with low (or negative) net worths were put under much closer supervisory scrutiny and control (pp. 131–132).

In September 1986, the Federal Home Loan Bank Board (FHLBB) established a higher net worth target of 6 per cent of liabilities. Although the 6 per cent was a target that would be gradually implemented, it was double the 3 per cent standard established in 1982. It was at this time also that the Bank Board began phasing out RAP standards in favour of a return to GAAP. For its part, the thrift industry during this period lobbied vigorously for leniency and forbearance as it sought to repair the accumulated damage to its balance sheets.

In its efforts to remain solvent, Germania had benefited from the previous climate of lenient regulation and RAP standards. As of March 31, 1987, the FHLBB found Germania's net worth to be 3.8 per cent as compared to the regulatory requirement of 3.4 per cent. But like much of the thrift industry, Germania's accumulated losses had taken it below the 5 per cent pre-1980 standard and well short of the 6 per cent FHLBB target.

The need to improve its net worth was clear to Germania management. One avenue pursued by Germania to bolster its regulatory capital was to acquire an ailing local thrift institution in 1986. Regulators at this time were anxious to place insolvent thrifts with acquirers. Such transactions allowed the hard-pressed Federal Savings and Loan Insurance Corporation (FSLIC) to avoid costs typically associated with the closure of failed thrifts. An acquiring thrift would find such a transaction desirable because it would then allow the creation of a goodwill asset referred to as 'supervisory goodwill'. This asset, which reflected the difference between the value of the insolvent thrift's assets and its liabilities, could then be counted as part of its regulatory capital. Germania availed itself of this accounting device and used the asset to help it meet its regulatory capital requirements.

Another stratagem that Germania employed to improve its net worth was the use of subordinated debt, which under regulatory accounting principles, contributed to its net worth. In December 1987, Laclede Gas Company, headquartered in St. Louis, agreed to invest $5.8 million in the form of convertible debentures. Also in late 1987, Germania undertook the sale of $10 million in subordinated debt, which it commonly referred to as 'subordinated capital notes' or 'Schnotes' in its marketing literature, primarily to its existing depositors. After approximately $9 million of the $10 million Schnote issues had been sold, the bank announced that it would increase its loan loss reserves an additional $8.8 million over its earlier proposed levels. This resulted in Germania reporting a loss of $5.9 million for 1987. Sales of the Schnotes were temporarily suspended, but then resumed after the bank's announcement of its 1987 results. The final $1 million of the initial $10 million target was then raised.

The Laclede investment and the Schnote purchases allowed Germania Bank to meet its regulatory capital requirements. However, the passage of the Financial Institutions Reform, Recovery, and Enforcement Act (FIRREA) of 1989, which effectively accelerated the trend toward tighter regulation and higher net worth standards, disallowed both subordinated debt and supervisory goodwill to count toward an S&Ls net worth position. As a result, the Resolution Trust Corporation (RTC) seized Germania in 1990 for being undercapitalized.

Legal Perspective

In November 1993, Germania Bank's former chairman, Edward Morris, and former president Steven Gardner, were convicted and sentenced to prison on federal charges arising from the sale of subordinated capital notes (Schnotes) to their depositors and new customers. The Schnotes became worthless after the bank failed in 1990.

Although numerous charges were originally made, the defendants went on trial only for the very specific federal violations of mail and wire fraud (18 U.S.C., Sec. 1341 and U.S.C., Sec. 1343) in connection with the sale of the Schnotes. The federal statutes under which Morris and Gardner were convicted address 'any scheme or artifice to defraud' executed by mail or wire.

At trial, the jury heard testimony that within weeks before launching a very vigorous sales campaign to sell the Schnotes, the bank's Executive Committee rejected a proposal prepared by the bank's financial managers to increase its loan loss reserves by about $9 million. The proposal was rejected, prosecutors argued, because such action would have caused the bank to show a loss and, consequently, hurt its ability to raise much-needed capital. Prosecutors also maintained that the decision and subsequent concealment of the management analysis and recommendations from auditors as well as potential investors constituted the 'scheme to defraud'.

Further testimony revealed a very aggressive plan for marketing the Schnotes. The plan involved sales incentives such as cash awards and prizes for bank personnel as well as promotional materials and advertising. Specific investors were identified and targeted. Internal communications referred to these customers as 'woopies' (well-off older people). This potential customer was profiled as a rather unsophisticated, risk-averse investor who traditionally purchased certificates of deposit or other savings instruments (Indictment p. 20, *United States of America* v. *Edward L. Morris and Steven M.*

Gardner, 1996 WL 146703 (7th Cir. (Ill.))). The sales materials included scripted responses for use by bank sales personnel in case a customer asked about the safety of the notes (which were, in fact, uninsured) or about the financial stability of Germania Bank. Neither the printed materials distributed to promote purchase of the Schnotes nor the sales scripts initially gave any indication that loan loss reserves would have any effect on these investments. Later, when additional reserves were taken in the quarter following the beginning of the Schnote campaign, one response developed for the sales staff was: 'The loss [of profits for that quarter] resulted from a special loan reserve. This was a prudent move that *protects* Germania and your Schnote rather than harms it' (Indictment p. 19).

Investors who appeared at the trial testified that they relied on assurances that their money was secure. A single 73–year old woman who had retired from a retail job and who had worked as a baby-sitter for several years at $1 per hour had this to say about her $15,000 investment:

> I told her that this was my life savings, that I didn't want to invest in something that wasn't fool proof [sic] ... and I asked her three or four times are you sure, Sharon ... I can't lose it, it's all I have ... (Brief for Appellee fn. 20, *United States of America* v. *Edward L. Morris and Steven M. Gardner*, 7th Cir., 1996).

Another retiree gave a similar account:

> Well, I had a CD[2] come due, and I went down there, and well I trusted the bank, I had done business there for over 50 years and this girl told me ... this is your lucky day. I asked her, I said is this safe and she said yes, ma'am ... (Brief for Appellee fn. 20, *United States of America* v. *Edward L. Morris and Steven M. Gardner*, 7th Cir., 1996).

The jury concluded that the Executive Committee's decision to conceal the information about the inadequacy of its loan loss reserves and, at the same time, to proceed with the sale of the Schnotes constituted a 'scheme to defraud'. Since the mails and telephone were used in the sales campaign, the scheme came within the parameters of the mail and wire fraud statutes. Morris and Gardner argued that regulatory changes in 1989, which redefined the net worth of the bank, such that the net worth then fell below standards acceptable for continued operation, actually caused the bank to fail and the investors, therefore, to lose their money. The court did not agree and attributed the cause of the losses to management's decision to ignore the need to increase loan loss reserves and, further, to conceal that decision from investors.

---

[2] Certificate of Deposit, a federally insured (to $100,000) instrument.

Personal Account

In January 1986, Morris joined Germania Bank as president and chief executive officer and became chairman in May 1986. Prior to this appointment, he was an investment banker, a principal in two respected and major regional securities firms operating in the midwest United States. His activities at both of those firms dealt with the origination and trading of registered and unregistered securities. With the exception of charges associated with Germania Bank, Morris was never the subject of a complaint or action by any individual, regulatory body, or any other entity.

In defending his actions and decisions, Morris laid the blame for the bank's collapse squarely in the lap of the US Congress. In a commentary, entitled 'RTC, Don't Blame Me; Blame Congress', published in the *Wall Street Journal* (1993), Morris turned the tables on his accusers by charging them with the same five counts of which he was accused: negligence, gross negligence, breach of contract, breach of fiduciary duty, and undue enrichment. In that article, he suggested that these same charges could be levelled at the Congress. His account reads as follows:

- *Negligence*. The thrift crisis began in 1980, when Congress ... voted to lift the ceiling on federally insured deposits from $40,000 to $100,000 and permitted the thrift industry to grow unchecked. Germania, once a sleepy home mortgage lender, doubled its deposits between 1980 and 1985 to 'grow its way out of its problems'. Other S&Ls grew even faster.
- *Gross Negligence*. The 1982 Garn-St. Germain Act, passed when the thrift industry looked insolvent, gave S&Ls wide-ranging powers to complement their rapid deposit growth. Though its officers then had little commercial banking experience, Germania booked about $150 million of commercial loans between 1982 and 1985, a large number of which eventually soured. It had taken Germania 92 years to develop the same level of home mortgages.
- *Breach of Contract*. In 1985 Germania changed hands. Joe Mason, then St. Louis's largest homebuilder, acquired controlling interest in the bank and quickly revamped the board with prominent St. Louis business people. I was recruited to be the new chief executive.

    Our first job was to raise capital and return the bank to stability after its foray into commercial lending. We studied all sanctioned capital-raising options, and with the regulators' approval and encouragement, sold $16 million of capital notes to our depositors and an affiliate of the local gas utility. The directors, led by Mr. Mason, bought about $5 million of Germania's stock, and the government awarded us a capital credit of $6 million for taking a busted thrift off its hands. As a result, capital grew from $19 million when we took over in 1985 to $42 million in 1989, a level about $20 million more than required.

At the beginning of 1989 we owned a 'healthy thrift'. But at that time the overall industry looked anything but healthy. So Congress did a remarkable flip-flop and passed the Financial Institution Reform Recovery and Enforcement Act in mid-1989.

FIRREA was as punitive as prior legislation had been lax, and gave regulators a new rulebook for computing bank capital. Unfortunately for Germania, not much of the capital we raised counted anymore. The act removed notes from the capital calculations and took away the capital credit for acquiring the failed S&L. Germania was redefined as a financial basket case by the end of 1989.

In 1990, the RTC seized Germania, because its capital under Congress's new rules was inadequate. Germania's depositors and the gas company lost the $16 million they invested in the bank's notes and my directors lost $5 million.

– *Breach of Fiduciary Duty.* After the RTC took over Germania, its spokesman said that it sold the bank's assets 'as fast as we could'. The RTC puts the loss from Germania's failure at $50 million. As both a former Germania shareholder and a taxpayer that is extremely disturbing, because, shortly before the RTC takeover, a major investment banking firm put the worst-case loss from liquidation at a small fraction of that amount. The bank also received a letter of intent from a larger St. Louis bank to acquire it, possibly at no cost to the taxpayer.

Who were the beneficiaries of Germania's failure? Wall Street and savvy real estate speculators. The losers? US taxpayers, as inept or indifferent RTC employees dumped assets at bargain prices into the willing hands of expert buyers.

– *Unjust Enrichment.* Under FIRREA, if the RTC alleges someone benefited unduly from an association with an S&L, his assets can be frozen. When I worked at Germania, my salary was set by my board at the midpoint received by other chief executives of public thrifts Germania's size. But the RTC now thinks it was too high and, without a nod to due process, ordered a freeze.

I had to give that agency a detailed listing of my assets – right down to the value of my watch – and a record of every dollar my wife and I made and spent since 1985. The RTC hired two private investigation firms to trail me as a part of its asset search. (A federal judge has since denied the RTC the right to continue its harassment.)

Why hasn't there been an inventory of the watches of the 'Keating Five'?[3] Why isn't there a freeze on the assets of the Congressmen who prospered through their S&L connections? And will there ever be the slightest admission from members who stocked their campaign coffers

---

[3] Five US Senators who were alleged to have unduly used their influence to assist Charles Keating, an S&L operator who was subsequently convicted of criminal activity.

with thrift industry PAC[4] money that Congress had anything to do with the S&L disaster? (p. A8).

Though the Securities and Exchange Commission investigated charges that the bank had issued inaccurate financial information with respect to its 1987 third-quarter operations, and that investors would thus have acted on inaccurate financial information, within a matter of a few months following this third-quarter report, Morris made personal investments on his own behalf and on behalf of relatives. Specifically, on January 12, 1988, Morris made his largest individual purchase of the common stock of Germania Bank. On that date, he purchased 4000 shares of Germania's stock for his own account. In addition, on February 4, 1988, $2500 of the bank's subordinated capital notes were purchased on behalf of his son by a family member. During that period neither Morris nor any member of his family sold any Germania securities that they themselves owned.

ANALYSIS OF THE ACCOUNTS

The Problem Stream

One of the key insights provided by Kingdon's model regarding policy problems is that such problems are neither obvious nor discrete. Where one wades into the stream and what one surfaces are all rather arbitrary actions that affect how problems are constructed. The history of the savings and loan scandal illustrates the point.

   The beginning of the problem can be traced mainly to financial legislation enacted during the great depression of the 1930s. Amid the collapse of a financial system that placed relatively few restrictions on the operations of financial institutions, legislation enacted in the 1930s sought to solve the problem of financial market chaos by eliminating price competition and by imposing a number of constraints on financial institutions.[5] Savings and loan associations, established in 1932, could not accept demand (checking) deposits but could accept federally insured savings deposits. They could not make commercial or most other types of loans and were restricted almost totally to the making of home mortgage loans in their local market. Subsequent regulation imposed in later years set ceilings on deposit interest rates

---

[4] Political Action Committee.

[5] A fundamental result of this 1930's financial legislation was the division of permissible activities among the various categories of financial institutions. Neither commercial banks nor their affiliates could engage in brokerage and other security market activities. Of course, securities firms could not engage in banking. Credit Unions, established in 1934, could not accept demand deposits and were largely limited to the provision of credit to people 'of small means' (according to the 1934 Federal Credit Union Act).

paid by all depository financial institutions but gave savings and loan associations a competitive advantage over commercial banks, in that the former were authorized to pay slightly higher interest rates on savings deposits than were the latter. Since legal maximum deposit rates were frequently less than what the market rate would otherwise be, the cost of money for savings and loan associations was held down. The combination of a low funds cost together with home mortgage usury ceilings imposed by the various states thus promoted a public policy goal of home ownership by the American public.

Continuing with the Kingdon framework, the legislative response imposed in the 1930s to cure financial chaos that then existed was not, for many years, recognized as potentially troublesome. Beginning in the late 1960s, however, and extending through the 1970s, inflation took hold and eventually resulted in dramatic increases in market interest rates. Savings and loan associations, relying almost entirely on deposits as a source of funds, and by law unable to raise rates above legally mandated ceilings, experienced substantial outflows of funds. Simultaneously, the market value of their assets, held mostly in fixed rate long-term mortgages, fell as market rates rose. Also, usury ceilings for residential mortgage loans were fixed at levels that made such lending unprofitable. Many savings and loans found that investment in one of the few assets that were legally permissible investments for them, such as short-term government securities yielding market interest rates, provided returns that exceeded those legally permitted on new mortgage loans. Thus the financial system was in disarray, the health of the savings and loan industry was questionable at best, and the public policy goal of a plentiful supply of low cost funds in support of home ownership had been impeded.

Kingdon's model of the problem stream focuses exclusively on how federal policy makers come to recognize and define a situation as a problem. The first element in this problem construction sequence is a change in indicators. As noted, by 1980, it was clear that the savings and loan industry was in trouble. Despite legislation designed to counter this trend, indicators assessing the financial health of these institutions continued to decline. By late 1987, the volume of S&L failures was double the previous year's pace.

An indicator of a problem is not a sufficient cause for a particular problem definition to take root. Values also play a role in shaping a particular problem definition, and in this case Congress placed a high value on the Federal Government's commitment to back with 'the full faith and credit of the United States' the insurance programme meant to protect depositors' savings up to $100,000. Thus, in 1987 Congress passed the Competitive Equality Banking Act. This act authorized the Federal Savings and Loan Insurance Corporation to borrow up to $10.8 billion to help troubled thrifts.

This legislation was also a focusing event signalling that the industry was indeed in crisis. Public faith in the savings and loan industry was declining.

And as Congress struggled to deal with what was now clearly perceived as a problem, it was still not clear as to how the problem should be categorized. It is this decision that ultimately gives the problem its shape and definition.

The three accounts above suggest the three major problem definitions floating in the problem stream. At the macro-analytic level, previous government policies combined with impersonal market forces may have signalled the fact that the continued viability of the savings and loan industry was questionable. In 1984, there were 3,418 savings institutions. By 1994, there were 2,152 such entities.

From a legal perspective, there appeared the need to fix culpability and blame. Thus historical, market, and policy forces only provided an opportunity for those so inclined to take advantage of others. In the case of Germania and many similar S&Ls, the 'others' taken advantage of were unsuspecting depositors and other investors.

From the point of view of the management, coping with the swirls and eddies of the financial market, it was the Congress, through its policies, that took advantage of the situation. By sponsoring and supporting laws that aided weak savings and loans, Congress made the situation worse while simultaneously enriching its members' campaign coffers through the largesse of lobbyists who urged such legislation. When that tack was no longer tenable, Congress reversed itself and blamed the 'victims', namely the S&L industry and its executives, for the financial debacle.

The eventual success of a particular problem definition in defining an event is in part dependent on another set of options. These consist of the available solutions to the problem. In a sense it is the feasibility and availability of particular solutions that help resolve competing problem definitions. Put another way, solutions come before problems.

The Policy Stream: The Available Solutions

A review of the above material suggests that at least six solutions floated in the policy stream. At the micro level, those who lost substantial amounts of money had available to them both the criminal and civil law. At the organizational level, savings institutions had investment strategies and the increasing ability to enter new markets. At the macro level, the Federal Government relied on both legislation and regulatory enforcement. As these strategies are measured against the benchmarks of technical feasibility, value acceptability, constraint recognition, and familiarity, decisions on those best to adopt are different at each level of concern.

Germania Bank failed in June of 1990. In November 1991, holders of Germania Bank notes filed a class action suit to recoup their investment. The suit was thrown out for technical reasons, specifically the failure on the part of the noteholders to say what each of about twenty different Germania officers, employees and directors did that was fraudulent. The suit was refiled, but in July of 1992, this second suit too was dismissed for improper drafting. As civil remedies to the problems of investors were losing steam, criminal prosecutions were proceeding.

Two years after the failure of Germania Bank, it was clear that both in St. Louis and nationally, the savings and loan crisis was going to be dealt with through a strategy that included heavy reliance on criminal law. Changes in government policies to regulate financial markets, civil law suits, and continued investment strategies to rescue troubled institutions were all gradually being obscured by the mechanisms of criminal law to both lock in a problem definition and apply a solution.

A number of factors seem to have led to this becoming a predominant means of problem amelioration. First, this solution appeared as the most technically feasible. While many of the participants in the drama faced civil proceedings, these were difficult for the public to understand and indeed, as noted, difficult for some of the plaintiffs to even get filed properly. A second important factor involved the suspicion that those who are involved in banking become wealthy at the expense of the less well off. Robert Reich (1987), in his *Tales of a New America,* captures this value dimension in his discussion of the cultural myth he terms 'Rot at the Top'. This is our fundamental cultural belief that 'power corrupts and absolute power corrupts absolutely'. Reich claims that a mirror for seeing our fundamental belief in this and other cultural myths can be found in the movie, *It's A Wonderful Life*. Recall the role of the wealthy bank investor who didn't care about the 'little' people who would lose their homes and savings as long as he was able to get as much money as he could from his investment. Unfortunately, the officers of Germania Bank were being cast in a role that fitted a cultural stereotype. Criminal proceedings against such individuals not only met the test of technical feasibility but of cultural values and familiarity as well.

Research by Christopher B. Colburn and Sylvia C. Hudgins (1993) suggests that Congressional support for under-capitalized/risk-seeking thrifts changed as the crisis became more apparent. Thus, these authors report that during most of the 1980s, Congress, through various pieces of legislation, tended to support under-capitalized thrifts by supporting policies that encouraged both forbearance and risk taking. By the end of the decade, as noted earlier, Congress began shifting to a policy of re-regulation as increasing financial constraints challenged the wisdom of these earlier policy initiatives. This move toward re-regulation further encouraged the criminalization of those activities seemingly given legislative support earlier in the decade.

At this point, it seems clear that rhetoric defining these complex matters as crimes had a number of advantages over other definitions. Both the problem definition and the strategies for dealing with such matters were familiar and easily understood by the public. Further, criminalization moved the focus from policy and politics to a relatively few individuals who could be held accountable. This was a welcome shift in emphasis for political leaders who were involved in policy issues that would eventually cost the American taxpayer billions of dollars.

The Political Stream

Kevin Phillips (1990) argues that by 1988, the political winds had shifted. Public support for the era of aggressive acquisition fostered by the Reagan years was on the wane. Concern was being expressed in opinion polls about the increasing gap between the very wealthy and those lower on the economic scale. Income for the bottom ten per cent of the population actually decreased in the period from 1977 to 1987 while it increased 24.4 per cent for the top ten per cent. For the top one per cent of the population the increase during this ten-year period was an astounding 74.2 per cent (Wills 1996). Income gaps between those running corporations and financial institutions and those who worked for them was also a concern, one highlighted by the fact that the seemingly more productive Japanese corporations did not come anywhere close to the salary differentials that separated American workers and their bosses.

As Phillips makes clear, George Bush was a different kind of Republican than Ronald Reagan. Phillips notes that the party had moved from the cloth coat Republicanism of Richard Nixon, through the aggressive, arrivalist philosophy represented by Reagan, to the Episcopalian, inherited wealth, Republicanism of George Walker Herbert Bush. This last type of Republicanism eschewed with considerable disdain the new wealth represented by those who took advantage of the economic climate fostered by deregulation, tax cuts, and negative views of government.

In 1988, at the end of Reagan's second term, the S&L crisis was beginning to occupy more and more space in the media. As might be expected, media attention focused not on the policy issues but on what seemed to be a hint of corruption in how government chose to deal with the problem. As noted, vigorous lobbying by the thrift industry resulted in policies that fostered leniency and forbearance. Such policies resulted in what have been termed 'Zombie Thrifts' (Kane 1989). Kane estimates that by 1984, one-forth of all S&Ls had been insolvent. Moreover, many of those benefiting from such leniency and forbearance seemed to be connected to powerful political interests.

The Competitive Equality Banking Act of 1987 was drafted, at least in part, to provide funds needed to close ailing thrifts. Vigorous lobbying on the part of the S&L industry slowed passage of the bill and weakened its provisions. Consequently, as the result of these lobbying efforts, the final version of this act encouraged forbearance and leniency (White 1991). Legislators who responded favourably to this lobbying activity included those who later became known as the 'Keating Five'. The Act seemed to protect those who had taken advantage of the public trust for their own self-enrichment. By 1988, the media was commonly referring to actions of the Federal Government to save ailing S&Ls as 'bailouts', a term that implied unwarranted government expenditures to benefit the industry.

This changing political climate helped accelerate and support a rhetoric that focused blame on individuals rather than on policies or institutional dynamics. As a result, criminal indictments became a more common governmental tool for addressing the crisis. After several months of heated public hearings covered extensively by the media, public officials concluded that the true culprits were the directors and officers of the troubled thrift institutions. One politician referred to the thrift officials as bank robbers participating in the grandest financial scandal of this century (*St. Louis Post Dispatch* 1990). They agreed that the situation could only be remedied if these individuals were targeted with vigorous investigation and strong sanctions where wrongdoing was discovered.

The outcome was the passage of 'get tough' legislation in October 1990. It specified severe, mandatory criminal and civil penalties for bank fraud and gave regulators and the Justice Department enhanced authority to seize assets obtained from defrauding the financial institutions. It added millions of dollars for special prosecutors and FBI and US Treasury agents to be assigned to focus exclusively on financial crime (*Congressional Quarterly Almanac* 1990). Yet the term 'crime' was the result of rhetorical skirmishes that had winners and losers.

SUMMARY AND CONCLUSIONS

This paper has explored three primary accounts of the savings and loan crisis in the United States. The three accounts share certain commonalties. First they are 'after the fact' explanations of events. Second, they attempt to simplify very complex long-term dynamics to make an apparent crisis more understandable. Third, they seek to assess culpability. But the accounts also differ among themselves in significant ways.

The macro-analytic account, in terms of time, is the most removed from the events. While it attempts to simplify by providing a conceptual framework, it is simplification at a much higher level of abstraction than are the other accounts. Thus it contains neither the timeliness nor the rhetorical appeal of the other accounts. Nevertheless, since accounts are historically anchored, and their legitimacy and strengths for explaining events are variable over time, the analytic account remains potentially valid and a viable explanation to be called upon.

As we have seen, the accounting of these events within the framework of criminal law became the definitive explanation. Its rhetorical strengths lay in its cultural appeal, its simplicity, by being able to define 'clear villains', and its ability to command a technical apparatus (e.g., investigators, courts, and juries) to bring relatively rapid closure to a series of seemingly endless events.

The rhetorical appeal of the convicted wrongdoer's account is attenuated because it blames an institution, Congress, rather than an individual. Thus, its level of simplification is at the midpoint between the conceptual arguments of the analytic account versus the very personal focus of the criminal proceedings.

Rhetorical victories diminish over time. With the advantage of historical focus and emergent new facts and understandings, other explanations of events may appear more cogent. Thus explanations are anchored in time. As accounts change and as formerly legitimated accounts are challenged, assessments of culpability also change.

We have reviewed several competing explanations for the collapse of the S&L industry generally, and for the decline and fall of Germania Bank and Edward Morris in particular. Consider, however, *United States* v. *Winstar* which decision was announced July 1, 1996. Mr. Justice Souter writing for the majority essentially adopts part of Morris' argument: the government broke its word and was '... liable in damages for breach'. (*United States* v. *Winstar Corporation, et al.* 116 S. Ct. 2432 (Slip Op. 95–865, p. 1) In *Winstar*, a number of S&Ls found themselves in a situation quite similar to that of Germania Bank in that, at the 'suggestion' of FSLIC and/or other regulators, these entities had assumed the assets of a number of failed institutions. Like Germania Bank, these institutions were stunned when the FIRREA-inspired RTC disallowed capital or reserve items. However, unlike Germania Bank, these institutions were large enough (i.e. had enough 'traditional' capital) to survive the RTC decision. Furthermore, like lovers scorned, three of these entities (of some 90–odd in number) sued and eventually, it appears, won the rhetorical day. The 'winning' account has changed yet again.

REFERENCES

Ahmed, Safir (1990). 'Fraud Case Weighed in Germania Probe.' *St. Louis Post Dispatch*, August 16: 1A.

Colburn, Christopher B. and Sylvia C. Hudgins (1993). 'The Influence of Congress by the Thrift Industry.' Paper presented at the meetings of the Financial Management Association, October 13–16, 1993, Toronto, Canada.

Congressional Quarterly Almanac Vol. XLVI (1990). Washington, D.C.: Congressional Quarterly Inc.

Danziger, Marie (1995).'Policy Analysis Postmodernized: Some Political and Pedagogical Ramifications.' *Policy Studies Journal*, Vol. 23, No. 3, 435–450.

Ermann, M. David and Richard J. Lundman (eds.) (1996). *Corporate and Governmental Deviance: Problems of Organizational Behavior in Contemporary Society*, 5th edition. New York: Oxford University Press.

Kingdon, John W. (1984). *Agendas, Alternatives, and Public Policies.* Boston: Little, Brown and Company.

Morris, Edward L. (1993). 'RTC, Don't Blame Me; Blame Congress.' *Wall Street Journal*, March 12: A8.

Philips, Kevin (1990). *The Politics of Rich and Poor: Wealth and the American Electorate in the Reagan Aftermath.* New York: Random House.

Reich, Robert B. (1987). *Tales of a New America.* New York: Random House, Inc.

White, Lawrence J. (1991). *The S&L Debacle: Public Policy Lessons for Bank and Thrift Regulation.* New York: Oxford University Press.

Wills, Gary (1996). 'It's His Party.' *The New York Times Magazine*, August 11: 30.

ROBIN MACKENZIE

10. Private Risk, Trust, Money and Handling the Proceeds of Corruption: Steps towards an Ecology of Financial Systems Design[*]

The terms handling, proceeds, corruption and risks are all essentially contestable, that is, incapable of being assigned a fixed meaning, whether this is based either on common sense or legal definitions. The study of corruption, for example, has been seen as an attempt to follow a moving target, as certain transactions move in and out of being seen as acceptable ways of behaving.[1] Similarly, the term handling raises a plethora of legal issues: must the item in question therefore be in the possession of the accused? What relationship to ownership, agency, bailment or trusteeship is involved? Which standard of knowledge is required? Are legally untried terms, such as suspicion, to be introduced? And how widely is the net to be cast: only as far as those in official or quasi-official positions or further? Proceeds is also problematic. Money as fungible gives rise to specific legal questions such as availability or tracing remedies, with the ensuing issues of how far down chains of transactions can specific sums be clawed back, whether intermingling or an overdrawn account destroys the possibility of restitution, or whether mixing legitimate and illegitimate funds taints the clean money so that it might become forfeitable. Yet much of the currency of corruption is not money but favours – a job for a nephew, a property sold under value, a contract awarded. Should these count as proceeds? Issues of proof and the consequences for innocent third parties are also seldom straightforward here. Finally, risk raises the same issues of how far and to whom or to what it should apply, together with theoretical concerns in that definitions of risk from an economist, a lawyer and a sociologist or anthropologist would differ markedly in terms of the preoccupations and assumptions upon which each discipline draws.

Any consideration of the risks involved in handling the proceeds of corruption, then, must specify its scope and theoretical provenance quite

[*] This paper forms part of *Banking and Finance Law: Cultural Dimensions of Risk Management Strategies in the World of Money* (forthcoming, 1997). It is dedicated to Dave Campbell, in gratitude for sustained intellectual comradeship.

[1] D. Nelken and M. Levi, 'The Corruption of Politics and Politics of Corruption', 23 *Journal of Law and Society* (1996), 1.

Barry A.K. Rider (ed.), Corruption: The Enemy Within, 149–165
© *Kluwer Law International. Printed in the Netherlands.*

closely. This paper aims to suggest that an approach which might help resolve some of the apparent conflicts of interest here is the project of designing financial systems which accept diversity at the same time as addressing concerns of distributive justice. It will draw upon recent social science approaches to risk theory, money, trust and corruption, using as examples some of the legal issues here which affect banks, in order to provide some modest demonstration of how this might be so.

SOME ECONOMIC APPROACHES

Economic theories have always had risk as a focus, since profit, a central concern, is commonly defined as the reward for innovation and for assuming risk.[2] Classically, risk management techniques enable those seeking profit to choose an acceptable level of risk in order to calculate risk/return trade-offs so that they might maximize returns.[3] In financial economic theory, the size of the risk matches the size of the possible reward or possible loss. *Homo economicus* will act rationally and maximize his own self-interest by choosing the course of action which matches his preferred risk profile. The various techniques which exist for measuring and dealing with risk strive for quantitative accuracy above all: much debate centres on the appropriate measures for risk assessment so that risk-specific investment strategies and new financial instruments can reliably return more or less predictable profit. Crises or collapses in the marketplace, such as the fall of Barings and the disaster at Daiwa, may then be seen as due to a failure of mechanisms to manage risk[4] or to an inability to assess it accurately as regulators lag behind financial innovations.[5] There is undoubtedly some merit to this view. Senior staff in the Bank of England, according to its Governor, had little understanding of financial conglomerates: their decision to allow Barings an unlimited informal concession to exceed their statutory 25 per cent limit on large exposure on OSE, TSE and SIMEX for two and a half years, so that the Baring Group's combined exposures to SIMEX and OSE exceeded 100 per cent of group capital by February 1995, evidences an equivalent lack of comprehension of the inherent risks here. Similarly, the management in Barings Bank itself reportedly failed to understand the risk characteristics of

---

[2] J.K. Galbraith, *A History of Economics: The Past as the Present*, London, Penguin (1987).

[3] D.G. Uyemura and D.R. van Deventer, *Financial Risk Management in Banking*, Chicago, Bankers (1993).

[4] M.J.B. Hall, 'A Review of the Singapore Inspectors' Report on Baring Futures (Singapore) Pte. Ltd.', 9 *Butterworths Journal of International Banking and Finance Law* (1995), 525.

[5] J. Jeremie, 'At the Strait Gate: Swaps, Derivatives and Regulatory Indecision in Global Capital Markets', 16 *Company Lawyer* (1995), 149.

the newer financial instruments and hence ignored or underestimated the operating risk that Nick Leeson's improbable reported profits were fictions.[6] Both Toshide Iguchi, who incurred unauthorized trading losses for Daiwa of $1.1 billion, and Nick Leeson, whose losses of £700 million caused Barings to collapse, were able to sustain their reputations as star traders as they each had dual responsibility for the trading and settling of accounts and so were able to conceal their activities, despite the obvious risk of wrong-doing such internal arrangements permitted.

Yet these bank scandals cannot be seen solely in terms of anomalous rogue traders and the need for continuing education on risk management techniques and the risk characteristics of innovative financial instruments. Corruption played a clear part in the scale of the losses, as those whose responsibility it was to ensure that unauthorized risks were not taken attempted to conceal the results of the illegal trading and thus their own shortcomings. Subsequent investigations into the Barings and Daiwa debacles have implicated Daiwa's New York management, the Japanese Ministry of Finance and senior Barings staff. They have also revealed that regulators' sophisticated supervisory mechanisms failed to detect or prevent the lax internal controls and risk management procedures which enabled the traders' transgressions.[7] Both the Bank of England and the Federal Reserve Bank had evidence of irregularities which should have prompted them to at the very least investigate further, yet no such steps were taken.

How would an economic theory of risk explain this? Giving in to a temptation to take advantage of another, whether this is seen as acting dishonestly or rationally seeking one's own best interests, is often couched in terms of moral hazard: strategic or opportunistic behaviour. When the risk of loss is not shared equally between parties to a transaction, those who bear the lower risk are tempted to engage in high risk activities, secure in the knowledge that if they succeed, they will retain the proceeds, but if they fail, the consequences of their loss will largely fall elsewhere. Strategies which aim to manage risk do take this into account. For years central banks, the Bank for International Settlements, the Basle Committee on Bank Super-vision, the G30 and the International Organization of Securities Commis-sions have all published reports which attempt to manage risks, including moral hazard, by instituting ever more stringent risk assessment techniques, closer prudential supervision of internal control procedures, fuller disclosure requirements and so forth. Yet rogue traders with secret accounts still clearly succumb to moral hazard. So do those managers whose responsibility it is to ensure that unauthorized trading does not take place, but instead turn a blind eye as long as profits, allegedly, keep rolling in. And regulators fail to enforce the letter of the law. The inherent difficulties of the accurate risk

---

[6] G. Millman, *Around the World on a Trillion Dollars a Day*, New York, Bantam (1995).

[7] R. Sarker, 'Daiwa and Barings: A Blueprint for Disaster', 17 *Company Lawyer* (1996), 86.

assessment of innovative financial instruments, the creation of appropriate internal controls and audit procedures and the maintenance of cooperative disclosures between regulatory authorities do not add up to a sufficient rationale for why this should be so.

Nonetheless, economic theory offers two ideas which are valuable for any consideration of the risks inherent in handling the proceeds of corruption. The emphasis on individuals making rational choices in order to maximize their own self-interest and the notion of moral hazard can be used to support arguments made by criminologists and others when discussing the difficulties of obtaining successful detection, prosecution and sentencing for those involved in financial wrongdoing. Classically, the likelihood of being caught, convicted and given a significant sentence has been so small that the rewards of financial corruption have far outweighed the risks. Logically, then, a solution might be to remedy the chronic underfunding of the forces which investigate financial wrongdoing, institute trials by judge rather than by jury and pass legislation to confiscate the proceeds of corruption and to impose substantial prison sentences. The risks might then match the rewards more closely.

CRIMINOLOGY, MORAL HAZARD AND CORRUPTION

Criminological research reveals that things are not quite that simple. Financial corruption tends to be discovered not via police investigation, audits or internal control systems but as a result of tip-offs, management changes or by chance, and four out of five frauds are committed by staff, often those who are trusted and long-serving.[8] Yet whistleblowers who tip off the authorities in the United Kingdom have had little incentive to do so and largely ineffective protection against victimization and job loss: how far any new measures may remedy this is a moot point since the proposed Whistleblowing Bill failed to survive its third reading.[9] Nor is it unproblematic, however, to create an incentive to blow the whistle by offering a bounty, as in the up to 30 per cent of damages received claimable under the False Claims Act 1863 for a successful civil action for defrauding the Federal Government of the United States. In the United Kingdom, the risks clearly outweigh the rewards; in the United States, the rewards may be such (in the GE case, $11.5 million was awarded to the whistleblower, despite opposition from GE and the US Justice Department) as to render considerations of moral hazard only too relevant.[10] In any case, in employment

---

[8] Ernst & Young, *International Fraud Survey*, London, Ernst & Young (1996).

[9] D. Lewis, 'Whistleblowers and Job Security', 58 *Modern Law Review* (1995), 208; and R. Sarker, 'Blowing the Whistle on Fraud', 17 *Company Lawyer* (1961), 24.

[10] L.M. Seagull, 'Whistleblowing and Corruption Control: The GE Case', 22 *Crime, Law and Social Change* (1994/5), 381.

situations where 'perks' are informally accepted as going with the job – and this includes most if not all employment situations – there may be considerable lack of agreement on what constitutes corruption and its proceeds.[11] Nor is corruption likely to be reported by an employee unless, after engaging in a personal cost/benefit analysis, that employee believes that it is safe to do so and that corrective action will be taken.[12] Certainly auditors are reluctant to see themselves as having a responsibility to blow the whistle on their clients and risk losing clients as a consequence. Similarly, in the wider business arena of internationalism and deregulation, accusations of corruption are likely to stem largely from firms who resent being excluded from the protectionism and competitive advantages offered by corrupt networks.[13]

Perceived self-interest in relation to perceived risk is also a prime factor when it comes to the prosecution of corruption. Take bank fraud and bank failures. While the market appears healthy, financial wrongdoings attract little attention. When the stability of the financial system appears to be under threat, however, resources flood into damage control efforts. Parliament found extra millions of pounds for the usually underfunded Serious Fraud Office's investigation of BCCI.[14] And, after revelations of widespread fraud in the US Savings and Loans thrift industry in 1989, the US government declared war on financial corruption and poured an unprecedented amount of resources into prosecuting it. Congress passed the Financial Institutions Reform, Recovery and Enforcement Act 1989, which authorized $75 million per year for the next three years to enable the Justice Department to track down and prosecute financial fraud. The FBI's funding here was raised from under $60 million in 1990 to over $125 million in 1991. However, these funds were applied selectively. Fraudsters in the thrift industry formed a focus and, unusually, after conviction they received significant jail sentences. Yet corporate and business crime in other sectors was virtually ignored, along with violations of other regulations such as health and safety; only the alleged fraudsters whose activities had led to thrift failure tended to be investigated. Criminologists thus explain this crackdown on financial corruption as not so much an effort to control crime

---

[11] H. Cornwall, *Data Theft: Computer Fraud, Industrial Espionage and Information Crime*, London, Heinemann, 1987; G. Mars, *Cheats at Work: An Anthropology of Workplace Crime*, Alkdershot, Dartmouth, 1994; A. Gorta and S. Forell, 'Layers of Decision: Linking Social Definitions of Corruption and Willingness to Take Action', 23 *Crime, Law and Social Change* (1995) 315.

[12] A. Gorta and S. Forell, 'Layers of Decision: Linking Social Definitions of Corruption and Willingness to Take Action', 23 *Crime, Law and Social Change* (1995) 315.

[13] V. Ruggiero, 'France: Corruption as Resentment', 23 *Journal of Law and Society* (1996) 112.

[14] D. Nelken and M. Levi, 'The Corruption of Politics and the Politics of Corruption', 23 *Journal of Law and Society* (1996) 1.

in itself as an attempt to contain damage in institutions seen as vital to the health of the United States economy.[15] They point out that fraud in the thrifts was not at all new, but was not taken seriously until the frauds resulted in losses which jeopardized the stability of the financial system, and hence compromised the positions of the political party in power and the regulatory bodies in question, both of whom are seen as responsible for ensuring a healthy economic system. Interviews with those concerned confirm this approach: regulators typically ignored 'technical breaches' as long as thrifts appeared to be flourishing financially. These 'technical breaches' in fact concealed huge costs to the United States economy. Thrift officers at insolvent or zombie thrifts typically formed mutual support networks whereby illegal transactions such as nominee loans to straw borrowers, daisy chains of reciprocal loans, trading bad assets (dead cows for dead horses) and linked financing provided the illusion of solvency, at a cost to the taxpayer of over $40 billion.[16] The thrifts have thus been described as an overwhelmingly crimogenic environment with structural incentives to commit fraud because of the deregulation which enabled a single person to control an institution, corrupt relations between thrift directors and politicians based on political campaign contributions and regulatory capture.[17]

These structural incentives can be couched in terms of moral hazard created by a failure to ensure that those who took the risks also bore the loss. In 1933, a year when 4004 banks had failed or been closed down, the United States Senate passed legislation to set up a government insurance fund to guarantee bank deposits, the Federal Deposit Insurance Corporation, in order to prevent the runs on banks which led to the bank failures.[18] A year later, in 1934, only 62 banks failed. Sixty years later, however, in 1993, the American taxpayer was faced with tax bills of untold tens of billions of dollars, since the Federal Deposit Insurance Corporation had been unable to provide the funds which would, in fact, guarantee the thrifts' lost deposits. The knowledge that the deposits were guaranteed allowed thrifts to engage in high-risk activities without fear of loss, once the safety-and-soundness regulations which protected the deposit insurance funds were relaxed in the 1980s' deregulation. The 1980s' deregulation also weakened further an

---

[15] K. Calavita and H.N. Pontell, 'The State and White Collar Crime: Saving the Savings and Loans', 28 *Law and Society Review* (1994), 297.

[16] J.G. Brenner, 'S & L Bailout: How Delays Drove up Cost', *Washington Post*, 11 March 1990, H1; K. Calavita and H.N. Pontell, 'Savings and Loan Fraud as Organized Crime: Toward a Conceptual Typology of Corporate Illegality', 31 *Criminology* (1993), 519.

[17] *See* K. Calavita and H.N. Pontell, *supra* notes 15 and 16; and K. Calavita and H.N. Pontell, 'Heads I Win, Tails You Lose: Deregulation, Crime and Crisis in the Savings and Loan Industry', 36 *Crime and Delinquency* (1990), 309.

[18] J.K. Galbraith, *Money: Whence It Came, Where It Went*, new ed., London, Penguin (1995).

accounting information system (already inadequate since it was based on past rather than market value valuations) which should have allowed the regulators to monitor the thrifts' exposure to risk but instead made it easier for thrift executives to misrepresent their assets. Regulatory controls which would have put the deposit insurance scheme on a sound commercial footing by controlling moral hazard and providing up-to-date accounting information in order to establish risk-based premiums failed to be implemented by a government where deregulation was treated as a magic wand which would automatically enhance market competition.[19]

Yet the regulatory controls based on accurate risk assessment economists would recommend here clearly failed to prevent the Barings bust or the Daiwa debacle. The problem here may be the paradigm. A simplistic version of the underlying model of the relationship between risk, regulation and corruption for significant numbers of economists and some criminologists appears to be as follows. Individuals rationally maximize their own self-interest by entering transactions in the market which create maximum gain, or profit. Markets allocate resources efficiently and profit (which is fed back in) ensures the growth of the financial system, which needs growth to stay healthy. Regulation is simply a system of rules which places boundaries about this praiseworthy enterprise in order to contain moral hazard – strategic or opportunistic behaviour which hinders the efficient functioning of the market and hence threatens the financial system. Once precise risk assessments have been carried out, the approximate mix of sanctions, guarantees, disclosure requirements and so forth crystallizes into a regulatory fence which ensures that the potential disinformation engendered by moral hazard is prevented from rendering the market inefficient. Corruption here results in disinformation as profits leave and enter the market through a tunnel under the fence, rendering risk assessment more difficult. It is simply a continuation of rational maximization of self-interest. Although rational maximization of self-interest may be expressed in strategic or opportunistic actions which result from a failure to contain moral hazard, this does not alter its nature; corruption is not qualitatively different.

WHAT IS WRONG WITH THIS PICTURE? TRUST, MONEY AND CORRUPTION

Critics point out that the market cannot exist without rules; it is, in fact, constituted by them. The market's efficiency results from the savings on transaction costs made when regulations ensure that there is no need to check on the credentials of each transactor, the stability of their currency

---

[19] L.J. White, *The S & L Debacle: Public Policy Lessons for Bank and Thrift Regulation*, Oxford, Oxford University Press (1991).

and the enforceability of agreements.[20] Markets and other monetary networks, then, are inherently fiduciary in very important ways. There must be a level of trust in the other transactors as well as trust in the stability of the network which ensures the validity of money over time and place. At the same time, money is inherently profoundly ambivalent in that it depends on a generalized level of trust in its properties for its existence and circulation in society, yet nevertheless inevitably embodies a site for conflicts of interest over the unequal distribution of power and resources in societies. The institutional practices and principles which enable monetary networks to survive over time, and hence to continue to be seen as trustworthy, also structure the reproduction and at times the exacerbation of these asymmetries.[21]

What can this analysis tell us about corruption? If we define trust as having the correct expectations about the actions of other people when these actions affect one's own actions, and when we must choose how to act without being able to check how they are acting first, then we see that trust must always involve a risk of loss.[22] What the preceding analysis tells us is that distrust, equally, involves risk of loss, and that loss here is more likely. Research into societies characterized by distrust confirm that these are usually characterized by widespread corruption and economic futility.[23] Studies of the lasting results of Spain's domination of Southern Italy in particular reveal how trust along with economic health can be deliberately destroyed by those who wish to exploit a society, as well as how distrust can be manipulated to increase demand for protection rackets and to maintain monopolies which ensure economic stagnation.[24] Conversely, institutions which promote trust can be set in place or may evolve via cooperation,[25] with the additional benefit that trust as a resource is increased rather than depleted by use.

---

[20] D. Campbell, 'Note: What is Wrong with Insider Dealing?', 16 *Legal Studies* (1996), 185.

[21] N. Dodd, *The Sociology of Money: Economics, Reason and Contemporary Society*, New York, Continuum (1994).

[22] P. Dasgupta, 'Trust as a Commodity' in D. Gambetta (ed.), *Trust: Making and Breaking Cooperative Relations*, Oxford, Blackwells (1988).

[23] D. Gambetta, 'Mafia: The Price of Distrust', in D. Gambetta (ed.), *Trust: Making and Breaking Cooperative Relations*, Oxford, Blackwells (1988); G. Hawthorn, 'Three Ironies in Trust' in D. Gambetta (ed.); and A. Pagden, 'The Destruction of Trust and its Economic Consequences in the Case of Eighteenth Century Naples' in D. Gambetta, (ed.).

[24] See *supra*, note 23.

[25] K. Hart, 'Kinship, Contract and Trust: The Economic Organization of Migrants in an African City Slum' in D. Gambetta (ed.), *Trust: Making and Breaking Cooperative Relations*, Oxford, Blackwells (1988); D. Good, 'Individuals, Interpersonal Relations and Trust' in D. Gambetta (ed.); and E.H. Lorenz, 'Neither Friends Nor Strangers: Informal Networks of Subcontracting in French Industry' in D. Gambetta, (ed.).

Is the solution to the problem of the risks of handling the proceeds of corruption, then, simply to set up institutions which promote cooperation? Would corruption then simply disappear? Sadly, this seems hardly likely because of the ambivalence inherent in money. Although we want to trust that it will retain its value and believe that we can also trust the people we deal with, at the same time we resent the rules that make this possible, as we want a bigger slice of the monetary cake than these rules allocate us. As a consequence, we are likely to cooperate with others of similar outlook to make sure that we do get a bigger slice of the cake. Corruption may then result from cooperation and trust. Take the workplace. Studies of cheats at work reveal that fiddling is endemic to almost all occupations; job situations create covert reward systems whereby employers and employees collude in an agreement that although certain activities are illegal, they will be tolerated within the framework of extra-legal rules.[26] Studies in the tradition of cultural theory have succeeded in evidencing a connection between the structural characteristics of occupations and their typical modes of corruption. Occupations can be placed within a fourfold classification based on the two dimensions grid/group according to how tightly peoples' behaviour is constrained by social roles (grid) and how collectively a culture operates (group).

The four quadrants and their typical crimes are as follows. Where a job promotes individualism and personal freedom (low group, low grid), as with journalists, dealers or entrepreneurs, rewards such as bonuses or commissions go to those who deliver the goods fast, and getting things done fast often involves bending the rules. Blind eyes will be turned to this as long as results are delivered. The selective inattention of supervisors and regulators to Nick Leeson and to risk-prone S & Ls as long as profits were reported exemplifies this. Where work groups are tight because of cultural values of strong collective feeling and little personal autonomy (strong grid/strong group), as with garbage collectors, prison workers and longshoremen on the docks, hierarchy, order and internal controls lead to highly organized pilferage. Where employees are isolated and highly constrained by rules (strong grid, weak group) as with supermarket cashiers or bus drivers, petty theft and sabotage often take place. Finally, those with high personal autonomy along with group support (low grid/high group) such as sales representatives and delivery drivers, embark upon individual fiddles such as delivering less and selling the surplus privately. Although the jobs mentioned here are contemporary and Western, this typology has explanatory force over many cultures and times.

If 72–95 per cent of employees engage in the extra-legal activities, and if current estimates of the size of the underground economy in Western nations can run as high as 20 per cent of GNP, how much sense does it

---

[26] *See supra*, note 11.

make to label these activities as criminal or corrupt? How many of us can say that we have never paid or accepted cash 'under the counter' simply because it saved us money? If this cash passes to someone else, may they then be handling the proceeds of corruption?

The point being made here is that if most of us do these things, moral panic about corruption is an inappropriate, or at least insufficient, response. As globalization and national deregulation proceed, more of this 'informal-ization' is likely: income-generating activities which bypass legal regulation through various types of political, personal or familial entrepreneurial cooperation proliferate.[27] Scholars agree that globalization is most advanced in the financial markets, as the exchanges between them become 'tokenized' (that is, symbolically mediated), de-centred and are increasingly carried out unconstrained by time and space via twenty-four-hour trading and instanta-neous telecommunication of transactions.[28] Yet to see this as the inexorable evolution of a perfect market unfettered by national regulations is to oversimplify, since markets can be conceptualized accurately only as an ongoing series of relationships in specific historic contexts. These ongoing relationships typically reveal at least some degree of continuing symbiosis or informal cooperation between official and alternative monetary networks. Indeed, regulatory extension is likely to provoke either regulatory arbitrage, as those who wish to escape it take their capital to less regulated jurisdic-tions, or to non-banking institutions such as bureaux de change; or to stimulate technological innovation, as in the new smart cards, which can now conduct significant transactions anonymously in different currencies around the world, bypassing the banking system altogether.[29] The offshore capital markets without regulatory frameworks, which have developed partly as a result of states' regulatory policies, depend on national monetary authorities to maintain fiscal sovereignty in order that offshore transactions remain competitive. National fiscal strategies, in turn, are able to rely on the capacity of offshore markets to soak up or supply funds at times of unwanted current account surpluses or deficits. Similarly, strong arguments can be made to suggest that BCCI was able to offer its illegal goods and services as long as it did, simply because these were provided to powerful world politicians, intelligence agencies and government officials, and that it was exposed as corrupt only through geopolitical changes which reduced its

---

[27] E. Fiege, 'Defining and Estimating Underground and Informal Economies', 18 *World Development* (1990); V. Ruggiero, 'France: Corruption as Resentment', 23 *Journal of Law and Society* (1996), 112; and M. Waters, *Globalization*, London, Routledge (1995).

[28] D. Harvey, *The Condition of Postmodernity: An Enquiry into the Origins of Cultural Change*, Oxford, Blackwells (1990); and A. Giddens, *The Consequences of Modernity*, London, Macmillan (1990).

[29] G. McCormack, 'Money Laundering and Bank Secrecy', 16 *Company Lawyer* (1995), 6.

usefulness and so lost its protection.[30] Hence the BCCI case has been seen as evidencing that such misconduct is common, and takes place in an environment of pervasive corruption.[31]

How realistic or even accurate is it, then, to see these alterative monetary networks solely in terms of corruption? And is some sort of partnership, then, acknowledged or unacknowledged, between officially acceptable and corrupt alternative monetary networks, a serial monogamy interrupted by the occasional scandalous divorce, inevitable?

RISK, TRUST AND THE ECOLOGY OF FINANCIAL SYSTEMS DESIGN

In order to argue that this may not be the most helpful perspective here, theories of risk must be put together with the promise offered by globalization in order to sketch out the beginnings of a different paradigm. Popular among sociologists at the moment is Ulrich Beck's claim (simplistically represented here) that we now inhabit a 'risk society'; that today's legal and political institutions are based inappropriately upon 19th century premises of a provident state where rational control allows hazards to be calculated and insured against.[32] As a consequence, these institutions are unable to restrain the risks which characterize the late 20th century, since these ignore national borders, frequently evade perception and are subject to alarming uncertainties over incidence, potential harm and susceptibility to control. Risks therefore force people to think globally, and can no longer be insured against. Beck suggests that as the environmental crisis is actually thus a social crisis, now that particular groups of experts can no longer be accepted as able to make decisions based on the prediction and control of risks, groups of citizens will be inspired to participate in an ecological democracy enabling a self-critical throttling-back of the self-endangering momentum of the global risk society.[33]

Beck's analysis has been criticized for largely ignoring the unchallenged identification of the power of capital with the good of mankind. In the context of this paper, however, his ideas seem to raise two interesting

---

[30] N. Passas, 'The Genesis of the BCCI Scandal', 23 *Journal of Law and Society* (1996), 57.

[31] N. Passas, 'The Mirror of Global Evils: A Review Essay on the BCCI Affair', 12 *Justice Quarterly* (1995), 801.

[32] U. Beck, *Risk Society: Towards a New Modernity*, London, Sage (1992); U. Beck, 'Risk Society and the Provident State' in S. Lash *et al.* (eds.), Risk, *Environment and Modernity: Towards a New Ecology*, London, Sage (1996), 27; and F. Ewald, *L'Etat Providence*, Paris, Editions Grasset (1968).

[33] *See* U. Beck, *supra*, note 32; U. Beck, *Ecological Enlightenment: Essays on the Politics of the Risk Society*, New Jersey, Humanities Press (1995); U. Beck, *Ecological Politics in an Age of Risk*, Cambridge, Polity (1995).

possibilities.[34] One is the scenario whereby a global crisis stimulates groups of citizens to reflect on the social institutions which relate to the crisis and to construct alternatives which allow for more people to participate in deciding upon the best means to deal with the relevant risks. How far might an endangered global financial system stimulate this sort of activity? Certainly, the consequences for the world at large, if systemic risk led to the collapse of the global financial system, are such as to merit its being seen as a crisis. Systemic risk is usually seen in terms of the failure of a group of banks linked by a chain of financial transactions pulling down the rest, as in the great crash of 1929. Regulators tend to deal with this by imposing strictures which limit or spread the risks of failure. The effectiveness of the strictures depends directly on the accuracy of risk assessment. Arguably, corruption skews the assessment process so that accuracy is impossible, thereby increasing the likelihood of systemic collapse. Yet if the proceeds of corruption were not fed into the system, what effect would this have on the high level of short term profits upon which contemporary capitalism depends? The macroeconomics of corruption is imperfectly understood: possibly if all attempts to contain it succeeded overnight, the financial system would cease to function.[35]

The likelihood of groups of citizens getting together to debate the optimum means of maintaining the health of the global financial system seems regrettably small. Although luminaries as far apart as Will Hutton and Margaret Thatcher have dreamed of financially literate populations, this remains a fantasy. Most people who regard present-day capitalism as providing reliable rewards through the global financial system do not care to question too closely its promises of endless passive enrichment. The materialist explanation for this is that as societies increasingly move from industrial capitalism, where money comes from labour, to financial capitalism, where money comes from money, money becomes fetishized as a commodity, so that the social relations which generate the money somehow become invisible and hence outside debate. An additional factor would be that if regulators and supervisors are unable to understand the intricacies of the latest financial instruments and how these impact on the global financial system, the chance that the public at large will be able to do so seems remarkably slight.

Nonetheless, since research into corruption in the workplace reveals that it is present in almost all workplaces, and that certain ways of structuring employment are reliably associated with certain sorts of crime at different times in history and different places in the world, it may be assumed that there is indeed widespread local knowledge of corruption and how it affects our

---

[34] M. Rustin, 'Incomplete Modernity: Ulrich Beck's Risk Society', 67 *Radical Philosophy* (1994), 3.

[35] International Monetary Fund, *Highlighting the Link Between Bank Soundness and Macroeconomic Policy*, IMF Survey (1996), 165; and International Monetary Fund, *Tougher Measures Needed to Counter Macro Effects of Money Laundering*, IMF Survey (1996), 245.

lives. Apprehension of the global nature of the risks involved in corruption, then, could conceivably lead to the kind of democratic participation in reforming social structures, here, financial systems, envisaged by Beck. So far, however, although the media regularly makes much of how corruption endangers the financial system and hence our way of life, few such changes have resulted. Despite valiant efforts to contain it, corruption continues. Undoubtedly, many of the reasons for this are structural, as when corrupt institutions such as BCCI are able to offer services which those in power find useful.

Yet many of the reasons must also rest on the ambivalence inherent in money which promotes so many alternative monetary networks. The institutions which purport to regulate monetary matters in order to guarantee the reliability of the financial system in doing so constitute the means whereby economic resources are distributed inequitably and may exacerbate economic asymmetries. Consequently, unless attempts to elicit popular support in order to get rid of corruption address the question of how resources might be allocated in a just manner, they are unlikely to persuade anyone to abandon alternative monetary networks in order to contribute more fully to a system which is widely regarded as unjust. Similarly, while efforts to ensure that corruption does not pay by confiscating its proceeds may undoubtedly prove useful in the short term, both to create a moral panic in order to capture the law and order vote, and to contribute to the funding of policing agencies, they are likely to prove ineffective in the long term now that e-cash and cybercash may be transferred instantaneously around the world in a way which bypasses traditional banking systems.

Legal measures which seek to control corruption by instituting strict reporting and compliance procedures, or to eliminate it by identifying and punishing those who handle its proceeds, then deeming the proceeds themselves subject to forfeiture, are thus likely to fail unless the inherent conflicts of interest here are addressed. Regulatory arbitrage determines that the proceeds of corruption are most likely to be placed in jurisdictions offering fewer regulations, or regulations which are on the books but remain unenforced.[36] Failing this, the proceeds will pass to financial institutions which are more lightly regulated or to alternative monetary networks. International cooperation is thus necessary to deal with transnational manipulation of the proceeds of corruption. Conflicts of interest between richer nations urging strict regulatory regimes and poorer nations with other priorities are inevitable here, and indeed insoluble unless the ambivalence at the heart of money is addressed at the same time. Issues of distributive justice must form part of the regulatory agenda, both internationally and within nation-state boundaries.

---

[36] J. Robinson, *The Laundrymen: Inside the World's Third Largest Business*, London, Pocket (1994).

Beck's notion that ecology offers an appropriate model whereby social institutions might be constructed and evaluated offers a conceptual forum whereby this debate might be explored. What might an ecologically sound financial system look like? An ecological economic theory? How might these come about? The concept of ecology here must be distinguished from a simple environmentalist adherence to green economics which insists that small is beautiful. Ecology as the study of ecosystems reveals that within one ecosystem evolving species compete for distinct ecological niches but amongst ecosystems typically symbiosis is the rule, that is, through cooperation between diverse ecosystems borders become blurred and a more sophisticated, more geographically-extensive, integrated whole results.[37]

This seems a fair description of one of the things that appears to be taking place as monetary networks globalize[38] and 'informalization' increases.[39] This ecological favouring of diversity amongst ecosystems appears to be borne out by research into financial system design. The different relationships between commercial banks and companies in Germany, Japan, the United Kingdom and the United States all possess their own unique advantages.[40] As a consequence, blanket monocultural global financial regulation may be inappropriate. Different nations' inter-bank clearing networks experience different degrees of systemic risk. Optimum levels of regulation of S & Ls vary according to their diversification into non-traditional assets. Experts in financial system design are clear about the need to rethink the way that institutions and markets have traditionally been seen as distinct and competitive while in fact they are complementary in many ways, and indeed can create new business opportunities for one another. The present relationship between Islamic and Western banking provides an example of this. Islamic beliefs prohibit *riba*, or interest: money is intended to be put towards productive use which benefits the community.[41] The risks and rewards of financial enterprise are to be shared. Both Western and Islamic banks have expanded their ranges of financial services as a result of

---

[37] J. Cohen and I. Stewart, *The Collapse of Chaos: Discovering Simplicity in a Complex World*, London, Penguin (1995).

[38] *See* D. Harvey, *supra*, note 28; and A.J. Thakor, (1996) 'The Design of Financial Systems: An Overview', 20 *Journal of Banking and Finance* (1996), 917.

[39] *See supra*, note 27; and A. Portes, 'Paradoxes of the Informal Economy: The Social Basis of Unregulated Entrepreneurship' in N.J. Smelser and R. Swedberg (eds.), *Handbook of Economic Sociology*, New York, McGraw Hill (1994).

[40] J.R. Macey and G.P. Miller, 'Corporate Governance and Commercial Banking: A Comparative Examination of Germany, Japan and the United States', 48 *Stanford Law Review* (1995), 73; and *supra*, note 37.

[41] M. Faruqui, 'A Paradox of Our Times', *New Horizon*, 3 March 1996; N. Angell, 'Islamic and Western Banking: I: Major Features, Structural Forms, Comparison with Western Banks, *Riba*' 17 *Middle Eastern Executive Reports* (1994), 9; and N. Angell, 'Islamic and Western Banking: II: Legal Status and Appraisal of Current Islamic Banking', 18 *Middle Eastern Executive Reports* (1995), 9.

mutual competition and cooperation. Increasing numbers of Western banks have now set up independent Islamic banking sections, while Islamic banks have been stimulated to modernize their accounting procedures and to diversify their range of financial products so as to confirm with Shari'a but offer competitive advantages.[42] The emphasis within Islam upon risk-sharing and the imperative that money should benefit the community together also offer a potential to combat the fetishization of money which renders its connection with social relations invisible and so enables the sort of public debate envisaged by Beck on these matters.

But the issue here is not whether a national or global economy is indeed made up of separate financial ecosystems inhabited by eager entrepreneurs ensuring the survival of the fittest business enterprise. Instead, what should be asked is whether an image of the economy as ecosystems promotes new and useful questions. If we see corruption as analogous to pollution, does this help us to justify placing a legal duty on corporations whose activities give rise to corruption to prevent it or to pay cleanup costs? Does it help us to decide how far auditors' liability for failing to detect fraud should stretch? Should the bonuses awarded the rogue traders and their senior staff then be seen as the proceeds of corruption? Does accepting such a bonus therefore count as handling the proceeds of corruption? If so, should it therefore be able to be clawed back in legal proceedings? And does this view of corruption change how we see the conflict between bank secrecy and anti-money laundering regulations? Does it in fact allow us to address the central ambivalence inherent in money as a site of trust but also a means of maintaining fundamental economic, political and social inequalities? Where what have been called 'alternative' monetary networks are concerned, how might a border between corrupt and acceptable diversity be put in place? How far might this border be subject to diversity or fuzzy as well? Could the global financial system be seen as a 'global commons' like Antarctica? What differences would this make?

What might constitute an ecologically sound financial system or trans-national market economy is a sensible question today, when threats of systemic risk and corrupt or muddled ideas are married to socially costly legal measures which promise, but do not necessarily deliver, justice and efficiency in the economic sphere. Or, in other words, shotgun weddings performed in haste in an atmosphere of moral panic to preserve virtues (of economies) and purity (of economic theories) are unlikely to result in the delivery of legitimate newborn transnational economies where appropriate legal regulation sustains the economy and promotes human flourishing. The economic inefficiencies of the community reinvestment banking legislation

---

[42] W.D. Knight, 'Islamic Investments in the U.S.', *New Horizon* 10 July 1996; M.A. Elgari, 'Islamic Banking Brought to You by Non-Islamic Banks', *New Horizon* 3 February 1996; and M.T. Usmani, 'Futures, Options, Swaps and Equity Investments', *New Horizon* 10 June 1996.

in the United States and the uncertainties of EC and national anti-money laundering regulations demonstrate these shortcomings only too clearly.[43]

How, then, might an ecological financial system deal with the risks of handling the proceeds of corruption? Legal rules here might be expected to express diversity of manifestation over underlying agreement on fundamental principles. One such principle here might be expected to be a consensus on the prohibition of unjust enrichment. This would be consonant with restitution under civil law, the emphasis on risk-sharing under Shari'a in Islamic law and the increasing acceptance of the principle in common law jurisdictions. It would translate in ecological terms as there being no such thing as a free lunch, or indeed as many equitable maxims. The central legal issue then, once a definition of corruption had been settled upon as being in some sense wrongly acquired, would be to whom should the risk pass and who should bear any loss. Grid/group analysis, which was used to classify structural inducements to crime for various types of jobs, may provide some initial suggestions on how diversity in the legal regulation of financial systems might express itself here. Cultural theory suggests that all societies can be seen as being made up of people from each of the four quadrants: individualists (weak grid/weak group), hierarchists (strong grid/strong group), communitarians (weak grid/strong group) and fatalists (strong grid/weak group). The sectors complement one another: the degree of social power each sector has fluctuates over time.[44]

Each sector has a characteristic perspective on risk and on nature – here, the financial system. For individualists, risk is opportunity and the financial system a cornucopia of excess. If individualists saw a possible profit in handling the risks of corruption, preferred legal regulations would set high thresholds of culpability necessitating disgorging the proceeds – actual knowledge in all likelihood – and recourse to alternative monetary networks would be a strong possibility. Those who were unable to bend the rules or to evade them would deserve loss. Hierarchists are concerned to contain risks: the financial system is seen as bountiful within strict limits. Handling the proceeds of corruption would be seen as endangering the whole financial system. Alternative and official monetary networks would be tightly regulated. Thresholds for disgorgement would be relatively high as important institutions and people would be assisted in maintaining their positions.

---

[43] S.A. Johnson and S.K. Sarkar, 'The Valuation Effects of the 1977 Community Reinvestment Act and its Enforcement', 20 *Journal of Banking and Finance* (1996), 783; M. Klausner, 'Market Failure and Community Investment: A Market Oriented Alternative to the Community Reinvestment Act', 143 *University of Pennsylvania Law Review* (1995), 1561; S. Whitehead, 'Disclosure Dilemma', *Law Society Gazette* (1995), 20; E. Radmore, 'Money Laundering Prevention – Effect of the New Law on Solicitors', 16 *Company Lawyer* (1995), 155; and R.D. Marisco, 'The New Community Reinvestment Act Regulations: An Attempt to Implement Performance-Based Standards', 29 *Clearing House Review* (1996), 1021.

[44] M. Thompson *et al.*, *Cultural Theory*, Boulder, Westview (1990).

Hence the rights of creditors would be protected by limitations on the scope of the doctrine of unjust enrichment. Those lower in the hierarchy would obtain some protection, but would not expect the legal privileges accorded their betters. Egalitarians would be concerned with community wellbeing and purity. The financial system would be seen as in need of protection from corruption. Thresholds for the disgorgement of proceeds would be low, as in suspicion or constructive notice: institutions would be expected to know their customers and follow detailed reporting procedures. Those who were seen as possessing more resources would be allocated more of the risks. Alternative monetary networks would be viewed with suspicion as potentially corrupt unless they manifested equivalent practices. Fatalists would be unable to cohere to organize a legal or financial system. They would be unsurprised if the risks fell upon them. Penalties for handling the proceeds of corruption or legal requirements, that they be disgorged, would be nonexistent or ignored.

Since every society is made up of a combination of all four types in varying proportions, finding societies which conform in all respects to any of the four possibilities traversed above is not to be expected. Nonetheless, some similarities with the real world stand out. English legal structures today reflect a transition between hierarchical order and Margaret Thatcher's individualist enterprise culture.[45] Islamic financial institutions' reliance upon panels of Shari'a scholars to pronounce upon the purity of proposed transactions and the concern to avoid the corruption of *riba*, along with their risk-sharing practices, are typical of a communitarian stance towards corruption and risk. Finally, the passive noninvolvement of the fatalists corresponds fairly closely to descriptions of the social relations in Southern Italy when distrust and corruption prevailed.

CONCLUSION

This paper has attempted to traverse some issues concerning the risks involved in handling the proceeds of corruption using sociological, criminological and anthropological approaches to risk, trust, corruption and economics. It has argued that the ambivalence inherent in money renders any attempt to combat corruption which does not address distributive justice issues ineffectual. Hence an ecological approach to financial systems design which investigates and promotes diversity is seen as potentially helpful. Cultural theory has been put forward as a promising analytic tool. It is hoped that these suggestions might provide a helpful framework from which legal systems might disempower corruption, manage risk and enhance trust.

---

[45] S.H. Heap and A. Ross (eds.), *Understanding the Enterprise Culture: Themes in the Work of Mary Douglas*, Edinburgh, Edinburgh University Press (1992).

IV. Controlling Corruption

SUSAN TAYLOR

11. Taking the Profit out of Corruption:
A UK Perspective

INTRODUCTION

Corruption is about obtaining a benefit; the corrupted obtains the benefit of the bribe, the corruptor obtains a preference or advantage over others. This advantage often leads to significant profit being made by the corruptor. Significant profits are in turn made by the corrupted; as the stakes become higher, the bribes become larger. Those who engage in corruption should not profit. The criminal courts have recently been given significant powers to ensure that this is more than mere words; they now have the means to make orders to ensure that the profit is taken out of corruption through using the confiscation powers given in the Criminal Justice Act 1989, as amended by the Criminal Justice Act 1993 and the Proceeds of Crime Act 1995.

The criminal courts may make orders of forfeiture and confiscation to ensure that benefit from crime is not retained. The courts also have power to compensate the victim through making a compensation order in his favour under Section 35, Powers of Criminal Courts Act 1973. In common English usage, the words forfeit and confiscate are often used interchangeably. In law, however, there is a substantial difference between a forfeiture order and a confiscation order. In the law of England and Wales, forfeiture orders are made against specific tainted property, such as the instrumentalities used in the offence. As a result of the forfeiture order, the rights in the property are transferred to the Crown.

A confiscation order, however, is a requirement to pay a sum of money based on an assessment of the value of the proceeds derived from drug trafficking or the criminal conduct to the Crown. It is an order directed against the defendant rather than, as with forfeiture, the property. As a result of a confiscation order, rights in the property are not immediately transferred to the Crown. However, the Crown has a financial claim against the defendant; if the order is not paid, action may be taken to compel payment by the enforced sale of any property (whether tainted by the offence or not)

Barry A.K. Rider (ed.), Corruption: The Enemy Within, 169–180
© *Kluwer Law International. Printed in the Netherlands.*

deemed to belong to the defendant. The order is enforced as though it were a fine or using civil court orders.[1]

As well as the civil remedies, victims may seek redress in the criminal courts. Compensation orders are made by either the Crown Court or the Magistrates' Court under Section 43 of the Powers of the Criminal Court Act 1973 to reimburse the victim for the loss that he has sustained as a result of the defendant's actions. A compensation order is applied for by a prosecutor after conviction and is part of the sentence of the court. The machinery of a compensation order made in the criminal courts is, however, intended for clear and simple cases.[2] Whilst corruption is not a victimless crime, it is often difficult to quantify the loss to the victim with ease and this may mean that the victim's primary recourse lies in the civil courts.

When making a compensation order, the court must have regard to the defendant's means. The defendant must provide the court with the information about his means, rather than the prosecution or the court making inquiries. A compensation order should not affect the penalty[3] imposed for the offence, although a compensation order has priority over a fine. The court may allow time to pay or direct payment by instalments.

THE CONFISCATION SCHEME

The powers of the courts to order forfeiture of assets arise in limited circumstances and there is little or no provision for the reservation of assets pending the making of the forfeiture order. Indeed, it was the very limitations of the forfeiture provisions that led to the enactment of the confiscation legislation in the late 1980s. Through the implementation of the Proceeds of Crime Act 1995, further significant steps have been taken against lifestyle white-collar criminals; those convicted of corruption fall squarely into this category.

Investigation

The Proceeds of Crime Act 1995 gave police officers power in domestic cases and, in order to obtain material for a foreign investigation, to make an application to a Circuit Judge to obtain material likely to be of substantial value in an investigation into whether a person has benefitted from the crime or the location of the proceeds of criminal conduct. This is of considerable

---

[1] In England and Wales, Receivership Orders in the High Court or Garnishee Orders in the County Courts.

[2] *See Kneeshaw* 1982 98 CR.App.R. 439.

[3] It is seen as inappropriate to impose a compensation order as well as a custodial sentence.

assistance both in the investigation of the offence and in the removal of the profit from the offence. If a production order has not been complied with, or there are grounds for thinking that similar circumstances exist as are required for a production order but immediate access is required, or it is not practicable to communicate with the holder of the material, the Circuit Judge may, upon application by a police officer, grant a search warrant.[4]

Preservation of Assets

Within the confiscation scheme there are extensive powers given to the prosecutor to obtain orders to preserve property. Under Section 76 of the Criminal Justice Act, Part VI, as amended by the Criminal Justice Act 1993 and the Proceeds of Crime Act 1995, the prosecutor may apply to the High Court for a restraint order to prevent dealings with sufficient property to enable payment of any confiscation order which may be made by the trial court. An application for a restraint order can be made before a person is charged with a criminal offence or before an application is to be made, so long as a decision to charge or to apply has been made.

The application for a restraint order is made in the High Court Queen's Bench Division *ex parte* in chambers by the prosecutor. The court has a discretion whether or not to grant a restraint order. It should only be granted if there is a reasonable apprehension that without it, assets may be dissipated. If the risk is just fanciful, the restraint order ought not to be made.[5] The application of a restraint must be supported by an affidavit containing the information detailed in the Rules of the Supreme Court, Order 115. This includes details of the realizable property and the grounds for believing that the defendant has benefitted from the proceeds of criminal conduct or from drug trafficking. The affidavit may contain hearsay.

As the application is made *ex parte*, the prosecutor is under a duty to make full and frank disclosure to the court of all facts which are material to the application.[6] This duty of full and frank disclosure is a continuing duty. If the prosecutor does not make full and frank disclosure, the court has a discretion to set aside the restraint order. Even if there is material non-disclosure in applying for the restraint order, the court will be reluctant to discharge the order.

---

[4] CJA Section 93.
[5] *Johnson & Johnson*, 9 December 1992, unreported.
[6] In *Re A Defendant*, *The Times*, 7 July 1987.

Realizable Property

The concept of realizable property is central to the confiscation scheme. It is defined as any property held by the defendant or in which he has an interest, together with any property held by a third party to whom the defendant has directly or indirectly made a gift caught by the acts. It follows, therefore, that even if the defendant has laundered his assets through third parties, these can still be traced and taken under the confiscation regime. In proceeds of criminal conduct cases, a gift is a transfer at a significant undervalue made by the defendant at any time after the commission of the earliest offence with which he is charged.[7]

Although a limited company is a separate legal entity, the court may be willing to lift the corporate veil and regard the assets held by the company as the realizable property of the defendant, if the prosecution can successfully argue that the company is a mere vehicle to conceal the true ownership of the property.[8]

The Effect of a Restraint Order

A restraint order prohibits any person from dealing with any realizable property subject to such conditions or exceptions as may be specified in the order. The restraint order is made to ensure that a defendant is able to pay any confiscation order that may be made against him. Property that may be affected by the restraint order may be clean property and not in any way tainted by the criminal offence. The restraint order may prohibit the defendant from dealing with specified property to a certain value or prohibit him from dealing generally with his property. The latter is most likely in cases where the prosecutor will trigger the assumptions, as in these cases the prosector is alleging that the whole of the defendant's assets are derived from crime.

Repatriation

Although restraint orders operate worldwide, there is a greater risk that assets may be dissipated if they are held outside the jurisdiction of the High Court. If assets are held overseas, to ensure that dissipation does not occur, the restraint order may contain an order for the transfer of all moveable property into the jurisdiction of the court.[9]

---

[7] CJA Section 74(1).

[8] *Hare & Others* v. *Commissioners of Customs & Excise and Another*, *The Times*, 29 February 1996.

[9] *See Re WJT* 1990 3 All ER 263.

Living and Legal Expenses

The defendant is entitled to living and legal expenses. In *Re Peters*,[10] the Court of Appeal held that the court had to strike a balance between preserving the assets to satisfy a confiscation order if one was made and meeting the reasonable requirements of the defendant. Reasonable legal costs are permitted; this will be subject to taxation if not agreed by the prosecutor.[11]

Appointment of a Pre-conviction Receiver

Once a restraint order is made, a receiver may be appointed to take possession of any realizable property and manage or otherwise deal with it in accordance with the court's directions in order to preserve the value of the defendant's realizable property.[12]

Disclosure Affidavits

Once a restraint order has been made, the defendant may be ordered to swear an affidavit disclosing the full nature, value and whereabouts of his assets and serve it on the prosecutor. Whilst there is no statutory provision for this to occur, the Court of Appeal held in *Re O and Another*[13] that it was inherent in the statutory power granted to the High Court that it should have power to make a disclosure order. If the court orders that a disclosure affidavit must be sworn, a mandatory condition must be inserted into the restraint order, in order to protect the defendant's right against self-incrimination.[14] The courts also have the power to order a third party to make a disclosure affidavit, disclosing the full nature, value and whereabouts of all his assets.[15]

If a restraint order is disobeyed, the prosecutor will return to the High Court and apply to have the defendant committed to prison for contempt of court or for a financial penalty to be made against him.

---

[10] 1988 3 All ER 43.

[11] *The Commissioners of Customs & Excise* v. *Norris*, 1991 2 All ER 395.

[12] CJA Section 77(8), *Mason* (1994) 98 Cr. App. 31.

[13] 1991 1 All ER.

[14] This states: 'No disclosure made in compliance with this order shall be used as evidence in the prosecution of any offence alleged to have been committed by the person required to make that disclosure or by any powers of that person.'

[15] In *Re D, The Times*, 25 January 1995.

MAKING THE CONFISCATION ORDER

Once a defendant is convicted of corruption in the Crown Court, either the prosecutor will trigger the confiscation determination by giving written notice to the court, or the court may itself decide that it considers it appropriate.

Once the confiscation determination has been triggered, the court must then determine:

(1) whether the defendant has benefitted from any relevant criminal conduct;[16]

(2) if he has so benefitted, the court must determine the amount of benefit;[17]

(3) the amount that might be realized;[18]

(4) the court must make a confiscation order in an amount equal to the lower of the 'benefit' and the 'amount that might be realized',[19] unless the court is satisfied that a victim of any relevant criminal conduct has instituted or intends to institute civil proceedings against the defendant. If so satisfied, the court has a discretion to make a confiscation order in an amount up to the lower of the benefit and the amount that might be realized;[20] and

(5) once the court has fixed the amount of the confiscationorder, it must fix a period of imprisonment to be served in default of payment[21] and may give time to pay.

Determining Benefit from Any Relevant Criminal Conduct

Benefit may be either simple benefit or extended benefit. Simple benefit involves the court in calculating benefit from the offences of which the defendant is convicted together with any offences which the defendant asks to have taken into consideration. Extended benefit is much wider; the court may make assumptions as to the defendant's benefit from his criminal conduct, which will include benefit from crime of which the defendant is not convicted and which he does not admit.

Simple benefit[22] is calculated by calculating the gross value of the property obtained as a result of or in connection with the offence: there is

---

[16] CJA s. 71(1A).

[17] CJA s. 71(1B) and s. 71(6)(a).

[18] CJA s. 71(1B) and s. 71(6)(b).

[19] CJA s. 71(1B) and s. 71(6).

[20] CJA s. 71(1C).

[21] CJA s. 75(1).

[22] CJA Section 71(4).

no reduction to take account of expenses, and benefit does not mean profit. In calculating benefit, the court must value the property obtained as a result of or in connection with the offence. Sections 74(5) and (6) provide a scheme for the valuation of property. These provisions require the court to treat the value as the greater of either the value of the property at the time it was obtained (adjusted to take inflation into account) or its value (or that which it directly or indirectly represents) at the time of the making of the confiscation order.

Extended benefit[23] enables the court not only to confiscate the benefit arising from or in connection with the offence of which the defendant has been convicted, and those which he has asked to be taken into consideration but, by the use of assumptions, to confiscate also the proceeds of offences with which the defendant has not been charged, and of which he has not been convicted. If the prosecutor is alleging that the defendant has financed his lifestyle from corruption, then he will trigger the extended benefit provisions which permit the court to make the assumptions. In order for the court to exercise this power, two preconditions must be met:

(1) the prosecutor must trigger the procedure by giving written notice under Section 71(1)(a); that notice must contain a declaration that, in the prosecutor's opinion, it is appropriate to trigger the assumptions;[24] and

(2) the defendant must be convicted of two or more 'qualifying offences'.[25] One of those offences may be a previous conviction, provided it meets the requirements of a 'qualifying offence' and was committed during the 'relevant period'.[26]

A 'qualifying offence' is defined in Section 72AA(2) as an indictable offence (not drug trafficking or terrorism), which was committed after 1 November 1995[27] and that the court is satisfied is an offence from which the defendant has benefitted. If the defendant is convicted of two corruption offences or a corruption offence and an acquisitive offence of a different type, such as burglary, the extended benefit may be triggered.

The assumptions are that the whole of the defendant's lifestyle is financed from his proceeds of criminal conduct or from drug trafficking. It can be assumed that all property held by the defendant and all expenditure made by the defendant came from the proceeds of criminal conduct.

These assumptions can be made both to determine whether the defendant has benefitted from the relevant criminal conduct, and if he has, to assess

---

[23] CJA Section 72AA.

[24] CJA s. 72AA(1).

[25] CJA s. 72AA(1)(c)(i).

[26] CJA s. 72AA(1)(c)(ii). The 'relevant period' means the period of six years ending when the proceedings were instituted against the defendant.

[27] The commencement of s. 2 of the Proceeds of Crime Act 1995.

the value of his benefit. The court may also assume for the purpose of valuing such benefit that he received the benefit free of any other interests in it.

Once the court has made the assumptions, the onus is on the defendant to rebut them by demonstrating to the court that he has obtained the property or made the expenditure from legitimate sources. The court should not make the assumptions if the defendant's benefit from the offence has already been the subject of a previous confiscation order, or if the court is satisfied that there would be a serious risk of injustice in the defendant's case if the assumption was to be made in relation to that property or expenditure.

The Amount That Might Be Realized

Once the benefit has been determined, the court must calculate the amount that might be realized. This is the value to the defendant of all his assets, whether legitimately derived or not, and the value of any gifts.[28] The court must value the defendant's realizable property. Property is realizable if the defendant holds any interest in the property,[29] unless it is property which has previously been the subject of a forfeiture order under the Misuse of Drugs Act 1971, or the Prevention of Terrorism (Temporary Provisions) Act 1989 or the Criminal Procedure (Scotland) Act 1975; or a deprivation order under the Powers of the Criminal Courts Act 1973.[30] The value for the purposes of confiscation of that identified realizable property is the market value of the property less any sum required to discharge any incumbrance.[31]

Obligations having priority at the time the confiscation order is made must be deducted.[32] An obligation having priority would be such if it was a fine or other order made following a previous conviction[33] or was a preferential debt within the meaning of Section 386 of the Insolvency Act 1986.[34] The court has discretion to add to that net figure the value of any gift. Where some consideration has been given for the asset, the gift is to be valued proportionately to its actual value and the consideration given by the donee.[35] The value of the gift is not the value at the time it was received

---

[28] *See* the consecutive paragraphs: 'These assumptions can be made...' and 'Once the court has made the assumptions...', which appear immediately before the sub-heading 'The Amount That Might Be Realized', above.

[29] S. 74(1)(a) and 102(7) CJA (interest includes right: 102(1) CJA).

[30] CJA s. 74(2).

[31] CJA s. 74(4) (a) & (b).

[32] CJA s. 74(3).

[33] CJA s. 74(9).

[34] S. 74(9)(b) CJA and section 386 of the Insolvency Act 1986.

[35] CJA s. 74(12)(b)

by the donee, unless it is greater than its value on the date of the confiscation order, as a result of the change in the value of money[36] or because the gift has itself increased in value.[37]

Once the prosecution has proved on the balance of probabilities that the defendant has benefitted and if so, the amount, the burden is on the defendant to show that he does not have the necessary property to be realized.

Making the Confiscation Order

The court must make a confiscation order in the lower of the two amounts (benefit and the amount that might be realized) that it has calculated. If the court is satisfied that a victim of any offence in which a confiscation determination is under consideration has instituted, or intends to institute, civil proceedings against the defendant, the court has no obligation to make a confiscation order, but retains a discretion to do so. If it makes an order, it may make an order for less than the full amount of benefit which it would otherwise be obliged to order.

Once the court has made a confiscation order, it must fix a term of imprisonment to be served in default of payment. The terms to be served are the same as those applicable to fines. The court has power to give time to pay and to order payment in instalments.[38] If the court assesses the amount that might be realized in an amount lower than the amount of benefit, the court must issue a certificate to that effect.[39]

Where a court makes a confiscation order, it must take account of that before imposing any monetary order, such as a fine, a compensation order under Section 35 of the Powers of Criminal Court Act 1973, a deprivation order under Section 43 of the Powers of Criminal Court Act, or a forfeiture order under Section 27, Misuse of Drugs Act 1971. Other than that, it must ignore the fact that a confiscation order has been made when it determines the appropriate sentence.

In every case, once the confiscation determination has been triggered, the prosecutor must give the court a statement dealing with whether the defendant has benefitted from any relevant criminal conduct, or to an assessment of the defendant's benefit from that conduct. The court also has power to require the prosecutor to give it such statements where it has decided of its own volition to make a confiscation determination.

The court can order the defendant to give it any information it requires to made a confiscation order. If the defendant fails, without reasonable

---

[36] CJA s. 74(7) explained in *Foxley* 16 Cr. App. R. (S).
[37] CJA s. 74(8).
[38] S. 31(2)(b) Power of Criminal Courts Act 1973.
[39] CJA s. 73(6).

excuse, to comply with such order, the court can draw adverse inference from that failure.

The court is able to sentence the defendant first and consider the making of the confiscation determination later. If the confiscation determination is postponed, then the court cannot sentence the defendant to a monetary order until after the confiscation determination is made. More than one postponement can be made in the same case, but unless there are exceptional circumstances, the total postponements should not be for more than six months.

Compensating Victims in Proceeds of Crime Cases

The court can make both a confiscation order and a compensation order in the same proceedings, leaving the confiscation order out of account when considering the amount of the compensation order. If the defendant has sufficient assets to satisfy both orders, then the court has the power to make both a confiscation order and a compensation order against the defendant in the same proceedings. If that occurs, enforcement of both orders will take place in parallel. The enforcement powers of the magistrates' courts are similar for both types of order.

If the defendant does not have sufficient means to satisfy both orders, the court can direct payment of the amount of compensation that will not be recoverable out of any sums recovered under the confiscation order. The victim will obtain the advantage of all the High Court orders which are ancillary to the making and enforcement of a confiscation order, such as restraint, disclosure, repatriation and receivership orders. A restraint order which preserves assets for the satisfaction of the confiscation order will automatically preserve assets for the satisfaction of the compensation order. Any receiver appointed by the High Court to sell sufficient assets of the defendant in order to satisfy the confiscation order will be selling sufficient assets to satisfy the compensation order. The costs of such a receiver are borne proportionally between the Crown and the victim.

Enforcement

Once a confiscation order has been made by Crown Court, the onus is on the defendant to satisfy the order in full and he can take steps to pay the order voluntarily. The terms of the restraint order permit this to occur. If the defendant fails to take steps to satisfy the confiscation order in full voluntarily, then enforcement will occur. Enforcement may occur in two ways:

  (1) through the magistrates' court. The magistrates' courts are the principle enforcers of confiscation orders. The money is paid to the

consolidated fund of the Treasury through the magistrates' court. The magistrates' courts have all the usual powers of enforcement as they would were the order a fine. In addition, where the defendant serves a term of imprisonment, or detention in default of paying any amount due under a confiscation order, it does not expunge the confiscation order. In appropriate cases, an application can be made to appoint a receiver, even though the defendant has served a term of imprisonment in default of payment of the confiscation order. Interest is added to an unpaid confiscation order at the civil judgment debt rate; and

(2) in addition to those powers, the prosecutor has a specific power to apply to the High Court to appoint a receiver to realize sufficient of the defendant's realizable property to satisfy the order. This may mean litigation if third parties are affected.

The Application

All persons with an interest in the property which is liable to be subject to the receivership must be served with the receivership application and may obtain legal aid and attend the hearing. At the hearing, the court will determine the defendant's rights and interests in the property and appoint a receiver. Thereafter, the receiver takes office and will sell sufficient of the property to satisfy the order.

Variation and Review of Confiscation Orders Downwards

The defendant can obtain the reduction of a confiscation order made under the acts where the amount that might be realized turns out to be less than that assessed by the Crown Court.

The courts have power to make a confiscation order where none has been made or increase one where it has been so made.[40] This power is restricted to cases where the prosecution discovers, after the defendant was dealt with, further evidence to prove benefit or more benefit from relevant criminal conduct. The application is made by the prosecution, can only be made up to six years after the defendant was dealt with, and the assumptions do not apply.

---

[40] CJA Sections 74A, 74B, 74C.

Effect of a Restraint Order on Assets Held Overseas

The effects of the CJA are worldwide. When a criminal court makes a confiscation order, account will be taken of the defendant's realizable property held abroad. Ancillary High Court orders of restraint may include orders requiring the repatriation of funds from outside the jurisdiction as well as preventing any person from dealing with the defendant's realizable property worldwide. To give effect to these orders by preventing dissipation of the property before any confiscation order is made, and once an order is made, to take action worldwide to enforce the confiscation order, requires considerable international cooperation.

Some alternative to international cooperation lies in the power the High Court has to make a restraint order against a defendant who is within the jurisdiction. A restraint order may obviously extend to property situated outside the jurisdiction.[41] A dealing by the defendant after the restraint order has been served upon him would therefore put him in contempt of the restraint order. An order may be made requiring the repatriation of property outside the jurisdiction. A defendant or third party outside the jurisdiction may have a restraint order made against him and leave may be given to serve him outside the jurisdiction.[42]

Mutual legal assistance occurs under those obligations assumed by the UK through ratification of the Vienna and the Council of Europe Conventions and under the numerous bilateral treaties that have been concluded between the government of the UK and other countries to permit the investigation, restraint, registration and enforcement of confiscation orders and forfeiture orders against assets held in jurisdictions other than where the orders were made. Once a country has ratified the appropriate convention, it will be designated under an Order in Council and in law the UK can provide cooperation.[43] Restraint orders and the enforcement of overseas confiscation orders in England and Wales are only available to foreign countries which have been designated by Order in Council.

If a country is not designated, assistance from them to recognize a restraint order or enforce a confiscation order may still be available. Whether or not the requested country could restrain or enforce on our behalf would depend simply upon whether their law would permit such action to be taken by them. A request for assistance merely asks that action be taken by the foreign requested state in accordance with the provisions of their domestic law. Any sum realized from the realizable property held overseas will generally remain in the requested country.

---

[41] DTA s. 62(2) and CJA s. 102(3).

[42] RSC O11 r. 1(1)(q)/(s).

[43] The basis of the designation procedure arises from the primary legislation. The CJA makes provision for further legislation through Orders in Council.

LINDA J. CANDLER

12. Taking the Profit out of Corruption: A US Perspective

While much has been done to ensure that proceeds of drug trafficking offences are confiscated, as demonstrated by the signing of the Vienna Convention in 1988, procedures for seizing criminal proceeds in corruption cases are not as clear. There is no multilateral treaty for tracing and seizing proceeds of fraud and corruption cases, unless money laundering is involved. The United Kingdom has taken a very broad approach with the enactment of the Proceeds of Crime Act 1995, which provides for seizure and confiscation of proceeds of all crimes. In the United States, forfeiture for corruption offences is possible under the racketeering (RICO) or money laundering statutes, and may be brought as a criminal action, which requires a conviction, or civil action, which requires jurisdiction over the property. This paper will discuss the different approaches taken by the United States and the United Kingdom to seize criminal proceeds in fraud and corruption cases.

OVERVIEW

The United States and the United Kingdom take an entirely different approach in forfeiture cases. In the United Kingdom, confiscation of property is based on the theory that a defendant should not be permitted to profit from crime. Thus, if the defendant is convicted, the court will make a post-trial assessment of the amount of benefit derived from the criminal activity, and any property can be used to satisfy the order, whether involved in the offence or traceable to the offence, or not. In the United States, forfeiture actions may be civil or criminal. A civil forfeiture action may be filed directly against property involved in an offence, and a conviction is not required. However, there are requirements for tracing the criminal proceeds. In civil forfeiture proceedings, the property itself is considered the wrong-doer, and the value of the seized property may be unrelated to the proceeds derived from the offence. This has led to constitutional challenges based on the Excessive Fines Clause and the Double Jeopardy Clause. Criminal forfeiture must be alleged in the indictment, and again will depend on tracing or proof that the criminal proceeds have been dissipated.

Barry A.K. Rider (ed.), Corruption: The Enemy Within, 181–194
© *Kluwer Law International. Printed in the Netherlands.*

In the US, a forfeiture order is considered part of a criminal sentence, whereas in the UK, it is not. Also, the government must connect the property to the crime, or show the original proceeds have been dissipated. In the UK, the confiscation order is a money judgment against the defendant based on the court's determination of the amount of benefit and the property available to satisfy the order. It does not matter if the criminal proceeds have been dissipated, co-mingled, or reinvested; any available assets, whether or not derived from the criminal activity, can be used to satisfy the order.

Another difference is that UK law now permits confiscation of the proceeds of all crimes. In the United States, there are numerous laws providing for forfeiture of specified criminal activity, including narcotics offences, money laundering, and racketeering, but fraud proceeds are not always subject to forfeiture – some sort of nexus is required, for example, a federally-insured bank.

Finally, the ability to return seized funds to victims is quite different. If a confiscation order is entered, the UK court has the power to endorse a compensation order to reimburse the victims first. In the US, title vests with the government at the time the offence is committed and the funds are transferred to the asset forfeiture fund upon entry of the final order. At that time, the Attorney General or Secretary of Treasury may, but is not required to, pay restitution out of forfeited funds.

US FORFEITURE LAWS

In the United States, forfeiture is based on the theory that the property itself is tainted, whereas in the United Kingdom, confiscation is directed at the proceeds of crime – that is, the amount by which the defendant benefitted from his criminal conduct. The US forfeiture order is entered against the property, not against the defendant. The property is transferred to the government as soon as the forfeiture order is final.

In the United States, the government may file a civil *in rem* forfeiture action directly against the property, or bring a criminal forfeiture charge against the defendant as part of a criminal prosecution. In a civil forfeiture proceeding, the identity of the wrongdoer is irrelevant. Civil forfeiture merely requires proof that the property itself was the proceeds of a crime or was involved in a crime. The doctrine that the property itself is considered the offender in a civil forfeiture action 'has a venerable history in our case law'.[1] Civil forfeiture may be imposed even where the owner of the property is not legally guilty of the criminal offence, or 'where the in-

---

[1] *Austin v. United States*, 491 U.S. 600, 113 S. Ct. 2801, 2808–09 (1993).

nocence of the owner was "fully established"'.[2] Criminal forfeiture actions
are charged in the indictment, and if the defendant is convicted, the jury is
then required to render a special verdict concerning the property subject to
forfeiture. The standard of proof for criminal forfeiture is beyond a reasonable doubt, as in all criminal convictions. In civil forfeiture actions, the
standard of proof is probable cause to initiate the action or seize property.[3]
Once probable cause is shown, the burden shifts to the owner to demonstrate
that the property is not forfeitable.[4]

In criminal forfeiture actions, the government must prove that the property
was proceeds of the offence, used to facilitate the offence, traceable to such
property, or substitute assets if the original assets have been dissipated.[5]
Substitute assets can be forfeited if any of the property subject to forfeiture,
as a result of any act or omission of the defendant '(1) cannot be located
upon the exercise of due diligence; (2) has been transferred or sold to, or
deposited with, a third party; (3) has been placed beyond the jurisdiction of
the court; (4) has been substantially diminished in value; or (5) has been
commingled with other property which cannot be divided without difficulty...'.[6] This is vastly different from the UK system, where any asset
belonging to the defendant (or gifts made by him within the relevant time
period) may be used to satisfy a confiscation order. In addition, US courts
are divided over whether the government can restrain substitute assets
pretrial in fraud and racketeering cases.

Unlike the UK confiscation laws, forfeiture orders are not available for
all crimes. The government can bring criminal forfeiture actions in narcotics
cases, racketeering (RICO) cases, and money laundering cases, for specified
unlawful activities, including fraud.[7] There is no general forfeiture provision

---

[2] *Calero-Toledo* v. *Pearson Yacht Leasing Co.*, 416 U.S. 663, 684, *reh'g denied*, 417 US
977 (1974).

[3] *United States* v. *Monsanto*, 491 U.S. 600 (1989) (Government may 'seize property based
on a finding of probable cause to believe that the property will ultimately be proven forfeitable'); *United States* v. *One Twin Engine Beech Airplane*, 533 F.2d 1106 (9th Cir. 1976);
United States v. *1982 Yukon Delta Houseboat*, 774 F.2d 1432 (9th Cir. 1985).

[4] *United States* v. *One 1970 Pontiac GTO*, 529 F.2d 65 (9th Cir. 1976).

[5] Title 18 United States Code Sec. 982(a)(1) – court shall order that any person convicted
of specified money laundering offences forfeit to the United States 'any property, real or
personal, involved in such offence, or any property traceable to such property'. For fraud
affecting US financial institutions, Sec. 982(a)(2) provides that the court shall order forfeiture
of 'any property constituting, or derived from, proceeds the person obtained directly or
indirectly as the result of such violation'. The substitute assets provision of 21 U.S.C. Sec.
853(p) is applicable to fraud and money laundering offences listed in 21 U.S.C. Sec. 982
pursuant to Sec. 982(b)(1).

[6] Title 21, U.S.C. Sec. 853(p).

[7] *See* Title 18, U.S.C. Section 982(a)(1) for money laundering violations (Title 31, Sections
5313(a), 5316, or 5324; or Title 18, U.S.C. Sections 1956, 1957, or 1960); Title 21, U.S.C. Section
853 for narcotics offences, and 18 U.S.C. Section 1963, for racketeering offences.

for fraud; forfeiture is only possible if the proceeds of the fraud have been laundered, or a federally-insured bank or financial institution was defrauded.[8] This is a real limitation in the United States and a key difference between the United States and the United Kingdom. The Department of Justice has proposed amendments to the forfeiture statutes to make the proceeds of all federal financial crimes in Title 18 of the United States Code subject to forfeiture, so that forfeiture would be available as a sanction in white-collar crimes such as fraud and public corruption.[9]

In addition to not covering all crimes, the fact that the forfeiture is based not on the amount of benefit, as in the United Kingdom, but rather on the 'taint' or 'criminality' of the property itself, has resulted in disproportionate forfeitures in the United States, and has resulted in recent decisions curtailing the government's ability to bring both civil and criminal forfeiture actions.

In *Austin* v. *United States*,[10] the court held that civil forfeiture constituted punishment, and was subject to the Eighth Amendment prohibition against excessive fines.[11] Austin was charged with drug offences, and pleaded guilty to one count of possession of cocaine. He was sentenced to seven years' imprisonment. The government subsequently filed a civil forfeiture action seeking forfeiture of Austin's mobile home and auto body shop. The evidence showed that Austin sold two grams of cocaine at the body shop, which he retrieved from his mobile home. Small amounts of marijuana and cocaine and $4,700 in cash were also discovered at the body shop and mobile home pursuant to a search warrant. The Court of Appeals reluctantly affirmed the District Court's order of forfeiture, holding that in civil forfeiture, when the government is proceeding against property *in rem*, the guilt or innocence of the property's owner 'is constitutionally irrelevant'. Thus, '[i]f the Constitution allows *in rem* forfeiture to be visited upon innocent owners ... the Constitution hardly requires proportionality review of forfeiture'.[12]

The Supreme Court reviewed the history of the Eighth Amendment and concluded that the Excessive Fines Clause was not limited to criminal cases. The Court determined, after an extensive review of civil and criminal forfeiture proceedings, that forfeiture, whether civil or criminal, operates as

[8] *Id.*
[9] Forfeiture Act 1995, Title III.
[10] *Id.*, note 43.
[11] The Eighth Amendment provides that '[e]xcessive bail shall not be required, nor excessive fines imposed, nor cruel and unusual punishments inflicted'. U.S. Const., Amdt. 8.
[12] *United States* v. *One Parcel of Property*, 964 F.2d 814, 817 (8th Cir. 1992), reversed, *Austin* v. *United States*, 491 U.S. 600 (1993), quoting *United States* v. *Tax Lot 1500*, 861 F.2d 232, 234 (9th Cir. 1988), *Cert. denied sub nom.*, *Jafee* v. *United States,* 493 U.S. 954 (1989).

punishment,[13] and that the Excessive Fines Clause of the Eighth Amendment was applicable because '[t]he purpose of the Eighth Amendment ... was to limit the governments' power to punish... The Excessive Fines Clause limits the government's power to extract payments, whether in cash or in kind, "as *punishment* for some offence"'.[14]

The Court also relied on *United States* v. *Halper*,[15] another case which limited the government's ability to proceed both civilly and criminally. In *Halper*, the government, following a criminal conviction, brought a civil RICO action and sought treble damages. The Court ruled that 'the government may not criminally prosecute a defendant, impose a criminal penalty on him, and then bring a separate civil action based on the same conduct and receive a judgment that is not rationally related to the goal of making the government whole'.[16] As a result, a civil case resulting in civil sanctions that are punitive as well as remedial is barred by the Double Jeopardy Clause, and a criminal case brought after a civil case would also be barred where the sanctions 'cannot fairly be said solely to serve a remedial purpose, but rather can only be explained as also serving either retributive or deterrent purposes, is punishment, as we have come to understand the term'.[17]

Applying the rationale of *Austin* and *Halper*, the Court of Appeals for the Ninth Circuit held in *United States* v. *$405,089.23 US Currency*,[18] that a civil forfeiture proceeding which followed a criminal conviction was barred by the Double Jeopardy Clause, stating that '[i]n light of the decision in *Austin*, and applying the *Halper* test here, we find the conclusion inescapable that civil forfeiture under 18 U.S.C. Sec. 981(a)(1)(A) and 21 U.S.C. Sec. 881(a)(6) constitutes "punishment" which triggers the protections of the Double Jeopardy Clause'.[19] Accordingly, the court ordered that the forfeited funds be returned to the defendants. The court rejected the

---

[13] The Court, citing *Calero-Toledo* v. *Pearson Yacht Leasing Co.*, 416 U.S. 663, 94 S.Ct. 2080 (1974), noted that three kinds of forfeiture were established in England at the time the Eighth Amendment was ratified: *deodand*, which involved forfeiture of an inanimate object directly or indirectly causing the accidental death of a King's subject; forfeiture upon conviction for a felony or treason, which was based on conviction and required forfeiture of property, real and personal, to the Crown in cases of treason and forfeiture of chattels to the Crown and land escheating to his lord for convicted felons; and statutory forfeiture, for seizure of offending objects used in violation of the customs and revenue laws.

[14] *Austin* v. *United States*, 491 U.S. 600, 113 S.Ct. 2801 at 2805, citing *Browning-Ferris Industries* v. *Kelco Disposal, Inc.*, 492 U.S. 257 (1989), at 265.

[15] 490 U.S. 435, 109 S.Ct. 1892 (1989).

[16] *Id.*, at 450–451.

[17] *Id.*, at 448, 109 S.Ct. at 1902.

[18] 33 F.3d 1210 (9th Cir. 1994), *amended and reh'g denied*, 56 F.3d 41 (1995), *cert. granted*, 64 U.S.L.W. 3484, 12 January 1996 (No. 95–346), reversed, 116 S.Ct. 2135 (24 June 1996).

[19] *Id.*, at 1219.

government's argument that the forfeiture action was simply an attempt to forfeit the illegal proceeds, noting that the narcotic forfeiture statute is broader and covers any money 'used or intended to be used' to facilitate a narcotics transaction. Following *$405,089,23 US Currency*, the Sixth Circuit overturned a *criminal* conviction which followed a civil forfeiture on double jeopardy grounds in *United States* v. *Ursery*.[20]

The Supreme Court overturned these decisions in *United States* v. *Ursery*, 116 S.Ct. 2135 (24 June 1996) and concluded that for purposes of the Double Jeopardy Clause, civil forfeitures do not constitute punishment. The Court noted that under common law, the right of forfeiture did not attach until conviction, and a holding that a civil forfeiture would be prohibited by the prior criminal proceeding 'would have been directly contrary to the common-law rule, and would have called into question the constitutionality of forfeiture statutes thought constitutional for over a century'. Citing previous decisions in *United States* v. *One Assortment of 89 Firearms*, 465 U.S. 354 (1984), and *Various Items of Personal Property* v. *United States*, 282 U.S. 577 (1931), the Court held that '*in rem* civil forfeiture is a remedial civil sanction, distinct from potentially punitive *in personam* civil penalties such as fines, and does not constitute a punishment under the Double Jeopardy Clause'.

The Court distinguished *Halper*, as it involved an excessive civil penalty, 'so extreme and so divorced from the Government's damages and expenses as to constitute punishment', citing *Halper*, 490 U.S. at 442. The Court held that 'forfeitures ... are designed primarily to confiscate property used in violation of the law, and to require disgorgement of the fruits of illegal conduct ... it is virtually impossible to quantify, even approximately, the nonpunitive purposes served by a particular civil forfeiture'. Thus, 'the case-by-case balancing test set forth in *Halper*, in which a court must compare the harm suffered by the Government against the size of the penalty imposed, is inapplicable to civil forfeiture'. The Court also distinguished its holding in *Austin* that civil forfeiture constituted punishment under the Eighth Amendment Excessive Fines Clause, stating that while '[f]orfeitures effected under 21 U.S.C. § § 881 (a)(4) and (a)(7) are subject to review for excessiveness under the Eighth Amendment after *Austin*; this does not mean ... that those forfeitures are so punitive as to constitute punishment for the purposes of double jeopardy'.

In reaching this decision, the Court made three findings: (1) Congress intended forfeitures under 21 U.S.C. § 881 and 18 U.S.C. § 981 to be civil proceedings; (2) there is little evidence that forfeiture under these statutes 'are so punitive ... as to render them criminal despite Congress' intent to the contrary'; and (3) the statutes serve important nonpunitive goals of prevent-

---

[20] 59 F.3d 568 (6th Cir. 1995), *cert. granted*, 64 U.S.L.W. 3484 (12 January 1996), reversed, 116 S.Ct. 2135 (24 June 1996).

ing further illegal use of such property and 'ensuring that persons do not profit from their illegal acts'.

As these cases illustrate, the fact the forfeiture is not based on the amount by which the defendant benefited, but instead on the illegal use of the property, has led to confusion and constitutional challenges. Under the Excessive Fines Clause, forfeiture is considered punishment. Under the Double Jeopardy Clause, it is not. In another recent case, the Supreme Court held that forfeiture is considered an element of the sentence imposed following a conviction or a guilty plea, and as such, is not covered by the constitutional right to a jury trial.[21] The defendant had argued that despite his plea agreement, he was still entitled to a jury trial on the criminal forfeiture count. The Court held that the judge need not determine whether the assets to be forfeited pursuant to a plea agreement are tied to the defendant's criminal activity. Justice Stevens, in a dissenting opinion, cautioned that this decision could allow 'a wealthy defendant [to] bargain for a light sentence by voluntarily "forfeiting" property to which the government had no statutory entitlement'.

PRETRIAL RESTRAINT

The RICO statute, 18 U.S.C. Section 1963, provides for pretrial restraint of assets. The statute provides that:

> (d)(1) Upon application of the United States, the court may enter a restraining order or injunction, require the execution of a satisfactory performance bond, or take any other action to preserve the availability of property ... [subject to] forfeiture under this section.

This is a criminal *in personam* action against the defendant, and the restraining order may be sought upon the filing of an indictment or information. The purpose of this provision is to preserve, pending trial, assets which may be subject to forfeiture upon conviction.[22] For criminal forfeiture actions brought under the general criminal forfeiture statute, 18 U.S.C. Section 982, pretrial restraint is governed by the narcotics pretrial restraint provisions.

The courts are divided on whether substitute assets may be restrained pretrial in fraud cases. In *United States* v. *Billman*,[23] the government proved that Billman and other conspirators transferred $22 million in misappropriated funds to Swiss bank accounts. The government sought a pretrial restraining order for a wire transfer of $499,935 which Billman, who

---

[21] *Libretti* v. *United States*, 116 S.Ct. 356 (1995).

[22] *United States* v. *Regan*, 858 F.2d 115, 119 (2d Cir. 1988).

[23] 915 F.2d 916 (4th Cir. 1990), *cert denied*, 500 U.S. 952 (1991).

had fled the country, ordered transferred to a codefendant in Maryland from a bank account in London. The government could not prove that the funds in the London bank account had been transferred from the Swiss accounts. The Court of Appeals held that even if the wire transfer could not be traced to the proceeds deposited in Swiss bank accounts, the court would be authorized by statute to order forfeiture of substitute assets post conviction. The court concluded that the RICO statute should be construed to authorize pretrial restraint of substitute assets, to avoid permitting a defendant 'to thwart the operation of forfeiture laws by absconding with RICO proceeds and then transferring his substitute assets to a third person who does not qualify as a *bona fide* purchaser for value'.[24]

The opposite conclusion was reached in *United States* v. *Field*,[25] where the Court of Appeals for the Eighth Circuit affirmed the District Court's order vacating a pretrial restraining order on the grounds that it did not have the power to restrain assets before trial that were not fruits or instrumentalities of the crime. In *Field*, the government sought a restraining order preventing the defendant in a fraud case from dissipating assets allegedly obtained by fraud, or other property up to the value of the money obtained by fraud. In this case, forfeiture was alleged under 18 U.S.C. Section 982. The defendant argued this statute did not permit pretrial restraint of substitute assets. The court agreed, holding that the statute only authorizes post-conviction seizure of substitute property if forfeitable property is no longer available.[26]

As these cases illustrate, there is a split among the circuits on whether pretrial restraint of substitute assets is possible in fraud cases, either under the RICO statute or under the general crime forfeiture statute.[27] As a result, the Department of Justice has recommended legislation authorizing the pretrial restraint of substitute assets in all criminal cases.

The conflict in the US over preservation of substitute assets pretrial emphasizes the simplicity of the UK system. The British court is not concerned with whether the assets represent actual proceeds of the crime;

---

[24] *Id.*, at 921.

[25] 62 F.3d 246 (8th Cir. 1995).

[26] 18 U.S.C. Sec. 982(b)(1)(B) provides that in cases of mail fraud, forfeiture is governed by 21 U.S.C. Sec. 853(b),(c),(e), and (g) through (p) (the narcotics forfeiture provisions). Section 853(a) only refers to property associated with the crime. A separate provision, 853(p), allows forfeiture of substitute assets post conviction. Sec. 853 does not specify whether pretrial restraint of substitute assets is permitted.

[27] *Compare United States* v. *Ripinsky*, 20 F.3d 359 (9th Cir. 1994) (pretrial restraint not permitted); *United States* v. *Floyd*, 992 F 2d 498 (5th Cir. 1993) (pretrial restraint not permitted); *In re Assets of Martin*, 1 F.3d 1351 (3rd Cir. 1993) (pretrial restraint not permitted under RICO); with *In re Billman, supra*, n. 131 (pretrial restraint permitted under RICO); and *United States* v. *Regan*, 858 F.2d 115 (2d Cir. 1988) (court should consider pretrial restraint under RICO when restraining fruits of crime would be a burden to third parties).

any asset may be used to satisfy a confiscation order, and consequently any asset may be restrained pretrial.

Although not as widely used as *Mareva* injunctions, preliminary injunctions have been granted in civil RICO cases to prevent dissipation of assets. In a civil RICO action brought by the Republic of the Philippines, the Court of Appeals for the Ninth Circuit upheld a preliminary injunction restraining assets of deposed leader Ferdinand Marcos, his wife, and others.[28] The Republic of the Philippines sought an injunction enjoining the Marcoses from disposing of any of their assets, including real estate in Beverly Hills, California, of $4 million, $800,000 on deposit at a bank in California, and $7 million in money, jewels and property transported to Hawaii by the Marcoses when they left the Philippines.

The Republic alleged that Marcos abused his position of power to convert government funds to his personal use and established that the Marcoses had bank accounts in Switzerland of approximately $1.3 billion, notwithstanding that their total salaries from 1966 to 1985 were less than $800,000. Marcos argued that the 'act of state' doctrine barred the suit. The court held that while the 'act of state' doctrine might be applicable to prevent judicial challenge in US courts of acts of a dictator in power, 'No estoppel exists insulating a deposed dictator from accounting ... [t]he doctrine is meant to facilitate the foreign relations of the United States, not to furnish the equivalent of sovereign immunity to a deposed leader'. The court enjoined the disposal of worldwide assets, not just those in the United States, holding that '[b]ecause the injunction operates *in personam*, not *in rem*, there is no reason to be concerned about its territorial reach'.[29]

In a civil RICO and securities fraud case, *Hoxworth* v. *Blinder, Robinson & Co. Inc.*,[30] the Third Circuit Court of Appeals upheld a preliminary injunction against a securities firm and its president preventing the defendants from transferring funds overseas and ordering the president to repatriate funds he had transferred overseas since litigation had been commenced. The Court of Appeals modified the order, however, because the District Court did not tailor the injunction to the expected recovery; the order encumbered all of the assets of the defendants, worth tens of millions of dollars.[31] The defendants argued that the District Court did not have the power to issue a preliminary injunction to protect a future damages remedy. The Court of

---

[28] *Republic of the Philippines* v. *Marcos*, 862 F.2d 1355 (9th Cir. 1988), *cert. denied*, 490 U.S. 1035 (1989).

[29] *Id.*; *see also United States* v. *First National City Bank*, 379 U.S. 378, 380 (1966), ('Once personal jurisdiction of a party is obtained, the District Court has authority to order it to "freeze" property under its control, whether the property be within or without the United States...').

[30] 903 F.2d 186 (3rd Cir. 1990).

[31] A default judgment was later entered against the defendants for $73 million. *Hoxworth* v. *Blinder, Robinson & Co., Inc.*, 980 F.2d 912 (9th Cir. 1990).

Appeals upheld the order, noting that, although not necessarily appropriate in a run-of-the-mill damages action, it was appropriate upon a showing that the plaintiffs are likely to become entitled to the encumbered funds and that without the injunction, the plaintiffs will be unlikely to recover. In other words, the criteria for a preliminary injunction – the likelihood of success on the merits and the probability of irreparable harm if the relief was not granted – had been met.

Most of the other circuits have also held that a preliminary injunction is available to prevent dissipation of assets in order to protect an eventual money judgment.[32]

In the United Kingdom, the Court of Appeal upheld a worldwide *Mareva* injunction against Jean-Claude Duvalier, his wife and his mother, preventing them from disposing of assets, wherever located, which represented funds allegedly embezzled from the Republic of Haiti. The Republic of Haiti filed proceedings in France to recover $120 million, then sought a restraining order in England and an order compelling the defendants to disclose information relating to their assets. The Duvaliers did not reside in England, nonetheless the court concluded that 'there is jurisdiction to grant a *Mareva* injunction, pending trial, over assets worldwide',[33] although cases where it will be applied are rare.

The *Mareva* injunction was granted even though the defendants did not reside in England, because the court felt that 'what ... is determinate is the plain and admitted intention of the defendants to move their assets out of the reach of the courts of law, coupled with the resources they have obtained and the skill they have hitherto shown in doing that, and the vast amount of money involved. This case demands international cooperation between all nations'.[34]

REPATRIATION OF ASSETS

Once the assets are restrained, it still may prove difficult to transfer the assets, or proceeds thereof, back to the jurisdiction of the court. In the US, the defendant may be required, as part of a plea agreement, to liquidate his overseas assets and repatriate the proceeds to the United States for forfeiture. This puts the responsibility on the defendant, and saves the government the cost of liquidation and maintenance. In addition, there may be restrictions on the US government's ability to own or sell foreign property. Requiring the defendant to liquidate the property eliminates these problems. Unlike in the UK, a receiver is not appointed to liquidate the property; the burden falls

---

[32] *See In re Estate of Ferdinand Marcos*, Human Rights Lit., 25 F.3d 1467, 1478–80 (9th Cir. 1994), *cert. denied*, 115 S.Ct. 934 (1995), and cases cited therein.

[33] *Republic of Haiti* v. *Duvalier*, [1990] 1 QB 202 at 215.

[34] *Id.*, at 216–217.

on the government because the property is transferred immediately upon entry of the order. Thus, there is no leverage against the defendant after the forfeiture order is entered. In the UK, the liquidator can seek a court order to secure the defendant's cooperation, and failure to comply is punishable by contempt. In the US, if the plea agreement does not provide for repatriation or if the court does not order it, the United States must seek assistance from the foreign government in enforcing a forfeiture order or repatriating the assets.

If the defendant is uncooperative, the court can nonetheless order the defendant to repatriate his assets pursuant to a protective order or a sentencing order. A defendant may be ordered to repatriate funds from foreign bank accounts pursuant to 18 U.S.C. Section 982, which empowers the court to take any action to preserve the availability of forfeitable property.[35] Specifically, pursuant to 18 United States Code, Section 982(b)(1), which incorporates the narcotics-related provisions of 21 United States Code, Section 853(e)(1)(A), the government can seek a protective order directing the defendant to repatriate funds from foreign banks to the jurisdiction of the US court pending the outcome of the forfeiture proceeding where funds which the government alleges are subject to forfeiture have transferred outside the United States after the indictment.

ENFORCEMENT OF FOREIGN CONFISCATION ORDERS

The UK can enforce foreign confiscation orders in fraud cases under the Criminal Justice (International Cooperation) Act 1990.[36] Section 9 provides that overseas forfeiture orders may be enforced in the United Kingdom where there is an Order in Council.

Restraint orders may also be enforced pursuant to the 1995 Act.[37] This provision was extended to the United States on 1 August 1994, thus allowing the UK to enforce US restraint and forfeiture orders in criminal cases.

The United States can enforce foreign forfeiture orders in drug cases pursuant to 18 United States Code, Section 981(b)(1). There is no statutory provision for enforcement of foreign forfeiture or confiscation orders in fraud cases unless the offences can be classified as money laundering or a

---

[35] *See United States* v. *Lopez*, 688 F. Supp. 92 (E.N.D.Y. 1988) (defendants ordered to execute release needed to transfer foreign funds subject to forfeiture); *United States* v. *Sellers*, 848 F. Supp. 73 (E.D. La. 1994); *United States* v. *Rutgard*, Case No. 94–408–GT, Order dated 24 January 1995 (S.D. Ca.) (defendant ordered to repatriate funds from Isle of Man to registry of US District Court pending conclusion of trial and forfeiture determination; funds were subsequently forfeited upon conviction).

[36] Entered into force 5 April 1990.

[37] Proceeds of Crime Act 1995, para. 14(3).

RICO violation. The Department of Justice has recommended legislation to provide for enforcement of overseas forfeiture orders in fraud cases.

RESTITUTION

A US court does not have the authority to award restitution out of forfeited funds. Upon entry of an order of forfeiture, title passes to the United States, and the Attorney General may award restitution out of forfeited funds. Title 18 United States Code Section 981(e)(6) provides that 'the Attorney General, the Secretary of the Treasury, or the Postal Service, as the case may be, is authorized to ... restore forfeited property to any victim of an offense...'. The offence must be one described in the statute, and includes fraud, theft and embezzlement offences involving federal financial institutions, fraudulent loan applications to US federal agencies, counterfeiting or forgery of US securities or postage, and customs violations. The statute thus provides for restitution where the victim is a federally-insured bank or a US government agency or the crime involves use of a federal financial institution; however, it does not provide a basis for restitution to private parties in all cases. Moreover, this provision is discretionary, just as a restitution order by the court is discretionary.

The RICO forfeiture statute,[38] which was used in the BCCI case, also gives the Attorney General the authority to restore forfeited property to victims of an offence. In the BCCI case, BCCI, through its court-appointed liquidator, pleaded guilty in January 1992 and agreed to the forfeiture of all of BCCI's assets in the United States.[39] More than $550 million has been ordered forfeited,[40] and the United States Department of Justice has identified nearly a billion dollars in forfeitable assets. Pursuant to the plea agreement, 50 per cent of the forfeited funds were to be transferred to a Worldwide Victims Fund. In September 1995, $223 million was transferred to the court-appointed liquidators in London for distribution to the innocent depositors.

Courts in the United Kingdom may award compensation to victims of crime under the Powers of Criminal Courts Act 1973. Section 35 provides

---

[38] 18 United States Code, Section 1963(g)(1) provides that the Attorney General is authorized to '... restore forfeited property to victims of a violation of this chapter, or take any other action to protect the rights of innocent persons which is in the interest of justice and which is not inconsistent with the provisions of this chapter...'.

[39] BCCI pleaded guilty, on 19 January 1992, to operating a racketeering conspiracy, in violation of 18 United States Code, Section 1962.

[40] Order of Forfeiture dated 24 January 1992; Order and First Supplemental List of Forfeited Property dated 31 January 1992; and Order of Forfeiture and Second Supplemental List of Forfeited Property dated 29 July 1992, United States District Court for the District of Columbia, Criminal Number 91–0655 (JHG).

that courts in the United Kingdom are empowered to order persons convicted of an offence to pay compensation 'for any personal injury, loss or
damage resulting from that offence or any other offence which is taken into
consideration by the court in determining sentence'.[41] If appropriate,
compensation must be considered before imposition of a fine.

A compensation order can be imposed in addition to a confiscation order,
and is entered before or during the criminal proceedings, not after the trial
as in confiscation cases. Unlike a confiscation order, which is imposed in
addition to the sentence on an offender, a compensation order may be in
addition to, or instead of, any other sentence. If there are insufficient funds
to pay both, the compensation order is paid first.[42]

In *R. v. Edward Albert Hunter*,[43] the court ordered that a compensation
order be paid out of realizable property, where there were insufficient funds
to satisfy both orders. The trustee in bankruptcy argued that to use the
confiscation procedures for the ulterior purpose of making a compensation
order would give the victims preferential treatment over the creditors in
bankruptcy. The court held, however, that '... [T]he aims of confiscating ill-
gotten gains on the one hand and of returning them to the victim on the
other are about as complementary as can be. One would expect them to be
considered together and the Court's powers to be used to that end'.[44]

CONCLUSION

The United Kingdom's Proceeds of Crime Act expands the ability to seize
and confiscate proceeds of fraud and corruption. While the United States'
powers are broader, in some respects, with the availability of civil forfeiture,
in other respects, the ability to seize proceeds in corruption cases is narrower, as proof of racketeering or money laundering is required. In addition,
as discussed above, since forfeiture is considered part of the criminal
sentence, this has led to constitutional challenges. Moreover, the United
States' ability to compensate victims is discretionary, and may not be
awarded if the court imposes a fine or a substantial jail sentence, or if the
defendant demonstrates an inability to pay.

---

[41] Powers of Criminal Courts Act 1973, para. 35, entered into force 1 July 1974.

[42] Criminal Justice Act 1988, Sec. 72(7). 'Where – (a) a court makes both a confiscation
order and an order for the payment of compensation under Section 35 of the Powers of
Criminal Courts Act 1973 against the same person in the same proceedings; and (b) it appears
to the court that he will not have sufficient means to satisfy both the orders in full, it shall
direct that so much of the compensation as will not in its opinion be recoverable, because of
the insufficiency of his means, shall be paid out of any sums recovered under the confiscation
order'.

[43] Southwark Crown Court Order No. T94 0361, dated 10 October 1994.

[44] *Id.*, at 16.

The United Kingdom's system of awarding compensation first out of confiscated funds aids the victims, and can be significant in corruption cases if public funds are involved.

JOHN GLOVER

13. Taxing the Proceeds of Corruption

Illegally acquired gains are taxable in most countries,[1] though revenue
codes are almost uniformly silent on the subject. A number of inconsistencies have resulted. Proceeds of crime have been brought into the revenue
net, accompanied by a range of jurisprudential and accounting problems.
Consider the United States: Congress received legislative power to tax
'incomes from whatever source derived' by the passage of the 16th Amendment in 1913. In the same year, a tax was imposed on income derived from
'any *lawful* business carried on for gain or profit'.[2] In 1916, without debate,
Congress omitted the word 'lawful', substituting an unqualified form of
words which still endures.[3] Senator Williams, moving the Senate's acceptance of the 1913 Bill, said that its 'object' was

> to tax a man's net income: that is to say, what he has at the end of the
> year after deducting from his receipts his expenditures or losses. It is not
> to reform men's moral characters; that is not the Act at all.[4]

Does this mean that wrongdoers are indiscriminately taxed on the amount
of their wrongful booty? Does it mean that they are entitled to deductions
for their most reprehensible expenses?

The theory of income tax describes it as a levy on persons, measured by
an index of their gains and advantages, or their 'control over society's

---

[1] E.g. UK: *Partridge* v. *Mallardaine* (1886) 3 TC 415; *Lindsay, Woodward and Hiscox*
v. *IRC* (1932) 18 TC 43; *IRC* v. *Aken* [1990] STC 197; P. Whiteman, etc., *Whiteman on
Income Tax* (3rd ed. (1988), 152–153; Canada: *R.* v. *Poynton* (1972) 72 DTC 6329; *Tax
Bulletin* IT 256R; Australia: Tax Ruling TR 93/25; R. Parsons, *Income Taxation in Australia*,
(1985), 32; US: *Commissioner of Internal Revenue* v. *Wilcox* 327 US 404 (1946); *James* v.
United States, 366 US 213 (1961); M. Chirelstein, *Federal Income Taxation*, 5th ed. (1988),
51; *but cf.* Ireland: *Hayes* v. *Duggan*, [1929] IR 406.
[2] Revenue Act of 1913, § 2B.
[3] Revenue Act of 1916, §2(a): *see now* the Internal Revenue Code of 1996, § 61(a)(1).
[4] Quoted in *Commissioner* v. *Tellier* 383 U.S. 687, 691 (1966).

Barry A.K. Rider (ed.), Corruption: The Enemy Within, 195–208
© *Kluwer Law International. Printed in the Netherlands.*

resources'.[5] Taxes which place significantly different burdens on taxpayers in similar economic circumstances are manifestly unfair. Taxes may also be unfair for failing to discriminate between persons according to their abilities to pay.[6] What are 'similar economic circumstances' and how much tax should increase with the ability to pay are matters of 'tax equity', which can be expressed as dimensions.[7] 'Horizontal' equity requires that persons in similar economic circumstances be treated equally. 'Vertical' equity requires that persons in different situations should be treated differently, so that those who are better off bear a greater share of the tax burden. Measurement by value of taxpayers' gains for the purpose of either dimension is the same. Leaving illegal income out of the tax base will mean that people with similar taxpaying capacities will not be taxed equally and the greater taxpaying ability of some will not be recognized. Allowing disapproval of illegal income sources to affect the relevant tax base is a kind of category mistake. Taxation's business has nothing to do with moral gestures. Its purpose is to raise money for the activities of government. All citizens, lawful or unlawful, should contribute according to their capacity to pay.

In *Rutkin* v. *United States*, the Supreme Court of the United States said:

An unlawful gain, as well as a lawful one, constitutes taxable income when its recipient has such control over it that, as a practical matter, he derives readily realizable economic value from it.[8]

Gains from immorality, the investment of lottery winnings, as well as from diligence and hard work are all taxed in an undiscriminating way. Indeed, it may be 'incongruous' for the gains of an honest labourer to be taxed, whilst the gains of the dishonest labourer are left immune.[9] Taxation laws are not penalties.[10] They are not concerned to discipline the source of gains. Other laws fulfil this task. Police and more coercive arms of government are better adapted to law enforcement. Taxpayer compliance with revenue laws is a resource to be employed for revenue purposes only.

---

[5] Henry C. Simons, *Personal Income Taxation: The Definition of Income as a Problem of Fiscal Policy* (1938), 49.

[6] *See Reform of the Australian Tax System:* Draft White Paper (1985), 14.

[7] *The Structure and Reform of Direct Taxation:* Report of a Committee Chaired by Professor J.E. Meade (1978), 7–11, 43–44.

[8] 342 U.S. 130, 137 (1952); *see also James* v. *United States* 366 U.S. 213, 218, Warren CJ (1961).

[9] *James* v.*United States* 366 U.S. 213, 218, Warren, CJ (1961).

[10] *See Bailey* v. *Drexal Furniture Co.* (the Child Labour case) 259 U.S. 20 (1922); *Fairfax* v. *FCT* 114 CLR 1, 17, Menzies J (1965), and text at note 61 below.

PROPERTY INTERESTS IN THE PROCEEDS OF CRIME

Assessability of the proceeds of crime differs between countries. Revenue systems sometimes exempt illegal income from the tax base, according to whether or not wrongdoers obtain title to the wrongful proceeds. Title is obtained when wrongdoers receive property rights by legal transfer from third parties. Title is not obtained where the proceeds are forcibly or fraudulently taken, or are otherwise misappropriated. A wrongdoer who consensually receives the funds of third parties might run an illegal betting ring or call-girl service, or sell illegal drugs. Third parties trading with the wrongdoer are usually not deceived or pressured into exchange, nor do they labour under a mistake of fact as to the nature of the business conducted. Instead, the wrongdoer's customers are *in pari delicto* with him or her and have, in consequence, no restitutionary right to recover money paid in the transaction.[11] Title to the proceeds superior to the wrongdoer's title cannot be shown – until, at least, a forfeiture or confiscation order is made after the wrongdoer's apprehension. Misappropriated funds are in a different category. Whoever was deprived against his or her will remains the true owner of the funds and the wrongdoer obtains, at best, a voidable title. Proceeds are subject to restitutionary entitlements. A wrongdoer's victim can oblige him or her to disgorge a misappropriated fund and pay the same to the person truly entitled. It has been observed of 'a common thief' that he or she acquires

> not a semblance of right, title or interest in his plunder, and whether he spends it or not, he is indebted to his victim in the full amount taken as surely as if he had left a promissory note at the scene of the crime.[12]

In terms of property interest, the question for this paper is whether the fruits of corruption fall into the irrecoverable *in pari delicto* category, or into the category for which restitutionary claims are made. Fruits of corruption are primarily bribes. Do people bribed obtain superior title to the payments made to pervert their integrity in the performance of public or private duty? The answer is 'no', provisionally, although for long it was thought to be 'yes'. Bribes are now in the restitutionary category. A short excursus into history is needed to put this answer into perspective.

'By the early years of the nineteenth century', said Lord Diplock in the British House of Lords,

> it had become an established principle that an agent who received any secret advantage for himself from the other party to a transaction in which

---

[11] *See* R. Goff and G. Jones, *The Law of Restitution* (4th ed. 1993), 505–512.
[12] *James* v. *United States* 366 U.S. 213, 251, Whittaker J (dis.) (1961).

the agent was acting for his principal was bound to acquire it for his principal ... The remedy was equitable, obtainable in a Court of Chancery.[13]

The latter part of the 19th century, however, was a time of high popularity for the English legal remedy of 'money had and received'. This was an action which resulted in a money judgment *in personam* against the defendant. No property right was conferred.[14] For many years, wronged principals recovered bribes as 'money had and received' by their agents and they were allowed no more than personal remedies.[15] Interlocutory proceedings in *Lister & Co.* v. *Stubbs*[16] demonstrate how equity's proprietary reach was curtailed.[17] Stubbs was Lister & Co.'s dishonest purchasing officer, who accepted bribes in the course of his duties. He invested the proceeds in land. Lister & Co., in the course of proceedings, sought an injunction to restrain Stubbs from dealing with the land. The issue arose whether the deceived employer had a proprietary interest in the bribes and the land in order to justify the injunction. A strongly constituted British Court of Appeal denied the employer's claim. It represented, Lord Justice Lindley said, 'the unsoundness of confounding ownership with obligation'.[18] Stubbs was under an obligation to account to his employer for the bribes and no more. Property in the bribes themselves (and their product) remained in the bribee. Such an approach was affirmed in the Court of Appeal seven times, most lately in 1986. Until lately it still received respectable academic support.[19]

In 1994, the Privy Council in *Attorney General for Hong Kong* v. *Reid*[20] decided in that an equitable proprietary right did flow from a breach of fiduciary duty constituted by the receipt of bribes. Mr. Reid was a New

---

[13] *Thambiah* v. *Malaysia Government Officers' Co-operative Housing Society Ltd.* [1979] AC 374, 380 (PC).

[14] *See* A. Burrows, *The Law of Restitution* (1993), 29–30; S. Stoljar, *The Law of Quasi-Contract* (2nd ed., 1989), 7–10.

[15] *See Metropolitan Bank* v. *Heiron* (1880) 5 Ex D 319 (CA) and *Boston Deep Sea Fishing and Ice Co.* v. *Ansell* (1888) 39 Ch D 339 (CA) – bribed company directors; *Lister & Co.* v. *Stubbs* (1890) 45 Ch D 1 (CA) – bribed purchasing agent; *Andrews* v. *Ramsay & Co. Ltd.* [1903] 2 KB 635 (CA) – bribed auctioneer; *Powell & Thomas* v. *Evan Jones & Co.* [1905] 1 KB 11 (CA) – bribed borrower's agent; *Attorney General* v. *Goddard* (1929) 98 LJKB 743 – bribed police officer; *Reading* v. *R.* [1948] 2 KB 268 (1st. inst. only) – bribed army sergeant.

[16] (1890) 45 Ch D 1 (CA).

[17] *See* discussion of *Keech* v. *Sandford* (1726) Sel. Cas. Ch. 61 in *Attorney General for Hong Kong* v. *Reed* [1994] 1 AC 324, 335 (PC), Lord Templeman.

[18] *Ibid.*, 13, Cotton and Bowen LJJ agreeing.

[19] Attorney General's Reference (No. 1) of 1985 [1986] 1 QB 491 (CA); *see* P. Birks, *Introduction to the Law of Restitution*, rvd. ed. (1989), 377–399; P. Watts (1994) 110 LQR 178; R. Peace [1994] LMCLQ 189; D. Crilley [1994] RLR 73.

[20] [1994] 1 AC 324 (PC).

Zealand national. He rose to become the (acting) Director of Public Prosecutions in Hong Kong. In breach of the fiduciary duty which he owed as a servant of the Crown, Reid accepted bribes as an inducement to hinder certain prosecutions. He was eventually arrested, imprisoned and ordered to pay a sum equal to the value of those of his assets which could only have derived from bribes. Among Reid's assets was some freehold land in New Zealand, registered in his own and his solicitor's names. Against this, the Attorney General for Hong Kong lodged caveats. Action was commenced to sustain the caveator's entitlement. The New Zealand Court of Appeal,[21] relying with misgivings on the settled authority of *Lister* v. *Stubbs*,[22] held that the Crown had no caveatable property interest. Lord Templeman for the Board in *Reid*'s case reversed this and upheld the submission that equitable proprietary interests can be based in no more than a fiduciary's receipt of bribes. 'Property', he said,

> acquired by a trustee as a result of a criminal breach of trust and the property from time to time representing the same must belong in equity to his *cestui que* trust [the Crown] and not to the [wrongdoer], whether he is solvent or insolvent.[23]

This decision, though not binding on common law jurisdictions outside New Zealand, is yet the persuasive view of a high tribunal. It puts most of the fruits of corruption clearly within the second, restitutionary category. Corrupt bribees have no beneficial interest in bribes they receive and must pass them to the principal properly entitled. It is as though the relevant proceeds had been stolen from a bank.

MISAPPROPRIATED FUNDS

Long after illegal gains were generally considered assessable, no gain was thought to be realized in the absence of beneficial title. Receipt of criminal proceeds consisting of misappropriated funds was conceived to be no more taxable than receipt of borrowed funds.[24] The 'off-setting obligation to repay' was the thing said to disqualify receipt of funds of either type from being a taxable gain.[25] Misappropriation negatived income derivation. Say, a violent thief stole money from a bank – and perhaps obtained funds by deceptions practised on his neighbours as well. How, it was thought, could

---

[21] [1992] 2 NZLR 385 (CA).
[22] (1890) 45 Ch D 1 (CA).
[23] [1994] 1 AC 324, 311 (PC).
[24] *See James* v. *United States* 366 U.S. 213, 227 (1961), Black J (dis.).
[25] *McKnight* v. *Commissioner of Internal Revenue* 127 F. 2d 572, 573 (1942), Sable J.

the misappropriator 'gain' or, in a taxable sense, 'enjoy', what at all times rightfully belonged to others?

This was the one-time view of the US Supreme Court, reversed in 1961. In that year, the *James* v. *United States*[26] majority decided that an obligation to repay funds did not deflect a tax liability on the same as income. Repayment was due after the taxable event occurred. Liability for income tax on a gain did not depend on possessing title to it. Rather, the taxpayer's 'control' over the misappropriated funds prior to restoring them was the taxable thing. Control gave access to 'readily realisable economic value' that the funds represented until the time for repayment came.[27]

Canadians take a similar view. In *Sura* v. *Minister of National Revenue*,[28] the Supreme Court of Canada considered the matter in relation to a matrimonial regime in Quebec which provided for a spousal 'community' of property acquired during a marriage. Husbands were legally entitled to administer and dispose of the property whilst a marriage subsisted. Mr. Sura argued that a fiscal consequence of the 'community' was that he was only liable for the tax on half of his salary and rentals income during a particular year – his wife being liable for the other half. The claim was denied. Justice Taschereau said that 'the Income Tax' is imposed on 'the person and not the property':[29]

> The Act does not address itself to capital or ownership of property. It addresses itself to the person and the amount of tax is determined by the benefits that the person receives.[30]

Australian and United Kingdom laws differ from North American laws on this point. First, we will consider Australia, where in relevant ways the taxation system is comparable to those in the United States and Canada. A 'global' sense of income is employed. Income character depends on conformability to concept, in a sense undefined by statute. Definition is left to the courts. One persuasive statement is contained in *Commissioner of Inland Revenue* v. *Glenshaw Glass Co.* 'Income', Warren CJ said, is comprised of 'undeniable accessions to wealth, clearly realized, and over which taxpayers have complete dominion'.[31] Australian thieves are not

---

[26] 366 U.S. 213 (1961), Warren CJ, Brennan, Stewart, Clark and Frankfurter JJ.

[27] *Ibid.*, 218, Warren CJ.

[28] (1962) 62 DTC 1005.

[29] *Ibid.*, 1006 (for the Court), quoting *McLeod* v. *Minister of Customs and Excise* (1926) 1 DTC 85, Mignault J (SC of Can.).

[30] *Ibid.*, 1009.

[31] 348 U.S. 426, 413 (1955); *see also* FCT v. *Dixon* (1952) 86 CLR 540, 564–565, Fullager J, FCT v. *Whitfords Beach Pty. Ltd.* (1982) 39 ALR 521; and R. Parsons, 'The Meaning of Income and the Structure of the Income Tax Assessment Act' 23 *Taxation in Australia* (1978), 378.

taxable on proceeds they misappropriate. Nor can they be liable for the offence of failing to disclose those proceeds in their tax returns in the years of theft. Such an outcome is associated with a supposed Australian orthodoxy in revenue matters that 'the character of a [taxable] gain' must involve the same being 'derived by the taxpayer beneficially'.[32] Confusion concerning the application of United Kingdom authorities decided in relation to a different system of income taxation is evident, as we will see.[33]

The decision in *Zobory* v. *FCT*[34] confirmed the Australian property interest requirement. Mr. Zobory was a thief. He stole more than $1 million from his employer and invested it in interest-bearing accounts in his name. For two years Zobory filed income tax returns which showed interest earned on the money taken from his employer as part of his own income. Then he was found out. Zobory was convicted of theft and consented to judgment in a civil suit brought by his employer to recover the $1 million. The sum was duly repaid, together with the interest that had accrued during the period that it was wrongfully possessed. Zobory then objected to previously being assessed in accordance with his returns – contending that the money taken was at all times held by him for the employer on constructive trust. The intended effect was that the employer would be at all times liable for the tax. The Full Court of the Federal Court overturned Zobory's prior assessment. Speaking for the Court, Burchett J made reference to the 'fundamental principle' that the Income Tax Assessment Act 1936 (Com) is 'directed to income to which a taxpayer is beneficially entitled'.[35] Liability to pay tax on the interest that Zobory earned and had the use of was diverted to the employer beneficially entitled.[36]

Misappropriated funds are similarly exempt from taxation in the United Kingdom, although the word 'income' in the Revenue Code functions in a manner different from Australia, the United States, Canada and comparable jurisdictions.[37] The basis of the difference is historical, as tax lawyers know. It reflects the form of the earliest British 'income tax', introduced during the Napoleonic wars. Only a small and affluent minority were liable. Species of income were described by schedules, each referring to a different source. These include income from employment, income from trading, income from rents, income from woodlands, and so forth. Payers of wages, rents, interest and other sums identified by the schedules as income in the payees' hands are required to deduct basic income tax and transmit it to the

---

[32] R. Parsons, *Income Taxation in Australia* (1985), 36–38: 'propositions' 4 and 5 on the nature of income.

[33] Unqualified use of United Kingdom authorities was made in Taxation Ruling TR 93/25: *see below*, note 37.

[34] (1995) 129 ALR 484; *also MacFarlane* v. *FCT* (1986) 13 FCR 356.

[35] *Ibid.*, 486.

[36] *Ibid.*, 487.

[37] *See* the Income and Corporations Taxes Act 1988 (UK), ss. 18 and 19.

revenue. Tax is deducted from the income flow before the payee has a chance to spend it.[38] Hence gains today made by United Kingdom taxpayers are liable to income tax only to the extent that they have a source within one or more of the schedules described in the Revenue Code. The web is not seamless. Gains of criminals must fall within schedule D, case 1, 'profits or gains arising from [a] trade'. Otherwise they are essentially outside the net. Criminals are rarely in 'employment' in deriving the gains that they do. Nor do they derive income as 'rent', or from the 'occupation of woodlands', referred to in other schedules. The inquiry as to whether a given criminal is taxable centres on whether his or her activities have 'the indicia of trade'.[39] Britain's regime has limited potential for taxing the proceeds of crime. For the purpose of schedule D, case 1, British courts do not acknowledge the trades of 'burglary', bank robbery or murder-for-hire.[40] Illegality can be at most 'incidental' to a recognized trade.[41] Beyond this, an antimony between criminality and trade exists. 'Where illegality goes to the root of a trade', Keith Day remarks, '[its] profits or gains may be viewed as the proceeds of crime and, as such, are not chargeable to tax'.[42]

TAXATION AND FORFEITURE

Over the last few decades, organized crime has become the preoccupation of law enforcers. Dangers to the institutions of modern society posed by organized crime are perceived to far outweigh those resulting from solitary criminal acts.[43] Strategies for controlling organized crime are 'targeted upwards', to removed higher echelon criminals,[44] and targeted *consequentially*, to remove the fruits of crime. Law enforcers have sought to 'financially incapacitate' offenders by seizing and forfeiting the profits of crime.[45] Confiscation legislation has been introduced in the United

---

[38]   J.A. Kay and M.A. King, *The British Tax System*, 2nd ed. (1980), 64–67.

[39]   M. Mulholland and R. Cockfield, 'The Implications of Illegal Trading' [1995], *British Tax Review* 572, 573–575; *also* K. Day, 'The Tax Consequences of Illegal Trading' [1971] *British Tax Review* 104, 108–109.

[40]   *See J.P. Harrison (Watford) Ltd.* v. *Griffiths* (1962) 40 TC 281, 299, Lord Denning.

[41]   K. Day, note 39, 108; e.g. a regulatory infringement – like loading a ship over the Plimsoll line.

[42]   *Ibid.*, 115.

[43]   Noted by M. Beare, 'Efforts to Combat Money Laundering: Canada' 18 *Commonwealth Law Bulletin* (1992), 1435; *see also* A. Freiberg 'Criminal Confiscation, Profit and Liberty' 25 *ANZJ Crim* 44 (1992), 48.

[44]   M. Beare, *ibid.*, 1437–1438.

[45]   *Id.*; *also* C. Corns, 'Inter-agency relations: some hidden obstacles to combatting organized crime?' (1992) 25 *ANZJ Crim* 169, 169–170.

States,[46] the United Kingdom,[47] Australia,[48] and Canada[49] – with the common purpose of 'tracing, freezing and confiscating' the proceeds of criminal activity.[50]

Confiscation under the forfeiture legislation in part has an administrative (or civil) nature, although the statutory mechanisms are in form adjunctive to criminal proceedings.[51]

In the United States, confiscation orders under RICO and similar statutes[52] have certain civil law characteristics. For example, § 1963 (c) of Title 18 of the United States Code provides that

> [A]ll right, title, and interest in [property derived from racketeering activity] vests in the United States[,]

which is similar to relation-back in bankruptcy.[53] Since Jacobean times, property which belonged to a bankrupt at the time of his or her earliest act of bankruptcy vested in the bankruptcy trustee.[54] Fraudulent dealings perpetrated by the insolvent on the eve of bankruptcy are thereby overcome.

---

[46] *See* esp. Racketeer Influenced and Corrupt Organizations Act of 1970 (Title IX of the Organized Crime Control Act); USCA §1961–§1968 ('RICO').

[47] Following the Hodgson Committee Report (1984), forfeiture was introduced as an ancillary but little used sanction for offences under the Drug Trafficking Offences Act 1986 and the Criminal Justice Act 1988. The Proceeds of Crime Act 1995 has now made forfeiture obligatory, unless the offender is impecunious, or the victim intends to bring restitutionary proceedings: *see* K. Talbot, 'The Proceeds of Crime Act 1995', *New Law Journal* (1995), 1857.

[48] The Proceeds of Crime Act 1987 (Com); Confiscation of Proceeds of Crime Act 1989 (NSW) [*see also* the Drug Trafficking Civil Proceedings Act 1990 (NSW)]; Crimes (Confiscation of Profits) Act 1986 (Vic); Crimes (Confiscation of Profits) Act 1989 (Qld); Crimes (Confiscation of Profits) Act 1986 (SA); Crimes (Confiscation of Profits) Act 1988 (WA); Crimes (Forfeiture of Profits) Act 1988 (NT).

[49] The Canadian Criminal Code was amended in 1989 by Bill C-61 to allow forfeiture of the proceeds of 'enterprise crime offences', associated with organized criminal activity: *see* s. 462.3.

[50] A. Freiberg, 'Criminal Confiscation, Profit and Liberty', 25 *ANZJ Crim* (1992), 44, 45.

[51] *See* A. Freiberg and R. Fox, 'Forfeiture, Confiscation and Sentencing' in B. Fisse, D. Taylor and G. Coss (eds.), *The Money Trail: Confiscation of the Proceeds of Crime, Money Laundering and Cash Transaction Reporting* (1992), 106, 127–128; A. Freiberg, '"Civilising" Crime: Parallel Proceedings and the Civil Remedies Function of the Commonwealth Director of Public Prosecutions', 21 *Aust. and NZ Journal of Criminology* (1988), 129, 131–132.

[52] E.g., the Comprehensive Drug Abuse Prevention and Control Act of 1970: s. 511 – forfeiture of controlled substances, raw materials and equipment used in manufacture, and conveyances including aircraft used in transportation, etc.

[53] *See US* v. *Delco Wire and Cable Co. Inc.* 722 F. Supp. 1511 (1991); *US* v. *Ianniello* 621 F. Supp. 1455 (1985).

[54] The Act of 1604 (1 James I, c.15) introduced the relation-back idea, whilst treating bankruptcy as a crime: *Lewis's Australian Bankruptcy Law*, D. Rose (9th ed., 1990), 12–15. *See now* Bankruptcy Act 1966 (Com), s. 116(1); Insolvency Act 1986 (UK), s. 238.

In another *simulacrum* of the civil law, the government can bring *ex parte* proceedings prior to trial to obtain a 'restraining order' – comparable to a '*Mareva* injunction'.[55] The agency can be permitted to seize criminal proceeds if 'there is a substantial probability' that a conviction will one day result and that the 'need to preserve [their] availability ... outweighs the hardship on any party'.[56]

Confiscation legislation in Australia, by contrast, is conviction-based.[57] The Australian Proceeds of Crime Act 1987 (Com) is an example. The statue empowers courts to make a 'forfeiture order' under Section 19, in respect of property which is 'tainted property in respect of the offence'. A 'pecuniary penalty order' under Section 26 may be made in respect of money or property that came into the possession of the wrongdoer by reason of the commission of the offence. In both cases the court's jurisdiction is conditional on the defendant being convicted, found guilty of, having admitted or absconded in relation to a crime.[58]

Forfeiture proceedings are to be contrasted with the way in which revenue authorities create tax liability. By way of example, we will examine how the Australian Commissioner of Taxation ('the Commissioner') generates an assessment under Section 166 of the Income Tax Assessment Act 1936 (Aust.) and this matures into taxpayer indebtedness. Relying on self-assessment under Section 169A, a return of income that the taxpayer may have lodged, or any other information in his or her possession, the Commissioner computes both the taxpayer's taxable income and the tax payable thereon. Computation is an administrative act. Regard is not paid to fairness considerations, including whether the taxpayer should be given a hearing. Any exercises of discretion involved are reviewable, administratively, by a tribunal under Section 14ZZ(b). Then, on a question of law, or directly from an assessment, the matter may be appealed judicially to the Federal Court.[59] Before this judicial tribunal, the applicant taxpayer has the burden of proving that the assessment is excessive and/or incorrect and/or should not have been made. All this contrasts with forfeiture procedure. By contrast, an agency seeking to confiscate assets must usually have established beyond reasonable doubt that the wrongdoer has committed an offence. Disparity between tax and forfeiture procedures has prompted some commentators to suggest that governments should employ the taxing power

---

[55] *Viz.*, an injunction to restrain the defendant from dealing with assets under his or her control so as to frustrate judgment in the plaintiff's favour – as in *Mareva Compania Naviera SA* v. *International Bulk Carriers SA* [1975] 2 *Lloyd's Reports* 509.

[56] 18 USC § 1963 (e): *see US* v. *Perholtz* 622 F. Supp. 1253 (1985), *US* v. *Musson* 802 F. 2d 384 (1986) and *US* v. *Regan* 699 F. Supp. 36 (1988).

[57] With two exceptions: proceedings under the Customs Act 1901 (Com) and under the Drug Trafficking (Civil Proceedings) Act 1990 (NSW).

[58] *See* ss. 14(2), 26(1) and 5(1) of the Proceeds of Crime Act 1987 (Com).

[59] *See* paragraphs 14ZZ(a) and 14ZZ(c) of the Income Tax Assessment Act 1936 (Com).

more in the fight against organized crime.[60] Criminals, it is thought, could as easily be disabled by punitive tax assessments as by forfeitures. Proceedings with an imprisonment sanction might be commenced for the non-declaration of illegal income gains.[61]

Can a tax law be used as a forfeiture or penalty in this way? This is a question which only arises where lawmakers are bound by constitutional limitation. Parliament in the United Kingdom is omnipotent, of course. Not even an established British custom requires that taxes and forfeitures be kept distinct.[62] Things are otherwise in the United States. In *Bailey* v. *Drexal Furniture Co.*,[63] the Supreme Court was concerned with the constitutionality of a tax on manufacturers which imposed a differential rate, according to the state of child working conditions. Its purpose was to ameliorate the children's lot. The Court struck down this levy as a penalty 'plainly within state power' and not a proper subject for a taxing Act.[64] In the early years of the Australian federation, too, it was thought that a law was not 'with respect to taxation', within Section 51 (ii) of the Constitution, if the purpose of the statute was to achieve some end other than the raising of money.[65] However, in *Fairfax* v. *FCT*[66] it was held that a tax could be valid even though its purpose was collateral to the proper exercise of a taxing power. Validity of a tax law depended on the 'substance of the enactment', Justice Fullagar said, and that 'substance' was the obligation that the Act imposed.[67] Levies imposed by justiciable criteria and expressed to be of general application were sufficiently 'a tax'. Menzies J in the same case, after agreeing, went on to express the view that 'a special prohibitive tax upon income derived from the sale of opium' was not a tax 'on its true nature and character'. It was instead 'a law to suppress heroin'. This suggests that a 'prohibitive' tax to suppress undesirable activities might be intrinsically invalid – at least, when its 'true character' was determined. However, it is hard to see how the investigation could proceed. For the *Fairfax* majority eschewed characterization of an Act by its economic consequences, or by speculation on the legislative motives which inspired

---

[60] E.g., F. Costigan, *Report of the Royal Commission on the Activities of the Federated Ship Painters and Dockers Union*, vol. 5, chap. 9, para. 9.027 (1985); D. Cameron, *Attacking the Proceeds of Crime: An Investigative Perspective*, paper presented to the National Crime Authority Proceeds of Crime Conference, Sydney, June 1993.

[61] Al Capone, the famous racketeer, was convicted in 1931 and sentenced to 11 years in prison for federal tax evasion. He died in gaol. *See* J. Kobler, *The Life and World of Al Capone* (1971).

[62] *See* W.R. Anson, *The Law and Custom of the Constitution: Part I: Parliament* (3rd. ed., 1897), 36–37.

[63] The 'Child Labour Case': 259 US 20.

[64] *Ibid.*, 43, Taft CJ.

[65] *R.* v. *Barger* (1908) 6 CLR 41, 74, Griffiths CJ, Barton and O'Connor JJ.

[66] (1965) 114 CRL 1.

[67] *Ibid.*, 13.

it.[68] Finally, in *State Chamber of Commerce and Industry* v. *Commonwealth* in 1987, the Australian High Court majority disapproved of the Menzies limitation, so far as it expanded the 'prohibitive' word.[69] Another view has been advanced by the commentator Leslie Zines.[70] A taxing obligation, he says, must allow a taxpayer to act or not to act so as to render him or her self liable to the imposition of the levy. Which is to say, a tax on the proceeds of organized crime, drug dealing, gangland killings, or other misdeeds, must be couched in a way which impliedly authorizes the events – a morally agnostic levy, as it were.

Precedent for such relativism exists in the United States. Some 18 state governments have lately enacted Marijuana and Controlled Substance Taxation Acts. The proceeds of drug dealing are assessed and the activity is not otherwise sanctioned. The purposes of these statutes seem to be as follows. State authorities desire to overcome a 'linkage' problem with forfeiture statues. Establishing a connection between illicit drug activities and assets to be seized is often problematic. Say, a drug dealer trades out of an expensive automobile – crawling along gutters and through deserted laneways. When he or she is apprehended, it may transpire that the vehicle is owned and registered in the name of the dealer's brother, or parent, or some other person whose knowledge of the drug dealing cannot be proven. The vehicle then cannot be forfeited as property 'tainted' with the crime. If, however, the same drug dealer fails to pay the assessed amount of the drug dealer's tax, his or her general assets can be sold until the liability is satisfied. Another reason why state governments impose the tax may be concerned with a desire to take a 'cut' of the proceeds of a lucrative trade conducted within state borders. The (Federal) Drug Enforcement Agency funds much of its activities from the sale of the forfeited assets of wrongdoers within its reach.[71] State governments in the United States may intend something as parasitic as the former federal tax on coin-operated gaming devices, wagering and bookmaking activities.[72]

---

[68] *Ibid.*, 11–12, Kitto J, 17, Menzies J (Barwick CJ agreeing).

[69] (1987) 163 CLR 329, 353, Mason CJ, Wilson, Dawson, Toohey, Gaudron JJ.

[70] *The High Court and the Constitution*, 3rd. ed. (1992), 33.

[71] (Unsigned article) 'Levying a Tax on Drugs and Dealers', *BJA Asst Forfeiture Bulletin* (Dec. 1989), 3, 4.

[72] US (federal) stamp taxes were imposed on coin-operated gaming devices (26 USC 4461–4), wagers (26 USC 4401–5) and bookmaking (26 USC 4411–24), repealed in 1981 after the 'Commission on the Review of the National Policy towards Gambling' reported: *see* R. King, 'Let's Not Deregulate Organized Crime' 13 *Tax Notes* (1981), 259.

PROBLEMS WITH THE TAXATION OF CRIME

Taxes which appear to legitimate illegal activities may be an unacceptable affront to public morals. Not only must the illegal activity be *permitted*, we have noted, for the levy to have the character of a tax, but information gathered must be *confidential*, if canons of revenue neutrality are to be observed.[73] Information which would assist in the criminals' detection and conviction must be withheld from law enforcement authorities. In the Minnesota Marijuana and Controlled Substance Taxation Act 1986, for example, 'marijuana' is defined as something 'possessed, transported, sold or offered to be sold in violation of Minnesota laws'.[74] Then the Act goes on to provide:

297D.13 *Confidential nature of information*
Subdivision 1. Disclosure prohibited.
... neither the commissioner nor any public employee may reveal facts ... obtained from a tax obligor; nor can any information ... obtained from a tax obligor be used against the tax obligor in any criminal proceeding.

Exposing criminals to a standard and non-discriminatory income tax might be less objectionable. Taxpayer criminality under the revenue codes, we noted, is something neither sanctioned nor approved.[75] The position of the Australian Commissioner is fairly typical. He or she is given a discretion to pass on confidentially acquired information to the National Crimes Authority, though that information can only be used in 'intelligence' operations and not as evidence in a criminal proceeding.[76]

Another problem with using income tax assessments to discourage crime occurs where criminal taxpayers attempt to deduct expenses and losses tainted by illegal activities. Say, a criminal assessed on the proceeds of a bank robbery incurs the cost of ropes used to bind bank staff and/or bullets with which to shoot them. Should deductions for these outlays be allowed? The question seems a little fanciful. Revenue authorities are usually not interested in assessing persons sentenced to long terms of imprisonment and whose assets are otherwise forfeited. 'Public policy', also, could be invoked to fortify the disallowance, if ever such expense claims were made. However, what of the deductibility of expenses which are not morally reprehensible, like a restitutionary payment to the victim of a crime? Can a thief deduct from his or her taxable income the $1000 he or she is ordered to repay to the crime victim? Paragraph 54(1)(b) of the Australian Income Tax Assessment Act 1939 (Com)

[73] *See* S. Ross and P. Burgess, *Income Tax: A Critical Analysis* (1991), 18.
[74] Minnesota Statutes 296–299, 297 D.01, Subdivision 1.
[75] At note 1.
[76] Income Tax Assessment Act 1936 (Com), s. 16(4) and the Taxation Administration Act 1953, ss. 3E, 3D; *see* R. Galbally, 'Corporate and Commercial Crime: The New Emphasis', 65 *Law Institute Journal* (1991), 826, 827–828.

is explicit on restitutionary payments. A taxpayer cannot deduct 'an amount ordered by a court, upon conviction of a person ... to be paid by the person'. Is there then a 'purpose' in the Australian revenue legislation to 'penalize illegal business by taxing gross rather an net income'?[77] We have noted revenue's moral agnosticism about crime and the source of income. Has a 'neutral mechanism to collect revenue' become to this extent 'an instrument to punish persons convicted of crime'?[78] The answer should be consistent with the position that revenue authorities take towards assessing the proceeds of crime. Alternatively, some principle of public policy in revenue matters must be found to the effect that *honest* taxpayers are to be assessed on their taxable income (after deductions are subtracted) and *dishonest* taxpayers are to be assessed on their gross income.[79] Are courts, indeed, the most appropriate bodies to find this sort of public policy? This is a problem with misappropriated funds which has only surfaced in the United States. In the United Kingdom and Australia it is avoided – so long as Zobory remains immune from assessment on funds to which he is not beneficially entitled.[80] Anglo-Australian bank robbers are still at large in this tax respect.

Another problem with taxing illegal income is allocation of that income between participants in a multi-party venture. Allocation in this respect parallels the 'linkage' problem in forfeiture: establishing connections between criminals and assets to be seized. Assume another 'misappropriated assets' case, an armed robbery. One participant drives the getaway car. Another covers the bank personnel with her gun. Another raids the cash drawers. The fourth accomplice carries the stolen proceeds. All are apprehended in the following tax year. Assume that the revenue is prevailed upon to raise an assessment on each robber. In what proportions have the robbers earned income constituted by the proceeds stolen? An equitable solution might be to attribute each robber with 25 per cent of the haul. A preferred solution for the Commissioner might be for each robber to be attributed with 100 per cent of the haul – leaving the robbers to bear the onus of proving that they derived some lesser proportion.[81] An arbitrary exercise of discretion, perhaps, but by what facts could it be impeached?

---

[77] R. Peace and C. Messere, 'Tax Deductions and Illegal Activities: The Effects of Recent Tax Legislation', 20 *Rutgers Law Journal* (1989), 415, 418.

[78] R. Manicke, 'A Tax Deduction for Restitutionary Payments? Solving the Dilemma of the Thwarted Investor', *University of Illinois Law Review* (1992), 593, 614.

[79] R. Peace and C. Messere, note 77, 421–422.

[80] (1995) 129 ALR 484: *see* note 18.

[81] Under paras. 14ZZK(b) and 14ZZO(b) of the Australian Taxation Administration Act 1953 (Com), the taxpayer has the burden of showing that the assessment is excessive. A comparable 'presumption of correctness' obtains in the United States and Canada: *see* L. Rosenblatt, 'The Allocation of Unreported Income Among Participants in a Criminal Enterprise: Can the Commissioner Impose Honour Among Thieves?' 64 *Taxes: The Tax Magazine* (1986), 415, 416.

HENRY H. ROSSBACHER AND TRACY W. YOUNG

14. The Foreign Corrupt Practices Act: An American Response to Corruption

INTRODUCTION

In King Henry VIII, Cardinal Wolsey, in his final speech of expiation, urges Cromwell to act honourably, arguing: 'corruption wins not more than honesty'.[1] Hopefully, the radical nature of this sentiment did not cause the historic burning of the Globe Theatre during the inaugural performances of the play.[2] Just as Wolsey's recantation of his past sins and practices came a little too late with much too little, so American and, especially, international anti-corruption efforts have been either nonexistent or, at the least, largely admonitory.

Wolsey's adjuration is unreflected in the international business climate of today. Regrettably, bribery and corruption, endemic to certain cultures and a mainstay of human greed, is now, as it has always been, a thorn in our righteous side. Corruption is as old as man. Yet throughout history good men have fought back. The Bible condemns corruption throughout, from the Old Testament's fire and brimstone threats of destruction after 'God looked on the earth, and ... [beheld], it was corrupt',[3] to the New Testament's more poetic approach, 'For oppression makes a wise man mad, and a bribe corrupts the heart'.[4]

In conjunction with religious condemnation, man has also fought back with laws seeking to expose and punish various forms of corruption. This article will address primarily that insidious form of corruption known as bribery, and more particularly the international aspects of corruption by bribery within the context of the American response to domestic corruption.

---

[1] Shakespeare, *King Henry VIII*, Act 3, Scene 2, Line 444 (New Cambridge Shakespeare 1996).

[2] *Ibid.*, pp. 1–4. Britain has hardly been a leader in anti-corruption efforts, as this headline from *The Independent* of London shows: 'Britain Spurns US Over Bribes'. The article noted that 'Britain has refused to join other governments in immediate action against bribery and corruption in trade between developed and developing countries. An appeal by a senior United States official for Britain to adopt measures to prevent companies paying bribes to obtain contracts overseas has failed to change the Government's stance.' (3 April 1994).

[3] *See* Genesis 6:12–13.

[4] *See* Ecclesiastes 7:7.

Barry A.K. Rider (ed.), Corruption: The Enemy Within, 209–230
© *Kluwer Law International. Printed in the Netherlands.*

Until the Watergate scandals and Nixon debacle during the 1970s, there was no specific law curbing the practice of Americans and American businesses bribing *foreign* officials, and the government had not expressed any official concern about such practices. The Watergate scandal and resulting investigation of illegal domestic political contributions helped to focus attention on what America would soon learn was a shockingly prevalent practice, the bribery of foreign officials by American nationals.

When the magnitude of the problem was finally exposed, the public outcry was deafening. Highly public Congressional hearings revealed that numerous prominent corporations, including Lockheed, Exxon and Gulf Oil, had engaged in such illegal practices on a grand scale. The hearings resulted in a call for legislation, as well as public condemnation rooted in the moral and religious underpinnings on which America was founded. Corruption was seen as antithetical to the concept of 'pure' competition underlying America's faith in capitalism and free-market enterprise.[5]

The resulting legislation, the Foreign Corrupt Practices Act ('the Act'), signed into law by then-President Jimmy Carter on 19 December 1977, and passed by both houses of Congress without a single dissenting vote, was sweeping, yet appears to be relatively ineffective in curbing the problem it addresses. I will discuss the details of the Act in a moment, but suffice it to say, it has not been demonstrably effective in eradicating the problem in American corporations or, more tellingly, in enlisting foreign cooperation in joint efforts to reform international business practices. It does not, however, represent an imperialist extension of unprecedented prohibitions solely to foreigners but, instead, the extension of American domestic rules to the foreign activities of American economic participants.

THE AMERICAN DOMESTIC ANTI-CORRUPTION RESPONSE

The Law's Prohibitions

American's shock was not confined to foreign sins; increased scrutiny was primarily directed at domestic offences. Throughout the years since, the American response to domestic corruption has led to a sweeping series of laws attempting to constrain and punish politicians and government bureaucrats and those who seek to corruptly influence them. Punishments, in fact, vary – some swift, some sure, some illusory – but all are aimed at eradica-

---

[5] Pines, Comment, 'Amending the Foreign Corrupt Practices Act to Include a Private Right of Action', 82 *Calif. L. Rev.* 185, 186–188 (1994) (hereinafter 'Pines'); *see* Donald R. Cruver, *Complying with the Foreign Corrupt Practices Act, a Guide for U.S. Firms Doing Business in the International Market Place*, 1–5 (ABA 1994) (hereinafter 'Cruver'). The Cruver pamphlet is an excellent treatment of the Act aimed at compliance issues. It can be purchased from the American Bar Association at an immodest price.

tion of domestic corruption. I include a brief sketch here of the domestic scene in order that the American foreign anti-corruption initiative can be seen to fit relatively comfortably within the American domestic scheme.

The first set of prohibitions affects our federal appointed officials. These strictures are based on federal statutes, regulations and executive orders.[6] The laws provide not only ethical rules but also severe criminal sanctions for illegal acceptance of bribes, gratuities and salaries from private parties or from any source other than the government. The laws penalize equally the payer and the recipient of the proscribed payments.[7] In brief, corruption is a crime, the rules are strict, and prosecution can be merciless.[8]

The second set of prohibitions affects Senators and Representatives. These rules, issued internally by the Senate and House of Representatives, have recently been tightened. In brief, they supplement the applicable criminal statutes, limiting and requiring the reporting of gifts to federal legislators.[9]

---

[6] The most current and comprehensive compendium of these legal restrictions are contained in *Standards of Ethical Conduct for Employees of the Executive Branch* (US Office of Gov't Ethics 1996). The publication cites and explains, with extensive discussion and examples, the rules and procedures. It also contains a comprehensive list of related statutes of government-wide application. It does not cover statutes limited in application to a particular government department (e.g., Meat Inspection Act of 1907, Title 21, U.S.C. §§ 601–691, applicable to employees of the Department of Agriculture). A more limited guide is also published by the United States Office of Government Ethics: *Do It Right* (1995). Both are available for modest sums from the United States Government Printing Office in Washington, D.C.

[7] *See* Title 18, U.S.C. §§ 201–225. For the United States Department of Justice's views on public corruption laws and prosecutions, *see* generally *The Department of Justice Manual*, Vol. 9A, Chapters 85 and 85A (PH Law & Business).

[8] Violations of the United States' domestic laws can also have international consequences. Oliver North, the loyal foot soldier of the Iran-Contra mess, was convicted of taking an illegal gratuity in the form of a security system for his home in return for his covert work funding the Contras in El Salvador. Although that conviction was ultimately reversed on procedural grounds, it reflects the American approach to domestic corruption. *United States* v. *North*, 910 F.2d 843, modified, 920 F.2d 940 (D.C. Cir. 1990).

[9] The Senate Gifts Rule, effective 1 January 1996, is contained in Rule XXXV (Gifts) of the Senate Rules. The Financial Disclosure Rule is Rule XXXIV (Financial Disclosure). The Rules are explained and interpreted in a 27 March 1996 Memorandum from the US Senate Select Committee on Ethics dated 27 March 1996.

The House Gifts Rule, Rule LII (52), is explained and interpreted in a Memorandum from the House's Committee on Standards of Official Conduct dated 7 December 1995. Each Rule is enforced by the relevant Congressional committee and, ultimately, by action of the relevant House of Congress. The custom is for the concerned committee to hire an independent lawyer to conduct the investigation. A current example is the pending investigation of the Speaker of the House of Representatives, Newt Gingrich, by the House Committee and its retained independent counsel. *New York Times* National Edition (26 September 1996). Violations of criminal laws that are uncovered are referred to the Department of Justice; however, all discovered violations may form the basis for House or Senate discipline.

A third source of restraints is the federal laws governing and restricting both the giving and the reporting of campaign contributions. These laws require extensive reporting, enforced by civil and criminal penalties, and place restraints upon amounts and, in particular, corporate contributions, whether made directly or disguised through conduits. The laws have led to both civil proceedings brought by the Federal Election Commission and prosecutions brought by both the Department of Justice and various Independent Counsel.[10]

A fourth source of domestic restrictions has been the United States securities laws. Publicly traded corporations in the United States are subject to a number of restrictions and requirements in relation to disclosing publicly and accurately certain financial information, as well as to make and keep books, records and accounts which, in reasonable detail, accurately and fairly reflect the corporations' transactions and the disposition of their assets. These laws have criminal penalties for their violation and have been applied to both illegal campaign contributions and to bribes.[11]

---

[10] *See* Title 2, U.S.C. §§ 431–455, the Federal Election Campaign Act. The Act establishes a comprehensive set of restrictions and reporting requirements, enforced primarily by the Federal Election Commission. The Act provides for criminal prosecutions by the Department of Justice as well as extensive civil proceedings by the Commission. The force of these statutes is exemplified by the recent conviction of Sun Diamond Growers of California, a mammoth agricultural cooperative in California with reported sales of $670,000,000 annually, of, *inter alia*, one count of making a prohibited political contribution to former Secretary of Agriculture Michael Espy's brother Henry (a Congressional candidate) in violation of 2 U.S.C. § 441b(a), and four counts of violating 2 U.S.C. § 441f by making the contribution through four individuals in an attempt to conceal the source of the contributions. Other convictions include payment of prohibited gratuities (18 U.S.C. § 201(c)(1)(A)) and wire fraud (18 U.S.C. §§ 1343 and 1346). Total penalties on the conviction include a maximum fine of $2,500,000. Criminal penalties for FECA violations are contained in 18 U.S.C. §§ 3571–3573. The prosecution was brought by the Independent Counsel in re Secretary of Agriculture Espy. *United States* v. *Sun Diamond Growers of California*, Cr. No. 96–0193 (D.C. 1996).

The case of Michael Goland is an excellent example of cases brought by the Department of Justice for violations of the election laws. The extensive litigation history is set forth in three separate opinions by the United States Court of Appeals for the Ninth Circuit. *United States* v. *Goland*, 859 F.2d 405, 959 F.2d 1449, 977 F.2d 1449 (9th Cir. 1990 & 1992). Goland was convicted of making an illegal campaign contribution to a candidate for the US Senate in violation of 2 U.S.C. §§ 441a(a)(1)(A) and 437(d). His challenges to this criminal conviction as well as an attempt to have the Act declared unconstitutional, *Goland* v. *United States*, 903 F.2d 1247 (9th Cir. 1990), proved unavailing and he ultimately served a prison term.

[11] Violations alleged domestically typically include keeping fake books and records (15 U.S.C. §§ 78m(b)(2)(A) and 78ff(a)), falsification of accounting records (15 U.S.C.§ 78ff(a) and 17 C.F.R. § 240.13b2–1), false statements to the corporation's auditors (15 U.S.C. § 77ff(a) and 17 C.F.R. § 240.13b2–2), and securities fraud (15 U.S.C. §§ 77l(a) and 77x). An example is the indictment of Crop Growers Corporation, a publicly traded corporation engaged in marketing federal agricultural insurance on behalf of insurance companies together with its Chairman of the Board of Directors and Executive Vice President. *United States* v. *Crop*

The next general set of proscriptions typically involved includes requirements that communications with the federal government and its investigators be truthful. Aside from the specific reporting and disclosure requirements, prosecutions often deal with attempts through false statements and misrepresentations to conceal the wrongful conduct and deflect the investigation. Federal criminal law penalizes false statements to a federal agency.[12]

Finally, the federal criminal laws penalize separately conspiracies to violate the law or to defraud the United States. Thus, both the substantive offences and the conspiracy to commit them in concert are criminally proscribed.[13]

The American response to corruption committed in the domestic economy and polity is to criminalize not merely the bribe itself but also all of the indicia of the illegal conduct. The laws are constructed deliberately in an attempt to deter the conduct by forcing the participants, in so far as possible, to violate multiple laws in the process of committing the corrupt act. This approach, as we will see eventually in this paper, is precisely the approach of the Foreign Corrupt Practices Act.

America, however, has not limited itself to enacting comprehensive laws; it has attempted to insulate the prosecution in politically sensitive cases through the use of 'Independent Counsel'. The American experience has justified enactment of extraordinary protections against conflicts of interest and undue influence being brought to bear in situations where investigations

---

Growers Corporation, Hemmingson & Black, No. 96–0181 (D.D.C. 1996). The gist of the securities charges is that Crop Growers Corporation and its executives funnelled illegal campaign contributions to Henry Espy, the Secretary of Agriculture's brother, for his Congressional campaign. The prosecution was brought by the Independent Counsel *in re* Secretary of Agriculture Espy. The charges await trial.

[12] Title 18, U.S.C. § 1001 provides: 'Whoever, in any matter within the jurisdiction of any department or agency of the United States knowingly and willfully falsifies, conceals or covers up by any trick, scheme, or device a material fact, or makes any false, fictitious or fraudulent statements or representations, or makes or uses any false writing or document knowing the same to contain any false, fictitious or fraudulent statement or entry, shall be fined under this title or imprisoned not more than five years, or both.'

[13] Naturally, both a conspiracy to violate any federal criminal law and a conspiracy to defraud the United States by impairing and impeding the lawful functioning of its government and agencies are separate crimes carrying additional criminal penalties. 18 U.S.C. § 371. Not unnaturally, these charges are often present in corruption cases. A prime example is the *Crop Growers Corporation* indictment (note 11 above) which alleges, *inter alia*, a conspiracy both to violate the securities and other federal laws as well as to impede the lawful functioning of the Federal Election Commission and false statements. Further, failure to report bribes or gratuities would subject the recipient to potential liability for criminal and civil violations of the Internal Revenue laws: 25 U.S.C. §§ 7203, 7206, etc. An example is the recent prosecution in Los Angeles, California, of now-former Congressman Walter Tucker for extorting $30,000 in bribes while Mayor of Compton, California. The charges on which he was convicted included tax evasion charges.

implicate officials of the government.[14] No explanation of America's attempts to battle corruption, thus, would be complete without a brief description of this somewhat unusual feature of American law. The Independent Counsel mechanism may also prove to be a helpful model for other nations seeking both to combat corruption and to insure that their anti-corruption efforts are perceived as unbiased by political influence. A brief explanation follows.

Independent Counsel Law

Its Use in Domestic Corruption Prosecutions

Where an investigation focuses on an individual who is also a member of the executive branch of the United States government such as the Presidency, the various Cabinets and the Department of Justice, the prosecution creates a conflict of interest. In those situations where the executive branch is incapable of investigating itself, upon request by the Attorney General, an Independent Counsel is appointed by the judicial branch to conduct an unbiased investigation and, if necessary, prosecution of criminal violations by government officials on a case-by-case basis.[15] Unlike the British system, private lawyers in the United States normally cannot and do not act as defence counsel one day and prosecutors the next. American prosecutors are appointed by the federal or local state governments exclusively to prosecute violations of the criminal laws.

The Independent Counsel statute was invoked to appoint Lawrence E. Walsh to investigate the involvement of members of the Reagan White House and Cabinet in the Iran-Contra debacle.[16] It was also recently invoked to appoint an Independent Counsel to investigate President Clinton's and his wife, Hillary's, alleged involvement in the Whitewater investment scandal while President Clinton was Governor of Arkansas. At present, there are three Independent Counsel actively conducting investigations.[17]

---

[14] An excellent treatment of the historical record from the Bible to the present is Professor Noonan's scholarly exegesis on the subject: John T. Noonan, Jr., *Bribes* (Macmillan 1984). Chapters 15 through 20 chronicle America's extensive and admitted familiarity both with the conduct and its prosecution.

[15] 28 U.S.C. §§ 591–599 (1994).

[16] *See Secord* v. *Cockburn*, 747 F.Supp. 779 (D.C. Cir. 1990).

[17] In addition to the Whitewater investigation, Independent Counsel are actively investigating the former Secretary of Agriculture Michael Espy and Secretary of Housing and Urban Development Henry Cisneros. The investigation of Secretary of Commerce Ron Brown has been discontinued due to his death. The investigation of the former Secretary of Housing and Urban Development Samuel Pierce is finalizing its report.

Brief History

The Independent Counsel statute was promulgated as part of the Ethics in Government Act (the 'Ethics Act') passed in 1978.[18] The Ethics Act was passed by Congress to 'create and reorganize certain agencies of the federal government and to enhance the probity of public officials and institutions'.[19] The Ethics Act creating the Independent Counsel provisions was intended to eradicate further abuses of presidential power like that displayed by then-President Nixon during the Watergate affair.

At that time, 'special prosecutors' appointed to investigate the executive branch were not fully independent. After the burglary at the Watergate Hotel in Washington led to allegations of espionage and sabotage involving the Nixon administration, Nixon ordered then Attorney General Elliot Richardson to appoint Archibald Cox as the special prosecutor to investigate members of the executive branch. After Cox demanded the production of tapes and documents from the President, Nixon ordered the Attorney General to dismiss Cox as special prosecutor. Both the Attorney General and his deputy refused to carry out Nixon's order, then resigned. Ultimately, then-Solicitor General Robert Bork carried out Nixon's order and fired Cox.[20]

Independent Counsel and the statute have since had a rocky road. The Iran-Contra investigation, which took five years and cost $32,000,000, was roundly criticized by Congress. Additionally, both Iran-Contra and the subsequent debacle over reported loans by the United States to Iraq used by Saddam Hussein to obtain weapons just before the invasion of Kuwait, exposed weaknesses in the statute. Independent Counsel Walsh was unable to obtain classified information held by the Attorney General that was necessary for prosecutions of Iran-Contra defendants. As to Iraq, the Attorney General refused to request the appointment of an Independent Counsel, revealing the inherent weakness of the statute which gives the Attorney General sole discretion in this regard.[21] Further problems have arisen over disputes as to the extent of the grants of investigative jurisdiction by the Attorney General and whether or not newly discovered matters are, or should be, within the purview of the Independent Counsel.[22]

---

[18] *See* Ethics in Government Act of 1978, Pub. L. No. 95–521, 92 Stat. 1824 (codified as amended in scattered sections of 2, 5, 18, 26, and 28 U.S.C.).

[19] *See* John M. Kelly, Janet P. McEntee, Note, 'The Independent Counsel Law: Is There Life After Death?', 8 *St. John's J.* Legal Comment (1993) 561.

[20] *Id.* Bork's nomination as a Supreme Court Justice was eventually defeated by the United States Senate. Many consider his role in firing Cox to have been a significant factor in his rejection.

[21] *Id.*, at 574–579; 28 U.S.C. §§ 591–592.

[22] *See In re Espy*, 80 F.3d 501 (D.C. Cir. 1996); *In re Olson*, 818 F.2d 34 (D.C. Cir. 1987). As these cases show, these matters have not been without controversy.

Congress failed to reauthorize the Independent Counsel provisions of the Ethics Act in 1992.[23] The provisions were, however, reenacted in 1994.[24]

THE UNITED STATES AND FOREIGN CORRUPTION BEFORE THE ACT

The Reach of the Law

Domestic bribery, defined generically as the 'offering, giving, receiving, or soliciting of something of value for the purpose of influencing the action of an official in the discharge of his or her public or legal duties',[25] had long been prosecuted as a crime by both federal and state authorities in the United States resulting in extensive prison terms and fines. For example, the federal offence of bribing a United States government official can result in a maximum sentence of fifteen years in prison.[26] Before the enactment of the Act in 1977, however, American corporations and individuals caught bribing foreign officials could only be prosecuted indirectly.[27] Domestic bribery statutes did not reach directly foreign activity.

The Securities and Exchange Commission, known colloquially as the SEC, responded to revelations of foreign misconduct by taking the position that United States corporations were obligated to disclose payments to foreign officials as part of the securities laws.[28] The SEC has jurisdiction to regulate transactions in securities conducted on securities exchanges and over-the-counter markets in the United States.[29] Additionally, federal prosecutors with the Department of Justice sought to invoke the Bank Secrecy as well as the Mail and Wire Fraud statutes.[30]

The Bank Secrecy Act requires banks and other financial institutions to submit reports to the Internal Revenue Service disclosing transactions involving more than $10,000 in cash, or other bearer negotiable instruments and to submit similar reports to the United States Customs Service whenever

---

[23] Kelly and McEntee, *supra* note 19, at 581–582.

[24] *See* Independent Counsel Reauthorization Act of 1994, Pub. L. 103–270, 108 Stat. 732 (1994).

[25] *Black's Law Dictionary*, 6th Ed. 191 (1990).

[26] 18 U.S.C. § 201.

[27] Pines, *supra*, note 5, 82 *Calif. L.Rev.* at 185–188; *see Defending Corporations and Their Officers in Parallel Administrative and Criminal Proceedings and Their Avoidance Through Preventive and Compliance Programs*, American Bar Association National Institute (hereinafter 'Defending Corporations') (1980); Cruver, *supra*, note 5, at 1–5.

[28] Pines, *supra*, note 5, 82 *Calif. L. Rev.* at 186–188.

[29] 15 U.S.C. § 78b.

[30] *See* The Bank Records and Foreign Transactions Act, 12 U.S.C. §§ 1951–1959; the Mail Fraud Act, 18 U.S.C. §§ 1341, 1343.

transporting more than $5,000 across the border.[31] The Mail and Wire Fraud statutes, which prohibit the use of the United States mails and wire communications to engage in a fraudulent scheme, are limited to use of the United States mails and wire communications and thus are not designed to deal with acts undertaken exclusively abroad. Use of these laws to curb the particular practice of bribing foreign officials proved inadequate.[32]

The Extent of the Problem

A voluntary disclosure programme implemented by the SEC during the first half of the 1970s revealed that more than 450 companies had made collectively over $400,000,000 in questionable payments to foreign concerns. Over 117 of these companies were ranked in the Fortune 500 listing. The corrupting activities engaged in by these companies included bribery of high foreign officials to secure favourable foreign government action as well as facilitating or 'grease' payments made to ensure that lower level government employees performed desired ministerial functions.[33]

The American public was shocked to learn that companies such as Bell Helicopter, Gulf Oil, General Tire and Rubber, Exxon, Occidental Petroleum, Lockheed, Mobil Oil and other prominent corporations had engaged in such activities. For example, it was disclosed that Lockheed paid $1,000,000 to Prince Bernhardt of the Netherlands, who was forced to resign from his national defence functions as a result of an inquiry into the allegation. Gulf Oil reported spending $10,300,000 on gifts and gratuities related to political activity in the United States and abroad, including $4,000,000 given to the political party of South Korean President Park Chung Hee.[34]

The American Response

The public outcry resulted in passage of the Foreign Corrupt Practices Act on 19 December 1977.[35] President Carter noted,

> [B]ribery is ethically repugnant and competitively unnecessary. Corrupt practices between corporations and public officials overseas undermine the

---

[31] *See Economic Crime Workshop, International Trade – the Fraud Risks*, Chapter 2 (January 1987).

[32] Pines, *supra*, note 5.

[33] Cruver, *supra*, note 5, at 2–4.

[34] *Id.*

[35] 15 U.S.C. §§ 78m(b), 78dd-1, 78dd-2, 78ff (1988), originally enacted as Pub. L. No. 95–213, 91 Stat. 1494 (1977); *see* Arthur Aronoff, *Antibribery Provisions of The Foreign Corrupt Practices Act* (30 June 1994).

integrity and stability of governments and harm our relations with other countries....[36]

The Act most importantly upholds a valued moral standard underlying the history and culture of the United States. As noted in the Report issued by the House of Representatives on the Act,

> The payment of bribes to influence the acts or decisions of foreign officials, foreign political parties and candidates for foreign political office is unethical. It is counter to the moral expectations and values of the American public.... [I]t rewards corruption instead of efficiency and puts pressure on ethical enterprises to lower their standards or risk losing business.[37]

The Act was amended in 1988 to clarify and strengthen its provisions in response to the business community's expressed concern that, as originally drafted, the Act inhibited the ability of United States companies to compete abroad.[38]

BREAKDOWN OF THE ACT'S PROVISIONS

The Act prohibits American companies and their agents, as well as individuals, from using the mails or other means of interstate commerce to make a payment 'corruptly', either directly or indirectly through an intermediary, to a foreign official or politician to use his or her power or influence to help the American firm or individual to obtain or retain business.[39] The Act is broad-reaching in defining potential targets, curbing illicit practices of corporations under the auspices of the SEC, otherwise known as 'issuers', as well as the practices of all 'domestic concerns', that is any other corporation, partnership, association, joint-stock company, business trust, unincorporated organization, or sole proprietorship principally doing business in the United States or organized under United States laws or the laws of any United States territory, possession, or commonwealth.

The Act also reaches illicit practices of any United States citizen, national or resident.[40] Although other countries prohibit the bribing of their own officials, the United States is the only nation in the world that I know of

---

[36] Pines, *supra*, note 5.

[37] Pines, *supra* note 5, 82 *Calif. L. Rev.* at 212, quoting H.R. Rep. No. 640, 95th Cong., First Sess. 4–5 (1977).

[38] *See* Omnibus Trade and Competitiveness Act of 1988, Pub. L. No. 100–418, Title V, Subtitle A, Part I, 102 Stat. 1107, 1415–25 (1988).

[39] Pines, *supra*, note 5, 82 *Calif. L. Rev.* at 188–189.

[40] 15 U.S.C. § 78dd-2(h)(1).

which punishes criminally its business community for bribing another country's public servants.[41]

Accounting Provisions

The Act's use of comprehensive accounting standards is particularly American in its approach to the detection and ultimate prosecution of financial crime through the use of disclosure requirements and regulatory oversight. Section 102 of the Act requires corporations subject to the jurisdiction of the SEC (1) to make and keep accurate books, records and accounts which properly detail the corporation's business activities, and (2) to create and maintain a system of internal accounting controls.[42] These provisions were intended to clarify that corporations' books and records should reflect transactions that conform to accepted accounting standards, should be designed to prevent off the books transactions such as bribes, and should increase corporate accountability.[43]

The accounting controls required by the Act are not limited to quantitative accuracy and fairness but also include a requirement of qualitative disclosure. Under the Act, corporations' books must correctly record all information which may be necessary to call an auditor's attention to any possible qualitative illegality or impropriety. The financial details of a particular transaction may not tell the whole story. If the transaction is being entered into as a result of a 'suggestion' by a foreign official, if the sums being disbursed exceed sums paid in comparable transactions, or if there are apparent conflicts of interest between the foreign parties engaging in the transaction and the foreign official from whom a particular entity wishes action, all this information must be disclosed.[44]

Criminal liability for violations of the accounting standards requires that the accused have knowingly circumvented a system of internal accounting controls or have knowingly falsified records or books maintained under the accounting requirements of the Act.[45]

Bribery and 'Grease' Payments

Sections 103 and 104 create a new criminal offence intended to reduce bribery of foreign government officials by United States-based businesses.[46]

---

[41] Pines, *supra*, note 5, 82 *Calif. L. Rev.* at 205–206, 227 n. 147.
[42] 15 U.S.C. § 78m(b)(2).
[43] Cruver, *supra*, note 5, at 20–22.
[44] *Id.*, at 22–23.
[45] 15 U.S.C. §§ 78m(b)(4) and (5).
[46] 15 U.S.C. §§ 78dd-1 and 2; *supra* note 27, *Defending Corporations*, at 197–198.

The 'foreign corrupt practices' prohibited by the Act include five separate elements:

1. the use of an instrumentality of interstate commerce (such as the telephone, telex, telecopies, air transportation, or the mails) in furtherance of
2. a payment of, or even an offer to pay, 'anything of value', directly or indirectly
3. to any foreign official, foreign political party, or foreign political candidate,
4. if the purpose of the payment is the 'corrupt' one of getting the recipient to act (or to refrain from acting)
5. in such a way as to assist the company in obtaining or retaining business or in directing business to any particular person.[47]

These provisions apply to both businesses subject to the SEC's jurisdiction, that is 'issuers', and to all individuals and other entities coming under the Act. The accounting provisions differ in their reach, covering only the activities of 'issuers'.

Prosecutions can be brought not only for direct corrupt payments but also for indirect corrupt payments made by third parties if there is actual knowledge of the intended results or if there is a conscious disregard or deliberate ignorance of known circumstances that should reasonably alert the offender to the high probability of violation of the Act.[48]

As amended in 1988, the Act provides an explicit exception to the bribery prohibition for small payments made to foreign officials to ensure their performance of customary duties, known as 'grease' payments, or more specifically,

any facilitating or expediting payment to a foreign official, political party, or party official the purpose of which is to expedite or to secure the performance of a routine governmental action by foreign official, political party, or party official.[49]

'Routine governmental action' does not include a decision by a foreign official to award new business or to continue business with a particular party or any action taken by a foreign official involved in the decision-making process to encourage a decision to award new business to, or to continue business with, a particular party.[50] Rather, 'routine governmental action' is understood to mean commonly performed official actions, such as:

---

[47] Cruver, *supra*, note 5, at 15.
[48] 15 U.S.C. §§ 78dd-2(a)(3), (h)(A) and (B); Aronoff, *supra*, note 35, § III E.
[49] 15 U.S.C. § 78dd-2(b).
[50] 15 U.S.C. § 78dd-2(h)(4)(B).

- obtaining documents or permits to qualify to do business in a foreign country;
- processing government papers, such as visas or work permits;
- providing for police protection, delivery, or scheduling inspections in connection with contract performance or transit of goods through the country;
- providing phone service, power and water supply, cargo-handling services, or protection for perishable commodities; and
- actions of a similar nature.[51]

Affirmative Defences

There are also a variety of affirmative defences under the Act as amended in 1988. These defences include:

(1) the payment, gift, offer, or promise of anything of value that was made, was lawful under the written law and regulations of the foreign official's, political party's, party official's, or candidate's country; or
(2) that the payment ... was a ... reasonable and *bona fide* business expenditure ... related to–
(A) the promotion, demonstration, or explanation of products or services;
(B) the execution or performance of a contract with a foreign government or agency thereof.[52]

The accounting requirements of the Act should serve to flush out bribes that are concealed as business expenses. Nor can American businesses avoid criminal and civil enforcement by arguing that bribery and graft are customary in a foreign country, as opposed to legally authorized, no matter how much the custom permeates the fabric of business in that country.

Penalties

The maximum amount of the potential fines to firms violating the Act is $2,000,000 and $100,000 for individuals and for officers, directors and stockholders acting on behalf of the firm, as well as imprisonment for up to five years, or both.[53] The Department of Justice and the SEC can also bring civil actions and seek substantial civil fines, as well as injunctive relief.[54]

---

[51] Cruver, *supra*, note 5, at 16.
[52] 15 U.S.C. § 78dd-2(c).
[53] 15 U.S.C. §§ 78ff(c) and 78dd-2(g).
[54] 15 U.S.C. §§ 78dd-2(d), 78dd-2(g)(1)(B), 78dd-2(g)(2)(C), 78ff(c)(1)(B), 78ff(c)(2)(C).

Advisory Opinions

An extraordinary provision of the Act creates a review procedure by the Department of Justice in which the Attorney General is required to issue an opinion in response to a specific inquiry from a person or firm. The opinion is meant to enable companies to obtain a 'before the fact' opinion as to whether prospective conduct will conform to the Department of Justice's current enforcement policy regarding the anti-bribery provisions of the Act. Such an opinion creates a rebuttable presumption of compliance with the Act, yet it is not binding on the SEC.[55] In spite of this governmental effort to be helpful, businesses have not displayed much interest in the opinion procedure, relying more on the advice of private counsel. There were only twenty opinions released between 1980 and 1989.[56] The Department of Justice, pursuant to the 1988 amendments to the Act, has adopted new procedures which make supporting documents unreachable through a Freedom of Information Act ('FOIA') request.[57]

Enforcement

The SEC is responsible for civil enforcement of the accounting provisions of the Act and the anti-bribery provisions with respect to issuers. The Department of Justice is responsible for all criminal enforcement, for civil enforcement against individuals, and against entities that are not under the SEC's jurisdiction.[58]

PROBLEMS REMAINING WITH THE ACT

Despite amendments, the Act still has a variety of problems that prevent it from fully achieving its goals. One of these problems is limited enforcement by the agencies entrusted with enforcement jurisdiction, the SEC and the Department of Justice. Only sixteen separate bribery allegations have been prosecuted under the Act.[59] Many factors can contribute to limited enforcement. Initially, Congress has expressed concern about the effectiveness of

---

[55] 15 U.S.C. §§ 78dd-1(e), 78dd-2(f), 78m(b)(2) and (3); *see* Department of Justice Manual 1993–1 Supplement, §§ 9–47:140 and 9–47.140A, Part 80, § 80.13.

[56] *See* Beverley Earle, 'The United States' Foreign Corrupt Practices Act and the OECD Anti-Bribery Recommendation: When Moral Suasion Won't Work, Try the Money Argument', 14 *Dick. J. Int'l L.* (1996) 207, 220–221.

[57] *Id.*

[58] Pines, *supra*, note 5, 82 *Calif. L. Rev.* at 189; Aronoff, *supra* note 35, § III C.

[59] *See* Pendergast, 'Foreign Corrupt Practices Act: an Overview of Almost Twenty Years of Foreign Bribery Prosecution', 7 *Int'l Quarterly* 187 (1995).

the agencies entrusted with the Act's enforcement, the SEC and the Department of Justice. Neither agency has complete control over enforcement of the Act, instead sharing that responsibility. Some believe the agencies have displayed an inability to cooperate effectively.[60] In addition, both agencies have of late been overwhelmed by ever-expanding demands on resources that have not been commensurately increased. Further, changing priorities (as in the Department's recent offensive against 'deadbeat dads' for delinquent child support payments) can reduce the resources brought to the anticorruption fight.

Other factors impeding enforcement under the Act include exceptionally high standards for the initiation of prosecution, as well as the obvious difficulties in investigating and prosecuting sophisticated and complex international commercial transactions. Investigation and prosecution under the Act require interviews with witnesses and the obtaining of documents from individuals and entities in foreign countries, a task complicated by financial, diplomatic and political concerns.[61]

The United States has entered into mutual assistance treaties with other countries, including the Netherlands, Switzerland, Greece, Nigeria and Colombia, which oblige a signatory nation to assist in locating witnesses, in compelling persons to appear and testify, and in producing documents and records. Where these treaties are limited to the investigation and prosecution of crimes recognized by the laws of both the United States and the other nation, they would not include investigations of criminal violations of the Act. There are also bilateral agreements governing the transfer of information between the Department of Justice and foreign law enforcement agencies, which are limited to the activities of specified companies in the host countries.[62]

The Act also continues to suffer from vagueness that hinders its effectiveness. The scarcity of judicial decisions emanating from prosecutions and civil actions has cut down on judicial clarification of the grey areas in the Act. This is unfortunate in that lack of clarity can have a chilling effect on business activities abroad. It is not precisely clear what is meant by the Act's prohibition against corporate use of the mails 'corruptly' in furtherance of payments to foreign officials. It is also unclear what constitutes a 'payment', what is meant by the 'knowing' standard in relation to liability for intermediaries' illegal acts of bribery, when a foreign official is engaged in an 'official capacity' or a 'legal duty', and what constitutes a 'routine governmental action'.[63]

For example, businesses, of necessity, often use foreign consultants. It is unclear under what circumstances a United States business and the people

---

[60] Pines, *supra*, note 5, 82 *Calif. L. Rev.* at 192–195.
[61] *Id.*
[62] Cruver, *supra*, note 5, at 65–68.
[63] Pines, *supra*, note 5, 82 *Calif. L. Rev.* at 200–203.

who work for and invest in that business can be held responsible for the corrupting practices of such a consultant. It can also be problematic to distinguish between a foreign official's 'official' conduct and conduct undertaken for personal or business reasons, a problem exacerbated by the lack of substantive and administrative law in the countries involved.[64]

Some commentators have argued that the Act should be amended to allow a restricted private right of action in order to facilitate fair competition.[65] In short, give a competitor harmed by violations of the Act a right to sue. This would supplement scarce government resources with motivated, well-financed private litigants. Although this approach would seem logical and appropriate, there does not appear to be any domestic political support for further 'tilting the playing field' against American competitors, given the lack of foreign action to crack down on foreign corrupters of public officials.

Perhaps the lack of enthusiasm reflects the disinclination of government officials and businessmen to equip private parties with an economic incentive and the legal right to challenge their actions, either domestic or foreign. In addition, it is doubtful if American or transnational businesses are interested in supplementing the scarce government resources now available to enforce the Act. Similarly, salutary attempts by the private securities bar to imply a right of action for violation of the Act and bring litigation against corporate managements have been disallowed by the courts.[66] Enactment of both would revitalize anti-corruption efforts in the United States.

INTERNATIONAL RESPONSE TO THE ACT AND TO BRIBERY

International Reaction to the Act

The fall-out from this American condemnation of American concerns engaging in 'business as usual' overseas has been harsh, with some critics calling the Act a form of 'cultural imperialism'.[67] The foreign criticism may have been particularly vitriolic because the Act was partially motivated by an endemic, expressed American fear that the contagion of corruption, supposedly caught abroad, would emigrate to the United States, corrupting

---

[64] *Id.*, at 200–202.

[65] *Id.*, at 215–227.

[66] See *Lamb* v. *Philip Morris, Inc.*, 915 F.2d 1024, 1029 (6th Cir. 1990), *cert. denied*, 498 U.S. 1086 (1991); *Citicorp Int'l Trading Co.* v. *Western Oil & Ref. Co.*, 771 F.Supp. 660, 606–07 (S.D. N.Y. 1991); *Shields ex rel. Sundstrand Corp.* v. *Erickson*, 710 F.Supp. 686 688 (N.D. Ill. 1989); *Lewis ex rel. National Semiconductor Corp.* v. *Sporck*, 612 F.Supp. 1316, 1328–34 (N.D. Cal. 1985).

[67] Pines, *supra*, note 5, 82 *Calif. L. Rev.* at 204.

otherwise law-abiding domestic business. The Act was conceived as a vigorous inoculation against this disease.

There is also overwhelming evidence that the exportation of corruption by transnational companies, including American companies, has had disastrous effects on foreign nations, destabilizing their governments, causing existing corrupt governments to retain power at any cost, all resulting in poor economic development.[68] Payments of bribes by United States corporations to foreign officials and exposure of the practice figured significantly in the fall of governments or officials thereof in Japan, Bolivia, Honduras, the Cook Islands, Italy and the Netherlands.[69] The United States Congress cited the 'world-wide outcry against the corrupting influence of some United States-based multinationals on foreign governments' in passing the original Act.[70] Yet no one is so naive as to believe that only American corporations' activities have had these effects. Other national governments have been slow, however, to decry their own corporations' illicit overseas activities.

International Action

Prior to passage of the Act in late 1977, certain international agencies and organizations had expressed concern over the growing problem of foreign bribes. Since passage of the Act and under sustained lobbying efforts by the United States, these organizations have increased their efforts to take concrete actions curbing such illicit activities. To date, however, the United States is the only nation to have criminalized overseas bribery.

In 1975, the United States obtained a resolution from the General Assembly of the United Nations condemning bribery and other corrupt practices in international commerce. Section five of that resolution called for nations' cooperation to prevent such practices. Thereafter, in 1979, the United Nations' Committee on an International Agreement on Illicit Payments presented the United Nations Economic and Social Council ('ECOSOC') with a treaty outlawing overseas bribery that was heavily supported by the United States. It was never adopted.[71]

The Act, as amended in 1988, directed the President to pursue an international agreement among the members of the Organization for Economic Cooperation and Development ('OECD') to create legislation in their own countries aimed at attacking the problem of international corrup-

---

[68] Earle, *supra*, note 56, 14 *Dick. J. Int'l L.* at 221–223.

[69] *Id.*

[70] *Id.*, at 206–207.

[71] *See* Stephen Muffler, 'Proposing a Treaty on the Prevention of International Corrupt Payments: Cloning the Foreign Corrupt Practices Act is not the Answer', 1 *ILSA J. Int'l & Comp. L.* (1995) 3, 8–13.

tion.[72] On 27 May 1994, the OECD Council approved a Recommendation in which the members agreed that bribery distorts international competitive conditions, that all countries share a responsibility to combat bribery in international business transactions, and urging member countries to criminalize overseas bribery. The OECD's Committee on Investment and Multinational Enterprises established a working group to follow up on the recommendations.[73] Most recently, on 11 April 1996, the OECD '[u]nder intense pressure from the United States', agreed that bribes paid to foreign officials should no longer be tax-deductible, and committed its 26 member nations to rewrite their tax codes.[74] Efforts by the United States to forge a binding agreement among member nations of the OECD criminalizing overseas bribery have failed, in large part due to the efforts of a coalition led by Britain.[75] The United States is continuing its lobbying efforts to forge an international agreement making foreign bribery a crime.[76]

In March 1996, the Organization of American States ('OAS') adopted the Inter-American Convention Against Corruption. The Convention calls for the criminalizing of transnational bribery by member states, makes such acts of corruption extraditable offences, and calls for increased cooperation among member states, including the establishment of 'Central Authorities' to facilitate such cooperation.[77] On 15 June 1994, Justice Ministers from the Council of Europe adopted a programme to combat corruption at the close of the Council's Nineteenth Conference. The United Nations, through its Commission on International Trade Law, has also adopted model laws for the procurement of goods and services which challenge corruption in host countries.[78]

In March 1996, the International Chamber of Commerce ('ICC') announced a revised set of 'Rules of Conduct to Combat Extortion and Bribery in International Business Transactions', which prohibit extortion or bribery for any purpose. These rules are non-binding and self-regulating. In 1977, the ICC had passed an earlier set of rules which prohibited extortion and bribery only in connection with obtaining or retaining business. In its corresponding March 1996 Report, the ICC recommends that all govern-

---

[72] 15 U.S.C. § 78dd-1 note.

[73] Aronoff, *supra*, note 35, § VII D; Earle, *supra*, note 56, 14 *Dick. J. Int'l L.* at 224–225.

[74] *See* Marlise Simons, 'United States Enlists Other Rich Countries in a Move to End Business Bribes to Foreign Officials,' *New York Times*, 12 April 1996, at A7.

[75] Earle, *supra*, note 56, 14 *Dick. J. Int'l L.* at 224–225; Muffler, *supra*, note 71, 1 *ILSA J. Int'l & Comp. L.* at 13–14, notes 60–61; *see also* note 2, *ante*.

[76] Simons, *supra*, note 74.

[77] *See* Inter-American Convention Against Corruption, adopted 29 March 1996, Organization of American States, OEA/Ser.K/XXXIV.1CICOR/doc.14/96 rev.2.

[78] *See* Jay M. Vogelson, 'Corrupt Practices in the Conduct of International Business', 30 *Int'l Law* (1996) 193, 196–198.

ments implement the May 1994 OECD Recommendation on Bribery in International Business Transactions.[79]

A private organization named Transparency International ('TI'), modeled on the structure and tactics of Amnesty International, was formed in 1993 to tackle the ethical dilemmas faced in international business, which its supporters believe neither governments nor corporations can successfully address. Based in Berlin with offices around the world, TI receives financial support from United States corporations and European aid agencies. Through the use of public exposure, introduction of legislation in other nations similar to the Act, and other tactics, TI is dedicated to ending international kickbacks, bribes and corruption.[80]

THE ACT'S RECORD

Has the Act been successful? No one really knows, or even agrees on the criteria for success: stopping American participation in foreign corruption or assisting American firms to be competitive? Enactment certainly galvanized the United States to press for international action. Yet, as shown above, progress has been slow or nonexistent. United States Trade Representative Mickey Kantor has bitterly protested foreign indifference: 'Last year from April 1994 to May 1995 the US government learned of almost 100 cases in which foreign bribes undercut US firms' ability to win contracts valued at $45 billion.'[81] Secretary of State Warren M. Christopher claims that the Act's effectiveness has had a deleterious economic impact on American business abroad.[82] While there is, as yet, to my knowledge no official study confirming these claimed effects,[83] it appears reasonable to assume they exist.

There are also concrete examples of American businesses invoking the Act to avoid the continuous blackmail and extortionate relationships which an initial bribe or gift can yield, significantly driving up the cost of doing business abroad. Colgate-Palmolive successfully deflected demands for bribes from Chinese officials by citing the Act's prohibitions against such payments. Colgate-Palmolive ultimately opened a $20,000,000 factory in Guang Dong in January of 1992 without the use of bribes.[84]

---

[79] *See Report and Revised Rules on Corruption and Bribery in International Business Transactions*, International Chamber of Commerce (March 1996).

[80] Earle, *supra*, note 56, 14 *Dick. J. Int'l L.* at 232; Muffler, *supra*, note 71, 1 *ILSA J. Int'l & Comp. L.* at 12–13.

[81] *New York Times*, *supra*, at note 74.

[82] Pines, *supra*, note 5, 82 *Calif. L. Rev.* at 207–214; Earle, *supra*, note 56, 14 *Dick. J. Int'l L.* at 226.

[83] Pines, *supra*, note 5, 82 *Calif. L. Rev.* at 207–214.

[84] *Id.*

There is also a record of sixteen successful prosecutions. Seventeen companies and thirty-three individuals have been charged with violating the Act through the use of foreign bribes. Fines on the corporate entities have ranged from $10,000 to $3,450,000. Yet few executives have gone to jail. A brief discussion of a few of these prosecutions shows the magnitude of the commercial transactions and the bribes involved, the latter representing sometimes up to twenty per cent of the business obtained. In July 1992, the General Electric Company, in the *Dotan* case, admitted it had conspired with an Israeli general and others to create bogus bills for fictitious Israeli Air Force projects. General Electric pleaded guilty to four federal charges, including violation of the Act, and agreed to pay $69,000,000 in fines and settlement.[85]

The SEC filed a civil injunctive action against Ashland Oil Company and its former Chief Executive Officer, alleging that in 1980 they agreed to pay an entity controlled by an Omani government official approximately $29,000,000 for a majority interest in Midlands Chrome Inc., a Zimbabwean mining operation, in order to obtain crude oil at a highly favourable price. The mining claims were not profitable and in 1982 Ashland wrote off its investment. In December 1982, Ashland was awarded a crude oil contract by the Omani government for 20,000 barrels a day for one year at a $3–per-barrel discount from the 'selling price'.[86]

In a criminal proceeding against Crawford Enterprises, the Department of Justice alleged a scheme to bribe officials of Pemex, the Mexican national oil company, to obtain orders for compression equipment systems for use in Mexico's oil and natural gas industry. The main defendants were convicted following a trial. Thereafter, Pemex itself filed a major civil action against eighteen known defendants and other unknown conspirators seeking more than $45,000,000 in direct damages.[87]

The multiple actions against Lockheed exemplify the tenacity of corruption in the international marketplace and how some companies treat financial sanctions as a cost (albeit substantial) of doing business abroad. In June 1979, after Lockheed admitted to bribing Prince Bernhardt of the Netherlands, Lockheed entered a plea of guilty based on its disclosure to the SEC of payments to Japanese Prime Minister Tanaka. Thereafter, in June 1994, Lockheed was indicted yet again for violations of the anti-bribery provisions of the Act based on allegations of payments to an Egyptian Parliament member, a Dr. Takla, who served as Lockheed's consultant in Egypt between 1980 and 1990. The indictment alleged that Lockheed agreed to pay Dr. Takla $600,000 for each C-130 aircraft sold to Egypt under an FMS programme. After auditors discovered the arrangement, Lockheed told the Pentagon it would not pay the fee. It then paid Takla $1,000,000 into a

---

[85] Cruver, *supra*, note 5, at 56; Pendergast, *supra*, note 59, at 10–29.

[86] Cruver, *supra*, note 5, at 52.

[87] *Id.*, at 54–55.

Swiss bank account as a 'termination fee'.[88] A Lockheed executive pleaded guilty, and Lockheed was also convicted. A Lockheed regional vice-president is a fugitive in Syria. Lockheed paid a fine of $28,100,000 and $3,000,000 in civil false claims damages.[89]

It also appears clear that the Act may only have succeeded in causing firms to be more circumspect. Most recently, allegations have surfaced in the press regarding IBM's payment of $20,000,000 to a subcontractor in connection with a $250,000,000 contract awarded to IBM in 1994 to computerize Banco de la Nacion in Argentina. As reported in the news, the contract, although beneficial to IBM, is allegedly damaging to the Argentine state. On July 31, a magistrate in Argentina charged 18 suspects, including IBM executives and provincial bankers, with plotting to defraud the Argentine government and inflating the price of the computer contract with unnecessary costs and services. The investigation focused on a $37,000,000 subcontract awarded to CCR, a small software company linked to Juan Carlos Cattaneo, alleged to be a power broker of Argentine's ruling party. The money disappeared and was allegedly diverted to bank accounts in Switzerland, Uruguay and the United States. The company apparently performed no identifiable services in exchange for the money. American prosecutors are looking into whether violations of the Act have occurred and if they have, enforcement and prosecution should be forthcoming.[90]

The uncomfortable fact, however, is that these few are the only prosecutions in almost twenty years. And many were uncovered not by the SEC or Department but almost adventitiously by the press. It beggars the imagination to believe that corporations which reported $400,000,000 in bribes so few years ago have been reformed so totally. Without comprehensive international investigations, no one will ever know.

CONCLUSION

The Foreign Corrupt Practices Act is a good-faith effort by the United States to combat the use of bribery abroad by United States companies that degrades and harms other nations' economic development and our own moral welfare. The Department of Justice and the SEC have tried to enforce the Act. Yet the problems experienced by the United States in creating a workable enforcement structure, solving investigatory needs, and clarifying

---

[88] Pendergast, *supra*, note 59, at 28–29; Earle, *supra*, note 56, 14 *Dick. J. Int'l L.* at 211–213.

[89] *See* Evan Jay Cutting, *Foreign Corrupt Practices Act: ABA-CLE White Collar Crime 1996, Representing Corporations, Financial Institutions and their Directors, Officers and Employees*, I-17–21.

[90] *See* Sebastian Rotella, 'IBM Scandal is Equal Parts Spectator Sport and Lesson', *Los Angeles Times*, 11 August 1996, at D1.

the activities outlawed under the Act, have hindered and will continue to hinder its use. In fact, the most promising change to spur legal action and enforcement, the addition of private rights of action, have not to date been enacted, although such changes might well result in an explosion of private enforcement. In spite of these problems, the United States has had some success in prosecuting a few egregious violations.

The United States has also tried to negotiate international cooperation in fighting corruption. It has attempted to lead the way both by criminalizing directly not merely the conduct involved but also the corporate shenanigans necessary to conceal the corruption. Although efforts by the United States to forge effective international agreements criminalizing such practices have failed to date, there has been significant movement and dialogue about the issue resulting from the United States' repeated calls for international enforcement and an apparent realization in some foreign climes that corruption is a real threat to their own national security. Yet, the entrenched nature of 'influence peddling', 'competition' as a pernicious form of nationalism and other unethical practices in many parts of the world may render them immune from effective international condemnation. We can only hope that is not the case.

MARVIN G. PICKHOLZ

15. The United States Foreign Corrupt Practices Act as a Civil Remedy

INTRODUCTION

The Foreign Corrupt Practices Act ('FCPA' or the 'Act'), contrary to common sense, is not limited to 'foreign' activities, nor to 'corrupt' practices, nor even to 'practices' in the sense that more than one occurrence is necessary. Any United States company, or United States subsidiary of a foreign corporation, which does or is considering doing business abroad must seriously consider the limitation placed on its actions by the provision of the FCPA.[1] Failure to do so could lead to costly litigation, government action, and even more costly negative publicity.

The FCPA also covers conduct of domestic companies with no foreign business. These companies must equally be wary of transgressing the provisions of the FCPA.

Often addressed as an 'anti-bribery' statute, in fact the FCPA has two prongs that affect publicly owned corporations. One prong is the anti-bribery provision. The second prong is the accounting and books and records provisions found in section 13(b) of the Securities and Exchange Act of 1934. This article will attempt to provide some illumination in these areas.

BACKGROUND AND OVERVIEW OF THE FOREIGN CORRUPT PRACTICES ACT

The Foreign Corrupt Practices Act is one of the more interesting and controversial legacies of the Watergate conspiracy that drove President Richard M. Nixon from office. As a part of the investigation into the allegedly illicit conduct of the Nixon Administration, the Special Prosecutor uncovered numerous corporate political slush funds that had been used for illegal domestic campaign contributions. An investigation by the Securities

---

[1] References here will be companies or corporations. However, the FCPA uses the word 'person' and defines that term to mean natural or artificial persons including partnerships and joint ventures.

Barry A.K. Rider (ed.), Corruption: The Enemy Within, 231–252
© *Kluwer Law International. Printed in the Netherlands.*

and Exchange Commission (the 'SEC') into these illegal contributions revealed that the payments were made possible by falsified corporate financial statements which were used to conceal the source and application of the corporate funds. Additionally, the SEC investigation revealed the existence of corporate 'slush funds' from which money was discharged for bribes and other illicit purposes.

This discovery propelled the SEC to undertake a broad ranging independent investigation of corporate conduct abroad in order to determine (1) the extent to which such funds upset the federal disclosure system and (2) the accuracy of corporate accounting practices and the truthfulness of financial statements. As a result of the investigation, the SEC uncovered information that the slush funds were used to make large-scale bribes to foreign officials, as well as domestic bribes.[2]

The SEC had also become aware of bribery through routine investigations, such as the one conducted by the SEC in connection with *SEC* v. *United Brands*, in which the SEC investigated United Brands after the suicide of its Chief Executive Officer, Eli Black. The SEC inquiry disclosed that United Brands, one of the world's largest banana producers, had paid an Honduran official $1.25 million in order to reduce a new export tax on bananas. It had paid the official through a foreign subsidiary, which had accounted for the payment on its books as 'commission' and had deposited the money in a Swiss bank account for the official.

The SEC believed that these corporate contributions to domestic politicians and payments to foreign officials were of material significance to investors who were entitled to disclosure of them and of their significance to the operations, revenues, profits and risks of doing business of those public corporations which engaged in such activities. Consequently, the SEC initiated a voluntary disclosure programme for publicly held companies, inviting them to make these disclosures on their own initiative. It provided an open window in which companies could make voluntary disclosures of questionable payments to foreign officials and thereby diminish their chances of being prosecuted. The response was staggering. Prior to the adoption of the FCPA, more than 450 companies reported making questionable or illegal payments involving hundreds of millions of dollars to foreign officials. For example, the Exxon Corporation acknowledged paying $1.2 billion in 15 foreign countries 'to secure or influence governmental action'. Additionally, Exxon's Italian subsidiary made unauthorized commercial payments and political contributions totalling $19 million.

Despite the success of the voluntary disclosure programme, the SEC also encountered a number of problems. First, the programme led to consent

---

[2] The discovery of the depth and breadth of bribery of foreign officials, particularly in many developing countries but also in developed countries, and the amassment of individual wealth by government officials, produced a new term: 'Kleptocracy' – government by thieves known as 'Kleptocrats'.

decrees which required the companies to create and implement compliance programmes.[3] To achieve this, the SEC depended on the desire and the ability of a company's independent directors[4] and outside counsel to compel accurate disclosure of payments. Second, consent decrees entered into between a company and the SEC were often ambiguous. Finally, the Freedom of Information Act and the media prevented the SEC from keeping the disclosures completely confidential. The bad publicity that resulted made corporations reluctant to comply with the voluntary programme.

In response, Congress enacted the Foreign Corrupt Practices Act of 1977. The FCPA replaced the indirect and ineffectual methods of prosecuting such payments[5] with a seemingly clear and direct posture. The FCPA was a statement by Congress that 'competition in overseas markets should be based on the merits – on price and product quality – rather than on questionable payments to foreign political leaders'.[6] Congress desired to stop illegal foreign bribes in order to 'restore public confidence in the integrity of the American business system'.

Congress had several additional objectives in mind: (1) Congress believed that the payment of bribes was counter to the moral expectations and values of the American public; (2) Congress wanted to prevent the distortion of commercial competition; and (3) Congress was concerned about the public scandals engendered by bribery and the resulting foreign policy problems for the United States when friendly governments are embarrassed. The FCPA, and the growing number of similar anti-corruption statutes worldwide are a recognition that 'public corruption is the ultimate non-tariff barrier to trade'.

---

[3] These SEC-imposed requirements for the creation and implementation of 'compliance programmes' were the early forerunners and the conceptual ancestors of the compliance programme requirement embedded in the Organizational Sentencing Guidelines passed almost twenty years later.

[4] The SEC discovered that, too often, 'outside directors' were friends or business associates of the chief executive officers and not truly 'independent'. Directors traded board memberships. So grew an inbreeding of directors more interested in protecting each other than in recognizing their duty to manage a public corporation in the best interests of the shareholders. Like 'compliance programmes', this SEC-imposed requirement sprang to full vigour in the early 1990s when corporations began to open their board rooms to individuals willing to exercise a genuine oversight and managerial function.

[5] Before the enactment of the FCPA, United States corporations that bribed foreign officials could only be prosecuted through indirect means, such as the disclosure requirements of the Securities Exchange Act of 1934, the Bank Secrecy Act, which required disclosing of funds which enter or exit the US, false Shipper Export Declarations to the US Department of Commerce and the catch-all Mail Fraud Statute. *See* Daniel Pines, 'Amending the Foreign Corrupt Practices Act to Include a Private Right of Action', 82 *Calf. L. Rev.* (1994) 185, 198.

[6] Assistant Attorney General Philip B. Heyman.

The FCPA Accounting Provisions

The first prong of the FCPA, and the net that frequently catches bribery by publicly-held corporations, are the accounting provisions found in section 13(b) of the Securities Exchange Act of 1934. This section requires a corporation to keep accurate accounts of all transactions it conducts.[7]

While it is certainly true that the accounting provisions of the Act were geared to work in tandem with the anti-bribery provisions, there was a recognition at the time of the Act's consideration by Congress that the accounting provisions would have an effect extending beyond so-called 'questionable payments' made in connection with foreign business.[8] The SEC Report stated that

> Whatever their origin, the Commission regards defects in the system of corporate accountability to be matters of serious concern. Implicit in the requirement of a public corporation to file accurate financial statements is the requirement that those financial statements be based on truthful books and records. Accordingly, the integrity of corporate books and records is essential to the entire reporting system administered by the Commission.[9]

In turn, the 'accounting provisions' have two distinct prongs: the first relates to the maintenance of the books and records themselves; the second addresses the creation and implementation of an adequate system of internal controls to measure and assure compliance with the first requirement.

> The 'books and records' provision contained in Section 13(b)(2)(A) of the FCPA has three basic objectives: (1) books and records should reflect transactions in conformity with accepted methods of reporting economic events,[10] (2) misrepresentation, concealment, falsification, circumvention, and other deliberate acts resulting in inaccurate financial books and records are unlawful, and (3) transactions should be properly reflected on books and records in such a manner as to permit the preparation of

---

[7] 15 U.S.C. § 78M. (West Supp. 1994). *See also* the companion Rule 13b-2 (17 C.F.R. 240.13b-2) often referred to as the 'thou shalt not lie to thy auditor' rule.

[8] The SEC's 'Report on Questionable and Illegal Corporate Payments and Practices' Senate Committee on Banking, Housing and Urban Affairs, *Report of the Securities and Exchange Commission on Questionable and Illegal Corporate Payments and Practices*, 95th Cong., 1st Sess. (1976) at 3 ('SEC Report').

[9] *Id.,* at 49–50.

[10] 'Accepted methods of reporting economic events' is a more broadly worded phrase than 'generally accepted accounting principles' ('GAAP'). Under the former, a company would be in compliance with the FCPA if its recordation met the requirements of either GAAP, the Internal Revenue Code, or rules relating to how municipalities and local governments, public institutions, charities and similar organizations with specialized accounting principles normally record their business affairs in a truthful manner.

financial statements in conformity with GAAP and other criteria applicable to such statements.[11]

The elements of a violation of the books and records provision of the FCPA's accounting provisions are:

1. public companies
2. which fail to make and keep books, records and accounts
3. which *accurately and fairly reflect*
4. in *reasonable detail*
5. the *transactions and depositions of the assets* of the company.

Subsection (B) requires a company to maintain adequate controls to assure that the books and records provision will be complied with. The internal controls provision requires:

1. public companies to *devise and maintain* a system of *internal accounting controls*
2. *sufficient* to provide *reasonable assurance* that
   a. transactions are recorded as necessary (i) to permit preparation of financial statements in conformity with generally accepted accounting principles (GAAP) or *any other criteria applicable to such statements*,[12] and (ii) to maintain accountability for assets;
   b. access to assets is permitted only in accordance with management's *general or specific authorization*; and,
   c. the recorded accountability for assets is compared with the existing assets at reasonable intervals and *appropriate action is taken* with respect to any differences.[13]

The FCPA Anti-Bribery Provisions

The second prong of the FCPA makes bribery of foreign officials by United States businesses – whether publicly or privately held and whether they are partnerships, joint ventures or other forms of business entities – a violation of the Act.[14] Enforcement authority for the FCPA was given to both the Department of Justice ('DOJ') for all criminal offences and for civil cases against non-public corporations, and the SEC for civil actions against publicly owned corporations.

---

[11] *SEC* v. *Worldwide* (N.D. Ga. 1983).

[12] *See supra* note 10.

[13] The requirement of 'appropriate action' was the early predecessor to the Organizational Sentencing Guidelines' requirement that there be not only a 'compliance programme' but that it be 'effectively implemented'.

[14] 15 U.S.C. §§ 78dd-1(a) – 2(a) (1977) (amended 1988).

Despite the unanimous adoption of the Act by Congress, and the politically appealing nature of its principles, the FCPA was subject to almost
immediate criticism by United States businesses. First, critics complained
that the Act's provisions were extremely vague. Second, they complained
that the FCPA's provisions covered such a broad scope that the FCPA
threatened to unduly impair the conduct of United States business abroad.
The critics were not limited to United States businessmen; the late Senator
Heinz, for example, also believed that many of the FCPA's provisions
would cripple the ability of American companies to compete in certain
foreign countries.[15]

In response to these criticisms, Congress enacted the Omnibus Trade and
Competitiveness Act of 1988 to amend the FCPA.[16] The 1988 Amendment
contained several major changes, including the exclusion of certain types of
payments to foreign officials, and addition of affirmative defences against
prosecution.[17]

As amended, the elements of a violation are:

1. A company, officer, or employee
2. who uses the mails or any instrumentality of interstate [which would
   include foreign] commerce[18]
3. corruptly in furtherance of an offer, payment, promise to pay, or
   authorization of the payment of any money, or offer, gift, promise to
   give, or authorization of the giving of anything of value
4. to any foreign official, foreign political party, political party official or
   candidate for political office,
5. for the purpose of influencing any official act or decision (including
   omission to act) or to induce such official to use influence to affect any
   act or decision),
6. in order to assist in obtaining or retaining business for, with or to any
   person.

---

[15] 'Sen. Heinz Reintroduces Proposal to Amend FCPA', *Sec. Reg. & L. Rep.* (BNA) No.
7 at 318 (15 February 1985). As discussed later in this Chapter, neither Senator Heinz nor these
critics envisioned an emerging global economy where well-run corporations selling top quality
goods or services at fair prices would come to dominance and where competitors who relied
on bribes would find their business relationships fragile, short-lived and extremely damaging
to their reputations in the marketplace. These corporations failed to understand that politicians
without scruples who govern by corruption are the first to deny knowledge of illegal acts, quick
to condemn the perpetrators, and even quicker to engage in a few public executions whether
by killing or imprisoning individuals or by confiscating corporate property and refusing to make
payments due for goods and services.

[16] Pub. L. No. 100–418 (1988) (codified at 15 U.S.C. §§ 78dd-1(a)(3) – 2(a)(3) (West
Supp. 1977).

[17] 15 U.S.C. 78dd *et seq.* These issues will be addressed more fully in later sections of this
Chapter.

[18] The Mail Fraud Statute has been modified to include use of private courier services.

Penalties

The penalties for violating the FCPA are substantial. Individuals who violate the Act are subject to up to five years in prison and may be fined up to $100,000 for each act. Any fine imposed on an individual may not be paid, directly or indirectly, by the corporation. Corporations may be fined up to $2,000,000 for each act.

It is with this significant risk in mind, that we turn to a more detailed consideration of the elements of an FCPA violation.

ELEMENTS OF FCPA VIOLATIONS

Accounting Provisions

Sections 13(b)(2)(A) & (B), the accounting provisions, are designed to provide reasonable assurance that corporations make and keep their books, records, and accounts in a fashion which will enable them to fulfil their disclosure obligations. Although Congress intended the internal controls section to strengthen the anti-bribery provisions, the law does not limit internal control requirements to the prevention or detection of foreign bribery. Therefore, despite the title of the Act, the accounting provisions are in no way linked to either overseas business activities or to corrupt practices. As former Chairman of the SEC, Ray Garrett, Jr. said, 'If this Act were a prospectus, the issuer would be jailed for using a misleading title'.

The accounting requirements apply to all business activities of all United States companies that are either registered or file reports, or both, with the SEC under the Securities Exchange Act of 1934 Act.

The law requires publicly held companies to (1) devise and maintain a system of internal controls sufficient, among other things, to provide reasonable assurance that transactions are properly recorded and (2) keep records which 'accurately and fairly' reflect financial activities in reasonable detail.

Record-keeping Standard
The record-keeping provision was directed at three basic problems which were uncovered by the SEC's improper payments investigations in the 1970s:

1. Records that simply failed to record improper transactions at all.
2. Records that were falsified to disguise aspects of improper transactions otherwise recorded correctly.
3. Records that correctly set forth the quantitative aspects of transactions but failed to record the 'qualitative' aspects of those transactions

which would have revealed their illegality or impropriety – such as the true purpose of particular payments to agents, distributors or customers.

In response, the law places the responsibility on publicly held companies to: '... make and keep books, records, and accounts, which, in reasonable detail, accurately and fairly reflect the transactions and dispositions of the assets of the issues...'

a) The Meaning of 'In Reasonable Detail'
The 'in reasonable detail' qualification was added to the originally proposed Senate bill to avoid implying an unrealistic degree of exactitude. The phrase indicates that records should be maintained which are sufficient to allow an understanding of the real nature of the transactions and to prevent the occurrence of off-book slush funds and bribes.

b) The Meaning of 'Accurate and Fairly'
'Accurate and fairly' was a compromise and substitute for the more stringent, and more easily – albeit innocently – violated requirement of 'truthful' books and records. It constitutes recognition of how modern day accounting principles operate. This phrase merely requires that the books and records should reflect transactions in conformity with accepted methods of recording economic events. GAAP and IRS accounting methods, among others, are considered acceptable.[19]

Internal Controls Standard
The law requires publicly held companies to devise and maintain internal control systems sufficient to provide reasonable assurance of meeting the objectives set in the disclosure requirements Securities Laws. Therefore, the controls must be sufficient to provide 'reasonable assurances' concerning the use and disposition of assets, that is, not an absolute standard. Controls must be sufficient to prevent off-book bank accounts, cash hordes and misclassification of transactions.

The Materiality Standard
The internal controls provision is not limited to material transactions or to those above a specific dollar amount. In other words, there is *no* materiality standard. This means that *any* deviation is, theoretically, enough for liability under the Act.

---

[19] *See supra* note 10.

Despite this ambiguity in the Act, the legislative history makes it very clear that Congress expected management to estimate and evaluate the cost/benefit relationships of the steps to be taken to fulfil its responsibilities and to reject controls that could not be justified economically. Among the factors that Congress anticipated that management would consider were (1) the size of the business, (2) the diversity of operations, (3) the degree of centralization of financial and operating management, and (4) the amount of contact by top officers with day-to-day operations.

The Anti-Bribery Provisions

The Corrupt Party: The Definition of 'Domestic Concern' and Public Company ('Issuer')

The foreign bribery provisions of the Act apply to *all* United States companies and officers, directors, employees, *agents*, or stockholders acting on behalf of such companies. The law comprises two similar sections – one which covers publicly held companies, or 'issuers', and the other which applies to all other 'domestic concerns'.

An 'issuer' is simply any company registered under section 12 of the Securities Exchange act of 1934 and any company required to file reports pursuant to section 15(d) of that Act.

A 'domestic concern' is broadly defined as (1) *a business entity which either has its principal place of business in the United States* or which is organized under the laws of the United States or any state, territory, or possession; or (2) *an individual* who is a *United States citizen, national, or resident.* Thus, activities by wholly owned United States subsidiaries of foreign corporations, or those entities controlled by foreign companies, are within the ambit of the FCPA. Significantly, actions outside the United States by United States citizens, nationals or residents even if performed for foreign corporations, are swept up into the Act's prohibitions and, at a minimum, could create liability for those persons with attendant negative publicity for the entities that employ them. As a practical matter, it is difficult to envision a situation involving a totally foreign corporation, whose securities are not traded in and which is not based in the United States, having a United States citizen, national or resident charged under the FCPA for an activity undertaken in a third nation on behalf of his foreign employer. However, that having been said, it would be equally unwise for a foreign corporation to assume that, for political reasons, the United States government would not employ the FCPA, antitrust laws or any other statute, to attempt to 'level the playing field' for United States economic or political interests.

a) Foreign Subsidiaries

Although foreign subsidiaries of United States business are not *specifically* mentioned in the law, the actions of foreign subsidiaries is incorporated into the reach of the law through the language which prohibits *indirect* foreign payments or offers. The question of whether the percentage of ownership interest by the parent in the subsidiary (that is, whether it is more or less than 50 per cent) affects its liability is still open. Additionally, the question of whether a joint venture with a foreign company exposes the domestic company to liability also remains unresolved. Both situations will turn on the facts of a particular transaction.

b) The Requisite Intent: 'Corruptly' to Influence An Official Action
The FCPA prohibits United States concerns and issuers from 'corruptly' using the mail or any other means or instrumentalities of interstate (including foreign) commerce for making a payment or providing anything else of value for various business purposes to foreign government officials. The term 'corruptly' is not defined in the FCPA. As a result, several possibilities have been postulated for how the term should be defined in the context of the FCPA; however, the legislative history indicates that the term 'corruptly' is to be construed in a fashion which is analogous to the use of that term under the domestic bribery statute, 18 U.S.C. § 201(b).[20]

The courts have adopted this viewpoint and given support to the position that 'corruptly' should be interpreted the same way under the FCPA as it is under the domestic bribery statute. For example, in *United States* v. *Liebo*,[21] the court held that a jury could properly infer corrupt intent from the defendant's act of giving a gift to a close relation of the foreign official where the surrounding circumstances sustained the reasonable inference that the 'gift' was made for the purpose of influencing the foreign official's decision-making process.[22]

It is interesting to note that the payment, or 'gift', in *Liebo* was not made to, nor did it benefit, the particular government official that Liebo 'intended' to influence. Liebo had bought airline tickets which benefited the cousin of the foreign official.[23] It is also interesting to note that in *Liebo* subjective intent of the defendant was inferred from the surrounding circumstances. Since the prosecution of a FCPA violation is necessarily *post facto*, it is important to be mindful that activities will be judged with the benefit of

---

[20] S.Rep. No. 114, 95th Cong., 7th Sess. at 10. Occasionally, the claim is made by the bribe-giver that, in fact, the payment resulted from extortion and not bribery. In the United States, generally, prosecutors will look to whether the payment was made after a threat to a person's life or property occurred. If so, it is more likely that an extortion occurred. However, making a payment in response to being told that not to do so would eliminate a company from consideration for a project or some other business is considered a bribe since the giver had free will and made a voluntary choice.

[21] 923 F. Supp. 1308 (8th Cir. 1991).

[22] *Id.*, at 1312.

[23] Although the cousin was also a foreign official, the facts are clear that Liebo intended to influence the Maintenance Chief of Nigeria. *Id.*, at 1310.

hindsight. If the transaction results in an economic benefit conferred on a decision-making official (or on a close friend or family member), the inference of corrupt purpose is substantial.

The Recipient of the Corrupt Payment: Any 'Foreign Official'
Unlike with the term 'corrupt', the FCPA does define the term 'foreign official'.[24] A foreign official is 'any officer or employee of a foreign government or any department, agency, or instrumentality thereof, or any person acting in an official capacity for or on behalf of any such government or department, agency or instrumentality'.[25]

The FCPA requires that the 'foreign official' be engaged in an official capacity or lawful duty when the alleged illegal conduct occurs. In effect, this makes the definition of foreign official analogous to the term 'public official' as defined in the domestic bribery statute.

Under the domestic statute, all that is required to qualify as a public official is that the 'individual must possess some degree of official responsibility for carrying out a federal programme or policy'.[26] In other words, it is not necessary that the individual be an employee of the government.

While this presents what could be termed a difficult situation under the domestic bribery statute, it may be treacherous under the FCPA. Often, officials in foreign countries act in a public and private capacity simultaneously. For example, payments to officials of state owned companies has constituted a violation of the FCPA.[27] Care must be exercised in this area because 'foreign officials' may apply to anyone who exercises 'official' influence over an 'official' enterprise.[28]

---

[24] 15 U.S.C.A. §§ 78dd-1(f)(1) – 2(h)(2) (West 1994).

[25] *Id.* Within this definition would be government-created corporations or entities as well as consultants, or advisors, to the foreign government entity.

[26] *Dryson* v. *United States*, 465 U.S. 482.

[27] *See, e.g., United States* v. *Young L. Rubicam, Inc.*, 741 F. Supp. 334 (D. Conn. 1990); *United States* v. *Sam P. Wallace Co.*, 617 Sec. Reg. & L. Rep. (BNA) A-4 (D.D.C. 13 August 1981).

[28] In some Third World countries, the infrastructure development needs of the nation crimp its ability to pay for all the government services needed and 'foreign policy officials' are expected to obtain a portion, or all, of their compensation from duties, taxes or service charges imposed upon foreign companies doing or seeking to do business in that country. Where such a procedure is set forth in the statutes or official rules and regulations of that nation, there should be no violation of the FCPA. The difficulty is that virtually all nations make bribery of their officials a crime. In those countries the line between paying for services and 'bribery' may be too thin to be perceived. More important, when a United States government prosecutor confronts such a situation, in the absence of a foreign statute on point, there will be a request for some official government paper from the foreign nation stating that this practice is lawful, encouraged by the government, and does not violate any of that country's laws. A corporation faced with such a request may find to its great sorrow that obtaining such an official statement is not possible.

The Medium of Payment: 'Anything of Value'
The FCPA prohibits the corrupt payment, offer, gift or authorization of the giving of 'anything of value'.[29] Although the medium of corrupt payment is often cash or cash equivalent, the term 'anything of value' reaches payments of non-cash items. For example, charitable donations,[30] travel expenses,[31] loans with favourable interest and repayment terms,[32] trips and the services of a prostitute have all been held to constitute corrupt payments under the FCPA and the bribery statute. In short, the gift or promise need not be shown to have a specific economic value. Indeed, it need not be something that anyone else in the world would find 'valuable'. The test is whether it was something that the intended recipient wanted, asked for, or placed a value on whether real, psychological, physical or emotional. If so, the test for 'anything of value' has been met.

As is obvious, the phrase 'anything of value' is interpreted very broadly. In fact, the medium of corrupt payment may not even have any monetary value whatsoever or even in fact exist. In *Williams*,[33] a domestic bribery case resulting from the ABSCAM investigation into payments to members of the United States Congress, the 'thing of value' was stock in a fictitious titanium mining venture. Objectively, stock in a non-existent company has no negotiable value; however, under the anti-bribery provisions, its perceived value is sufficient to uphold a conviction.

Payments to Third Parties: 'Knowing' the Payment Will Be Made to a Foreign Official
As noted above, the FCPA also prohibits payments to third parties with the knowledge that 'all or a portion' of the payment will be made, 'directly or indirectly' to a foreign official.[34] The substitution of the term 'knowing' for 'reason to know' was one of the concessions made in the 1988 Amendment to the FCPA.

The FCPA defines a person's state of mind as 'knowing' if either:

a) the person is 'aware' that he or she is engaging in the conduct; or

---

[29] 15 U.S.C. §§ 78dd-1(a) – 2(a) (West Supp. 1994).

[30] *Lamb* v. *Phillip Morris, Inc.*, 915 F.2d 1024 (6th Cir. 199) (agreement to make donations totalling $12.5 million to the Children's Foundation of Caracas, whose president was the wife of the President of Venezuela, in exchange for elimination of cigarette price controls and other tax considerations).

[31] *United States* v. *Liebo*, 923 F.2d 1308 (8th Cir. 1991).

[32] *United States* v. *Hare*, 618 F.2d 1085 (4th Cir. 1980).

[33] *United States* v. *Williams*, 705 F.2d 603 (2d Cir.), *cert. denied*, 464 U.S. 1007 (1983). Therefore, a 'thing of value' has been broadly construed, and may involve only the perception of the item held by recipient. It is the corrupt intent of the giver which is likely to be determinative in cases arising under the FCPA.

[34] 15 U.S.C. §§ 78dd-1(a)(3) – 2(a)(3) (West Supp. 1994).

b) if the person has a 'firm belief' that a result 'is substantially certain to occur'.

The FCPA further provides that where 'knowledge' of a circumstance is required, such knowledge can be established 'if a person is aware of a high probability of the existence of such circumstances...'.[35] Exception is made 'if the person actually believes that such circumstances do not exist'.

Although 'simple negligence' and 'mere foolishness' are not a basis for culpability under the FCPA, the concept of 'conscious disregard' and 'willful blindness' are incorporated into the definition of 'knowing' conduct.[36] Thus, liability cannot be avoided by turning a blind eye to the practices of subordinates within a company, or to the realities of the situation in the foreign country.

However, it should be noted that at this point the exact scope of the term 'knowingly' has not been developed in the context of the FCPA.[37] Corporations which have been facilely advised by their lawyers or others not to make too broad an inquiry in order to escape liability under the anti-bribery provisions of the FCPA may well be maneuvering themselves into a violation of the accounting and internal controls provisions applicable to public corporations. Not only would these corporations be in derogation of their responsibility to know the use and disposition of corporate assets and that such be in accordance with general or specific management directives, but those involved could face civil or criminal suits on another ground. Assets of a corporation not used to advance the business or interests of the corporation may come within the concepts of wasting of corporate assets, breach of fiduciary duty or self-enrichment.

'For the Purpose of Influencing' an Official Act or Decision
The intent of the giver controls the determination of the purpose of the payment or gift. Like many of the other phrases in the FCPA, determination of this element involves a backward look at the facts. The examination will entail looking at the recipient, the relationship of the recipient to the activity desired by the giver and whether the recipient or someone the recipient was intended to influence had the ability to act or omit to act in a matter that affected the giver's obtaining or retaining of business. Payments for the performance of ministerial functions or to induce a government official to

---

[35] 15 U.S.C. § 78dd-(1)(f)(2)(B) (West Supp. 1994).

[36] 1988 Conference Report at 919.

[37] The concept of 'knowledge' and 'wilfully' have recently found expression in several decisions by the United States Supreme Court. *Cheek* v. *United States*, 498 U.S. 192 (1991) (Internal Revenue Code issue); *Ratzlaf* v. *United States*, 510 U.S. 135 (1994) ('structuring', a money laundering offence). In essence, the Supreme Court held that to prove wilfulness and intent, the government must prove that the defendant knew of a legal duty and voluntarily and intentionally violated that known duty.

perform an act which they are already legally or contractually required to perform are not violative conduct.[38]

'Obtaining or Retaining Business'

The idea of 'obtaining' business should not require extended discussion except to note that gifts or payments to foreign officials to draft requests for contract proposals in such a manner as to disfavour competitors or make them unable to bid is within the statute. 'Retaining' business likewise affects elimination of competition and relates to multi-stage projects where each stage is separate and bids are made and approved separately.

DEFENCES AND EXEMPT TRANSACTIONS

Exempt Transactions

Under the revised provisions of the FCPA, there is an explicit exemption for certain 'facilitating payments' where the purpose of the payment is to 'expedite or to secure the performance of a routine government action'.[39] For the purpose of the Act, a 'routine government action' refers only to actions that are ordinarily and commonly performed by a foreign official in connection with:

1. obtaining permits, licences, or other official documents to qualify a person to do business in a foreign country;
2. processing governmental papers, such as visas and work orders;
3. providing police protection, mail pick-up and delivery, or scheduling inspections associated with contract performance of inspections related to transit of goods across country;
4. providing phone service, power and water supply, loading and unloading cargo, or protecting perishable products or commodities from deterioration; or

---

[38] For example, arranging for air transport to a remote area for a government inspector to perform a necessary inspection would not, in itself, be improper. Payment of a small gratuity to a customs official to promptly inspect fruit for export is another example of a non-violative act (but making the payment to secure issuance of documents might be a violation). Similar situations involve securing prompt berthing approval from a harbour master to off-load construction equipment or parts for a factory or project or to expedite processing of papers for the exportation of household goods and personalty of company employees seeking to leave the foreign country upon completion of their work. To assure that such actions will be deemed within the exception for lawful or contractually required official action, corporations undertaking projects abroad should negotiate these items into their contracts and secure official government approvals before beginning the work.

[39] 15 U.S.C. §§ 78dd-1(b) – 2(b). *See supra* note 38.

5. actions of a similar nature.[40]

The Act makes clear that the term 'routine government action' does not include 'any decision by a foreign official whether, or on what terms, to award new business to or to continue business with a particular party, or any action taken by a foreign official involved in the decision-making process to encourage a decision to award new business to or continue business with a particular party.[41]

The exemption for facilitating payments, thus, is quite limited in scope. Also note that even though a payment is exempt from the bribery provision of the FCPA, it is not exempt from the accounting provisions. It must be disclosed accurately in the financial statements and in the company's books of original entry.

Statutory Affirmative Defences

The 1988 Amendment recognizes two affirmative defences to liability under the Act: first, that the payment was lawful under the written laws of the foreign official's country; and second, that the payment was reasonable and *bona fide* and that it related to promotion of products and execution of the contract.[42]

Lawful Payments
The FCPA provides that it shall be an affirmative defence that:

> The payment, gift, offer or promise of anything of value that was made, was lawful under the *written* laws and regulations of the foreign officials, political party's, party official's, or candidate's country....[43]

It should be noted that the payment must be legal under the foreign country's written laws; therefore, 'custom' is not a defence to prosecution under the FCPA.

Reasonable and Bona Fide Promotional Expenses
The FCPA also contains an affirmative defence in the situation where the payment was made in association with (a) a promotional effort; and (b) the execution or performance of a contract:

---

[40] 15 U.S.C. § 78dd-1(b) – 2(b).
[41] 15 U.S.C. § 78dd-1(f)93)(A) – 2(h)(4)(A).
[42] 15 U.S.C.A. §§ 78dd-1(c)(1), 2(c)(2) (West Supp. 1994).
[43] 15 U.S.C. §§ 78dd-1(c)(1) – 2(c)(1) (West Supp. 1994).

The payment, gift, offer or promise of anything of value that was made, was a reasonable and *bona fide* expenditure, such as travel and lodging expenses, incurred by or on behalf of a foreign official, party, party official, or candidate and was directly related to:

a. the promotion, demonstration, or explanation of products or services; or

b. the execution or performance of a contract with a foreign government or agency thereof.[44]

It should be cautioned that this defence only applies when the payment was made in good faith; therefore, if the payment is, in reality, a bribe or is otherwise a corrupt payment intended to influence an official act, the defence would not apply.

It should also be cautioned that the above defences do not alter the basic requirement to accurately reflect these transactions in the company's records.

Rejected Proposed Defences: Business Courtesy and Due Diligence

A business courtesy exception was proposed by the Senate for inclusion in the 1988 Amendment. However, in the House-Senate Conference the provision was 'receded' by the Senate. This proposal would have provided an exception for 'nominal' payments or gifts that were a 'courtesy, a token of regard or esteem, in return for hospitality'. The FCPA, as amended, does not have such an exception leaving to the judgment of prosecutors whether a payment of this type had the purpose and intent prohibited by the FCPA.

A company may generally be held vicariously liable for the acts of its employees that were committed within the scope of employment with some intent to benefit the company.[45]

The House proposed that there be a 'safe harbour' from vicarious liability for FCPA violations of employees or agents for companies that had

---

[44] 15 U.S.C. §§ 78dd-1(c)(2) – 2(c)(z) (West Supp. 1994). Sponsoring a trip by a foreign official to the United States to visit a company's offices, production facilities, and to meet with various of its officers and employees would not be improper even if the trip entailed time for the official to engage in personal activities provided the predominant purpose and time were expended for business. Similarly, if the United States State Department or other governmental agency, the White House, a United States embassy, a foreign nation's United States embassy, invites a corporation to be a 'corporate sponsor' of a reception for or visit by a foreign official from a country where the corporation does business, that sponsorship generally will not be deemed improper. A closer question arises where the corporation is in the process of attempting to secure a contract from the foreign nation even if not from a department under the direct supervision of the visiting dignitary.

[45] *New York Central and H.R.R.R.* v. *United States*, 212 U.S. 481 (1908); *United States* v. *Cincotta*, 689 F.2d 239 (1st Cir.), *cert. denied*, 459 U.S. 991 (1982).

established procedures that were 'reasonabl[y] expected to prevent and detect' violations.[46]

This proposal was also rejected. Nonetheless, despite the absence of a formal defence of due diligence, a company's internal controls are at least a partial defence and may be argued to a jury as proof of a lack of 'intent' to commit a crime. At a minimum, the existence and effective implementation of a system of internal controls should support a request for a jury instruction that the jury may consider this as a factor in deciding whether a corporation had the 'intent' to violate the law.

COMPLIANCE AND DUE DILIGENCE

A programme for compliance with the FCPA can help a company detect and avoid potential violations of the Act by alerting the company to warning signs that a deal may involve questionable conduct on behalf of an agent of employee. Moreover, with the 'knowing' standard of third party conduct, a company will be in a better position in a prosecution to prove that it did not 'hide its head in the sand', if it has an on-going due diligence practice.

Written Policy

The company should adopt a written policy governing the selection and retention of foreign sales representatives. The policy should detail the steps involved in hiring an outside representative in a foreign country. For instance, it should clarify the type of documentation and background information that the company requires to make a decision, as well as the person ultimately responsible in the company to make the decision of whether or not to retain the foreign person.

The company should also include in its written policy, a section which outlines the basic provisions of applicable law, such as the FCPA.

Written Agreement

When a decision to hire a foreign representative is made, the agreement should be memorialized in a written agreement which designates the consultant an 'independent contractor'.[47] It should also contain a 'compliance with law' section that unequivocally states that the representative is not to engage in any acts which could be considered to violate the FCPA. The

---

[46] 1988 Conference Report at 922.

[47] Nevertheless, because the independent contractors will be acting for, and in the interests of, the company, they may be viewed as 'agents' of the company as defined in the FCPA.

contract should be made contingent on compliance with this term by the foreign agent. There should be documentation of a business need for the services of a foreign agent. In most legitimate business dealings abroad, this is not too difficult to do and will be helpful. Likewise, payments to the foreign agent should be in proportion to the services rendered and to the value of the business obtained. Disproportionately sized payments will raise questions and require justification. The contract should state that where there is a possibility that the action of the foreign agent could violate a provision of the FCPA, the representative will not engage in the act without having first secured approval from the company's legal staff. Finally, it should make clear that all expenditures must be properly recorded and promptly reported to the company.

Background Information

The company should ascertain information concerning the representatives' background. This information should be gathered from direct interviews with the candidate and through an independent background check.

A background evaluation should include as a first level:

1. contact with the country desk at the United States Department of State and the United States Department of Commerce;
2. the Commercial Attaché at the local United States Embassy;
3. banks doing business in the foreign country;
4. reporting services such as Dunn & Bradstreet;
5. international newspapers and periodicals and local publications in the foreign country likely to carry information about activities of the foreign agent; and
6. other companies, especially other United States companies, and 'strategic partners' doing business in the foreign country.

All the information collected should be reduced to writing and kept in the agent's files.

When the first-level background check raises questions and the company still perceives a need to utilize the particular foreign agent, additional inquiry should be made of:

1. United States government officials knowledgeable about the foreign country and likely to maintain files on significant personalities in those countries;
2. investigative services in the foreign country as well as a second such service less likely to be co-opted by local personalities;
3. writers who have lived and worked in that country;
4. university scholars specializing in the country;

5. experts at 'think tanks' who have devoted study to the foreign country; and
6. retired United States government officials who served in the foreign country.

Opinion of Counsel

In addition to the opinion of the company official who will make the ultimate decision, the opinion of foreign counsel should also be obtained and filed. The opinion of foreign counsel should include:

1. whether local law requires, permits or prohibits the type of representation contemplated in the agreement;
2. whether the proposed representative qualifies to represent the company (that is, whether there is a requirement that the representative be a citizen of the country or that the owners, officers or directors of the representative be citizens of the country);
3. whether there are registration or disclosure requirements that apply to the representative's activities on behalf of the company;
4. whether the terms of the agreement with the representative violate local law, particularly with regard to compensation;
5. whether there are restrictions or prohibitions concerning the sharing of commissions or fees with third parties;
6. whether the method and place of payment of compensation complies with the country's currency and tax laws;
7. whether the law of the country recognizes the representative's independent contractor status; and,
8. whether there are restrictions concerning the company's ability to terminate the representative.

Counsel can also provide general information regarding the conduct, with respect to payments, that is permissible under a foreign country's written laws or judicial decisions. Additionally, United States counsel can advise whether a proposed payment would be considered a 'facilitating payment' under the FCPA.

THE INTERNATIONAL DIMENSION

Acceptance of the FCPA both in the United States and abroad has been slow and grudging. Anti-corruption statutes often are seen by business managers as unrealistic in light of the normative behaviour pattern in a foreign country and likely to result in an unfairness which does not apply to foreign competitors. It is seen by many as weakening the ability of American companies to gain a foothold in some of the fastest growing international markets. A few companies called for repealing the FCPA. Other companies simply complain about it.

While one obvious solution would be to repeal the law, the better and more challenging solution is to encourage other nations to raise their standards so that they enact similar statutes to the FCPA. From the inception of the FCPA, this has been the goal. However, nearly twenty years after Congress passed the FCPA, the United States remains one of the few if not the only nation in the world which prohibits its businesses from bribing foreign officials.

In fact, European and Japanese competitors even can deduct bribes from their taxes. As one commentator put it: 'If a German bribes a German, he gets thrown in jail; if he bribes a foreign official he gets a tax deduction'. This is the situation in most European countries. In countries such as Germany, Greece, Luxembourg, Belgium and France foreign bribe payments are tax deductible in whole or part.

Even worse is the attitude of government officials of developing countries: the Kleptocrats. They often expect to become more wealthy through their involvement in politics. As a result, United States businesses often find themselves at a competitive disadvantage when bidding against foreign companies for contracts in Kleptocracies. As one writer said, 'Competitors grease palms that United States developers are legally bound to merely shake'.

However, the days in which United States businesses are forced to play by a different set of rules may be coming to an end. Surprisingly, perhaps, this is not because the United States has abandoned the FCPA, but rather it is the result of the rest of the world beginning to see the necessity for curtailing the practice of corruption in the international marketplace. In fact, remarkable progress is being made.

On April 11 of 1996, the Organization for Economic Cooperation and Development ('OECD'), whose member comprise the world's 26 leading industrial nations, passed a resolution stating that bribes made to foreign officials should no longer be tax deductible. Member nations are now expected – but not legally bound – to rewrite their tax laws accordingly; the OECD has set up a watchdog group to monitor the changes and report back on the progress within one year.

The OECD is also seeking to pass another resolution making bribery of a government official a criminal offence. On 22 May 1996, overcoming last-minute objections from France and Germany's resistance to the effort, the OECD members agreed to 'criminalise the bribery of foreign officials in an effective and co-ordinated manner' and to re-examine the tax deductibility bribes where this was still permitted. Ministers agreed to consider proposals on anti-bribery next year. The 52-member Commonwealth has come forth in support of the OECD efforts to contain international business corruption. The OECD has also recommended that their governments take action to introduce anti-corruption provisions into contracts funded by their aid budgets.

Also in March 1996, the International Chamber of Commerce ('ICC') issued guidelines to its 7,000 business members urging them to adopt enforceable codes against bribery and to insure transparency in accounting for political contributions. The ICC also called on governments to write tougher legislation and to repeal laws allowing tax deductibility for foreign bribes. The ICC intends to press the World Trade Organization at its December 1996 meeting for a study on the impact of bribery in distorting and hindering international trade. In March, it approved a series of guidelines which urge its members to adopt enforceable codes designed to counter bribery and ensure transparent accounting of any political contributions. It also calls on governments to toughen legislation on bribery and extortion, and to remove opportunities for companies to write off bribes against tax bills.

On 29 March 1996, 21 member states of the 34 member states of the Organization of the American States ('OAS') signed the Inter-American Convention against Corruption at an annual meeting. The treaty requires each signatory country to make bribery of foreign officials a crime and an extraditable offence. This is the first extension outside the United States of the approach taken in the FCPA. In a gesture more symbolic than substantive, on 2 June 1996, the United States has since become a signatory to this treaty.

The World Bank's chairman, James Wolfensohn, has spoken out on corruption and is expected to make it an important point in his speech to the World Bank's meeting later this year. Already the World Bank's board has approved reforms in the procurement process. On 23 July 1996 the Board of the World Bank adopted requirements that all commissions paid to agents be disclosed to the World Bank, giving to the Board the right to audit contractors and suppliers, and strengthened provisions for cancellation of bribe-tainted contracts and for debarment from contracting of violators.

The International Monetary Fund is exploring steps that it might take.

The Council of Securities Regulators of the Americas (COSRA) adopted an anti-bribery resolution to ensure enforcement of and compliance with internal control and accurate books and records requirements. COSRA also agreed to facilitate closer cooperation among securities and banking regulators in investigations and in criminal prosecutions for bribery.

The United States, in conjunction with other members of the United Nations, has drafted a proposed UN declaration for consideration at the ECOSOC General Assembly meeting in the Fall of 1996 to support the efforts of the OAS, OECD and to criminalize bribery and repeal laws allowing foreign bribes to be tax deductible.

Another group committed to the issue is Transparency International ('TI'). TI leads an international effort to curb corruption. It spreads the message throughout the world that there is an underlying logic to reducing corruption; that, if countries want to enjoy the benefits of growing foreign investment in flourishing trade, they must clean up their corrupt practices. It advocates that corporations and governments throughout the world should discontinue practices which encourage corruption; that they should place sanctions on both those who give and those who take bribes. The United States chapter of TI is supported by a growing number of prominent businesspeople and corporations, all of whom have recognized that corruption abroad can indeed by fought if major foreign and US companies join forces to discourage corruption and support the 'rule of law'.

While all of these efforts are encouraging to the writer of this Chapter (who worked at the SEC in the 1970s during the infancy of the fight against foreign corruption and helped with the FCPA), the reality is that these efforts remain largely aspirational and greatly in need of support by action.

V. International Initiatives

IBRAHIM F.I. SHIHATA

16. Corruption – A General Review with an Emphasis on the Role of the World Bank[*]

DIFFERENT PERSPECTIVES ON CORRUPTION

Societies may differ in their views as to what constitutes corruption, although the concept finds universal manifestations. Experts have different perspectives on the meaning, causes and effects of this universal phenomenon. While a few take an inter-disciplinary approach, positions are more often influenced by the respective discipline. The literature on the subject is vast and diversified. Any attempt to summarize it here would not do it justice. It may be useful, however, to begin this paper by sharing with the reader some of the main findings based on that literature.

Some economic writings tend to define corruption as a situation where the benefit (to a corrupt agent) of acting against the expectation of a principal outweighs the cost, or where a public good, service or office is sold for personal gain.[1] Others describe it in terms of the exploitation of economic rents which arise from the monopoly position of public officials.[2] In either sense, to quote one economist, corruption 'provides a market price where a market is not allowed'.[3] Economists find the causes of corruption embedded in the country's economic and administrative structures.[4] They note its prevalence where government intervention exceeds its ability to intervene efficiently and where discretion in the allocation of public goods, services or subsidies

---

[*] This paper is based on a paper submitted to the Fourteenth International Symposium on Economic Crime at the Jesus College in Cambridge, England, held September 8–13, 1996. The views in this article are the personal views of the writer and should not be attributed to the institutions he works for. The author wishes to recognize the assistance of Ms. Sabine Schlemmer-Schulte in the preparation of this paper.

[1] *See*, e.g., R. Klitgaard, *Controlling Corruption* 22 (1988); A. Shleifer & R. Vishny, 'Corruption', 108 *Quarterly Journal of Economics* 599 (1993); M. Naim, *The Corruption Eruption*, II The Brown J.W. Aff. 245, 248 (1995).

[2] *See*, e.g., M. Beenstock, *Economics of Corruption* (1977).

[3] R. Klitgaard, 'Bribes, Tribes and Markets that Fail: Rethinking the Economics of Underdevelopment', 11 *Development Southern Africa* 481 (1994).

[4] *See*, e.g., R. Klitgaard, *supra* note 1, at 38–47; E. Mason, *Corruption and Development* 17–30 (Harvard Institute for International Development Discussion Paper No. 50, 1978).

Barry A.K. Rider (ed.), Corruption: The Enemy Within, 255–283
© *Ibrahim F.I. Shihata. Printed in the Netherlands.*

is great, the risk of punishment is low and the pay-offs are sufficiently attractive. A broader view takes into account government policies (e.g. the level of civil service wages or import tariffs) and may further look into the honesty and integrity of both public officials and private individuals. Holding these factors constant, however, this view determines the incidence and size of corruption by the level of benefits available, the riskiness of corrupt deals and the relative bargaining power of its source and beneficiary.[5] Economists are also concerned about the effect of corruption on growth and development. They see bribery, when freely offered and accepted, as serving the immediate interest of the parties to it. As for the interests of the society, some writers have found corruption an important source of capital formation, which could promote flexibility and efficiency in the market and advance entrepreneurship.[6] Others have concluded, on the basis of questionnaires and interviews with businessmen, that a lack of political credibility (faith in the stability of government policies) was much more harmful than corruption, which they viewed 'more as a variable cost than as uncertainty factor'.[7] Other economists distinguish between 'efficient' and 'inefficient' bribes depending on the underlying regulation, arguing that a bribe to avoid regulations which restrict competition increases efficiency.[8] Beyond this efficiency argument, and in spite of the dearth of empirical research, an emerging consensus in modern economic writings seems to suggest that the *long term* effects of corruption on competition in the market, the investment climate and the people's welfare are disruptive and inequitable and that such negative effects tend to increase with the degree of monopoly in the provision of goods and services.[9] The

[5] *See* in particular S. Rose-Ackerman, *The Political Economy of Corruption – Causes and Consequences* (World Bank, Viewpoint Note No. 74, 1996) (hereinafter The Political Economy of Corruption) and S. Rose-Ackerman, *Corruption* 9 (1978) (hereinafter Corruption).

[6] *See*, e.g., J. Nye, 'Corruption and Political Development: A Cost-Benefit Analysis;, 61 *American Political Science Review* 421–422 (1967). Professor Nye, a political scientist, who approached the subject from an economist's point of view, is one of the most quoted sources for the argument that corruption can be useful for a country's economy.

[7] S. Borner, A. Brunetti & B. Weder, *Political Credibility and Economic Development* 58–61 (1995) (distinguishing between different forms of corruption and suggesting that some forms while having potentially serious distributional effects, may not be too damaging to economic activity as a whole).

[8] *See*, e.g., N. Leff, 'Economic Development through Bureaucratic Corruption', in *Bureaucratic Corruption in Sub-Saharan Africa: Toward a Search for Causes and Consequences* 325 (M. Epko, ed., 1979) (hereinafter Bureaucratic Corruption in Sub-Saharan Africa).

[9] *See*, e.g., S. Rose-Ackerman, Corruption, *supra* note 5, at 88; A. Shleifer & R. Vishny, 'Corruption', 108 *Quarterly Journal of Economics* 599, 600 (1993); P. Mauro, 'Corruption and Growth', 110 *Quarterly Journal of Economics* 681 (1995) (representing one of the few empirical studies finding a correlation between corruption and economic growth in the sense that the less corruption there is, the higher the GDP growth rate); P. Ward, *Corruption, Development and Inequality* 170 (1989) (emphasizing the negative effect of corruption on the income distribution in developing countries).

vested interests established through corrupt practices tend to weaken public institutions and delay attempts to reform the system, thus inhibiting the development of new activities and reducing economic growth.[10]

Political science speaks of corruption as a symptom of more deeply rooted problems in the society's structure related in particular to the means of attaining and maintaining power and the weak or non-existent safeguards against its abuse. Accordingly, it addresses this phenomenon in different patterns of the exercise of power and of outsiders' political influence on public offices. For many political scientists, the main causes of corruption are to be found in political structures. Some attribute it to those structures which are characterized by the lack of democratic rule.[11] They are aware that widespread corruption can be found under democratic governments, but find assurance in the checks and balances inherent in a democratic system.[12] They also seek to develop ways to reduce the opportunities for political corruption, including collusion between legislators and bureaucrats, and to increase the awareness and participation of voters in the democratic process especially through the efforts of civil society.[13] Political scientists differ on the effects of corruption, with some distinguishing between 'integrative' (positive) and 'disintegrative' (negative) forms of corruption.[14] However, a growing consensus is also emerging among political scientists on the adverse impact of corruption on political and bureaucratic stability and efficiency. To quote one of them, '[corruption] privatizes valuable aspects of public life, bypassing processes of representation, debate and choice'.[15]

Legal literature generally treats corruption in the context of the deviation (for private gains) from binding rules, the arbitrary exercise of discretionary powers and the illegitimate use of public resources.[16] Lawyers address it

---

[10] *See* S. Knack & Ph. Keefer, 'Institutions and Economic Performance: Cross-Country Tests Using Alternative Institutional Measures', 7 *Economics and Politics* (No. 3) 207, 227 (1995).

[11] *See*, e.g., G. Myrdal, 'Corruption – Its Causes and Effects', in *Asian Drama: An Enquiry into the Poverty of Nations*, Vol. II, 951, 952 (1968) (a professor of economics writing this article from a political perspective); C. Friedrich, *The Pathology of Politics: Violence, Betrayal, Corruption, Secrecy and Propaganda* 127, 128 (1972).

[12] *See* M. Johnston, 'Public Officials, Private Interests, and Sustainable Democracy: When Politics and Corruption Meet', in *Corruption and the Global Economy* 61, 67 *et seq.* (K.A. Elliott ed., 1997).

[13] *Id.* at 74 *et seq.*; S. Rose-Ackerman, Corruption, *supra* note 5, at 12.

[14] *See* M. Johnston, 'The Political Consequences of Corruption: A Reassessment', 18 *Comparative Politics* 459, 464 (1986).

[15] D. Thompson, 'Mediated Corruption – The Case of the Keating Five', 87 *American Political Science Review* 369 (1993).

[16] *See*, e.g., *Black's Law Dictionary* 345 (6th ed. 1990) (defining corruption as '[t]he act of an official or fiduciary person who unlawfully and wrongfully uses his station or character to procure some benefit for himself or for another person, contrary to duty and the rights of others').

in the implementation of economic, administrative and criminal law and in the performance of fiduciary duties in particular, noting its spread when law enforcement is weak and the probability of detection and punishment is low.[17] They agree on its devastating effect on the rule of law which, through corruption, is substituted for by the rule of whoever has the influence or the ability and willingness to pay.[18] They are particularly concerned when corruption reaches the ranks of the judiciary and distorts the system of justice.[19] And they are increasingly aware of the need for rules to address situations of conflict of interests and for the protection of state assets from corrupt and fraudulent practices.

Sociology finds corruption a 'social relationship' represented in the violation of socially accepted norms of duty and welfare.[20] Social scientists speak of it at times in patron-client terms. Some describe it as a form of 'patrimonialism' which is strongest in societies where communities are small and interactive relationships are highly personal, and the need to accumulate 'social capital' is great.[21] Others consider it an indicator of a dysfunctional society. They generally attribute it to historical and socio-cultural factors resulting from conflicts between different groups and varied values within the society.[22] It thrives, they say, in the conflict of values. While they also recognize negative and positive effects of corruption, their more recent studies emphasize such negative aspects as adverse effects on development and on national integration.[23]

---

[17] *See*, e.g., R. Ogren, 'The Ineffectiveness of the Criminal Sanction in Fraud and Corruption Cases: Losing the Battle against White-Collar Crime', 11 *The American Criminal Law Review* 959, 987 (1973); A. Morice, 'Corruption, loi et société: quelques propositions', 36 *Tiers Monde* 41 (1995).

[18] *See*, e.g., Rose-Ackerman, Corruption, *supra* note 5, at 81–83; A. Block, 'American Corruption and the Decline of the Progressive Ethos', 23 *Journal of Law and Society* 18 (1996) (noting that 'there is a loss of faith in the United States of America today in public institutions because of the sense that they do not work as intended, for they ... have been corrupted ...').

[19] *See*, e.g., M. Zalman, 'Can We Cure Judicial Corruption', 66 *Michigan Bar Journal* 365 (1987); J. Ramsyer, 'The Puzzling (In)Dependence of Courts: A Comparative Approach', 23 *Journal of Legal Studies* 721 (1994).

[20] *See*, e.g., M. Defleur, 'Corruption, Law and Justice', 23 *Journal of Criminal Justice* 243 (1995) (defining corruption as a 'colonization of social relations in which two or more actors undertake an exchange relation by way of a successful transfer of the steering media of money or power, thereby sidestepping the legally prescribed procedure to regulate the relation').

[21] *See* V. Tanzi, *Corruption, Governmental Activities and Markets* (International Monetary Fund 1994).

[22] *See*, e.g., J. Scott, 'The Analysis of Corruption in Developing Nations', in *Bureaucratic Corruption in Sub-Saharan Africa*, *supra* note 7, at 29, 31; R, Braibanti, 'Reflections on Bureaucratic Corruption', in *Bureaucratic Corruption in Sub-Saharan Africa*, *supra* note 7, at 11.

[23] *See*, e.g., Introduction to Part III, in *Bureaucratic Corruption in Sub-Saharan Africa*, *supra* note 7, at 307–309; W. Easterley & R. Levine, *Africa's Growth Tragedy: Policies and Ethnic Divisions* 2 (World Bank Draft Working Paper, 1996).

Public administration specialists are concerned with bureaucratic corruption, even though they realize that this is but one form of a more complex phenomenon. They see corruption in the abuse of public resources and the use of public offices for private gains contrary to prescribed norms.[24] They say that it undermines the implementation (and sometimes the making) of public policy. They attribute it mainly to poor pay of public officials, monopoly of public services, wide personal discretion, weak financial control systems, excessive regulation and procedures, and the failure to build a strong internal culture of public service and ethics.[25] They also agree on its overall negative impact where the allocation of public goods and services becomes the privilege of who pays first or most.[26] They are particularly alarmed by the intrusion of political corruption into the bureaucracy and the possible collusion between politicians and senior bureaucrats against public interest.

Business organizations treat corruption mostly as a trade and investment policy issue. While they are concerned about its impact on the volume and cost of transactions, their major worry is the uncertainty it brings to business dealings and their inability to predict the outcome of competition when corruption is widespread.[27] Some, especially in developed countries, worry about its impact on company values and financial controls.

Practically *all people who publicly address corruption* condemn it, even though it would not exist at a wide scale without the participation of many. In the poor countries, most people take it as a fact of life, an unalterable part of the rules of the game which they have no choice but to accept. Their perception of its scope may even exceed its real dimensions.

Most people recognize corruption as an additional cost, which some consider necessary to get things done (and by doing so, contribute to making

---

[24] *See*, e.g., G. Caiden & N. Caiden, 'Administrative Corruption', 37 *Public Administration Review* 301, 302 (1977).

[25] *See*, e.g., A. Bent, *The Politics of Law Enforcement: Conflict and Power in Urban Communities* 3–6 (1974) (particularly discussing the cause of too broad discretionary powers of public officials); B. Schaffer, 'Access: A Theory of Corruption and Bureaucracy', 6 *Public Administration and Development* 357 (1986).

[26] *See*, e.g., Introduction to Part III, in *Bureaucratic Corruption in Sub-Saharan Africa*, *supra* note 7, at 308.

[27] In its 1977 and 1996 Rules of Conduct, the International Chamber of Commerce (ICC), an international non-governmental organization having 7,000 member companies and business associations in more than 130 countries, condemns corrupt practices by member enterprises in connection with international commercial transactions because of their negative impact on international trade and international competition. *See* F. Heimann, 'Combatting International Corruption: The Role of the Business Community', in *Corruption and the Global Economy* 147 (K.A. Elliott ed., 1997). In 1995, under the auspices of the World Economic Forum in Davos, Switzerland, a 'Davos Group' was formed to work on an agenda to catalyze the adoption of international standards for business ethics and regulation.

it necessary). Some see corruption broadly as a violation of human rights and, at the extreme, as a 'crime against humanity'.[28]

All agree it may increase the wealth of those practising it but almost certainly reduces the revenue of the state and the welfare of society as a whole.

Yet corruption in one form or another exists in varying degrees in all human societies. Like other immoral practices, its egregious manifestations have been recognized and condemned since old times in practically all cultures; it continues nonetheless to be widely practised at all social levels.

CORRUPTION AS I SEE IT

I use the word 'corruption' here in a broad sense encompassing different forms of behaviour. This behaviour usually results from two types of situations. The first is where, in the allocation of benefits or even the mere allowance of opportunities, the temptation to realize private gains prevails over the duty to serve other interests which are usually common interests. And the second is where, in the application of rules, the opportunity to grant special favours undermines the general obligation to apply public rules without discrimination. In situations where rules are being circumvented, are applied with unwarranted differentiation, or are simply non-existent, a corrupt agent, acting on his own or at the behest of others, typically chooses to give preference to special interests over the broader interests he is legally required to serve. The resources put at his disposal or the office he holds are being used, or rather abused, in ways different from those set out by his principal. The principal varies according to the situation. It may be the agent's supervisors, the institution for which he works, the owners of such an institution or the public at large.

In this broad sense, corruption occurs when a function, whether public or private, requires the allocation of benefits or the provision of a good or service. The agent may have the opportunity to perform this function in the absence of any or adequate prior rules, substantive or procedural, and may thus have great discretion and a vast opportunity to make personal choices. He may also be acting when pre-established rules exist but chooses to violate them to achieve private profit for himself and his bribers. Alternatively, he may apply the rules as written but selectively, to benefit himself, his family, friends or whoever pays him for the favour. In all cases, a position of trust is being exploited to realize private gains beyond what the position holder is entitled to. Attempts to influence the position holder, through the payment of bribes or an exchange of benefits or favours, in

---

[28] *Corruption in Government* 24 (United Nations 1990), TCD/Sem. 90/2, INT-89-R56 (Report of an Interregional Seminar held in the Hague, the Netherlands on December 11–15, 1989).

order to receive in return a special gain or treatment not available to others is also a form of corruption, even if the gain involved is not illicit under applicable law. The absence of rules facilitates the process as much as the presence of cumbersome or excessive rules does.

Corruption in this sense is not confined to the public sector and, in that sector, is not confined to administrative bureaucracies. It is not limited to the payment and receipt of bribes. It takes various forms and is practised under all forms of government, including well established democracies. It can be found in the legislative, judicial and executive branches of government as well as in all forms of private sector activities. It is not exclusively associated with any ethnic, racial or religious group. However, its level, scope and impact vary greatly from one country to another and may also vary, at least for a while, within the same country from one place to another. While corruption of some form or another may inhere in every human community, the system of governance has a great impact on its level and scope of practice. Systems can corrupt people as much as, if not more than, people are capable of corrupting systems.

Some cultures seem to be more tolerant than others when it comes to certain forms of corruption, particularly favouritism and petty bribes. In some societies, favouritism is so pervasive in human behaviour that those who, in the performance of their public functions, decline to favour friends and relatives are generally criticized as being unhelpful or unkind. Petty bribes are also seen in many countries as a charity, an advance incentive or expression of gratitude, or an acceptable substitute for the low pay of public officials – not the extortion it is recognized to be in other countries. Such cultural variations, though real, should not be taken as acceptable excuses for what is basically a corrupt behaviour.

Corruption may be petty or grand, sporadic or systemic, casual or entrenched but the widespread practice of any of its forms has devastating effects in all societies:

– *In the application of law*, it creates a different law in practice from the one in the books. It transforms public rules and procedures based on democratic or meritocratic principles into *ad hoc* practices based on the willingness and ability to pay or on personal connections and reciprocated favours.
– *In the practice of government*, corruption turns the rule of law to a rule of individuals pursuing their private interests. It gives special interests priority over the public interest represented by majority rule. Its spread undermines public confidence in government and the government's ability to implement policies, leading to the weakening and possible disruption of democratic systems and in the extreme to the collapse of the public order. Collusion between political corruption and bureaucratic corruption is bound to accelerate this process. While this tends to destabilize political structures, spreading the benefits of corruption has often been used,

however, as a stabilizing tool, especially under non-democratic govern-ments.[29]

– *In the working of most economies*, the impact of corruption is not less harmful, whether we look at market or non-market economies. While the phenomenon is complex and the cost may fall on other areas and in future times, corruption can endanger the use of economic choices, increase the costs of transactions, reduce state revenue, increase public expenditures, penalize law abiders and produce adverse distributional effects. It is likely to tax the system in its entirety, although it works in particular against the poor and the underprivileged. Its prevalence could over time threaten macro-economic stability, raise the rate of inflation and push business into the informal sector. The scope and adverse impact of corruption, or at least the eruption of cases of corruption,[30] tend to increase in the periods of transition from non-market to a market system, and from a totalitarian to an open political system.

– *In the application of environmental rules and procedures*, corruption may enable those addressed by them, both in the public as well as the private sectors, to violate applicable standards, turning ideal environment laws and regulations into meaningless gestures for those who have the money or the influence.

– *In all cases*, and however you look at it, corruption deepens inequities. In doing so, it sows the seeds for social and political tensions, threatens the very fabric of society and undermines the effectiveness of the state and the political legitimacy of government.[31]

Once corruption finds its way in a certain place or sector, like a virus, it tends to spread out to other areas and sectors. It does not stop at political boundaries and it grows faster in environments of under-regulation or over-regulation. Corrupt and corrupting individuals have a vested interest in spreading the perception that corruption is dominant and prevalent. Through them, it becomes self-perpetuating. Foreign business, especially in develop-ing countries, often contributes to the spread of corruption by assuming that pay-offs and connections are inevitable facts of doing business – an attitude which often turns out to be a self-fulfilling prophecy.[32] If unchecked, corruption eventually distorts the values of the society, except for the few who manage to insulate themselves through strong moral shields, often based on strict religious and ethical values. Its effect on the society and on individuals in that society is thus as destructive as it is far reaching. Any

---

[29] *See* Rose-Ackerman, Corruption, *supra* note 5, at 80–81.

[30] *See* M. Naim, *The Corruption Eruption*, *supra* note 1, at 246 (1995) (arguing that the greater disclosure of corruption in recent years is a sign that democracy and markets are working).

[31] *See* Rose-Ackerman, The Political Economy of Corruption, *supra* note 5.

[32] Naim, *supra* note 1, at 255.

short-term benefits it may bring (such as practically deregulating a heavily regulated economy or 'greasing the wheels' of business transactions) will most likely be outweighed by the collective damage corruption is bound to bring about beyond the specific transaction at hand. Even at the transactional level, corruption often increases inefficiency in government projects and may raise the cost of public and private procurement alike. Quite often, large illicit payments, far from being invested in the country, are transferred abroad or diverted into other illegal business. Corruption may also increase the public debt of the country as a result of the higher cost of externally funded contracts secured through corrupt or fraudulent practices.

In short, corruption, in spite of some returns for its beneficiaries, retards the overall development of societies and their systems of governance. Historically, it declined with the rise of civilizations and increased with their fall. Its level and pace of growth may thus have an inverse relationship with the degree of development.

EFFORTS TO COMBAT CORRUPTION

Attempts to combat corruption may have a greater chance of success if they recognize from the outset the complexity of this phenomenon and the impossibility of eliminating it altogether. Those who are determined to fight corruption must realize that it results from forces which have accumulated over a long period of time and that it takes strong commitments as well as laborious and lengthy efforts to overcome such formidable forces. They are best advised to avoid simplistic solutions and the narrow approaches typically advocated in different social disciplines. A comprehensive approach encompassing the experiences of different disciplines and countries will inevitably consist of short-term and long-term measures which may have both domestic and international dimensions. It should address the economic, political, social, legal, administrative and moral aspects of the phenomenon and recognize the close linkages among these aspects. It must recognize that different types of corruption may need to be addressed by different strategies and methods. It cannot ignore that the prevalence of corruption is often based on deeply rooted causes related to the values with which people grow up and the system which governs their relationships, both among themselves and with their government. For this reason, a successful approach must also take into account the educational and mass communications' processes which influence such values and system of governance. The synergistic effects of all the measures included in this approach are likely to produce positive results over time. However, curbing corruption requires continued commitment by an adequate number of people as well as an *a priori* acceptance of possible frustration and failure.

A comparative survey of the literature, including different attempts by governments to combat corruption, leads to placing the emphasis on certain areas of reform which may have particular relevance in this respect. Although these relate mainly to government action, there is also a need for complementary efforts by business groups such as the adoption of international and domestic codes of conduct and internal systems for compliance with applicable law and codes against extortion and bribery.[33] Nor should the measures stated below obscure the fact that efforts to combat corruption have a much greater chance of success when they are not confined to the high ranks of government but become the responsibility of the largest possible numbers of individuals, acting individually and collectively through non-governmental organizations.

Economic Reform

Although macro- and micro-economic reforms may not necessarily target corruption as a specific objective, they do have a major positive effect on the situations which give rise to it.[34] On the general level, the adoption of sound development strategies creates an environment of hope in the future in the economy as a whole. The loss of such a hope contributes to the shift towards corrupt practices for many of those who see in them the only chance for the betterment of their own conditions. Liberalization of markets, demonopolization of services, and deregulation (i.e. reducing regulations to the level needed to protect competition and ensure transparency and accountability) certainly decrease the opportunities for arbitrary and corrupt practices on the part of public officials. The positive effects of these measures, especially in areas such as foreign trade (imports and exports licences), taxation (tax structures and administration, including customs), and entry and exit barriers for investment have been proven in many countries. Such effects are clearest when these measures are coupled with the development or strengthening of institutions which supervise the proper implementation of remaining regulations and ensure their effectiveness. In the absence of strong and effective institutions, economic liberalization may become counter-productive. It may increase the chances for corruption and create a vacuum for organized crime to fill. Even privatization authorities and regulatory institutions can themselves be subject to corruption.

In addition to general economic reform measures, specific anti-corruption actions enhance the chances of success. These may include the imposition

---

[33] *See* examples in 'Corporate Anti-Corruption Programs – A Survey of Best Practices' prepared by the US Chapter of Transparency International in June 1996.

[34] *See*, e.g., *World Development Report – From Plan to Market* 95–96 (World Bank 1996 (listing economic measures such as transparent privatization, liberalization, demonopolization of the economy, and deregulation as measures which, according to Bank experience, have reduced the scope for corruption and are supposed to also have this effect, if applied, in transition economies).

of user fees for government services (with a simultaneous increase in the salaries of public employees, practically replacing illicit bribes), or reducing the discretionary distribution of benefits (especially subsidized food and public housing allocations which can be delivered at market prices, with cash payments to the needy) as well as similar measures which, to the extent possible, replace administrative approvals with market mechanisms, thus obviating the need for influencing the officials in charge and reducing the scope for rent seeking. Governments must be careful however as all these measures may easily be exploited in the absence of efficient regulatory regimes and strong supervisory institutions.

Legal and Judicial Reform

Clarifying and streamlining the necessary laws and eliminating the unnecessary ones, strengthening the law enforcement capacity in the country while putting in place measures to ensure an efficient and just judicial process are not only general steps required for the creation of a sound investment climate;[35] they are also necessary for reducing the incidence of corruption.[36] Specific laws may also be issued to introduce a greater measure of transparency in government actions, to regulate procurement of goods and services for the government on a competitive basis and impose deterrent procedures on corrupting bidders, to create investigative, monitoring and evaluating authorities, to prohibit bribery of both local and foreign officials, and to impose severe punishment on both the giver and recipient of bribes, to end tax deductibility of bribes, to impose strict corporate auditing, accounting and disclosure rules, to forfeit corruptly gained assets and contracts, to protect witnesses and informers, and to reverse the burden of proof in cases of unjustified enrichment in order to facilitate the often elusive attempts to capture corrupt officials. Legislative action may also address political corruption by criminalizing bribery (and other advantages) of members of and candidates for law-making bodies and officials of public parties.

Such legislative anti-corruption measures may not be effective, however, in the absence of honest and efficient investigative and judicial bodies. Increasing the remuneration and training of clerks, prosecutors and judges

---

[35] On the role of legal and judicial reform for private sector development, *see* I. Shihata, *The World Bank in a Changing World*, Vol. II, 127–182 (1995), Chapter Three (Legal Framework for Development and the Role of the World Bank in Legal Technical Assistance) and Chapter Four (Judicial Reform in Developing Countries and the Role of the World Bank).

[36] *See generally* Rose-Ackerman, Corruption, *supra* note 5, Part II on bureaucratic corruption. *See also World Development Report – From Plan to Market 95* (World Bank 1996) (identifying uncertain rules and heavy regulation in many economy-related areas as causes of corruption and calling for legal order to reduce corruption).

and enhancing their career development opportunities as well as protecting their independence contribute greatly to the fight against corruption. The establishment of an anti-corruption commission, an ombudsman's office and the like may also be helpful, although experience has been mixed in this respect. Corruption is rampant in some countries with several such offices, filled with low-paid and ill-trained staff at all levels. Worse still, these offices have been actively used in some instances by incumbent governments against their political enemies.

Administrative (Civil Service) Reform

As in the cases of economic and legal/judicial reforms, general administrative reform (especially in the revenue-collecting departments) can significantly reduce corruption.[37] Reform of the civil service may also include specific measures which directly address this phenomenon. Obviously, the issue here is not merely the reduction of the size of the civil service, necessary as this may be. The required general reform includes as well all the measures needed to ensure *efficiency* and *honesty* of the civil service. Of particular relevance are:

– the restructuring of the civil service to make it responsive to actual needs;
– the streamlining of administrative rules and procedures, especially by eliminating meaningless approvals and programs riddled with corruption;
– the introduction of competition between government agencies and the private sector in the delivery of public services and the supply of goods;
– the professionalization of the service through adequate remuneration (especially for officials with discretionary powers over distribution of benefits), continuous training, skilled management, objective systems of recruitment and promotion based on qualification and performance and improved definition of tasks and work standards;
– the promotion of ethics in the civil service through the enactment and enforcement of clear rules governing conflicts of interest, elaboration on expected behaviour, obligatory disclosure of assets and investments above a certain threshold (including those of dependents) and meaningful sanctions in cases of violation;

---

[37] *See generally* Rose-Ackerman, Corruption, *supra* note 5, Part II on bureaucratic corruption, and *World Development Report – From Plan to Market 95–6* (World Bank 1996) (listing some administrative reform measures such as the strengthening of oversight and appeal mechanisms, as well as the increase in public officials salaries, etc. as efficient anti-corruption efforts). *See also Corruption in Government* 12–17 (United Nations 1990), TCD/Sem. 90/2, INT-89–R56 (Report of an Interregional Seminar held in the Hague, the Netherlands on December 11–15, 1989).

- paying special attention to the selection of managers, both from the professional and ethical viewpoints, and applying to them an effective system of incentives and sanctions;
- increasing the public's awareness of their rights to government services and the channels available to them for submission of complaints, while strengthening the capacity of these channels and access to administrative and judicial remedies;
- introducing an effective system of financial management, including serious and timely record keeping, auditing and supervision of performance, especially in the procurement of goods and services and the execution of public works;
- adoption of clear legislation and regulations on public procurement generally based on the principle of competitive bidding;
- adequate regulation, staffing and equipment in the agencies in charge of combating tax evasion and money laundering, including rewards and punishments needed to ensure effective compliance and implementation; and
- creation of oversight bodies and offices of client advocates to receive complaints from the public, as checks and balances throughout the bureaucracy.

Such general administrative reforms may also be complemented by specific anti-corruption techniques, such as creating several offices to provide the same function (e.g., to issue driving licences or passports), in order to reduce the monopoly rents of a single outlet and allow the public to opt out of the corrupt ones. They may also include anti-corruption measures, such as anti-bribery laws which impose penalties representing a multiple of the marginal benefits of the pay-offs, not just the amounts paid or received, in addition to mandatory dismissal of corrupt officials, and the disqualification (from bidding for government contracts or services) of corrupt firms or individuals and regulating the payment of commissions for public contracts with a view to limiting them to appropriate remuneration for legitimate services, if not eliminating them altogether.

Other Institutional Reforms

The above reforms may not produce their desired effect in the absence of a system of government endowed with adequate checks and balances to prevent collusion between the separate branches of government and the emergence of *de facto* centres of power which act above the law. Depending on the circumstances of each country, the introduction of such a system may require a massive effort of political reform, along with broad access to information and a free press. This, of course, may not always be feasible and cannot at any rate be sustained if it is merely imposed from the outside.

However, political reform may gradually develop from within the society, through the elimination of illiteracy, the strengthening of the education system, the development of civil society, the liberalization of economy, the building up of the citizens' confidence in their state's political and economic system, and the adoption of measures of legal and judicial reform to establish the rule of law, especially with emphasis on the due process of law.

Nothing in the above suggests that democratic governments are immune from corruption; it simply indicates that the more checks and balances exist within a society, and the more strong institutions are in place to protect such checks and balances, in an overall environment of liberalization, the fewer opportunities there may be for corrupt practices which remain unchecked or unpunished. Electoral laws can also be used to curb political corruption. They should regulate political contributions and provide for their disclosure. Immunity of members of Parliament should not be invoked in cases of alleged bribes or extortion to them or by them.

Moral Reform

Underlying all reforms is the commitment of the reformers, the pressure from the civil society that sustains this commitment, and the ability of the leadership to influence the public. This usually requires high moral standards at the leadership level. Such standards normally reflect the common aspiration of the society and are often embedded in the teachings of its predominant religion and ethics. It is not uncommon, however, to note a wide gap between such teachings and peoples' day-to-day behaviour. Rather than attempting to narrow this gap through a combination of reinterpreting the teachings and reforming the behaviour, most societies are content to live with it and to see it widening further over time. The effect on the level of corruption is then inevitable.

If corruption becomes rampant, combating it would require a major change in moral behaviour. The issue here is hardly the lack of an agreed set of moral values, but rather the prevalent hypocrisy which confines these values to public postures, with little impact on daily behaviour. While a new moral movement, with or without religious underpinnings, may emerge from time to time, it cannot be always relied upon as a practical remedy. The attitude of the elite in power can have demonstrable effects, however. The behaviour of parents at home, teachers at school, and political leaders in and outside government inevitably influence the behaviour of a new generation. An ideology of austerity may be useful in a poor society, but not if it is required only from the poor. Religious teachings may also have little effect if the public has little faith in the degree of their observance by those who are more privileged in the society or by the religious establishment itself.

International Measures

While domestic measures of reform such as those already mentioned may help in checking corruption, certain corrupt practices defy remedies by domestic measures alone. International collaboration is particularly needed with respect to activities which by their very nature are transboundary, such as corruption in international business transactions and money laundering (especially in connection with illicit narcotics trafficking). It is required in particular to enhance the capacity of states which need assistance in combating corruption and to strengthen mechanisms for exchange of information and for mutual assistance in the investigation.

It should be noted, however, that international measures addressing corruption are still in their infancy. Apart from the international measures for the criminalization of money laundering which started with the 1988 *UN Convention Against Drug Trafficking*,[38] other international measures are the product of more recent years (with the exception of the abortive attempt of the UN Commission on Multilateral Corporations referred to later on). Mostly regional in character, these measures have, for the most part, taken so far the form of draft agreements or non-binding recommendations.

At a universal level, the UN Commission on *Transnational Corporations* completed in 1978 a draft *International Agreement on Illicit Payments*. Covering both active and passive corruption, this draft requires the criminalization of corruption in international commercial transactions and establishes the jurisdictional basis for the prosecution of this offence. It requires the parties to provide for the obligation of transnational corporations to keep accurate records of payments related to their international transactions. It also requires civil sanctions for corrupt practices and mutual assistance among the states parties to it. Late in 1995, the UN resolved to reconvene work on this draft agreement. In December 1996, the General Assembly of the United Nations has also adopted a *Declaration Against Corruption and Bribery in International Commercial Transactions* by which states pledged

---

[38] Reference is to the UN Convention Against Illicit Traffic in Narcotic Drugs and Psychotropic Substances which was open for signature on December 20, 1988 and entered into force on November 11, 1990. This convention establishes that illicit trafficking in drugs and laundering of the proceeds from such trafficking shall be criminal offenses in the state parties. The Convention also requires parties to it to render mutual legal assistance with respect to the prosecution of the just mentioned offenses and particularly with respect to search and seizures. International measures against money laundering include, in addition to the above-mentioned UN Convention, the 1988 Statement on Prevention of Criminal Use of the Banking System for the Purposes of Money-Laundering issued by the Basle Committee on Banking Regulations and Supervisory Practices, the 1990 Council of Europe Convention of the Proceeds from Crime (in force), the 1991 EC Directive on Prevention of the Use of the Financial System for the Purpose of Money Laundering (in force), and the 1990 Forty Recommendations of the Financial Action Task Force (FATF) (created by the G-7 Summit in 1989) on Money Laundering. The Forty FATF Recommendations were revised in 1996.

to criminalize bribery of foreign public officials and to deny the tax deductibility of bribes paid by any private or public corporation or individual of a UN member state to any public official or elected representative of another country.

Recently, a Government Procurement Agreement covering the purchase of goods and services including public works and public utilities was prepared by the World Trade Organization (WTO) to ensure that the international procurement process was open and transparent. Only 24 WTO members are parties to this 1994 agreement which entered into force in January 1996. In the meantime, participants at the WTO ministerial meeting in December 1996 have agreed to negotiate an interim procurement arrangement on transparency, openness and due process in government procurement until such time as the 1994 agreement is more widely accepted. A Working Group on Transparency in Government Procurement has been established to facilitate the negotiation of this interim agreement.

At the OECD level, two recommendations to governments have been adopted. The 1994 Recommendation is directed against 'bribery of foreign public officials in connection with international business transactions'. Recommending the extra-territorial application of bribery law, the Recommendation suggests the criminalization of bribery and making its acts illegal in terms of civil, commercial and administrative laws and regulations, along with eliminating the indirect favouring of bribery in tax laws and introducing company and business accounting requirements and banking regulations to facilitate inspection and investigation as well as the denial of public subsidies, licences, and other public advantages in cases of bribery. The 1994 Recommendation also provides for cross boundary cooperation and consultation among the relevant authorities, regular reviews, and international legal assistance. By contrast to this broad recommendation, the 1996 OECD Recommendation is confined to the prohibition of tax deductibility of bribes to foreign officials – a practice which seems to have been tolerated earlier outside the United States.[39] In May 1997, the members of the OECD agreed to draft a treaty by the end of this year which would make it illegal for firms from member countries to bribe foreign officials.

At the regional level, several multilateral attempts to curb corruption have taken place. Among these is the one multilateral anti-corruption agreement which has been signed by 23 countries and has actually entered into force, the 1996 *Inter-American Convention Against Corruption* prepared under the auspices of the Organization of American States (OAS). This regional

---

[39] It is interesting to note in this respect that the new Trans-Atlantic Agenda (TA), a product of the 1995 United States-European Union Summit, urged EU members to combat illicit payments by implementing the 1994 OECD Recommendation. The private sector counterpart to the TA, the Trans-Atlantic Business Dialogue, later formed a separate issues group to deal exclusively with bribery and called on governments 'to implement promptly the 1994 and 1996 OECD recommendations.'

convention is open for accession by non-OAS members. It requires the states parties to take action against defined corrupt practices both within their territories and, subject to their respective constitutions, those committed by nationals and residents abroad. As defined in the convention, the actions to be outlawed cover corruption both in its active form (the offering or granting of any article of monetary value or other benefit to a government official in exchange for any act or omission in the performance of a public function) and passive form (the solicitation or the acceptance by a government official of such article or benefit for the same purpose). It also covers the fraudulent use or concealment of property derived from the afore-mentioned acts, the participation, in any manner, in their commission or attempted commission, and other acts of corruption which the states parties agree to include under the Convention. Subject to the constitutional law of each member, the Convention equally covers the offence of 'illicit enrichment,' that is any unexplained significant increase (in relation to lawful earnings) in the assets of a government official. (The US delay in signing the Convention has been justified by the possible inconsistency of this latter requirement with the constitutional protection in the US against self-incrimination.) In addition to requiring that such acts of corruption be established as criminal offences, and providing the jurisdictional basis for such state actions (including the possible extra-territorial application of bribery laws), the Convention also provides for mutual assistance among the agencies of the states parties in the investigation and prosecution of acts of corruption and in the tracing and seizure of their proceeds. It prohibits states parties from invoking bank secrecy as a basis for refusal to provide such assistance.[40]

The charter of the *North American Development Bank*, established under NAFTA, requires companies seeking loans from that Bank to certify that they have not engaged in bribery and to state that they have not been convicted of bribery within the past five years.

A number of *European draft conventions* are also worth mentioning. These include the two 1996 draft conventions which the Multidisciplinary Group on Corruption of the Council of Europe has still to finalize. The first of those is the draft *Framework Convention on Corruption* which focuses on the criminal law aspects of this phenomenon, requires the parties to outlaw corruption (and the laundering of its proceeds) 'at home and abroad,' and prohibits the granting of tax deductions for bribes or other economic advantages linked to corruption 'whether benefited at home or abroad'. It also requires parties to adopt 'appropriate legislation' for the procurement

---

[40] In June 1996, the Council of Securities Regulations of the Americas adopted a resolution on efforts to combat bribery of government officials by publicly held companies and to develop and promote laws that address such illicit payments, to strengthen auditing, assist in enforcing securities laws and improve access by securities regulators to investigatory information.

of public goods and services and for the restructuring of administrative procedures as well as codes of conduct for elected representatives, freedom of the press, auditing of businesses and the establishment of appropriate civil law remedies for victims of corruption.

The second draft convention of the Council of Europe is the draft *Convention on Corruption*. Unlike the previous one, this draft convention provides a detailed definition of the forms of corruption covered by this term. Those include both active and passive bribery as well as the trading in influence over the decision-making of public officials and money laundering. It is not limited in scope to public officials. Also covered are private, including foreign, entities, and senior officials of international organizations, elected representatives of international bodies and judges and officials of international courts. The latter draft convention also provides for cooperation and assistance between the parties in the investigation of corrupt acts and in the confiscation of their proceeds and the provision of additional remedies for their victims.

Other European initiatives include first a *Protocol on Corruption to the EC Convention on the Protection of the Communities' Financial Interests* which was signed by the EU Member States in September 1996 and which criminalizes corruption in which community and national officials are involved damaging or likely to damage the European Communities' financial interests. Another *Convention on the Fight Against Corruption Involving Officials of the European Communities or Officials of Member States of the European Union* has recently been signed by the Member States. This Convention requires EU Member States to make active and passive corruption involving community officials or officials of the Member States a criminal offence. Corruption committed by or against government ministers, elected members of national parliaments, members of the highest courts or the court of auditors, members of the Commission of the European Communities, the European Parliament, the Court of Justice and the Court of Auditors of the European Communities has equally to be criminalized according to the Convention. The Convention also includes a provision requiring the Member States to hold heads of businesses for the corrupt acts of persons under their authority criminally liable.

At a less formal level, the *International Chamber of Commerce* issued in 1996 a revised version of its 1977 *ICC Rules of Conduct* as a set of legally non-binding rules of ethical business conduct. While these Rules appeal to public international organizations, such as the World Bank, to take measures to combat corruption, they basically address the behaviour of member corporations.[41] They prohibit corruption in a broad sense which includes extortion, bribery, kick-backs, payments to agents which represent more than the appropriate remuneration for legitimate services and contributions to

---

[41] *See* Heimann, *supra* note 27.

political parties or committees or to individual politicians if undisclosed and made in violation of applicable law. The Rules also require proper financial recording and auditing by the enterprises and introduce control and review procedures within each enterprise to ensure compliance and sanctions against the responsible director or employee contravening the Rules. They also speak of the need for a code of conduct for each individual company (with examples provided) and of coordination between the ICC headquarters and its national committees in this field as well as for the promotion of the Rules themselves on the domestic and international levels.

Similarly, the International Bar Association issued in 1996 a declaration recommending to governments the adoption of several anti-corruption measures for international economic transactions and calling on international financial institutions to take up the matter in its activities.[42]

THE WORLD BANK'S EFFORTS

The Bank's Growing Concern with Corruption Issues

The World Bank is required by its Articles of Agreement to ensure that the proceeds of its loans will be used only for the purposes for which they are granted and to disburse its loans only as expenditures on the projects it finances are actually incurred.[43] It is also required by these Articles to finance such expenditures with due attention to considerations of 'economy and efficiency,' and without regard to political or other non-economic influences or considerations.[44] The Articles of Agreement do not specifically include curbing corruption among the Bank's purposes or functions. They generally prohibit the Bank from taking non-economic considerations

---

[42] Similar, recent unofficial international declarations were issued by the Council of Securities Regulations in the Americas (1996) and by the TransAtlantic Business Dialogue in 1994 and 1996.

[43] *See* Article III, Section 5 (c), 2nd sentence of the IBRD Articles of Agreement (providing, *inter alia*, that 'in the case of loans made by the Bank, it shall open an account in the name of the borrower and the amount of the loan shall be credited to this account in the currency or currencies in which the loan is made. The borrower shall be permitted by the Bank to draw on this account only to meet expenses in connection with the project as they are actually incurred'). *See also* Article V, Section 1(h) of the IDA Articles of Agreement (providing that '[f]unds to be provided under any financing operation shall be made available to the recipient only to meet expenses in connection with the project as they are actually incurred').

[44] *See* Article III, Section 5(b) of the IBRD Articles of Agreement (providing that '[t]he Bank shall make arrangements to ensure that the proceeds of any loan are used only for the purposes for which the loan was granted, with due attention to considerations of economy and efficiency and without regard to political or other non-economic influences or considerations'). *See also* Article V, Section 1(g) of the IDA Articles of Agreement to the same effect.

274 Ibrahim F.I. Shihata

into account in its decisions and from interfering in the political affairs of its members.[45] For this reason, the Bank has traditionally been active and explicit in ensuring that procurement under its own loans is done in a transparent manner and on a competitive basis but has avoided, until very recently, any full-fledged attempt to adopt an anti-corruption strategy. Since the early 1990s, the Bank, has however identified corruption as an issue to be taken into account in its work on governance and, in a few cases, began to raise it in the country dialogue. It has also sought to assist its borrowing countries in introducing economic, administrative, legal and judicial reforms through a series of structural and sectoral adjustment loans, technical assistance loans and grants and sectoral investment loans. While the Bank was not in this way directly involved in fighting corruption, it was aware that these reforms have a direct positive effect not only on the growth prospects of the borrowing countries but also on the level of corruption.

The Bank's explicit concern with corruption as a general development issue came with the assumption of James D. Wolfensohn of its Presidency in mid-1995. Soon thereafter, he highlighted the issue in his first speech before the Annual Meeting of the Board of Governors (in September 1995). He then asked this writer, as the Bank's General Counsel, to review all proposals and consider initiatives for possible actions by the Bank. Detailed discussion of such proposals and initiatives at the senior management level led to specific action which has been approved by the President and, as needed, by the Board of Executive Directors. Such action covers a number of different fronts, all related to measures deemed to be within the Bank's competence which will be detailed below. In the meantime, a comprehensive strategy to address corruption, both as an issue of the Bank's own effectiveness and more generally as a development policy issue, is being prepared for consideration by the Bank's Board in the near future.

Before addressing in the remaining part of this lecture past and current actions of the Bank in combating corruption, it may be useful to explain the reasons which prompt it, at this particular stage, to take a leading role in this area.

The Bank's involvement in addressing corruption issues beyond the projects it finances has not been free from controversy. On the one hand, it can validly be argued that the Bank is not a world government for the borrowing countries; its mandate is defined by its Articles of Agreement. Being subject to a weighted voting system and limited in its operations to the borrowing countries, its role as a world reformer beyond its defined purposes would inevitably carry the marks of rule by the rich countries of the poorer ones. In any event, the Bank should only be concerned, under

---

[45] *See* Article IV, Section 10 of the IBRD Articles of Agreement (stating that '[t]he Bank and its officers shall not interfere in the political affairs of any member; nor shall they be influenced in their decisions by the political character of the member or members concerned'). *See also* Article V, Section 10 of the IDA Articles of Agreement to the same effect.

this argument, with the functions provided for in its Articles of Agreement, the main among which is to help finance specific projects for productive purposes.[46] It should, in particular, avoid involvement in a subject matter which has obvious domestic political connotations and could otherwise entangle the Bank in complex political considerations which it is explicitly prohibited from taking into account under its Articles.

It should nonetheless be stated that as the world's major development finance institution and the coordinator of foreign aid to many of its members, the Bank cannot realistically ignore issues which significantly influence the effective flow and appropriate use of external resources in its borrowing countries. It has already been able to deal with a large number of governance and institutional issues which have direct relevance to its development mandate, without entanglement in partisan domestic politics. Its concern with public sector management in its borrowing countries has been an important factor in its operational and research work through the years. Any intervention by the Bank would, at any rate, take the form either of a financial instrument to which the country involved would be a contracting party, as a borrower or guarantor, or advice which must be related to the Bank's development mandate. In neither case can the Bank take a coercive stance or impose a particular direction on a borrowing member. It can only play a facilitating role, the effectiveness of which would depend largely on the borrower's full cooperation.

As a practical matter, the World Bank can hardly insulate itself from major issues of international development policy. Corruption has become such an issue. Its prevalence in a given country increasingly influences the flow of public and private funds for investment in that country. The Bank's lending programs and in particular its adjustment lending take into account factors which determine the size and pace of such flows. From a legal viewpoint, what matters is that the Bank's involvement must always be consistent with its Articles of Agreement. The Bank can in my view take many actions to help the fight against corruption. It can conduct research on the causes and effects of this world-wide phenomenon. It can provide assistance, by mutual agreement, to enable its borrowing countries to curb corruption. It may take up the level of corruption as a subject of discussion in the dialogue with its borrowing members. And, if the level of corruption is high so as to have an adverse impact on the effectiveness of Bank assistance, according to factual and objective analysis, and the government is not taking serious measures to combat it, the Bank can take this as a factor in its lending strategy towards the country. The only legal barrier in this respect is that in doing so the Bank and its staff must be concerned only

---

[46] *See* Article III, Section 4(vii) of the IBRD Articles of Agreement which reads: 'Loans made or guaranteed by the Bank shall, except under special circumstances, be for the purpose of specific projects of reconstruction or development.' *See also* Article V, Section 1(b) of the IDA Articles of Agreement to the same effect.

with the economic causes and effects and should refrain from intervening in the country's political affairs. While the task may be difficult in borderline cases, its limits have been prescribed in detail in legal opinions issued by this author and endorsed by the Bank's Board.[47]

According to one such legal opinion ('Governance Issues and their Relevance to the Bank's Work' issued in December 1990), the concept of governance in the sense of the overall management of a country's resources cannot be irrelevant to an international financial institution which at present not only finances projects but also is deeply involved in the process of economic reform carried out by its borrowing members. Clearly, the concern here is not with the exercise of state powers in the broad sense but specifically with the appropriate management of the public sector and the creation of an enabling environment for the private sector. It is a concern for rules which are actually applied and institutions which ensure the appropriate application of these rules, to the extent that such rules and institutions are required for the economic development of the country and in particular for the sound management of its resources.[48]

No doubt, the Bank has to address issues of corruption in this context with great caution, acting on the basis of established facts and only to the extent that the issues clearly affect the economic development of the country. It cannot, however, ignore such issues at a time when they have become a major concern, not only to the sources of international financial flows but also to business organizations and indeed to the governments and peoples of most of its member countries.

Ensuring a Corruption-Free Institution

For an institution like the World Bank to take a leading role in the international efforts to assist its members in curbing corruption, it must first introduce adequate safeguards against any corruption within its ranks. There is no evidence of any major instance of corruption in the more than 50 years of Bank's history; few incidents have been promptly dealt with, even

---

[47] *See Issues of 'Governance' in Borrowing Members – The Extent of Their Relevance Under the Bank's Articles of Agreement*, Legal Memorandum of the General Counsel, dated December 21, 1990 (SecM91–131, February 5, 1991), also published as Chapter Two in I. Shihata, *The World Bank in a Changing World*, Vol. I (1991), and *Prohibition of Political Activities in the Bank's Work*, Legal Opinion of the General Counsel, dated July 11, 1995 (SecM95–707, July 12, 1995).

[48] For details *see* I. Shihata, *The World Bank in a Changing World*, Vol. 1, 53–96 (1991), Chapter Two (The World Bank and 'Governance' Issues in Its Borrowing Members).

harshly in some cases, according to the Bank's Administrative Tribunal.[49] The Bank's Staff Rules include detailed provisions on conflicts of interest and the expected behaviour of staff in their dealings within and outside the Bank.[50] They require annual financial disclosures of all assets and financial transactions by senior staff[51] and disclosure by all staff of 'any financial or business interest of the staff member or of a member of his immediate family that might unfavourably reflect on or cause embarrassment to the Bank'.[52] An Outside Interests Committee, headed by a Deputy General Counsel, must approve any staff activity unrelated to the performance of Bank duties, other than a non-compensated position in a non-profit corporation or organization, to ensure that it is compatible with Bank Group work requirements and the principles of staff employment.[53] In addition, a statement on staff ethics, first issued in 1994, is now to be distributed annually under the President's signature.[54] As part of the recently approved measures, the Staff Rules will be amended to make termination of employment mandatory in any case of corrupt or fraudulent practice resulting in a misuse of Bank funds or other public funds. They will also clarify the duty of staff to report incidents of corruption and strengthen the reporting procedures in such cases. Focal points have been designated to receive corruption-related complaints and to investigate them or advise on how best they should be investigated. Programs for increasing staff awareness about corrupt practices will be launched. Periodic audits of internal activities will also take place over and above the normal auditing work of the Internal Audit Department, to establish whether any questionable practice has taken place.

Curbing Corruption Under Bank-Financed Loans

While the Bank has long been known for its stringent measures to insulate the projects financed by it from any possible corruption, such measures have

---

[49] So far three cases before the Bank's Administrative Tribunal have involved fraud committed by Bank staff. In all cases the Bank had terminated the staff for defrauding the Bank by submitting exaggerated overtime claims. This sanction was found, however, to be disproportionate by the Administrative Tribunal. *See W. Carew* v *IBRD*, Decision 142, WBAT Reports (1995); *A. Planthara* v *IBRD*, Decision 143, WBAT Reports (1995); *Th. D. Smith* v *IBRD*, Decision 158, WBAT Reports (1997).

[50] *See* Staff Rule 3.01, Paras. 1.01, 4.01–4.06, 5.01–5.03, 6.01–6.03 (setting forth the rules governing conflicts of interest including public and private activities of Bank Staff). *See also* Principle 3 of the Staff Manual summarizing the general obligations and general behaviour of Bank staff.

[51] *See* Staff Rule 3.01, Paras. 8.01–8.02.

[52] *See* Staff Rule 3.01, Para. 8.01.

[53] *See* Staff Rule 3.01, Paras. 10.01–10.05.

[54] *See* The World Bank Group Code of Professional Ethics.

recently been enhanced in a number of areas, some of which have broader objectives:

(i) *At the early stages of project design, preparation and appraisal*, the Bank now places emphasis on the participation of affected people and NGOs.[55] Such participation, while serving other purposes, indirectly improves the accountability of government agencies and allows the Bank to hear and verify possible complaints about corruption, such as the selection of the project location to accommodate some special interests. Also, during project appraisal, Bank staff are now required to place emphasis on confirming the adequacy of the project's accounting system and to make sure that loan agreements include adequate covenants on appropriate financial management.

(ii) *During project implementation*, the Bank now places a much greater emphasis on supervision, including the actual observance of auditing requirements. It reviews with borrowers the Bank's portfolio of on-going projects, both to identify problems and agree on solutions.[56] Through such close supervision and review, questions of corruption, if they arise at all, have a much greater opportunity to be addressed. The Bank's more open disclosure policy adopted in 1993 also allows concerned NGOs and the public at large to play a more effective role in monitoring Bank-financed projects.[57] The establishment, also in 1993, of the Bank's Inspection Panel gives affected parties access to an independent mechanism to review alleged deviations by the Bank from its policies and procedures with respect to the design, appraisal or implementation of projects financed or to be financed by it.[58]

(iii) In the preparation of the periodic *Country Assistance Strategies* for each borrowing member and more generally in the on-going *dialogue* between Bank staff and government officials, Bank senior staff are authorized to raise governance issues relevant to the Bank's mandate. Should an issue related to alleged corruption under Bank-financed projects arise, it would no doubt figure prominently in such discussions and might influence the Bank's position if they are not adequately dealt with by the government.

(iv) A *new Operational Policy Statement and Procedure* (OP/BP 10.02 – Financial Management) has recently been prepared. It requires the

---

[55] Pursuant to Operational Directive (OD) 14.70, NGOs may become involved at all stages of a Bank-financed project. Other Operational Directives such as OD 4.00 on Environmental Policies or OD 4.30 on Involuntary Resettlement ensure the participation of people affected by Bank projects.

[56] *See* Operational Policy Statement (OP) 10.02 which is discussed *infra*.

[57] *See* Bank Procedure (BP) 17.50 on Disclosure of Operational Information and the Bank's Operational Policy Statement on Disclosure of Information (OP 17.50).

[58] *See* Resolution Establishing the World Bank Inspection Panel (Resolution No. 93–10; Resolution No. IDA93–6). *See also* I. Shihata, *The World Bank Inspection Panel* (1994).

strengthening of accounting and auditing procedures for the borrowers and the project implementing agencies with respect to Bank-financed projects and tightens the rules regarding the borrowers' compliance with audit and other financial covenants in the loan agreements. This OP/BP includes specific procedures for the suspension of loan disbursement in cases of prolonged non-observance.

(v) Perhaps more importantly in the context of curbing corruption, the Bank's *rules, applicable to the procurement of goods and services under its loans*, which are incorporated in its loan agreements, have been further tightened by virtue of new rules and procedures approved by the Bank's Board on July 23, 1996. According to these new rules and procedures:

(a) The Bank can at any time cancel the financing of any contract under the loan, not only in cases of misprocurement as previously stated, but also whenever corrupt or fraudulent practices were engaged in by representatives of the borrower or a beneficiary of the loan during the procurement process or the execution of the contract, unless the borrower takes timely and appropriate action satisfactory to the Bank to remedy the situation. Both the General Conditions applicable to IBRD loans and IDA credits, and the Procurement Guidelines, have been amended to reflect this important change.

(b) Any supplier/contractor/consultant financed by a Bank loan which is found by the Bank, after appropriate investigation with adequate safeguards, to have engaged in a corrupt or fraudulent practice, will be declared by decision of the Bank's President, upon the recommendation of a high level committee, ineligible to bid for Bank-financed contracts, for a specific period of time or indefinitely, according to the gravity of the offence.

(c) The Bank will also reject a proposal for the award of a contract by the borrower if it determines that the bidder recommended for this purpose by the borrower has engaged in corrupt or fraudulent activities in competing for that contract.

(d) The Bank can now require its borrowers to include in the contracts financed by Bank loans a provision by virtue of which the Bank will have the right to inspect the accounts and records of the contractor/ supplier/consultant concerned relating to the performance of the contract and to have them audited by auditors appointed by the Bank.

(e) Bidders for Bank-financed contracts are now required to disclose in their bids any commissions or other payments paid to local or foreign agents in the context of the procurement or execution of such contracts.

(vi) In addition to the above, recently approved measures include additional, previously unannounced, audits of Bank operations in a specific country by outside firms, and regular post-review of procurements on a country basis. Three of the first type of audits have already started in large borrowing countries.

Assisting Borrowing Members in Curbing Corruption

The main vehicle for assisting its members in their fight against corruption as a general phenomenon is the Bank's policy lending instruments and its technical assistance loans. Other measures have also been used by the Bank, however, to good effect.

1. *Policy Lending*
    Although adjustment lending was initiated in 1980 to assist countries in improving their economic performance, many reform measures introduced under structural and sectoral adjustment loans (and other 'rehabilitation' and 'recovery' loans) have indirectly and at times specifically helped in stemming corruption.[59] These have included, in addition to general measures of deregulation, liberalization and privatization which aim at replacing administrative dictates with market mechanisms, such specific measures as the following:
    a) The introduction of banking laws and regulations to ensure the health of the financial sector and also to strengthen controls over fraudulent and imprudent practices and money laundering;
    b) The introduction of tax laws and regulations, not only to simplify tax structures and reduce tax rates but also to improve tax administration and collection;
    c) The introduction or amendment of procurement laws, regulations and documents as well as measures of financial management, not only for development projects but more generally of the government budget, accounting and auditing systems;
    d) Less specific measures of legal and judicial reform have also been introduced in the context of policy based lending, especially under sectoral adjustment loans in situations where agreement was reached with the borrower on the pressing need and the feasibility of short term actions;
    e) Specific civil service reform measures have often been agreed under adjustment loans, especially for downsizing and pay increases.

2. *Technical Assistance and Sectoral Investment Loans*
    Both free standing loans and components of technical assistance and sectoral investment loans have covered Bank financing of legal and regulatory reform, civil service reform, judicial reform and public sector reform, all with potential direct or indirect effects on the opportunities

---

[59] For details on the policy of adjustment lending as a response to macro-economic disturbances in the 1980s in most developing countries, *see The Social Impact of Adjustment Operations: An Overview* (World Bank Operations Evaluation Department, Report No. 14776, 1995) and *Structural and Sectoral Adjustment: World Bank Experience 1980–1992* (World Bank Operations Evaluation Department, Report No. 14691, 1995); *see also World Development Report – Poverty* 104–120 (World Bank 1990).

for and level of corruption.[60] While relatively large free standing loans have been made in recent years for legal and/or judicial reform in countries as diverse as Venezuela, Bolivia, China, Russia and Ecuador, public sector reform and civil service reform loans started earlier and have covered a large number of countries. The recently agreed measures by the Bank's top management to assist in combating corruption include the broadening of activities in these fields as may be needed in the circumstances of each country.

3. *Bank Grants*
   Since the establishment by the Bank of its Institutional Development Fund (IDF) as a trust fund to provide grants to borrowers for capacity building purposes (other than project preparation, which may be financed by other types of Bank grants), a number of grants have been made for purposes such as the preparation of new legislation, public procurement and associated training, or the carrying out of studies which diagnose the problems of the civil service or the judiciary. Some of these studies paved the way for technical assistance loans for these sectors. Among the recently agreed measures, IDF grants will also be made for capacity building in accounting and auditing in borrowing countries. Other grants have already financed a number of surveys to assess the level of delivery of public services in some borrowing countries.

4. *Seminars by the Economic Development Institute (EDI)*
   EDI has pioneered a number of 'Integrity Workshops' for specific countries to increase awareness of the causes and economic effects of corruption. These seminars are planned to cover more countries in the future. EDI has also provided training for economic journalists. Recently agreed measures for the Bank to assist in combating corruption include new procurement seminars to be provided by EDI for the training of specialists in borrowing countries.

5. *Bank Research*
   Corruption has been researched on a few occasions by Bank staff as a separate topic but has been more regularly addressed under more general reports. Examples include the two Bank reports on governance issues published in 1992 and 1994, private sector assessment reports carried out for most borrowing countries, service delivery surveys (financed mostly by IDF grants), surveys of manufacturing enterprises in transition economies, a few Country Assistance Strategy (CAS) reports and the 1996 World Development Report (WDR) on Transition. The 1997 WDR, which will deal with 'The State in a Changing World,'

---

[60] For a general overview of legal technical assistance by the Bank, *see The World Bank and Legal Technical Assistance* (World Bank Policy Research Working Paper No. 1414, 1995).

will treat the issue of corruption in a broader and more detailed manner. In depth analysis of the causes of corruption, the empirical evidence of its impact on development, and how best to address it in Bank's lending and non-lending operations, is now being considered as possible subjects to be specifically addressed by Bank research.

CONCLUSION

Although corruption can be seen in a much broader context, it has been addressed here mainly in terms of the use of public office or trust for private gain, the abuse of a public or private position in favour of the position-holder, his family, friends or bribers and the selective or arbitrary application of public rules to benefit the official in charge and those who pay him for the favour. Its causes and effects, both on the parties to a corrupt deal and on the society at large, have been discussed from different angles. In spite of direct material benefits to the corrupting and corrupt parties and possible facilitating effect on business transactions, the long term effects of corruption are found to be negative on the society, its government, law, ethics and economy. Businessmen may be content to live with it as long as it is fairly predictable, and the poor may accept it as a fact of life, but its devastating distributional effects are increasingly recognized on a world-wide scale.

In practically all societies, corruption has been recognized as a social malaise, if not a religious sin. However, its manifestations continue to exist in varying degrees in all societies. Measures to combat it have also had different degrees of success but have generally been more effective when they followed a comprehensive approach and combined the efforts of governments with those of business groups and non-governmental organizations.

Both in theory and practice, many ways have been proposed to achieve the reduction of corruption. However, as the discussion in this paper demonstrates, these proposals may remain empty gestures in the absence of some basic requirements: (i) real commitment from national and local leadership at the political and administrative levels, (ii) a broad and sustained campaign by civil society to keep that commitment alive, (iii) institutional capacity to implement and enforce, (iv) public disclosure and a free flow of information, (v) a social enabling environment of norms and values supportive of anti-corruption measures, (vi) the adoption by multinational corporations and international agencies of standards and practices which address corruption with a view to fighting it in their work, and (vii) international cooperative efforts to deal with trans-boundary corrupt and fraudulent practices.

International conditions seem to be more conducive now than any time in the past to address corruption as an issue of global concern. With the greater liberalization of trade and investment, the gradual globalization of the market place and overwhelming advances in technology, corruption is becoming not only a common domestic problem but an international problem as well. It is being recognized as a development issue in view of its possible impact on the cost of transactions, the volume of external flows, the stability and predictability of the investment environment, and eventually the rate of growth itself. Inevitably, it has become a concern for the world's premier development finance institution.

The World Bank has already played an extensive role in the fight against corruption, a role which goes beyond the confines of the activities of its staff and the projects it finances. As corruption becomes a major issue of development policy, with respect to aid, trade and investment, the Bank's role is bound to increase and take on new dimensions. Chances of success in this complex area are more limited, but the expected impact on development may well be worth the effort.

DAVID CHAIKIN

17. Extraterritoriality and the Criminalization of Foreign Bribes

It is over 20 years since the United Nations General Assembly recommended measures to tackle the problem of international corruption.[1] Since then, various institutions, such as Law Ministers of the Commonwealth countries,[2] have called for increased action to deal with the problem of international corruption. Much has been said but little has been done to adequately address the insidious effects of corruption. The failure by host governments and the international community has been evident in the wholesale looting of developing countries in Africa and Asia, the undermining of democratic institutions and market economies in Eastern Europe, and political and economic instability throughout the developing world.[3]

This paper considers the policy considerations relevant to enacting a law prohibiting foreign bribery and the principles of jurisdiction that may be relevant to such a law. It also briefly discusses the lessons to be learnt from the United States Foreign Corrupt Practices Act. Finally, the paper describes the main regimes of international cooperation in combatting economic crime, including bribery.

---

[1] *Report of the Economic and Social Council Committee on an International Agreement on Illicit Payments*, UN Doc. E/1979/104 (25 May 1979), reprinted in 18 ILM 1025 (1979). *See also Declaration on International Investment and Multinational Enterprises*, Organization for Economic Cooperation and Development Press Release A(76) 20 (21 June 1976), reprinted in 15 ILM 967 (1976).

[2] *See* comments by Law Ministers at Law Ministers' meetings held in Canada, Barbados and Sri Lanka, as well as communiques from those meetings: Commonwealth Secretariat, *Minutes of Meetings and Memoranda* (1977, 1980, 1983); *see also* B. Rider, Commonwealth Law Ministers Meeting Report No. LLM (80)2, *The Promotion and Development of International Cooperation to Combat Commercial and Economic Crime* (1980).

[3] For corruption in Asian countries, *see* Phongpaichit and Piriyarangsan, *Corruption and Democracy in Thailand*, Chulalongkorn University (1994); and T. Wing Lo, *Corruption and Politics in Hong Kong and China*, Open University Press (1993).

Barry A.K. Rider (ed.), Corruption: The Enemy Within, 285–301
© *Kluwer Law International. Printed in the Netherlands.*

POLICY CONSIDERATIONS

In 1979, the United States Congress passed a law which made it a criminal offence for a United States national or company to make a corrupt payment to a foreign official or politician. The United States is now encouraging other countries to pass similar laws. Certain policy considerations arise in deciding whether to enact a foreign bribery statute.

Increased Effectiveness of Bribery Laws in the International Context

Bribery offences are notoriously difficult to investigate and prosecute.[4] Bribery is usually carried out with great secrecy in the interests of both the donor and recipient of the bribe. Secrecy is essential because disclosure may result in criminal prosecution, commercial loss and political ruin. Since detection is problematical, prosecutions for serious corruption are rare.[5] Where a third jurisdiction is used to make the illicit payment, the problems of enforcement are compounded.

If bribery of a foreign official is criminalized in both the countries where the bribe giver and the bribe recipient are located, and under the law of the nationality of the participants in the bribe, there will be an improvement in detection and prosecution. The deterrent effects of a criminal law increase where the jurisdictional net is expanded. This also improves the scope and intensity of international mutual assistance and extradition. It puts an end to the double standard whereby corruption is punished at home but encouraged abroad. It is also consistent with the view that bribery of foreign officials is morally and ethically improper.

Improved Governance of Multinational Companies

Where a multinational corporation makes an illicit payment in a foreign corrupt environment, it is sometimes suggested that the harmful effects of that conduct may be limited. That is, the illicit foreign behaviour may be 'fenced in' and will not affect the moral behaviour of the company in its 'home jurisdiction'. The evidence suggests otherwise. For example, the creation of secret slush funds to finance the bribery of foreign officials has also been used for illicit domestic political contributions in the United

---

[4] The enforcement difficulties in international bribery cases are set out in M. Reisman, *Folded Lies: Bribery, Crusades and Reforms*, New York, Free Press (1979).

[5] Prosecutions are less difficult for offences such as Section 10 of the Prevention of Bribery Ordinance (Hong Kong), which creates a statutory presumption of corruption where Crown servants possess assets disproportionate to their official income.

States.[6] A company which permits its officers to engage in foreign bribery will find that this encourages the evasion of conventional corporate controls, including those pertaining to management information systems, audit and internal control mechanisms and legal compliance systems. If a company sanctions bribery in another country, there is an increased risk of commercial fraud, corporate abuse and illicit diversion of funds. Losses will be suffered by shareholders and creditors. Criminalizing foreign bribes will also lead to an improvement in the moral climate and more effective internal control and corporate accountability of officers and employees of multinational corporations. For these reasons, the distinction between bribery at home and foreign bribery should be eliminated.

More Even Playing Field in International Business Transactions

The payment of a bribe which results in the securing of an international commercial contract is offensive to the principles of competition. Bribery of foreign officials may be characterized as an 'unfair trade practice' which is contrary to the principles underlying GATT[7] and the World Trade Organization. International bribery enables the 'donor' to obtain an illicit trade advantage. The contract is secured not on the basis of price, quality, or other commercial considerations. It is the corruption of an agent and the breach of fiduciary duties which secures the contract. This is unfair to the companies which do not participate in the bribe. It is also unfair to the citizens of the country where the officials are bribed.

Cultural Dogmatism and Cultural Insensitivity

Are laws prohibiting foreign bribery an improper attempt to impose Western moral precepts on countries which have different cultural values and business practices and traditions?[8] Virtually all countries prohibit bribery of

---

[6] *See* US Securities and Exchange Commission, *Report to the Committee on Banking, Housing and Urban Affairs, US Senate, 94th Cong. 2d. Sess., on Questionable and Illegal Corporate Payments and Practices* (1976); *see* generally, Mankiewicz, *Nixon's Road to Watergate*, London, Hutchinson (1973); and C. Bernstein and B. Woodward, *All the President's Men* (1972).

[7] For a discussion of the institutional aspects of the principles of international trade, *see* D. Chaikin, 'International Economic Institutions', *Law of Transnational Business Transactions* in V. Nanda and Clark Boardman (eds.), *Law of Transnational Business Transactions* (1985), Ch. 17.

[8] S. FitzGerald, *Ethical Dimensions of Australia's Engagement with Asian Countries: Are There Any?*, St. James Ethics Centre, Sydney (1993); R. Armstrong, 'An Empirical Investigation of International Marketing Ethics: Problems Encountered by Australian Firms', 11 *Journal of Business Ethics* (1992), 165; and Asia-Australia Institute, *Perceiving Business Ethics* (1985). *See* generally, A. Prindl and B. Prodhan, *Ethical Conflicts in Finance*, Blackwells (1994).

public officials under the local criminal law. But how a country deals with bribery is not found only in national laws. Professor Noonan[9] has suggested that bribery may be defined from four perspectives: that of the more advanced moralists; that of the written law; that of the law as it is generally enforced; and that of common practice. Corruption – or at least certain species of corruption – is sanctioned by all the great religious traditions.

Professor Noonan also suggests that the core concept of a bribe – an inducement improperly influencing the performance of a public function meant to be gratuitous – has been remarkably constant throughout history. Although the precise constituent elements of the behaviour may change with the culture, the idea of bribery and its illicitness has been with us since antiquity. Noonan makes the following acute observation:[10]

> Bribes are a species of reciprocity. Human life is full of reciprocities. The particular reciprocities that count as bribes in particular cultures are distinguished by intentionality, form and content. What is a bribe depends on the cultural treatment of the constituent elements.

Interference in National Sovereignty

Is the enforcement of a foreign bribery law an unwarranted interference with the sovereignty of a foreign country?[11] A nation-state has the power to make its own criminal laws. A state also has the power and the right to decide whether or not to enforce its own laws. For example, a state may deliberately choose not to exercise its criminal jurisdiction over corrupt payments made by foreign nationals to its own government officials. Indeed, some states may view bribery as a 'legitimate means' of remunerating its public officials who are paid paltry salaries, even though its own laws do not permit such payments.

If a foreign state asserts its criminal jurisdiction over the nationals of a foreign state, then this may be considered in some circumstances to be an interference in the internal affairs of that state. But the FCP Act penalizes nationals or national corporations and does not criminalize the conduct of foreign officials who accept bribes. How can the exercise of jurisdiction

---

[9] J. Noonan, *Bribes*, Macmillan (1984), at xii.

[10] Noonan, *supra*, note 9, at xiii.

[11] For an outline of this and other international problems, *see* K. Meessen, 'Fighting Corruption Across the Border', 18 *Fordham Intl. L.J.* 1647 (1995); *see also* the recent US Supreme Court decision which held that the act of state doctrine did not preclude enquiry into the motivation of Nigerian government officials in awarding a contract allegedly on the basis of bribery: *W.S. Kirkpatrick & Co.* v. *Environmental Tetronics Corp. International* 110 S.Ct. 701, reprinted in 29 ILM 182 (1990).

against one's own nationals be said to be an interference or invasion of sovereignty?

Competitive Disadvantage to Corporations of National State

Given the intense competition that exists in international trade, it is the unofficial policy of some governments to advise their nationals as to the best method of making illicit payments to foreign public officials. Diplomats and trade officials of some countries gather information on the personalities and susceptibilities of foreign officials to corruption. Valuable intelligence concerning the manner and level of bribes of competitors, the market level of payments, and the appropriate foreign officials to whom payments are to be directed, is given to national corporations. Such intelligence is used to secure an unfair competitive advantage.

Does a law criminalizing foreign bribery impose a competitive disadvantage on the corporations of the national state? It is a belief of many states that the FCP Act has hurt US corporations. There is a real concern that enacting US-style legislation is harmful to one's own corporations. Unfortunately, there is little evidence on the impact of the FCP Act and it is difficult to judge the extent to which the Act has seriously undermined US corporations' competitiveness.

In practice, many US corporates have learned to live with the FCP Act.[12] This is in contrast to the early days of the Act, when there was substantial opposition and concerted effort to repeal the Act. The perception that US multinationals are no longer criticizing the FCP Act may be explained by political considerations. Some US corporates are lobbying for a multilateral convention on international bribery which may reduce any existing competitive disadvantage.

The Prisoner's Dilemma

Objections to a foreign bribery law are sometimes based not on principle but on the pragmatic concern that if a country acts alone or ahead of the 'pack', it will suffer economically. This is the so-called 'prisoner's dilemma'. How does one change the law without leading by example? How does one act first without incurring business losses to less scrupulous competitors? The solution to the prisoner's dilemma is the enactment of a multilateral

---

[12] One counsel to a multinational corporation has claimed to the author that the FCP Act has been used by the corporation as a 'defence' against officials in Mainland China who seek to extort payments. Middle-sized companies are less likely to be able to resist extortion payments. Contrast with the comments in 'Corruption Laws Would Hurt Australian Trade', *Australian Financial Review* (7 August 1994), 3.

convention on international bribery with full participation of the leading countries of the industrialized world.[13]

Government Monopoly on Bribery

Professor Reisman, an international law scholar and expert on intelligence matters, argued in his book, *Folded Lies*,[14] that the FCP Act was an attempt by the US government to monopolize international bribery. He suggested that after the enactment of the law, a US multinational corporation may bribe a foreign government only if it did it with the consent of or in cooperation with the US government/intelligence community. That is, US corporates should coordinate illicit foreign payment with the CIA!

Professor Reisman's argument is based on a worldly, if not cynical, view of international affairs. It draws some strength from the fact that one of the reasons that Congress passed the FCP Act was to prevent future scandals that might hinder the ability of the US government to control foreign policy. But it is difficult to judge the validity of Reisman's opinion, because it concerns matters which are not open to scrutiny.

The strongest retort to the Reisman view is the fact that the number of prosecutions under the FCP Act has increased, with legal suits resulting in substantial fines and prison sentences.[15] The Department of Justice and the Securities and Exchange Commission are interested in pursuing cases under the FCP Act, although other arms of the US government may have different policy agenda on this issue.

UNITED STATES PARADIGM

It is 19 years since the United States Congress passed the FCP Act in 1977, in the aftermath of the Watergate scandal and the SEC revelations of massive US corporate bribery of senior foreign officials.[16] The FCP Act[17] focuses on corrupt payments to foreign officials, foreign political parties, party officials, or candidates or intermediaries for any such persons. The

---

[13] *See* 'Submission to the Working Group on OECD Recommendations on Cross-Border Corruption', *Transparency International Australia* (August 1994), 8.

[14] Reisman, *supra*, note 4.

[15] For example, in 1995 there were 85 active investigations under the Act and the US government has brought 3 dozen law suits against US corporations to enforce the Act.

[16] Noonan, *supra*, note 7, at 655–676; D. Boulton, *The Lockheed Papers*, Jonathan Cape (1978), 109–110, 164–165; and *supra*, note 6.

[17] *See* generally, A. Bhachu, 'Foreign Corrupt Practices Act', 32 *American Criminal Law Review* (1995); Note, 'Civil RICO Misread: The Judicial Repeal of the 1988 Amendments to the Foreign Corrupt Practices Act', 14 *Fordham International Law Review* 946 (1990–91).

payments are criminal when made for the purpose of influencing official acts or decisions and so as to assist in the obtaining or retaining of business.

The anti-bribery provisions in the 1977 Act apply to two separate categories of persons:

(a) issuers:[18] entities whose securities are registered under section 12 of the Securities Exchange Act 1934, or which are required to file reports under section 15(d) of the same Act (SEC jurisdictional entities); and

(b) domestic concerns: individuals who are citizens, nationals or residents of the United States, and corporations, partnerships, associations, joint-stock companies, business trusts, unincorporated organizations, or sole proprietorships having their principal business in the United States or organized under the laws of a state, territory, or commonwealth of the United States (US nationals and residents or US-based entities).

It would appear that the jurisdictional scope of the anti-bribery criminal provision is not excessive to the extent that it relies on the active nationality principle, territorial (effects) principle and protective principle (*see* discussion below). One area of concern has been the extent to which the FCP Act applies to the foreign subsidiary of a US based or registered company.[19]

As originally enacted in 1977, the FCP Act prohibited any payment to a third party, 'while knowing or having reason to know' that all or part of the payment would be used to bribe a foreign official. The *mens rea* requirement was changed in 1988 by the deletion of the 'reason to know' standard. Consequently, it must now be shown that the accused had knowledge that the payment was for the purpose of bribery. The phrase 'knowledge' is defined in the FCP Act and includes 'deliberate avoidance of knowledge', 'wilful blindness' and 'conscious disregard of the facts'.

Where a company carries out due diligence enquiries into the background and business practices of its sales agents, this may assist it in establishing the absence of the requisite degree of knowledge under the anti-bribery provision. Compliance programmes in respect of the Act are now commonplace, especially where an American company enters into international distribution and sales agency agreements.[20]

---

[18] The FCP Act distinguishes between public and non-public companies on the assumption that public companies are larger and more sophisticated, and should be subject to a higher standard of conduct, especially in their audited statements.

[19] Baruch, 'International Transactions which Violate the Foreign Corrupt Practices Act or Other Criminal Statutes', in *Law and Practice of US Reg. Of Int'l Trade*, Release 89–1, Booklet 11, 49–57 (ed. C. Johnson, 1989).

[20] J. Impert, 'A Programme for Compliance with the Foreign Corrupt Practices Act and the Foreign Law Restrictions on the Use of Sales', *Int'l Law* (1990), 1009 at 1018 (Red Flags include an excessively large commission or a request that the commission be paid in a third country).

Additional protection is available under the 1992 Department of Justice Guidelines whereby an issuer or domestic concern may obtain advice and a recommendation as to whether a proposed payment is in conformity with the FCP Act. This provides a 'safe harbour' for US transactions and a greater security in international business deals.

The anti-bribery prohibition does not apply to a 'facilitation payment', that is, any payment made in order to expedite or to secure the performance of a routine government action, such as obtaining permits, licences, processing government papers, providing police protection, providing 'phone services, etc. There are also two affirmative defences available under the FCP Act: payments made in accordance with the written laws of the host country, and payments constituting 'reasonable and *bone fide* expenditure'.

The successful investigation of offences under the FCP Act has relied extensively on the used of 'whistleblowers' and informers. Little use has been made of undercover operations or other techniques of entrapment. This may explain in part why there have been few prosecutions under the Act, and why most of these have been for violation of the accounting provisions. Prosecution obstacles include: unavailability of key witnesses who cannot be located or are unwilling to be interviewed in foreign countries; difficulty of obtaining books and records of companies in offshore bank secrecy jurisdictions and/or non-cooperation of foreign governments where members of the political elite are beneficiaries of the secret payments; and foreign government-sanctioned phoney books, etc.

EXTRATERRITORIAL PRINCIPLES OF CRIMINAL JURISDICTION

It is well recognized that states have claimed jurisdiction over criminal matters on the following bases: the territorial principle; the principle of protection or security; the principle of passive personality; the principle of active personality or nationality; and the universality principle. An outline of these principles[21] and their relevance to a law on foreign bribery are discussed in detail below.

The Territorial Principle

The territorial principle expresses the idea that every state is competent to punish crimes committed within its territory. Each state must have jurisdiction over crimes committed within its territory because such power is

---

[21] For a detailed analysis, *see* D. Chaikin, Commonwealth Law Ministers Meeting Report No. LLM (83)29 *Mutual Assistance in Criminal matters: A Commonwealth Perspective* (Commonwealth Secretariat 1983); *see also* P. Butler and C. Thompson, Transparency International Australia Report, *The Legality of Foreign Bribes under Australian Law* (1955).

necessary for its very existence. Moreover, it is expected that a person should obey the laws of the country in which he is physically present.

In order to deal with the problem of crime across national borders, the territorial principle has acquired two extensions. The 'subjective territorial principle' established that a state has jurisdiction over crimes committed within the state but completed and consummated abroad. This principle gives jurisdiction to the state where the actor was physically present at the time of the crime. The second extension, called the 'objective territorial principle', establishes that a state has jurisdiction over crimes committed outside the state but consummated within its territory. The objective territorial principle gave jurisdiction to the state where the 'harmful effects' of the prohibited conduct were felt. There is considerable disagreement between the United States and other countries as to the scope of this principle, with the United States courts asserting jurisdiction where economic and socially ulterior effects occur within its territory.

It is difficult to ascertain how the territorial principle of criminal jurisdiction may be relied on as a basis for criminalizing foreign bribery. Even under the 'open-ended' formulation of US courts,[22] it is not apparent how a foreign bribe would have any relevance or precise effect in the United States.

The Protective or Security Principle

The protective principle is a claim that a state has jurisdiction over crimes committed abroad which are directed against the vital interests of the state. The justification of the protective principle lies in the inadequacy of national laws in punishing conduct within its territory which is directed against the vital interests of other states. Offences falling within the ambit of this principle include attacks on the security, credit, political independence and territorial integrity of the state. Counterfeiting of a state's currency or falsification of its official documents are examples of the application of this principle.

The bribery of a foreign public official would not *per se* fall within the ambit of this principle. One can think of examples, such as the corruption of a foreign Head of State, which may injure the national foreign policy interests of a state and in extreme circumstances may even lead to inter-state conflict. However, it would seem that the protective principle is not the most appropriate jurisdictional base to justify a general law on foreign bribery.

---

[22] For an analysis of the extraterritorial problem and the US courts, *see* D. Chaikin, 'Fraud Securities Laws and Extraterritoriality in the United States' in B. Rider (ed.), *The Regulation of the British Securities Industry*, Oyez (1979), Ch. 11.

The Active Personality or Nationality Principle

It is well accepted that a state has practically unlimited jurisdiction over crimes committed outside its territory by its nationals or national corporations. The justification for basing jurisdiction on nationality is that a national owes allegiance to his state and that a state's treatment of its nationals is not a matter of concern to other states or to international law. (This must now be qualified because human rights are a matter of international concern and a state is not considered to have an unfettered right to conduct itself as it pleases in dealing with its own nationals).

The nationality principle has been used by Australia in enacting laws prohibiting child sex tourism and war crimes, and in creating extraterritorial crimes concerning its defence forces. For example, the Crimes (Child Sex Tourism) Act 1994 (Cth) criminalizes sexual intercourse with a child under the age of 18 while outside Australia and creates a series of offences applying to certain classes of persons, such as tour operators. The 1994 Act applies to Australian citizens, Australian residents, and Australian corporations or any other corporate body whose principal activities are carried out in Australia.

The nationality principle is well-suited as a jurisdictional basis for prohibiting bribery of foreign officials in a foreign territory. It requires a genuine link between the state enacting the law and the individual, the subject of the law. One problem that may arise is the potential conflict between the territorial principle and the nationality principle. The conflict may exist if the laws are different, for example where the local law does not prohibit the conduct.

A solution to this problem is for the country with jurisdiction based on the nationality principle to exercise prosecutorial restraint. Another way of dealing with this problem is to provide an affirmative defence, such as the one that is now available under the US Foreign Corrupt Practices Act. It is a defence under that Act if the US corporation shows that the particular payment was made in accordance with the written laws of the host or local country. The scope of this defence is limited in that it must be shown to be legal according to the law as written; it is not sufficient to show that the law is disregarded as a matter of common practice or is not enforced by the government.

An alternative approach is to impose on the prosecution the burden of establishing dual criminality, that is, that the proscribed corrupt conduct is criminal under the law of Australia and under the law of the country whose public officials are being paid 'commission', etc. Under this approach, it would be the government who would bear the burden of establishing illegality under a foreign law.

The Passive Personality Principle

The passive personality principle endows jurisdiction on a state for crimes committed by any person outside the territory if the victim of the crime is one of its nationals. It has been doubted whether this principle exists as a separate basis of jurisdiction. In any event, it is an irrelevant basis of jurisdiction for the purposes of discussing foreign bribery, since there is no clearly identifiable victim of the crime and, if there is one, it is more likely to be a national of a third state.

The Universality Principle

Universal jurisdiction is a claim to jurisdiction over crimes committed against the international order. A state asserts jurisdiction on this ground if the criminal is found within its territory. The universal principle is of a residuary nature in that it becomes relevant where the municipal criminal law of the state does not apply to the offence by virtue of the other principles of jurisdiction.

Based on the universality principle, Australia has proscribed piracy and 'terrorist conduct', that is, offences found in the anti-terrorist conventions dealing with hijacking, internationally protected persons, hostages and torture.

For example, Section 5 of the Australian Crimes (Internationally Protected Persons) Act 1976 (Cth) provides:

This Act extends – except so far as the contrary intention appears –
(a) to acts, matters and things outside Australia, whether or not in or over a foreign country; and
(b) to all persons irrespective of their nationality or citizenship.

International corruption and bribery of foreign officials are not yet matters of sufficient international concern to justify the application of the universal principle of criminal jurisdiction. Most states would object if a state asserted jurisdiction over foreign nationals for conduct amounting to bribery in third states. What would be the interest of, say, the United States criminalizing the actions of a British corporation which paid bribes to a Middle Eastern sheik?

INTERNATIONAL COOPERATION

There are four distinct regimes of international cooperation that are relevant to the tracing and recovery of misappropriated assets, including illicit bribes. These are: international mutual assistance between the police and prosecutors in relation to criminal matters; international judicial assistance in civil litigation; cooperation between courts of different jurisdictions in insolvency matters; and international cooperation between regulators and supervisors in the financial services industry.

Criminal Mutual Assistance Treaties and Arrangements[23]

In 1987, Australia enacted specific legislation to enable it to provide assistance to foreign countries in relation to both the investigation and prosecution of crimes (including tax offences) and the tracing, freezing and confiscation of proceeds of crime. Prior to that date, the Australian government could provide only a limited measure of legal assistance to foreign countries and, as a consequence, Australia received little assistance from foreign countries.

The Mutual Assistance in Criminal Matters (MACM) Act 1987 (Cth) provides a legislative basis for Australia to enter into treaties and arrangements with other countries whereby it can request and grant assistance in criminal matters. In particular, the MACM Act has enabled Australia, in cooperation with other countries, to deprive criminals of their proceeds of crime.

Australia's MACM treaties and arrangements provide for assistance in the following areas:
- the obtaining of evidence, documents or other articles;
- the provision of documents and other records;
- the location and identification of witnesses or suspects;
- the execution of requests for search and seizure;
- the making of arrangements for persons to give evidence or assist investigations;
- the forfeiture or confiscation of property;
- the recovery of pecuniary penalties;
- the restraining dealings in property or the freezing of assets;
- the locating of property that may be forfeited, or that may be needed to satisfy pecuniary penalties; and
- the service and authentication of documents.

However, the type of assistance that is available will depend on the specific treaty and the law of the foreign country. For example, some countries do not have laws permitting the freezing and confiscation of the proceeds of crime and consequently assistance may not be forthcoming in this area. In some cases, a foreign country may be given important financial information obtained by AUSTRAC: *see* section 37A of the MACM Act.

---

[23] *See* D. Chaikin, *supra*, note 21; *see also* D. Chaikin, *Mutual Assistance Aspects of the Proceeds of Crime Act 1987*, Tenth Australasian Corporate Crime Investigators Course, Bathurst, Australia, 2–14 December 1987.

(At present financial transaction reports information gathered by AUSTRAC may be passed to its foreign counterparts in France (TRACFIN) and in the United States (FINCEN) pursuant to Memoranda of Understanding reached with those agencies.)

Australia has concluded bilateral MACM treaties and arrangements with over 20 countries, including Austria, Argentina, Canada, Finland, France, Germany, Hong Kong, Italy, Israel, Japan, Korea, Luxembourg, Mexico, the Netherlands, New Zealand, Papua New Guinea, the Philippines, Portugal, Singapore, Spain, Switzerland, the United Kingdom, the United States and Vanuatu. Australia is also a party to the Commonwealth of Nations Scheme of Mutual Assistance which was agreed to by Law Ministers from 60 countries in Harare, Zimbabwe, in August 1986.

Before the Australian Commonwealth Attorney General's Department (which is the central authority for the processing of requests) will act on a foreign request for assistance, it must be satisfied that there is a genuine foreign investigation into a criminal matter. The MACM Act cannot be used for collateral purposes, that is, for non-criminal matters, such as a general investigation in bankruptcy or insolvency.

Where an investigation into a bankrupt pertains to a criminal matter, international legal assistance may be forthcoming. In *Bond* v. *Rozenes & Ors*,[24] Allen Bond sought declarations that the continued investigation into alleged bankruptcy offences by him and the Australian government's requests for mutual assistance to the Swiss authorities were *ultra vires* and an abuse of power. He also sought an injunction against the Commonwealth Director of Public Prosecutions, the Chief Commissioner of the Federal Police and the Commonwealth Attorney General from pursuing the mutual assistance request. That investigation concerned whether Bond had assets in Switzerland and Jersey which he had either failed to disclose to his trustee in bankruptcy or subsequently lied about when giving evidence during an examination of his financial affairs. The applicant argued that the annulment of his bankruptcy annihilated the bankruptcy, so that it was to be treated as never having taken place, with the consequences that the applicant was never a bankrupt and could not have committed an offence. Sundberg J rejected this argument, holding that a person who, while bankrupt, commits an offence against the Bankruptcy Act, does not escape prosecution by reason of his later discharge or the annulment of his bankruptcy. It followed that the continued investigation into the alleged bankruptcy offences was lawful, including the MACM request of Switzerland.

MACM requests may be made with secrecy, with the defendant often finding out about their existence only when the matter gives rise to court proceedings in a foreign country. The making of such requests is not usually scrutinized by the courts of the requesting country, although the execution

---

[24] Unreported, Federal Court (Sundberg J), 13 February 1996.

of the requests involving compulsory measures (for example, freezing of assets) will require the sanction of the court of the requested country. There is considerable prosecutorial and executive discretion in the MACM field. This is recognized by the MACM Act, which contains wide-ranging 'executive safeguards' in respect of all requests by foreign countries. Under Section 8 of the MACM Act, the Commonwealth Attorney General is under a legal obligation to refuse assistance if the granting of the foreign request would prejudice the sovereignty, security, national interest or essential interests of Australia or a state or territory. Assistance must also be refused if the request relates to a political offence or purely military offence.

The scope and value of mutual assistance is still being worked out. One limitation is that many countries will not give assistance involving compulsory measures (for example, access to bank information) unless the conduct underlying the investigation is criminal in both the requesting and requested country. For example, Vanuatu and the Cayman Islands will not compel banks to disclose confidential information about their clients in cases of insider trading and warehousing of shares, because such conduct is not criminal in their jurisdictions. Similarly, Switzerland will not give assistance in relation to tax evasion, although it will cooperate in cases of tax fraud.

A significant difficulty in MACM matters is that there may be considerable delays in obtaining documents and other material, particularly where such documents are held by third parties such as banks or lawyers. This is one area where there is room for considerable improvement. Delays may be reduced by sending investigators overseas, by reducing the number of hands through which MACM requests pass, and by ensuring that investigators understand foreign laws, procedures and customs. In complex matters, a local law firm may be hired to assist in the freezing and recovery of assets.

International Judicial Assistance in Civil Matters[25]

The 1970 Hague Convention
Since 1992, Australia has been a party to the Hague Convention for the Taking of Evidence Abroad in Civil and Commercial Matters 1970. The Hague Convention provides for the taking of evidence or the performance of other judicial acts by the issue of letters of request by judicial authorities or by diplomatic officers, consular agents and commissioners. The Convention may assist in obtaining admissible evidence in an action for the tracing of assets, but it has no application to the enforcement of judgments or orders for provisional or protective measures (for example, freezing orders).

---

[25] *See* generally, D. McClean, *International Judicial Assistance*, Clarendon (1992); and L. Collins, *Essays in International Litigation and the Conflict of Laws*, Clarendon (1994).

The Convention applies to the following jurisdictions: Akrotiri and Dhekelia, Australia, Barbados, Belgium, the Cayman Islands, Cyprus, Czechoslovakia, Denmark, the Falkland Islands, Finland, France, Germany, Gibraltar, Guam, Hong Kong, Israel, Italy, Luxembourg, the Isle of Man, Monaco, the Netherlands, Norway, Portugal, Puerto Rico, Singapore, Spain, Sweden, Turkey, the United Kingdom, the United States, and the American Virgin Islands.

Foreign Evidence Act 1994 (Cth)
Various methods of obtaining foreign evidence are set out in Part 2 of the Foreign Evidence Act 1994 (Cth) and in similar state legislation. Section 7V of the Foreign Evidence Act 1994 (Cth) provides that a superior court may

(a) order the examination of a person outside Australia before a judge, court officer, or other person;
(b) issue a commission for the examination of a person outside Australia; and
(c) issue a letter of request to the judicial authorities of a foreign country to take evidence of person or cause it to be taken.

This procedure does not permit an Australian court to order the production of documents by a person outside Australia. Nor does it provide any assistance in the freezing or the recovery of assets. It has been criticized as being a slow and expensive method of obtaining evidence.

Evidence and Procedure (New Zealand) Act 1994 (Cth)
This Act enables parties, for the first time in Australia, to obtain an international subpoena. It provides for the service of Australian subpoenas in New Zealand and New Zealand subpoenas in Australia. It also provides for the receiving of evidence by video link or telephone between the two countries.

Cooperation Between Courts in Insolvency and Bankruptcy Matters[26]

Section 29 of the Bankruptcy Act 1966 (Cth) and Section 581 of the Corporations Law 1991 (Cth) empower Australian courts to 'act in aid of' and be auxiliary to foreign courts having jurisdiction in bankruptcy or external administration matters. The jurisdiction under both Acts applies to the following 'prescribed countries': Bailiwick of Jersey, Canada, Papua New Guinea, Malaysia, New Zealand, Singapore, Switzerland, the United Kingdom and the United States. The procedure involves the filing, in an

---

[26] *See* generally, A. Rose, *Global Commerce: The Need for Cross Border Remedies in Insolvency*, Australian Bankruptcy Congress, Sydney (1996).

Australian court, of a letter of request which has been issued by a foreign court requesting aid in an insolvency matter. The Australian court may exercise such powers with respect to the matter as it could exercise if the matter had arisen in its own jurisdiction.

Conversely, an Australian court may request a foreign court to act in aid of its insolvency jurisdiction. This is claimed to have the potential of facilitating the location and recovery of assets, although it is more likely to provide an avenue for the obtaining of admissible evidence to be used in civil or criminal proceedings, as distinct from asset recovery actions.[27] For example, Mr. Robert Ramsay, the trustee of bankruptcy of Allen Bond, obtained from the Royal Court of Jersey orders for the examination of certain partners of Touche Ross in Jersey and the production of voluminous documents from Touche Ross in relation to certain transactions and various entities allegedly controlled by Allen Bond. Similarly, Mr. Max Donnelly, the trustee of bankruptcy of Christopher Skase, has obtained from the High Court of England summonses for the production of documents and for the examination of certain witnesses (including Skase's London solicitors, his step-daughter, the National Westminster Bank and the Austrian Bank). The purpose of the London examination is to establish whether or not various companies or persons are holding certain assets in trust for Mr. Skase. If it is so established, then an application may be made to the Federal Court under Sections 120 and 121 of the Bankruptcy Act for an order that these assets be treated as assets of the bankrupt estate.

International Cooperation Between Regulators

Another trend is the increasing cooperation between regulators in different countries in respect of both the sharing of information and the investigation of corporate malpractice. A number of countries have enacted discrete legislation in order to enhance the ability of regulators to assist their foreign counterparts. For example, the United States International Securities Enforcement Cooperation Act 1988 facilitates the gathering of evidence in international securities fraud cases by promoting cooperation amongst international securities regulations.

In Australia, the Mutual Assistance in Business (Regulation) (MABR) Act 1992 (Cth) enables certain Commonwealth business regulating authorities, such as the Australian Securities Commission (ASC), to provide assistance to foreign regulators. The type of assistance available under the Act includes the obtaining of information, documents or evidence and the transmitting of

---

[27] D. Chaikin, *Asset Recovery: The Money Laundering Obstacle*, National Conference of Insolvency Practitioners of Australia, Brisbane, 3 May 1986.

such material to the foreign regulator. The Act envisages the use of the local powers of the regulating authority to assist the foreign regulator.

A significant limitation on the use of the MABR Act is that the information or evidence obtained under that Act may not be used for the purpose of criminal proceedings and, to the extent to which it is within the ability of the foreign regulator to ensure, may not be used by any other person, authority or agency for the purpose of criminal proceedings. This limitation is intended to impose a speciality requirement on the use of information or evidence gathered by compulsory means by the ASC. It is not surprising that the ASC faces a similar limitation when it obtains material from overseas securities regulators.

The MABR Act contains a complex and excessively bureaucratic mechanism for the processing of requests to the ASC by foreign regulators. In contrast to the position in the United States, the execution of a request in relation to securities regulatory matters entails not only the approval of the agency itself (that is, the ASC) but also the sanction of a third party (that is, the Commonwealth Attorney General or his delegate, namely, the Secretary or Deputy Secretary of his Department). This regime offends the basic principle of international cooperation, namely, the greater the number of hands involved in the execution of a request, the more likely is it that the request will not be responded to in a timely and effective manner.

Pursuant to the MABR Act, the ASC has concluded a Memorandum of Understanding with the following regulators: the Securities and Investment Board/HM Treasury of the United Kingdom, the Securities Exchange Commission and the Commodity Futures Trading Commission of the United States, the Securities and Futures Commission of Hong Kong, the Commission Operation de Bourse of France, the Ontario Securities Commission and the British Columbia Securities Commission of Canada.

CONCLUSION

Measures to deal with the extraterritorial aspects of corruption are being taken by individual countries and the international community. However, enactment of a US-style Foreign Corrupt Practices Act will not by itself reduce the level of corruption unless it is supported by political goodwill and a substantial increase in enforcement resources. In the first place, corruption must be tackled by the country which is the victim. International cooperation complements the efforts of national states. However, grand corruption, especially where a Head of State or senior government official is involved, raises difficult political and legal problems. Recent improvements in the range and intensity of international cooperation raise the hope that the insidious effects of international corruption will be contained.

GEORGE J. MOSCARINO AND MICHAEL R. SCHUMAKER

18. Beating the Shell Game: Bank Secrecy Laws and their Impact on Civil Recovery in International Fraud Actions

> Any German national who, deliberately or otherwise, activated by a base selfishness or any other vile motive, has amassed his wealth abroad or left capital outside the country, shall be punished by *death*.[1]

This decree by the Nazi government in 1933 is likely the single most important event leading to the advent of bank secrecy laws as we know them today. This criminal provision was enacted to halt the German Jews' movement of assets out of Germany and into Swiss banks – a movement that was occasioned by the government's attempt to seize the Jews' assets.[2] Swiss banks were chosen because of their geographic proximity, but more so because of Switzerland's then-unofficial policy of confidentiality over banking deposits and transactions.

One year after the law's enactment, three German Jews were executed.[3] These executions, as well as the pressuring of Swiss Bank employees for information by German Gestapo agents, prompted the Swiss government to codify its practice of maintaining the confidentiality of its customers' accounts.[4] This law provided for the assessment of both civil and criminal penalties against any violator.[5] Thus was born the first effective bank secrecy statute.

---

[1] Edouard Chambost, *Bank Accounts* 5 n. ‡ (1983) (emphasis added).

[2] Staff of Senate Comm. on Governmental Affairs, 98th Cong., 1st Sess., Crime and Secrecy: 'The Use of Offshore Banks and Companies' 7 (Comm. Print 1983) (hereinafter 'Staff Report'); *see also* Dennis Campbell, *Bank Secrecy* 664 (1992). In order to enforce the statute, the Nazi government required every German citizen to declare all assets held outside Germany.

[3] C. Todd Jones, 'Compulsion Over Comity: The United States' Assault on Foreign Bank Secrecy', 12 *J. Intl. L. Bus.* (Winter 1992) 454, 455.

[4] *Id.*; *see also* Ellen R. Levin, 'The Conflict Between United States Securities Laws on Insider Trading and Swiss Bank Secrecy Laws', 7 *J. Intl. L. Bus.* (Fall, 1985) 318.

[5] The Federal Law Relating to Banks & Savings Banks of 8 Nov. 1934, Art. 47(b) (penalties of up to Sf 50,000 or imprisonment of six months or both).

Barry A.K. Rider (ed.), Corruption: The Enemy Within, 303–318
© *Kluwer Law International. Printed in the Netherlands.*

The passage of this secrecy law proved financially profitable for Switzerland.[6] This success did not go unnoticed. Other European nations, such as Luxembourg and Liechtenstein, adopted similar bank secrecy laws not long after the Swiss. Based on their successes, a number of island countries located in the Caribbean and West Pacific seas adopted even more stringent bank secrecy laws with similar hopes of attracting foreign banking activity.

Without question these banking laws have worked in attracting substantial amounts of funds to these bank secrecy jurisdictions.[7] Unfortunately, the financial advantages that these laws offer their countries, offer even greater financial advantage to the sophisticated criminals that now use those jurisdictions to hide or obscure their illegal and ill-gotten gains.

The government officials in these bank secrecy jurisdictions have, for the most part, come to accept the fact that their laws have been manipulated by criminals in furtherance of their illegal deeds, and have taken cooperative steps with their international partners to terminate this abuse. For example, the United States has entered into over twenty mutual legal assistance treaties with foreign nations[8] to aid both parties to the treaties in the criminal prosecution of money laundering, as well as the underlying crime whose fruits are being laundered. In addition, numerous international directives, conventions and agreements have been entered into by a number of the world's nations, all of which are designed to assist one another in the prosecution of criminal offences and, in many cases, the use of the various bank secrecy laws to hide illicit funds.

These international agreements and treaties ignore, however, the civil side of the equation. Individuals and corporations that are victimized by the sophisticated white-collar criminals that are so prevalent today will certainly applaud any prosecutor that brings the individual or association that committed the crime to justice. But, if the individual or corporation has been victimized to the tune of several millions of dollars and the criminal's sentence is limited to prison time and a $500,000 fine, their applause may quickly subside.

For these individuals, the chief avenue of recovery is a civil action. To succeed in a civil action, you must be able to prove your case. The bank

---

[6] Although Switzerland, has less than .03 percent of the world's population, it is the world's third largest financial power. Staff Report, *supra* note 2, at 85.

[7] The Cayman Islands, for example, had 'one or two banks and virtually no offshore business' prior to their passage of a bank secrecy law. Staff Report, *supra* note 2, at 9. As of 1993, the Caymans had the 'sixth largest financial centre in the world, with 548 banks controlling over $400 billion in assets, and 23,500 corporations registered on the island.' Scott Sultzer, 'Money Laundering: The Scope of the Problem and Attempts to Combat It', 63 *Tenn. L. Rev.* 143, 198 (Fall 1995). All of this for a country with a population of approximately 26,000. *Id.*

[8] *See* Danforth Newcomb and John Landry, 'How Foreign Governments Gain Access to U.S. Information', 4 *Money Laundering Law Report* No. 3 at 1, 5 (Oct. 1993).

secrecy laws in these foreign jurisdictions, however, often prohibit civil plaintiffs from learning the facts that are necessary to meet this burden.

This article briefly discusses the tools that are available to a civil plaintiff in an American court who seeks discovery abroad, and the problems associated with these discovery devices. Given the unsuitable nature of these discovery mechanisms and the general hardship bank secrecy laws create for a civil plaintiff seeking recovery, this article next discusses the opportunity a parallel criminal prosecution of the civil defendant in the American courts presents a civil plaintiff. The article concludes by questioning the desirability of these bank secrecy laws considering the heavy costs associated with their existence.

CURRENT TOOLS OF INTERNATIONAL CIVIL DISCOVERY IN AMERICAN COURTS

There are primarily three tools available to a plaintiff seeking civil recovery in an international fraud case brought in an American court: (1) letters rogatory; (2) consent directives; and (3) subpoenas. A brief analysis of these tools illustrates that none constitute effective devices for a civil litigant seeking to pierce a foreign nation's bank secrecy law.

Letters Rogatory

A letter rogatory, in its simplest terms, is a written request from one court to a foreign court for assistance in discovery. As classically defined, letters rogatory are 'the medium ... whereby one country, speaking though one of its courts, requests another country, acting through its own courts and by methods of court procedure peculiar thereto and entirely within the latter's control, to assist the administration of justice in the former country ...'.[9] Letters rogatory can be used to facilitate a wide range of discovery that civil litigants usually avail themselves of in American courts, including written interrogatories, oral depositions and requests for production of documents.

The procedure for obtaining a letter rogatory for a civil litigant is substantial.[10] Letters rogatory are issued by a United States court upon a motion and usually after a hearing.[11] Typically, the letter rogatory will be channelled through the US State Department and the Ministry of Justice of the

---

[9] *The Signe*, 37 F. Supp. 819, 820 (E.D. La. 1941).

[10] Although substantial, there is no specific procedure for obtaining a letter rogatory. Different countries will require different procedures be followed. *See* generally Jones, *supra* note 3, at 471–472.

[11] The issuance of letters rogatory are governed by Fed. R. Civ. P. 28(b) and 28 U.S.C. § 1781.

foreign country.[12] The letter may, however, be sent directly from an American court to a foreign court. Once received, the foreign court will usually have a hearing of its own to decide if and how it will allow the discovery requested. If the foreign court decides that the discovery should be issued, it will use its local method of compulsory process to compel the discovery requested.[13]

Letters rogatory are the oldest form of obtaining civil discovery in a foreign jurisdiction,[14] and most likely the least effective. The expense and time associated with the letter rogatory process are its biggest drawbacks. The letter rogatory process often requires multiple hearings: at least one in the US and usually one in the foreign country. Involvement of the US State Department or a foreign Ministry of Justice can add substantial delays to the process. Of course, all of these hearings and administrative wranglings cost money. Usually, local counsel in the foreign jurisdiction must also be obtained adding to the expense of the process.[15]

These inefficiencies are particularly frustrating given the fact that following the process may not even lead to the discovery desired. Assuming a civil litigant can convince the US court to issue the letter, the foreign court is under no obligation to respond favourably to the request made in the letter. A foreign court can deny the discovery for any of a number of reasons, including that the country does not allow the discovery requested.[16] Moreover, even if the foreign court orders discovery, it may not be in the manner sought. For example, some foreign jurisdictions will require the judge or an appointed master be present at a deposition. The general antipathy that some jurisdictions hold for US litigation procedures may also jeopardize the potential success of any letter rogatory request.[17] One former US Attorney General succinctly expressed his frustration with the procedure: 'Letters rogatory involve unnecessary

---

[12]   7 Charles A. Wright *et al.*, *Federal Practice and Procedure* § 2083 (1994).

[13]   '[T]he party seeking discovery abroad must rely on the court conducting the examination to employ the sanctions available under foreign law.' 7 Charles A. Wright *et al.*, *Federal Practice and Procedure* § 2083 (1994).

[14]   Jones, *supra* note 3, at 471.

[15]   Some courts have even ordered the party requesting the discovery to pay the related costs of the opposing party. *See Leasco Data Processing Equip. Corp.* v. *Maxwell*, 63 F.R.D. 94 (S.D.N.Y. 1973) (plaintiff ordered to prepay defendant's costs, including attorney's fees, for attending deposition in London); *River Plate Corp.* v. *Forestal Land, Timber and Ry. Co.*, 185 F. Supp. 832, 838 (S.D.N. Y. 1960) (plaintiff/movant required to pay defendant's costs and fees for discovery).

[16]   *See*, e.g., *Taylor* v. *Costa Cruises, Inc.*, No. 90 Civ. 2630, 1992 US Dist. LEXIS 11435 (S.D.N.Y. 3 August 1992) (court refused to issue letter rogatory because Costa Rican and Honduran courts prohibit compelled discovery); *Moezie* v. *Moezie*, 192 A.2d 808, 810–11 (D.C. App. 1963) (law of Iran does not permit compelled testimony in civil matters). Foreign courts are also less likely to grant the requested relief if the case is non-criminal. *See* Jones, *supra* note 3, at 472.

[17]   *See* Jones, *supra* note 3, at 472.

formalities, unacceptable delays, unresponsive channels of communication, and ineffective procedures for obtaining evidence in a form for timely use'.[18]

Consent Directives

Unlike letters rogatory, consent directives are almost exclusively used by US courts to assist parties in obtaining discovery from bank secrecy jurisdictions. Most bank secrecy laws allow disclosure of an individual's bank records to a third party if the individual customer consents to the release. Courts responded by simply requiring the party whose records are sought, and who the court has jurisdiction over, to sign a document giving the foreign bank the customer's consent.

In signing the directive the individual does not admit that he has any signature authority over any account in the foreign jurisdiction. Rather, the directive usually commands the bank that 'if' a bank account exists and the bank 'thinks' the witness has control, the bank should produce the documents.[19]

Consent directives can be used in civil litigations, but have almost been exclusively used in criminal prosecutions before federal grand juries. In these cases, the grand jury will serve a subpoena on the defendant commanding him to sign a form consent directing the foreign bank to release the defendant's bank records. If the defendant refuses, the trial court may issue an order holding the defendant in civil contempt.[20]

The chief problem with consent directives is that there is no guarantee that the process will work. Some defendants have simply refused to sign.[21] If the defendant truly has something to hide in the account, he may believe he is better off being found in contempt than being found guilty of fraud or money laundering.[22]

Some foreign courts have held that a consent directive is not effective consent under the foreign jurisdiction's bank secrecy laws and accordingly denied discovery.[23] Consent directives can also be problematic if the court

---

[18] *In re Grand Jury*, 550 F. Supp. 24, 29 (W.D. Mich. 1982) (setting forth statement of Benjamin Civiletti).

[19] *See, e.g., In re N.D.N.Y. Grand Jury Subpoena*, 811 F.2d 114, 118 (2d Cir. 1987) (holding that form must explicitly state that it is signed under protest); *United States* v. *Ghidoni*, 732 F.2d 814, 815–16 n. 1 (11th Cir.), *cert. denied*, 469 U.S. 932 (1984).

[20] The constitutionality of this procedure was upheld by the US Supreme Court in *Doe* v. *United States*, 487 U.S. 201 (1988).

[21] *See, e.g., In re Doe*, 860 F. 2d 40 (2d Cir. 1988).

[22] An individual may also prefer to be found in contempt than disclose information that implicates other associates in an illegal scheme.

[23] *See Doe* v. *United States*, 487 U.S. 201, 218 (1988) (citing *In re ABC Ltd.*, 1984 C.I.L.R. 130 (1984)); *The Bank of Crete* v. *Koskotas*, No. 88 Civ. 8412, 1989 U.S. Dist. LEXIS 4289 (S.D.N.Y. 19 April 1989) (banks may not honour consent directive that discloses that the form was signed under protest).

does not have jurisdiction over the individual customer. This may be a considerable problem in civil litigation where discovery may not be aimed at a specific individual, but rather a group of individuals or an organization.

Subpoenas

The most popular way of obtaining discovery from a banking secrecy jurisdiction in the American courts is through a subpoena. As the term suggests, a subpoena is a court-sanctioned order compelling an individual or organization to comply with the terms of a request or be penalized, either through civil or criminal contempt sanctions. Most cases that address this procedure involve grand jury subpoenas, but subpoenas have also been utilized in civil proceedings.[24]

Prior to 1991, subpoenas were issued by the court's clerk upon presentment by counsel. Following the amendments to the Federal Rules of Civil Procedure in 1991, attorneys may issue subpoenas as officers of the court without receiving the clerk's stamp of approval provided the attorney is authorized to practice in the issuing court.[25] Given the unorthodox nature of a subpoena for records held by a bank in a bank secrecy jurisdiction, counsel should raise the matter with the court prior to the subpoena's issuance.

Although this is the most popular procedure for obtaining discovery against a bank located in a bank secrecy jurisdiction, it is often times no more successful than letters rogatory or consent directives. There is a split among the courts regarding whether a subpoena commanding production of bank records from a foreign bank is enforceable if the foreign nation's banking secrecy law prohibits such production.[26] The decision is usually based on the application of a balancing test which purports to take into consideration the importance of the foreign jurisdiction's interests in protecting the information and the United States' interest in obtaining such

---

[24] *See*, e.g., *In re Sealed Case*, 825 F.2d 494 (D.C. Cir.), *cert. denied*, 484 U.S. 963 (1987) (grand jury subpoena); *In re Grand Jury Proceedings, Bank of Nova Scotia*, 740 F.2d 817 (11th Cir. 1984), *cert. denied*, 469 U.S. 1106 (1985) (same); *United States* v. *First Nat'l City Bank*, 396 F.2d 897 (2d Cir. 1968) (same). *Cf. Richmark Corp.* v. *Timber Falling Consultants*, 959 F.2d 1468 (9th Cir.), *cert. dismissed*, 506 U.S. 948 (1992) (civil subpoena); *Reinsurance Company of America* v. *Administratia Asigurarilor*, 902 F.2d 1275 (7th Cir. 1990).

[25] *See* Fed. R. Civ. P. 45(a)(3).

[26] *See In re Grand Jury Proceedings, Bank of Nova Scotia*, 740 F.2d 817 (11th Cir. 1984) (court enforced grand jury subpoena against a Cayman Islands bank), *cert. denied*, 469 U.S. 1106 (1985); *United States* v. *Davis*, 767 F.2d 1025 (2d Cir. 1985); *In re Grand Jury Proceedings*, 691 F.2d 1384 (11th Cir. 1982). *But cf. In re Sealed Case*, 825 F.2d 494 (D.C. Cir.), *cert. denied*, 484 U.S. 963 (1987) (subpoena not enforced against unidentified foreign bank); *United States* v. *First National Bank of Chicago*, 699 F.2d 341 (7th Cir. 1983) (court refused to enforce grand jury subpoena against a Greek bank).

information.[27] Regardless, the procedure often involves substantial briefing at both the trial and appellate court levels. Even more importantly, there is no guarantee that the subpoena will be enforced following this process.

Another problem with the subpoena procedure is that it presupposes that the issuing court has jurisdiction over the subpoenaed party. Normally, the party issuing the subpoena serves the US branch of a foreign bank. The subpoena orders the US branch to produce all relevant records held at the branch of the bank located in the bank secrecy jurisdiction. In this situation, the court has jurisdiction over the bank via its US branch. If, however, there is no US branch of the foreign bank, it would appear that the US court would have no jurisdiction to enforce a subpoena issued upon it in the foreign locale. Consequently, the subpoena procedure is of no use to a litigant if the foreign bank has no branches located in the United States.

THE OPPORTUNITY A PARALLEL CRIMINAL PROSECUTION OFFERS A CIVIL PLAINTIFF

As the above discussion illustrates, discovery from a bank located in a bank secrecy jurisdiction can be accomplished, but not without substantial time and expense. In addition, there is no guarantee that the discovery sought will ever be obtained. In short, there presently is no effective and efficient means for discovering documents from a bank located in a bank secrecy jurisdiction.

Of course, the unavailability of practical discovery is only important to the extent it prevents the victim of an international fraud from proving a legitimate civil claim and receiving rightful compensation. In the American courts, the existence of a parallel criminal prosecution offers a civil plaintiff two significant opportunities to obtain the civil recovery sought and thus avoid the need to obtain discovery from a bank secrecy jurisdiction.

---

[27] The balancing test applied by the courts has historically been taken from the Restatement on Foreign Relations Law. Many cases were decided under section 40 of the Restatement Second. The test most likely to be applied by a court currently faced with this decision is section 442 of the Restatement Third. That provision suggests that the court consider the importance of the records requested to the litigation; the degree of specificity of the request; whether the information originated in the United States; the availability of alternative means of securing the information; and the extent to which noncompliance would 'undermine important interests of the United States ... [or] of the state where the information is located'. Restatement (Third) Foreign Relations Law § 442 (1987).

Restitution Under the Victim and Witness Protection Act

In 1982, the United States Congress passed the Victim and Witness Protection Act.[28] This law generally obligates the federal judge who is sentencing the criminal defendant to consider the effect and impact of the defendant's crime on the victim.[29] More important for our current purposes, the Act recommends that the judge routinely impose restitution as part of any sentence.[30] Restitution is proper for all federal criminal offences (as listed in Title 18 of the US Code), including mail fraud, wire fraud and RICO.[31] Thus, if an individual or entity is the victim of an international fraud, and the federal authorities convict the defendant of the offence, they may be entitled to restitution from the defendant.[32]

Restitution may not be ordered, however, if the court 'determines that the complication and prolongation of the sentencing process resulting from the fashioning of an order of restitution ... outweighs the need to provide restitution to any victims...'. 18 U.S.C. § 3663 (d). Consequently, an order of restitution is by no means a sure thing.

The inclusion of this qualification is significant. To illustrate, suppose a company is defrauded out of a substantial sum of money through a complicated and sophisticated scheme and the government and defendant reach a plea agreement on that offence. As a result, there may not exist a significant exposition of the evidence, either through in-court testimony or the indictment, demonstrating the individual's status as a victim of the complex fraud. In this circumstance, the court may decide that a restitution order for the company would unduly complicate or prolong the sentencing process and deny restitution.[33]

---

[28] Pub. L. No. 97–291, 96 Stat. 1248 (originally codified at 18 U.S.C. §§ 1512–1515, 3146(a), 3579, 3580 (1982)).

[29] *See* Lawrence P. Fletcher, Note, 'Restitution in the Criminal Process: Procedures for Fixing the Offender's Liability', 93 *Yale L. J.* 505, 509 & n.18 (1984).

[30] S. Rep. No. 532, 97th Cong., 2d Sess. 30 (1982), reprinted in 1982 U.S.C.C.A.N. 2515, 2536.

[31] Restitution may also be ordered for violations of sections 46312, 46502 and 46504 of Title 49. 18 U.S.C. § 3663(a)(1) (1994).

[32] 18 U.S.C. §§ 3663, 3664 (1994). 'The restitution provisions are intended to aid crime victims by requiring convicted defendants to compensate their victims to the greatest extent possible, thus achieving the "ultimate justice".' Lorraine Slavin and David J. Sorin, 'Congress Opens A Pandora's Box – The Restitution Provisions of the Victim and Witness Protection Act', 52 *Fordham L. Rev.* (Mar. 1984) 507, 508 (citing 128 Cong. Rep. H8207 & H8209 (daily ed. 30 Sept. 1982) (remarks of Rep. Fish and Rep. McCollum)).

[33] In determining the amount of restitution the court must consider the loss sustained by the victim, the defendant's financial resources, and the financial needs and earning ability of the defendant. 18 U.S.C. § 3664(a) (1994). The victim bears the burden of proving the amount of loss; the defendant bears the burden of proving lack of financial resources. *Id.* § 3664 (d). Both are judged by a preponderance of the evidence standard. *Id.* If restitution is ordered, payment becomes a condition for release or parole. 18 U.S.C. § 3663(g).

For this reason, if an injured company or individual believes that they are an appropriate candidate for restitution under the statute, they should contact the government prosecutors and present the merits of their claim as soon as possible. In most instances, however, the criminal offence will be proven at trial and the individual victim's role in the fraud or other offence will be patently obvious. A restitution order, therefore, should not unduly complicate or prolong the sentencing procedure.

Communication with the government's prosecutors and other criminal investigatory agencies is also a good idea if the injured company or individual believes they might ultimately have to file a civil case in the US courts to obtain adequate compensation for their damage. Government prosecutors and criminal investigatory agencies have much better opportunities for piercing foreign jurisdiction's bank secrecy laws. The mutual legal assistance treaties that the United States has negotiated with numerous countries generally do not allow the foreign nation to use the bank secrecy law as a shield to a request for documents relating to a criminal investigation.

Foreign courts are also much more likely to grant the relief requested in letters rogatory or allow the enforcement of a subpoena issued by an American court if the discovery requested relates to a criminal prosecution or investigation. For this reason, the government may be able to obtain documents that a civil plaintiff would otherwise be unable to obtain. A good working relationship with these officials increases the chance that the civil plaintiff will be able to discover information and documents obtained by the government.

The Use of Adverse Inferences in a Civil Proceeding

The United States Constitution provides that '[n]o person ... shall be compelled in any criminal case to be a witness against himself'. US Const. amend. V. This right, often called the privilege against self-incrimination, is a cornerstone of the American criminal legal system. Due to the importance of this right, a judge or jury cannot take an adverse inference from a defendant's decision to invoke this privilege in a criminal proceeding.[34]

Such a limitation does not exist, however, for an individual who invokes this privilege in a civil proceeding. In this situation, the judge or jury is entitled to take an adverse inference from the individual's invocation of the privilege.[35] This situation most often arises when the defendant in the civil proceeding is also being prosecuted in a parallel criminal proceeding.

The ability to draw adverse inferences is a powerful weapon in the hands of a skilled civil plaintiff. This is particularly true given some recent

---

[34] *Griffin* v. *California*, 380 U.S. 609 (1965).
[35] *Baxter* v. *Palmigiano*, 425 U.S. 308 (1976).

American court decisions that hold that a civil plaintiff can rely, in part, on the adverse inferences drawn from a defendant's failure to answer questions during discovery and in some instances obtain final judgment against the non-responding civil defendant.[36] This development may reduce the plaintiff's burden of producing evidence to support his case and may well eliminate the necessity of prolonged and difficult litigation in civil discovery while attempting to deal with foreign bank secrecy laws.

BANK SECRECY LAWS: ARE THEY WORTH THE COST?

Restitution and the use of adverse inferences may be of some help to a civil plaintiff who seeks to obtain recovery in American courts. But they by no means are cure-alls to the problem bank secrecy laws create for civil plaintiffs. A court may find restitution improper in a particular case or a plaintiff may need more evidence to support judgment even with the adverse inferences that can be drawn. In both situations, the victim is back where he started: trying to get around the bank secrecy laws in order to prove his case.

In the end, you may be left wondering why these bank secrecy laws exist and what purposes they serve given the high societal costs that are associated with their existence. The discussion below attempts to answer this question.

The Societal Costs Associated with Bank Secrecy Laws

Whatever the justification for the establishment and continued existence of bank secrecy laws, few can deny that they have become the primary weapon of the world's money launderers. Money launderers use these bank secrecy havens to transfer funds in and out of banks in order to clean and hide dirty money.[37] Because the launderers' accounts remain secret, no one can discover who owns the account, how much is deposited or where the funds originally came from.[38] As it is often said, 'dirty money is like water: it follows the path of least resistance'.[39]

---

[36] *See United States* v. *4003–4005 5th Ave.*, 55 F.3d 78 (2d Cir. 1995). The adverse inferences may not, however, form the sole basis for judgment. Plaintiff must be able to present some other evidence in support of their allegations. *LaSalle Bank Lake View* v. *Seguban*, 54 F.3d 387 (7th Cir. 1995); *Koester* v. *American Republic Invs. Inc.*, 11 F.3d 818 (8th Cir. 1993).

[37] Sultzer, *supra* note 7, at 198.

[38] Bank secrecy laws usually impose criminal and civil penalties on any party who discloses confidential banking information.

[39] Charles H. Morley, 'The Impact of Money Laundering on State Security', at 4 (Dec. 1995) (as printed in *Money Laundering, Asset Forfeiture & International Financial Crimes* (1994)).

Money laundering is the 'life-blood' of crime 'because, without cleansing the profits of crime, the criminal enterprise cannot flourish'.[40] Money laundering 'sustains every criminal activity engaged in for profit, which is to say all crimes but crimes of passion or vengeance'.[41]

Estimates of the amount of money that is laundered in a year are staggering. The Financial Action Task Force for money laundering created by the G-7[42] estimated that $300 billion is laundered by the nation's drug dealers.[43] The US Department of State estimates the amount at $500 billion.[44] And this is just the amount the illegal drug industry launders. It does not include individuals or organizations that run sophisticated fraud and racketeering schemes who also must launder their illicit funds. Money laundering is quite simply 'the crime of the 1990s'.[45]

Although certain bank secrecy jurisdictions have received substantial notoriety for the money laundering that occurs within their borders,[46] it has been estimated that money launderers use over 125 countries to launder their funds.[47] Money laundering now takes place in second and third tier countries that were of little concern only a few years ago.[48] As one US government official stated, 'if you physically get the money out of the United States ... you can do almost anything with it'.[49]

---

[40] Sultzer, *supra* note 7 at 143.

[41] *Id.* (citing 'Federal Government's Response to Money Laundering: Hearings Before the Committee on Banking, Finance & Urban Affairs', 103d Cong., 1st Sess. 200–01 (1993)).

[42] The 'G-7' is an organization that is made up of representatives from the seven economically strongest nations.

[43] Fletcher N. Baldwin, Jr. and Robert J. Munro, 'Overview of International and American Responses', at 4 (March 1994) (as published in *Money Laundering, Asset Forfeiture and International Financial Crimes* (1994)) (hereinafter Money Laundering Overview).

[44] *Id.*

[45] Michael Zeldin, 'Money Laundering 101: Everything You Wanted to Know About Money Laundering But Were Afraid to Ask' at C-6 (as published in *White Collar Crime* (1994)).

[46] Switzerland, Luxembourg, Panama, the Grand Cayman Islands, Hong Kong, the Netherlands Antilles and the Bahamas are the most often mentioned. Of course, the biggest money laundering country in the world is the United States. *See* Fletcher N. Baldwin, Jr., 'The United States and Int'l Cooperation: Are There Constitutional Flaws?' at 3 (Sept. 1995) (as printed in *Money Laundering, Asset Forfeiture & International Financial Crimes* (1994)). Its notoriety is due, however, to the large drug trade within its borders, not to any bank secrecy law.

[47] US Department of State, *Int'l Narcotics Control Strategy Report* 20 (Mar. 1995). Another commentator estimated it at sixty countries. Money Laundering Overview, *supra* note 43, at 4.

[48] Sultzer, *supra* note 7, at 198 n. 342.

[49] Robert E. Taylor, 'Ex-Smuggler Tells of Huge Drug Profits Laundered, Placed at Major U.S. Banks', *Wall St. J.*, 12 February 1988 at A-4 (statement of Robert Serino, general counsel for the Comptroller of the Currency).

While some countries actively combat money laundering and see it as a societal blight, other actively solicit the money launderers' funds and see them as a solid source of revenue.[50] For example, the Seychelle Islands reportedly enacted legislation in late 1995 that gives those who make a $10 million investment in the islands immunity from prosecution.[51]

Panama is another good example. In Panama, a country otherwise dependent on the operation of the canal and expenditures of the US military, the revenue from banking is of vital importance. As a result:

> ... Panamanians do not rush quickly to moral indignation over accusations that their bank secrecy is being used to launder money. 'In a church collection, no one checks to see whether money has been deposited by a nun or a prostitute: why should we check with our depositors?' commented one prominent banker when challenged over the abuse of bank secrecy.[52]

The societal cost of money laundering and hence bank secrecy laws is substantial. Corruption in the government is the greatest evil.[53] With billions of dollars in illegal money on the line, criminals pursue all avenues to protect their take, including hidden contributions, favours, and outright bribes. The prevalence of the bribes grows to the point that corruption becomes pervasive at all levels of the government and business community.

Once gained, political corruption is extremely difficult to dislodge.[54] The corrupted officials will work to enact laws that favour their activities and eliminate laws that do not.[55] Force and violence will slowly be introduced into the society to maintain the status quo. Eventually a society develops where the 'haves' are those who engage in crime; the 'have nots' are those who make an honest living.

The gap that develops between these two groups is dramatic due to the poverty level that is often present in these countries. It is not long before the youth of the country desire the wealth, power and easy lifestyle of the corrupt criminals. It is perhaps at this point that total corruption has invaded the society.[56]

Money laundering also exacts a price on a country's banking system.[57] At best, legitimate businesses have been known to avoid or pull deposits out

---

[50] Sultzer, *supra* note 7, at 198.

[51] Ellen Leander, 'How Money Launderers Are Fighting Back', *Global Finance* at 54 (Feb. 1996).

[52] Robert Graham, 'Panama Pressed On Bank Secrecy', *The Financial Times* at 26 (25 June 1986).

[53] *See* generally Sultzer, *supra* note 7, at 147.

[54] Morley, *supra* note 39, at 6.

[55] *Id*. at 7.

[56] Panama and Colombia are the most often cited examples of this phenomenon.

[57] *See* generally Staff Report, *supra* note 2, at 5–7.

of countries that they suspect are involved in substantial money laundering.[58] At worst, money laundering has lead to the collapse of significant banking institutions. For example, money laundering has been cited as a contributing cause to the collapse of Nugan Hand Bank in Sydney, Australia,[59] Banco Ambrosiano of Milan, Italy,[60] and most recently Bank of Credit and Commerce International ('BCCI') of London, England.[61]

Last, but certainly not least, is the personal toll that money laundering and bank secrecy laws impart, from the investor who loses all of his savings in the bank failure to the citizen who loses her savings to a sophisticated fraud scheme. These individuals may have been planning to take their money to the Caribbean islands, but this was not the way they planned to do it. Thanks in part to the bank secrecy laws, those funds likely will never be seen again.

The Justifications for Bank Secrecy Jurisdictions and the Alleged Benefits that Flow from Them

Given these costs, what justifies the continued existence of bank secrecy laws? Numerous justifications have been given, some proper, some questionable, others ridiculous.

The most often-cited justification for bank secrecy laws is the belief that financial secrecy is somehow part of an individual's fundamental right of privacy.[62] This assertion is inaccurate.

Financial privacy is a privilege that may be extended by a bank or foreign nation's law; it is not a right. If someone desires true privacy in their financial affairs, they have the right to stick their money in their mattress or bury their money on the land they rightfully own. If, however, they find

---

[58] Morley, *supra* note 39, at 5 (noting the substantial transfer of deposits out of Panamanian banks following the United States' announcement that it suspected these banks were laundering drug proceeds).

[59] The Nugan Bank went into liquidation in 1980 with $50 million unaccounted for – $20 million of this amount missing from its branch in the Cayman Islands. Staff Report, *supra* note 2, at 5. Nugan Bank 'was deeply involved in moving funds around the world for international heroin dealers and may have been involved in international arms trafficking'. *Id.*

[60] Banco Ambrosiano was crippled by $1.4 billion of loans to several mysterious Panamanian shell companies. Banco Ambrosiano was the largest private banking group in Italy and had operations in 15 countries. *Id.* at 5–6.

[61] *See* Fletcher N. Baldwin, Jr. & Robert J. Munro, 'The United States and Money Laundering', at 3 (June 1996) (as printed in *Money Laundering, Asset Forfeiture & International Financial Crimes* (1994)).

[62] *See* Richard J. Gagnon, Jr., 'International Banking Secrecy: Developments in Europe Prompt New Approaches', 23 *Vand. J. Transnat'l L.* (1990) 653, 657 & n. 15; Silvia B. Pinera Vazquez, 'Extraterritorial Jurisdiction and International Banking: A Conflict of Interests', 43 *U. Miami L. Rev.* (1988) 449, 467.

such manner of storage unsafe, and desire to turn that money over to a financial institution in hopes of receiving greater protection, they have relinquished – to whatever extent it previously existed – their 'right' to financial privacy. Banking is a service governed by principles of contract, not inalienable rights.[63]

Nor does the mere passage of a bank secrecy law change this fact. As one commentator explained, 'just because criminal or civil liability has been attached to the disclosure of certain information does not render that information "private" in the sense of pertaining to an individual's sphere of privacy'.[64]

Some commentators have attempted to justify bank secrecy laws by analogy to the common law privileges of lawyer-client or doctor-patient.[65] This analogy is also flawed.

Attorney-client and doctor-patient privileges exist because they further important societal interests. Individuals would not speak freely to counsel if they feared reprisal from the possible disclosure of their statements. Similarly, patients would not disclose known ailments or diseases for fear of public censure if doctors could be forced to disclose such communications. In both situations, society has determined that 'the value of professional secrecy generally outweighs the social utility of disclosure'.[66] Bank secrecy laws have no comparable societal justification.

Other commentators have argued that bank secrecy laws are justified because they offer a 'reasonable response to the unfairness of particular types of tax systems'.[67] In other words, they argue that bank secrecy laws are proper because they offer flexibility to those individuals who seek to avoid taxation in their home country.

Tax evasion is not a justification for bank secrecy laws, but rather a consequence of their existence. Whatever a given country's stance may be on taxation, many countries have determined that taxation of its citizens serves a socially beneficial function. To argue that bank secrecy laws are justified because they assist tax evasion, is equivalent to arguing that one country's right to have bank secrecy laws supersedes another country's right

---

[63] This principle is implicit in *Tournier* v. *National Provincial and Union Bank of England*, the British judicial decision cited by many as the origin for English-derived bank secrecy laws. 1 K.B. 461 (Eng. C.A. 1924). *See Jones, supra* note 3 at 464–65. In that decision, the court held that there is an implied contract between a bank and its customer to keep the customer's account secret.

[64] Gagnon, *supra* note 62, at 658 (citing S. Stromholm, *Right of Privacy and Rights of the Personality* 67 (1967)).

[65] *See* Gagnon, *supra* note 62, at 657 & n. 13.

[66] *Id*. at 658 n. 20 (citing S. Bok, *Secrets* 122 (1985)).

[67] *See* Gagnon, *supra* note 62, at 657; Jeffrey I. Horowitz, Comment, 'Piercing Offshore Bank Secrecy Laws Used to Launder Illegal Narcotics Profits: The Cayman Islands Example', 20 *Tex. Intl. L. J.* (1985) 133, 134 n. 5.

to taxation. Such an argument flies in the face of international comity and country sovereignty.

Probably the most legitimate of all justifications posed to date is that bank secrecy laws offer a safe haven for those whose funds may be seized pursuant to political, religious or racial persecution.[68] We have proven, as World War II and the recent Bosnian war graphically illustrate, that we cannot always trust our neighbours or our government. For this reason, the ability to move funds out of one's resident country to a bank secrecy jurisdiction is a useful alternative and of some societal benefit.[69]

The most realistic and practical justification for bank secrecy laws is money. Bank secrecy laws are enacted by most countries because they see it as a way to attract foreign funds and to make money off the management of these funds. All wish to experience the surge of financial activity and corresponding increase in government funds that the Bahamas and Cayman Islands experienced.[70] For many countries, the money made off of the banking community is the difference between a national deficit and breaking even.[71]

The Times Have Changed

Do the costs associated with strict bank secrecy laws outweigh the benefits? International comity demands that each country be allowed to make its own decision. In making this decision, however, each country must realize that the playing field has changed in recent years.

Bank secrecy laws facilitate large-scale money laundering and in turn exact a substantial toll on global society. If we ever truly wish to combat this pariah, bank secrecy laws must be relaxed to allow for both criminal and civil discovery. Simply put, what justified the creation of a strict bank secrecy law a couple decades ago, may no longer justify it today.

---

[68] *See* Fletcher N. Baldwin, Jr., 'The United States and International Cooperation: Are There Constitutional Flaws?', at 12 (Sept. 1995) (as published in *Money Laundering, Asset Forfeiture and International Financial Crimes* (1994)); Horowitz, *supra* note 67, at 134 n. 5.

[69] Even this noble justification is not without its problems. What one country views as proper regulation of its citizens, may be viewed as persecution by other countries. Consequently, one country's decision to regulate may be frustrated by another country's bank secrecy laws.

[70] Some commentators have questioned the extent to which bank secrecy laws actually benefit a country financially. They point out that the money that moves 'offshore' from banking centres in the US or Great Britain often times never leaves the major banking centres. Moreover, the brass plate banks and shell corporations in these locales offer little employment opportunity. One lawyer can operate 20 'banks' or shell corporations. Thus, the only revenue to be gained is from bank licensing. Staff Report, *supra* note 2, at 45.

[71] Richard H. Blum, *Offshore Haven Banks, Trusts and Companies* (1984) 48–50.

The current situation in Switzerland illustrates the changing times. The flight of Jewish capital out of Germany in response to Nazi tyranny was dramatic. Many estimate that millions of dollars – possibly even billions – were deposited by Jews who later died in the Holocaust.[72] Family members who survived the war ultimately sought to collect their loved ones' assets. Switzerland's bank secrecy law, however, prohibited them from discovering what funds were deposited and the ultimate retrieval of those funds. In figurative terms, the shield that once protected the Jews' assets from the Nazis, had now become a sword in the side of their descendants.

Although not swift to react, Switzerland has now recognized that times and circumstances have changed. On 2 May 1996, Switzerland announced that it had agreed to establish a six-member commission to assist the Holocaust victims in claims to lost relatives' bank accounts.[73] Switzerland promised 'unfettered access to all relevant files'.[74]

The war on international fraud and the money laundering associated with it, is a most difficult battle. Money laundering profit centres are allowed to exist by the laws of certain nations. Unless these laws are eliminated or greatly reduced, the ability of the corrupt to hide and disguise funds will continue to escalate. The world cannot afford to continue to fight corruption and money launderers with a pop gun rather than with real and sophisticated weapons and true international cooperation and discovery.

---

[72] 'Swiss Banks OK Search For Holocaust Victims' Assets', *L.A. Times*, 3 May 1996, at A13.

[73] *See id.*; 'Swiss OK Much Expanded Holocaust Funds Search', *Chicago Trib.*, 13 May 1996, at N8.

[74] Ian Katz, 'Swiss Banks Give Jews Access to Secret Records', *The Guardian*, 3 May 1996, at 12.

MIKE BISHOP

19. Hong Kong Beyond 1997: The Importance of International Cooperation in the Fight Against Corruption

INTRODUCTION

The aims of this paper are threefold; firstly, to present a brief description of the history and work of the Hong Kong Independent Commission Against Corruption (ICAC); second, to emphasize the importance of international liaison and cooperation as a strategy to transcend jurisdictional barriers in the fight against corruption and corruption-related crime; and third, to reconfirm the ICAC's continued role in and commitment to that strategy beyond 1997.

1997 – BACK TO THE FUTURE

On 1 July 1997, Hong Kong will revert to Chinese sovereignty to become a Special Administrative Region (SAR) of the People's Republic of China (PRC). The rest of the world waits and watches and speculates about the implications of the transition. Will Hong Kong continue to maintain its status as one of the world's most thriving and vibrant economies? To what extent will cultural and political metamorphosis affect the SAR's relationship with its international trading partners and foreign governments?

What about the future security of Hong Kong? Is there any reason to suppose that, beyond 1997, the law enforcement agencies entrusted with the task of maintaining law and order may not be able to provide the same high standard of professionalism and effectiveness the people of Hong Kong have rightly come to regard as their entitlement? Or that the Hong Kong judicial system will be any the less impartial or efficient than it is today? And what of that most insidious and destructive of social evils, corruption? Will a frantic scramble to exploit the commercial opportunities generated by Hong Kong's reunification with the PRC spawn a black economy of such dimensions that the forces of law and order will be unable to cope?

These questions – particularly on the topic of corruption – reflect anxieties harboured by some of the less optimistic Hong Kong watchers around the world, and are among the most frequently asked of those of us

Barry A.K. Rider (ed.), Corruption: The Enemy Within, 319–326
© *Kluwer Law International. Printed in the Netherlands.*

who live and work in the territory. As the agency with sole responsibility
for the fight against corruption in Hong Kong, the ICAC does not share
those anxieties. This is not to say that we are not concerned about corruption in Hong Kong – merely that we do not doubt our ability to continue to
deal effectively with the problem up to and beyond the transition of
sovereignty.

THE ICAC – A BRIEF HISTORY

The ICAC was formed in 1974, at a time when corruption in Hong Kong
was endemic. The catalyst that led to this historic event was a public outcry
in response to the fact that, in the previous year, a Chief Superintendent of
Police had succeeded in fleeing Hong Kong while under investigation by the
(then) Anti-Corruption Office of the Royal Hong Kong Police. The consequent Commission of Inquiry, conducted by Sir Alastair Blair-Kerr,
recommended that a new, independent organization be established and
charged with responsibility for tackling corruption in Hong Kong. But the
role of this new organization – the ICAC – was not to be solely one of law
enforcement. Adopting a unique strategy that targeted not only the criminal
manifestation of corruption, but also its causes, the newly-created ICAC
comprised three separate departments within the one organization: Operations, Corruption Prevention and Community Relations. This structured
approach to the problem, in which investigation, prevention and public
education were recognized as equally essential factors, came to be known
as the 'Three-Pronged Attack on Corruption'.

   In recognition of the fact that corruption is more often than not inextricably entwined with other forms of criminal activity, the ICAC was empowered
by ordinance to investigate not only offences of 'pure' corruption, but also
other criminal offences facilitated by, or arising out of, suspected corrupt
conduct, both in the public and private sectors. As a result, ICAC investigations over the years have inevitably embraced a broad spectrum of criminal
activity in which corruption was known or suspected to be a factor, including such diverse fields as drug trafficking, illegal immigration, smuggling,
vice, counterfeiting of currency and credit cards, textile export quota fraud,
banking and other commercial fraud.

   The ICAC model proved so successful in combatting corruption in Hong
Kong that it has been emulated by a growing number of anti-corruption
agencies elsewhere in the world. But although we may have blazed something of a trail in our formative years – a fact of which we are proud – we
remain ever conscious that, if we are to continue to live up to our early
success, we need to keep abreast of what is happening in other jurisdictions;
to exchange experiences, information and ideas with those countries and
organizations that share our goal – the eradication of corruption wherever
it surfaces. Moreover, we are convinced that international cooperation, not

only in the field of criminal investigation and intelligence, but also in such areas as organizational training and development, is the key to optimizing the scope for success in the global battle against corruption.

THE IMPORTANCE OF INTERNATIONAL COOPERATION IN THE FIGHT AGAINST CORRUPTION

From its earliest days, the ICAC has been anxious to develop and maintain mutual cooperation with other agencies, both locally and internationally, in the fight against corruption and related crime. In the investigation field we are fortunate enough to have established effective professional relationships with numerous overseas law enforcement agencies over the years. Some of these maintain a presence within their respective consulates in Hong Kong, thereby facilitating close and routine liaison with the ICAC. They include, for example, the Federal Bureau of Investigation, the Drug Enforcement Administration, the Royal Canadian Mounted Police and the Australian Federal Police.

Within Asia itself, we have long enjoyed valuable and productive working relationships with a number of agencies: the Corrupt Practices Investigation Bureau of Singapore, the Malaysian Anti-Corruption Agency, and, in Macau, both the Macau Judiciary Police and the High Commission Against Corruption are among those with which we deal on a regular basis.

Naturally, given the developing relationship between Hong Kong and the PRC, mutual cooperation between the ICAC and the Chinese authorities has long been recognized as essential if the problem of cross-border corruption is to be effectively addressed. By the cross-border corruption, we mean corruption employed to facilitate the unlawful trafficking of persons or goods across the border between Hong Kong and China. This includes corruption in either China or Hong Kong which links participants in such trafficking to current or future corrupt deals. The smuggling of proscribed, controlled or stolen goods into the PRC, and the unlawful trafficking of people and goods out of the PRC form the general pattern. Commodities illegally imported into the PRC include stolen luxury vehicles and cigarettes, while prostitutes, illegal immigrants, valuable antiques and narcotics are the main subjects of illegal trafficking into Hong Kong.

Cooperation between the ICAC and our appropriate counterparts in the PRC – the Supreme and Provincial People's Procuratorates – has increased steadily since 1987, when liaison was first established with the Guangdong (Canton) Provincial People's Procuratorate (GDPP) in Hong Kong's adjacent Chinese province. Since that time, the working relationship between the two organizations has steadily progressed to achieve some notable successes in corruption investigation. By the beginning of this year, the GDPP had already assisted in securing evidence in the Chinese mainland in connection with over 70 ICAC investigations, while the ICAC has reciprocated in a similar number of cases involving Hong Kong in GDPP investigations. Inter-agency training and education have also become features in the developing relationship between the two organizations. With the assistance of the GDPP, we run training programmes and cross-border educational visits to familiarize officers of both agencies with the laws, procedures and judicial systems of each other's jurisdictions. It is worth mentioning here, that the Hong Kong and PRC systems are very different in these respects – a fact which unfortunately, but unavoidably, limits to some degree the extent to which each jurisdiction can assist the other. From a purely criminal investigation point of view, for example, it would be helpful if mobile surveillance operations were able to routinely pass from one jurisdiction to the other, but as yet this is not possible.

There are occasions when the ICAC requires assistance on matters which fall outside the purview of the GDPP. In such instances, we call upon the services of the International Criminal Police Organization (Interpol), which deals directly with Beijing on our behalf.

THE SCOPE FOR INTERNATIONAL COOPERATION – CONSTRAINTS AND OPPORTUNITIES

Divergent and incompatible national legislation, bureaucracy and indifference are among the constraints that sometimes threaten to frustrate trans-jurisdictional criminal investigation, but a will on the part of those dedicated to the battle against the common enemies of crime and corruption can do much to minimize the impact of such constraints. Necessarily, legislation exists in most countries to govern the circumstances and extent to which law enforcement and, indeed, the judiciary itself, can cooperate with requests for assistance from foreign jurisdictions. And it would be quite wrong to suggest that attempting to circumvent such legislation – or other, procedural, requirements – is either a legitimate or justifiable means by which to pursue the desired end.

Commissions Rogatoire, Letters of Request and formal extradition treaties are among the internationally recognized mechanisms by which cross-jurisdictional investigative goals can be achieved. Naturally, such mechanisms are designed to meet a variety of demands in terms of, for example, the laws of the countries in question, natural justice and political implications, and it is right that this should be so. But procedures can vary considerably between jurisdictions, and sometimes throw bureaucratic obstacles in the path of the uninitiated. This is one area where effective liaison and inter-agency cooperation can make life so much easier.

The International Criminal Police Organization is an effective and useful medium through which inter-jurisdictional cooperation can be achieved, and the ICAC, through the Royal Hong Kong Police Interpol unit, makes regular use of this facility. But in terms of securing rapid, reliable assistance and feedback from foreign jurisdictions, there is, we have found, no substitute for the direct 'person-to-person' relationship, based on mutual trust. The ICAC has an entire Section of investigators dedicated to liaison, and it would not be an exaggeration to say that within the majority of leading national law enforcement agencies throughout the world (as well as in a good many less well-known ones), we have one or more personal contacts to whom we can turn for assistance at a moment's notice. It is important to emphasize here that there is nothing 'unofficial' about these otherwise special relationships. Indeed, whilst invariably informal on a personal basis, they are nevertheless no more than a reflection of the formal organizational policies upon which they are established.

Cooperation is often 'one-way', with one agency assisting another to achieve its individual goals, either directly in the field or by international communication, but there are occasions when two or more agencies share a common interest in a criminal enterprise which spans several jurisdictions. There have been numerous such instances in which the ICAC has joined together with overseas agencies in joint operations – sometimes with spectacularly successful results. More often than not, though, the value of liaison and cooperation lies in being able to achieve in minutes or hours what would otherwise have taken days, weeks or even months. Because the individual approached for assistance has detailed knowledge of his or her own jurisdiction and organization, it is usually possible to streamline the investigative process, not by circumventing the relevant law or procedures, but by addressing them in the most appropriate and effective manner.

Knowledge and information are valuable commodities indeed, and the key to acquiring them, in the law enforcement context, is liaison. In recognition of that fact, the ICAC periodically runs seminars in Hong Kong on corruption-related crime, at which delegates from interested agencies from around the Pacific Rim meet to exchange ideas and discuss strategies for optimizing effectiveness in international cooperation. At this year's seminar, in November, we intend to propose establishing in Hong Kong a central 'clearinghouse' for corruption-related information from all parts of the region. The facility, if agreed, would be staffed by a small secretariat of investigators responsible for receiving, processing and disseminating news and details of trends and developments on the corruption-related crime front.

We also recognize the value and potential of conferences and seminars, such as the Cambridge Symposium on Economic Crime, as a medium for sharing experiences, exploring new strategies and developing valuable contacts. Indeed, we have been represented at every session of the International Anti-Corruption Conference (IACC) since the event began, and in fact hosted the third such conference in Hong Kong in 1987. Last year we assisted in the organization of the Beijing conference and we are currently taking a consultative role in the preparations for next year's conference in Lima, Peru.

We, the Hong Kong ICAC, believe we have played a significant role in the fight against corruption, not only in Hong Kong, and not only, by our example, elsewhere in the world, but in a more practical sense also. As we have been aided by overseas agencies in our international pursuit of evidence, so we, too, have assisted them when their investigations led them into our jurisdiction. But there is fear, which has been expressed by some of these agencies, that this strategy of mutual assistance will be affected by Hong Kong's return to Chinese sovereignty. We hope and believe that it will not, for the reasons that follow.

BEYOND 1997 – BUSINESS AS USUAL

Business as usual – that is our message. The ICAC's continued existence in its present form is guaranteed beyond 1997 by Presidential Decree Number 26 of the People's Republic of China – the Basic Law – which also defines Hong Kong's status as a Special Administrative Region within the concept of 'one country – two systems'. The principal Articles of the Basic Law which are pertinent to the ICAC's future are:

– Article 8 – which gives continuing effect to existing Hong Kong law under the SAR government;
– Article 57 – which specifically states that there shall be a Commission Against Corruption which will be accountable to the SAR Chief Executive (who will replace the Governor), and that the Commission shall be independent – essentially the situation that exists today;
– Article 63 – which establishes a Department of Justice to 'control criminal prosecutions free from any interference';
– Article 80 and 81 – which preserve the Hong Kong judicial system, subject to the establishment of a special Hong Kong Court of Final Appeal to replace the British Privy Council as the ultimate appeal court; and
– Articles 100 and 101 – which permit foreign nations, including those currently employed by the Hong Kong government, to work for the SAR government; the exception being certain very senior posts, including that of the Commissioner of the ICAC, which must be occupied by Chinese citizens who permanently reside in Hong Kong and have no right of abode in any foreign country.

Our present commissioner is Chinese. Mr. Michael Leung Man-kin grew up in Hong Kong, speaking Cantonese as his first language. Among his staff there are numerous officers, both Chinese and expatriate, whose existing contracts take them well beyond 1997, and we envisage little, if any, change to our organizational structure as a result of the transition.

In law, the ICAC is independent, accountable at present only to the Governor, and from July 1997 to the Chief Executive, but we consider that our mandate comes essentially from the Hong Kong community, without whose support we would be unable to perform our task. We have that support now and believe that we shall continue to receive it in the future. And this is not mere speculation; our belief stems from the results of annual independent surveys commissioned by the ICAC's Community Relations Department. The most recent of these, conducted in 1995, produced, among other information, the following revelations:

- nearly 70 per cent of those surveyed considered that the work of the ICAC would become more important as 1997 approached. Less than eight per cent thought that it would be less so;
- 73 per cent considered the ICAC's anti-corruption work to be effective. Less than three per cent disagreed;
- over 97 per cent believe the ICAC should be supported in its endeavours. Only 0.8 per cent thought it should not.

But, surveys aside, the Hong Kong community confirms its faith in the ICAC in a more tangible way – by reporting corruption. In the three-year period between 1993 and 1995, nearly 9,000 people made reports of corruption to the Commission. Moreover, 70 per cent of them, by identifying themselves, demonstrated their confidence in the integrity of the ICAC and its ability to preserve their confidentiality, both now and in the future.

However, public support is not given recklessly. The Hong Kong community is only too aware that, although the ICAC's independence prevents unwarranted interference in its work, the organization is nevertheless accountable. It is accountable to the courts and to its independently-chaired overview committees, which not only monitor the Commission's work, but have the power to advise the Commissioner on a variety of issues and to draw to the attention of the Governor any matters they consider appropriate. Officers of the ICAC are individually accountable to the independent ICAC Complaints Committee, which deals with complaints of non-criminal misconduct and procedural abuse. And, in the event that allegations of a criminal nature are made against ICAC officers, they are liable to police investigation. But although community support is a vital factor in the ICAC's ability to tackle corruption in Hong Kong, it is by no means the only factor. Government support, the rule of law and the dedication and professionalism of our officers are also essential to the Commission's continued effectiveness.

Hong Kong continues to sustain a vibrant economy. Ranking as the world's eighth largest trading entity and fifth largest banking centre, in terms of external banking transactions, the territory has become firmly established as a major international financial centre. Over six million people call Hong Kong home, and commerce and tourism swell that number annually with a multinational transient population. That crime and corruption should exist within such a heady milieu of wealth and frenzied commercial activity is inevitable, but ease of modern-day travel and the ability to move vast amounts of money around the globe quickly and easily have internationalized these social evils. This phenomenon can only be effectively tacked by inter-jurisdictional cooperation; it is no longer enough to simply keep one's own house in order. International liaison and cooperation with other law enforcement agencies have proved to be most effective weapons in the ICAC's fight against corruption. We value highly the special relationships we have developed with those agencies over the years, and look forward to reinforcing them through future successes beyond Hong Kong's transition to Chinese sovereignty.

R.E. KENDALL

20. The Role of Interpol in Fighting Economic Crime and Corruption

CORRUPTION – A TRANSNATIONAL CRIME

The struggle against transnational organized crime by those who wish to uphold the law, has become one of the most topical issues in international fora, as is witnessed by numerous articles in the press, the agenda of corporate meetings and high profile political conferences. Economic and financial crime is described by these fora as typical examples of transnational organized crime. The increase in cross-border economic activities is directly proportional to the increase in transnational criminality. Whilst these criminals do not perceive the national boundaries as an obstruction to their activities, the adversaries in law enforcement usually find a whole array of obstacles, such as incompatible legislation and criminal procedures, and bank secrecy or confidentiality. It is within this arena that international cooperation in law enforcement aimed at reducing these obstacles becomes of the utmost significance. In a nutshell, what ICPO-Interpol focuses on is to constantly improve upon the international cooperation of law enforcement.

ICPO-INTERPOL

The General Secretariat of ICPO-Interpol is the permanent administrative and technical body through which Interpol speaks. It implements the decisions taken by the organization's deliberative organs, the General Assembly and the Executive Committee, as well as directing and coordinating various actions designed to combat international crime. The heart of the organization is its data base on crime and criminals, and its 'state of the art' communication network, through which all information is channelled either to or from any of its 176 member countries. Respect for our principles in day-to-day cooperation, such as respect for national sovereignty, obviously means that Interpol cannot have teams of detectives with supranational powers who travel around investigating cases in different countries. International police cooperation has to depend on coordinated

Barry A.K. Rider (ed.), Corruption: The Enemy Within, 327–331
© *Kluwer Law International. Printed in the Netherlands.*

action on the part of the member states' police forces, all of which may supply or request information or services on different occasions. To facilitate this exchange of information, each member state designates an office as an NCB (National Central Bureau). This, however, does not mean that Interpol cannot have contacts with other organizations. On the contrary, this possibility is expressly provided for in our constitution.

The Interpol General Secretariat provides the following services to its members:

- a criminal intelligence service, which assists members in identifying, arresting and prosecuting international criminals. The General Secretariat maintains its own criminal data base, which is reliant on the information provided by the member states. Crime analysis, conducted by the ACIU, is an integral part of the above service;
- a liaison function, which facilitates the exchange of information between member states. This occurs either by the numerous meetings/conferences which the IPSG hosts or attends, or through the efforts of its well-informed liaison officers, well-informed both in respect of their subject matter as well as the region they represent;
- a number of training courses, both at a regional and international level, designed to assist member states in improving their infrastructures regarding communication and criminal investigation; and
- a technical support service which has not only developed an independent and secure 'state of the art' telecommunications network, but is currently in the process of upgrading member states' systems, enabling them to send and receive information as quickly and securely as possible.

One of the sub-directorates at the General Secretariat has specifically been assigned to deal with economic and financial crime. The sub-directorate consists of three branches, each dealing with a distinct area of crime, such as economic crime in general, counterfeiting of currency and of travel or identity documents, and money laundering. The branch dealing with economic crime (general) has some interesting projects that merit notice.

Interpol, in taking the initiative to combat computer crime, has made significant international contributions, predominantly through the vehicle of the European Working Party on Computer Crime. Another project consists of the development of a universally-accepted standardized classification system for counterfeit payment cards. This initiative is supported by all the member countries as well as the relevant private sector entities. Once operational, it will be unique in its application as serving all international inquiries in this regard. Under the mantle of the economic crime branch (general), the General Secretariat covers an extensive 'range' of economic criminality, ranging from environmental crime to product counterfeiting, issues which no longer can be addressed by policing units alone. The fact that the crime situation varies from country to country further complicates this issue. It was, therefore, considered appropriate to adopt the following approaches, which now appear indispensable, in attempting to deal with international economic and financial criminals.

The first approach, termed appropriately the 'multi-agency approach', is based on the fundamental principle that he who engages in criminal activity should not also profit from it. The rationale being that, in an instance where a policing unit is, for whatever reason, incapable of bringing a criminal to book, the information should be shared with the tax, customs or banking regulations authorities. This process should also involve, where possible, the private sector, for example, financial institutions, telephone companies and credit bureaus, who have a great role to play in the campaign against crime in general. The greater this conspiracy against crime, the greater its or our success. This approach has already been put effectively to the test in the most recent form of organized criminality; the West African or Nigerian fraud. It is expected that exceptions in terms of the legal provisions relating to bank secrecy and tax confidentiality will have to be overcome. A further factor to be considered is the gradual harmonization and coordination of legislation, first on a regional basis, then eventually evolving into an international framework.

The second approach is a regional approach, which is calculated as being our response to the specific demands and needs of a region. While some of our members are concerned about the vulnerability of a cyber payment system, other members require an induction or assistance in basic computing. The General Secretariat is now diversifying its services according to the needs as dictated by a specific region. In certain regions, the experiences of others may now have the effect of a real proactive approach to law enforcement. In this context, a meeting on economic crime was recently held in Africa to identify the priorities of the region and to effect improved cooperation. This initiative was well received by the African member states and will be extended to Asia and Latin America in the near future.

Regionalization has already affected the area of computer crime; it was recently (at our 2nd International Conference on Computer Crime) agreed upon to create regional working parties, which would be represented internationally by their respective chairpersons through the vehicle of a steering committee. Other new initiatives include a proposed meeting relating to a free exchange of financial investigation techniques amongst law enforcement officers, development of a strategy to improve effectiveness in combatting fraudulent bankruptcies and a meeting on corruption, with the emphasis on practical law enforcement issues.

Money laundering has probably been the most prominent feature on the law enforcement agenda for the past decade. We share this concern on an issue which has led to the creation of 'underground or subverted' economies, which have developed so rapidly that they now pose a real threat to international trade or even to a country's economy as a whole. Our priority, as far as money laundering is concerned, is to consolidate the investigative infrastructure of member states, concentrating specifically on legislation. The

General Secretariat is therefore conducting detailed surveys of the economic environment in the former Eastern Bloc countries. The resulting reports on each country are distributed to the law enforcement agencies and will hopefully also serve to improve their own instruments in addressing this problem.

The General Secretariat received its mandate as the 'International Central Office for the Suppression of Counterfeit Currency' as early as 1929, when Article 15 of the Geneva Convention imposed this role on the predecessor of what is now the ICPO-Interpol General Secretariat. In essence, the role of the General Secretariat is to centralize, analyze and disseminate the currency counterfeiting information it receives from the various NCBs. It also compiles information to keep abreast of the developments in document printing and reproduction systems, which are utilized in the production of counterfeit currency. The General Secretariat also organizes and promotes international counterfeit currency conferences and meetings of experts involved in the combatting of these offences.

In recent years, we have seen a remarkable change in the publication of the incidences of corruption. This trend can no longer be apportioned to only specific countries, but seems to be of international application. A multitude of reasons exist for this phenomenon. However, a major spin-off has been a general increase in awareness (of corruption), especially within the private industry or corporate sector. Many companies have incorporated into their loss-control strategy corporate security departments, staffed by well-trained professionals. An important by-product of their work is the contribution in terms of additional sources of information made to the criminal intelligence. The flexibility and greater financial resources of the private sector also allow for exploring these resources, which would otherwise remain lost to law enforcement. In 1994, the oil industry provided the General Secretariat with the opportunity of taking forward the idea of cooperating with the private sector as far as corruption-related crimes were concerned. Five major oil companies formed a joint operation know as ICG (Information Coordination Group) to counter a form of contract corruption known as 'illegal information brokering'. It has been defined as 'the dishonest acquisition of confidential information, or the improper exertion of influence, by an agent (illegal information broker) on behalf, and to the benefit of, a principal (vendor, supplier, sub-contractor). Financial or other corruption inducements are made to produce the information or exert the required influence, thereby enabling the principal to enjoy a position of unfair advantage in seeking to gain an award of contract or other interest'.

This prompted the General Secretariat to circulate a survey on corruption-related crime to its member countries. The survey, apart from introducing the concept of 'illegal information brokering', sought to establish what obstacles law enforcement faced when dealing with corruption in its various forms, and to what extent an exchange of intelligence occurred, firstly among law enforcement units themselves and second, among law enforcement in general and in the private sector. The responses to the survey, thus far, have been extremely frank and encouraging. To this end, the General secretarial intends to host the 'First International Conference on Corruption-Related Crime' in September 1997. As most of the international initiatives regarding corruption have thus far dealt with academic aspects which are aimed at establishing an international legal framework within which a corruption investigation can be effected, the General Secretariat will restrict its efforts to the practical issues and techniques affecting the investigators of these offences. As an early analysis of the survey tends to suggest, the conference may seek to initiate new platforms for the exchange of intelligence regarding corruption-related crimes, both on a national and international level, within or as far as the existing legal frameworks will be able to accommodate such platforms.

Mention must be made of the fact that the efforts and successes of Interpol were highlighted when the senior expert group representing the G7 countries at the recent summit issued the Chairman's statement on combatting transnational organized crime efficiently, which has a direct bearing on Interpol or the work and projects in progress. Our aims may appear too ambitious; however, may I emphasize that although some of these may only be realized in the long term, we cannot reach our goal if we do not aim high.

In this regard, I would like to refer to an observation by Alain, in 'Propos': '*Le pessimisme est d'humeur; l'optimisme est de volonté*'. Concern alone will get us nowhere; we must have a certain will to succeed.

GERT VERMEULEN

21. The Fight Against International Corruption in the European Union

INTRODUCTION

Traditionally, the application of national criminal law is limited to the national territory. According to the territorial principle – which takes a central place in most jurisdictions – the active corruption of national officials or public officers,[1] provided it is committed on national territory, can give rise to prosecution, irrespective of the question whether the offender is a national or a foreigner. As for acts of passive corruption committed on national territory, the same principle applies: as a rule, prosecution of the corrupted national official will be possible by virtue of the national provisions concerning criminal proceedings and the determination of the competent court.

The situation is different where the corruption has an international dimension, either because the actual acts of passive or active corruption have taken place outside the national territory, or because it concerns corruption inside the national territory against a foreign official.

In principle, the active corruption of a national official by a foreign citizen outside the national territory will not be prosecuted, unless the national jurisdiction rules allow universal prosecution for corruption offences (universality principle) or at least provide for extra-territorial competence where – as in the case of corruption of national officials – the public function, and thus the state itself, is to be protected (protective principle). Often, the prosecution of the active corruption of a national official by a national citizen, committed outside the national territory, will only be possible on account of the nationality of the offender (passive personality principle), provided, moreover, that the double criminality rule is observed. Actually, the latter condition will only be met if the foreign jurisdiction rules allow universal prosecution for corruption offences. The prosecution of acts of passive corruption of a national official, committed outside the

---

[1] Corruption of non-officials is not dealt with in this paper. Under certain national laws, however, this form of corruption is a criminal offence as well. *See*, e.g., Article 328 of the Dutch Penal Code.

Barry A.K. Rider (ed.), Corruption: The Enemy Within, 333–342
© *Kluwer Law International. Printed in the Netherlands.*

national territory, meets the same problems. Perhaps a solution could here be found through an 'unlimited' application of the active personality principle, that is, without the double criminality rule having to be observed.[2]

Finally, the prosecution by the national competent authorities of corruption offences having been committed inside the national territory by foreign officials will be dependent on the existence of universal jurisdiction for such conduct.[3]

In short, the extent to which national jurisdiction rules provide for extraterritorial competence is decisive for the success of combatting international corruption.

Therefore, a harmonization of national jurisdiction policies throughout the world is to be recommended. Clearly, the best way to achieve this is through the conclusion of international treaties on a universal or regional scale.

During the past decades, several attempts were undertaken to reach an agreement on international rules relating to the fight against international corruption, for example, in the context of the EC, the Council of Europe and the United Nations.[4] At the time, none of them led to concrete results. In the context of Justice and Home Affairs (JHA) cooperation in the EU, the thread has been taken up. Actually, it looks as if two valuable instruments for combatting international corruption in the EU will be concluded at really short notice.

EUROPEAN UNION INITIATIVES

*Two Draft MultiLateral Anti-Corruption Instruments
on Active and Passive Corruption*

The question of international corruption of EC officials having been discussed in the EC from 1974, it looks as if, finally, the Member States are about to agree on the penalization of such conduct. Two draft multilateral anti-corruption instruments on active and passive corruption are to be adopted under Title VI TEU in the near or even very near future. Both of them are being drawn up on the basis of Article K.3.2(c) TEU, according to which the EU Council may draw up conventions which it will recom-

---

[2] As, e.g., in Article 6 Dutch Penal Code, pertaining to offences committed by officials in the exercise of their duties.

[3] As for the US, *see* in this respect the 1977 Foreign Corrupt Practices Act, making corruption by American citizens or businesses of foreign government agents, foreign political institutions, members of foreign parliaments or foreign election-candidates a punishable offence. About this issue, *see*, e.g., P.-H. Bolle, 'Pratiques de corruption et transactions commerciales internationales', *Revue Internationale de Droit Pénal* (1982), 345.

[4] *See*, e.g., P.-H. Bolle, *supra*, 346–365.

mend to the Member States for adoption in accordance with their respective constitutional requirements. This means that in principle the entry into force of both instruments, when approved by the Council, is dependent on adoption and ratification by all Member States. However, anticipated entry into force on a bilateral basis is sometimes possible: any Member State may then declare that the Convention shall apply to it in its relations with Member States that have made the same declaration.[5]

Draft Protocol to the Convention on the Protection of the European Community's Financial Interests

The first draft results from an initiative taken by the Spanish EU Presidency during the second half of 1995.[6] By 23 November 1995, at the occasion of the Brussels JHA Council,[7] a political agreement on the fundamental options could already be reached.

By its Act of 26 July 1995, the Council drew up, as a first agreement, the Convention on the protection of the EC's financial interests,[8] which is intended specifically to combat fraud that damages those interests. At a second stage, it has been considered necessary to supplement this Convention by a protocol directed in particular at acts of corruption that involve national and EC officials and damage, or are likely to damage, the EC's financial interests,[9] for those interests may particularly be damaged or threatened by acts of corruption by or against officials responsible for the collection, management or disbursement of Community funds under their control. Given that people of different nationalities employed by different public agencies or bodies may be involved in such corruption and that, in the interests of effective action against international corruption practices, it is important that the Member States' criminal laws perceive them in a similar way.

As was indicated above, most Member States' criminal laws on crime linked to the exercise of public duties in general and concerning corruption in particular, covers only acts committed by or against their national officials and do not cover, or cover only in exceptional cases, conduct involving EC officials or officials of other Member States. It was, therefore, considered opportune to extend jointly the range of the Member States' national laws to such conduct.

---

[5] *See*, e.g., Article 13 Draft Convention on the fight against corruption involving officials of the European Communities or officials of Member States of the European Union, doc.: 7751/96 JUSTPEN 75, 30 May 1996.

[6] Staten-Generaal (the Netherlands), 1995–1996, 23 490, nrs. 90 and 37, 4.

[7] Tweede Kamer (the Netherlands), 1995–1996, 23 490 nr. 41, 5.

[8] *Official Journal of the European Communities*, No C 316/49, 27 November 1995.

[9] Draft Protocol to the Convention on the protection of the European Community's financial interests, doc.: 8586/2/96 JUSTPEN 96, 7 August 1996.

According to the Draft, any 'Community' or 'national' official, including any national official of another Member State, is considered an 'official' for the purpose of the Protocol.[10] Those considered to be 'Community officials' are: all officials or other servants of the EC, all persons seconded to the EC by the Member States or by any public or private body who carry out functions equivalent to those performed by EC officials or other servants, as well as[11] – inasmuch as they are not regarded as EC officials or other servants – the members of bodies set up in accordance with the Treaties establishing the EC and the staff of such bodies.

As regards the term 'national official', reference is made to the definition of 'official' or 'public officer' in the national law of the concerned Member State.

Each Member State must take the necessary measures to ensure that passive or active corruption is made a criminal offence.[12] For the purposes of the Protocol, the deliberate action of an official who – directly or through an intermediary – requests or receives advantages of any kind whatsoever, for himself for a third party, or accepts a promise of such an advantage, to act or refrain from acting in accordance with his duty or in the exercise of his functions in breach of his official duties in a way which damages or is likely to damage the EC's financial interests, constitutes passive corruption. Whosoever deliberately promises or gives – directly or through an intermediary – an advantage of any kind whatsoever to an official for himself for a third party for him or to act or refrain from acting in accordance with his duty or in the exercise of his functions in breach of his official duties, is guilty of active corruption, provided the EC's financial interests are damaged or likely to be damaged.

Also participating in and instigating the conduct in question must be made punishable offences.[13]

Draft Convention on the Fight Against Corruption Involving Officials of the European Communities or Officials of Member States of the European Union
Apparently, the agreement on a Draft Protocol directed in particular at acts of corruption involving national or EC officials and damaging or likely to damage the EC's financial interests, is not considered an end. It has been

---

[10] Draft Protocol to the Convention on the protection of the European Community's financial interest, doc.: 8586/2/96 JUSTPEN 96, 7 August 1996.

[11] At its meeting on 21 June 1996, the Working Party on Criminal and Community Law agreed to this extension. On 28 June 1996 the K.4 Committee confirmed this agreement. It is expected that the same addition will be made to the Draft Convention on the fight against corruption involving EC officials or officials of the EU Member States. *See* doc.: 9042/96 JUSTPEN 103, 15 July 1996.

[12] Articles 2–3 Draft Protocol.

[13] Article 5 Draft Protocol.

further decided to step up and improve judicial cooperation in criminal matters in the fight against international corruption in the EU. At the beginning of 1996, the Italian Presidency of the EU introduced a Draft Convention[14] directed at acts of corruption involving EC officials or officials of the EU Member States in general.[15] Its concept and structure are identical to those of the Draft Protocol.

Except for the still outstanding question concerning the role of the Court of Justice of the EC regarding dispute settlement and preliminary rulings, a political consensus was achieved at the occasion of the Brussels JHA Council of 4 June 1996.[16]

The scope of the Draft Convention, no longer requiring that the acts of corruption are damaging or likely to damage the EC's financial interests, is actually very large. Simply any act of passive or active corruption by whomever against a Community or national official, including any national official of another Member State, is made a criminal offence.[17]

General Considerations

The Protocol and the Convention having been drafted according to the same plan; the main provisions of both instruments can easily be discussed jointly. Both drafts deal with, respectively, the following issues: corruption offences committed by or against members of the EC institutions, corruption on behalf of businesses, jurisdiction, international cooperation in criminal matters, *ne bis in idem*, dispute settlement and preliminary rulings.

Corruption Offences Committed by or Against Members of the EC Institutions

Each Member State undertakes to ensure that in its criminal law, the descriptions of corruption offences committed by or against its government ministers, elected members of its parliamentary chambers, the members of its highest courts or the members of its court of auditors in the exercise of their functions, apply similarly in cases where such offences are committed by or against members of the Commission of the EC, the European Parliament, the Court of Justice and the Court of Auditors of the EC in the exercise of their respective duties.[18]

---

[14] Draft Convention on the fight against corruption involving officials of the European Communities or officials of Member States of the European Union, doc.: 7751/96 JUSTPEN 75, 30 May 1996.

[15] Staten-Generaal (the Netherlands), 1995–1996, 23 490, nrs. 90e and 43, 4.

[16] Tweede Kamer (the Netherlands), 1995–1996, 23 490, nr. 51, 6.

[17] Articles 2–3 Draft Convention.

[18] Articles 4 Draft Protocol and Draft Convention.

Corruption on Behalf of Businesses

Regarding the question of corruption on behalf of businesses, the relevant provisions of the Convention of 26 July 1995 on the protection of the EC's financial interests have been copied. Each Member State shall take the necessary measures to allow heads of businesses and any persons having power to take decisions or exercise control within a business to be declared criminally liable in accordance with the principles defined by its national law in cases of corruption.[19]

Jurisdiction

As was already mentioned above, each Member State must take the necessary measures to ensure that any act of passive or active corruption by whomever against a Community or national official, including any national official of another Member State, is made a criminal offence. As for the Draft Protocol, this obligation only stands in as far as the EC's financial interests are damaged or likely to be damaged. In addition, it has been agreed that – in principle – each Member State shall undertake to establish its jurisdiction over corruption offences,[20] provided that either the offence is committed in whole or in part in its territory, or the offender is a national or one of its officials, or the offence is committed against a Community or a national official of its own or of another Member State or against a national, being at the same time a member of the Commission of the EC, the European Parliament, the Court of Justice or the Court of Auditors of the EC, or the offender is a Community official working for an EC institution or a body set up in accordance with the Treaties establishing the EC, which has its headquarters in the Member State concerned. In other words, only when – cumulatively – the offence is committed in whole outside its territory, the corrupted official is a national of another Member State or a member of one of the EC institutions without being one of its nationals and the corrupting person is neither a national, nor a Community official working for an EC institution or a body set up in accordance with the Treaties establishing the EC and having its headquarters in its territory, a Member State must not establish jurisdiction.

Except for offences having been committed in whole or in part on their respective territory, the Member States may, however, declare that they will not apply or only apply in specific cases or conditions one or more of the said jurisdiction rules.

---

[19] Article 7 Draft Protocol, referring to Article 3 Convention on the protection of the EC's financial interests; Article 6 Draft Convention.

[20] Article 6 Draft Protocol; Article 7 Draft Convention.

International Cooperation in Criminal Matters
Further, a Member State is not allowed to reject jurisdiction when one of its nationals is alleged to have committed a corruption offence outside its territory and provided it does not extradite its own nationals.[21] Next to this – in case of non-extradition of a requested person solely on the ground of his or her nationality – the Member State concerned must, if it is appropriate, submit the case to its competent authorities for the purpose of prosecution. The requesting Member State shall be informed of the prosecution initiated and of its outcome.

Given the obligation for each Member State to penalize corruption offences committed by or against Community officials or national officials of another Member State and to extend its jurisdiction to most of these offences, procedures in connection with international corruption offences will often concern at least two Member States. The case being that the Member States concerned must cooperate effectively in the investigation, the prosecution and in carrying out the punishment imposed, by means of, for example, mutual legal assistance, extradition, transfer of proceedings or enforcement of sentences passed in another Member State.[22]

With a view to enabling extradition in cases where a Member State has no jurisdiction or decides not to submit the case to its competent authorities for the purpose of prosecution, both draft instruments[23] call upon the Member States to take the necessary measures to ensure that – at least in serious cases – corruption offences are punished by penalties involving deprivation of liberty which can give rise to extradition, that is, exceeding the standard extraditional threshold.

If more than one Member State actually has jurisdiction over the same corruption offence, the Member States involved are urged to cooperate in deciding which of them shall prosecute the offender or offenders with a view to centralizing the prosecution in a single Member State where possible.[24]

Ne bis in idem
Clearly, the obligation for the Member States to extend their jurisdiction cannot be counterbalanced except by a strict application of the *ne bis in idem* rule. According to both drafts,[25] the Member States shall therefore

---

[21] Article 7 Draft Protocol, referring to Article 5 Convention on the protection of the EC's financial interests; Article 8 Draft Convention.

[22] Article 7 Draft Protocol, referring to Article 6 Convention on the protection of the EC's financial interests; Article 9 Draft Convention.

[23] Articles 5 Draft Protocol and Draft Convention.

[24] Article 7 Draft Protocol, referring to Article 6 Convention on the protection of the EC's financial interests; Article 9 Draft Convention.

[25] Article 7 Draft Protocol, referring to Article 7 Convention on the protection of the EC's financial interests; Article 10 Draft Convention.

apply the rule, under which a person whose trial has been finally disposed of in a Member State may not be prosecuted in another Member State in respect of the same facts, provided that if a penalty was imposed, it has been enforced, is actually in the process of being enforced or can no longer be enforced under the laws of the sentencing State.

Unfortunately, the rule may be put aside by a Member State in one or more of the following cases:[26] if the facts which were the subject of the judgment rendered abroad took place in its own territory,[27] if the facts constitute an offence directed against the security or other equally essential interests of that Member State or if they were committed by an official of that Member State contrary to the duties of his office. The recognition of these traditional exceptions must be criticized. The reintroduction of the principles of territoriality and nationality seem hardly compatible with the aforementioned appeal to establish Union-wide jurisdiction for most corruption offences involving officials of the EC or officials of EU Member States.

Unlike the Draft Protocol, the Draft Convention on the fight against corruption contains a clause relating to the situation where a Member State brings a further prosecution in respect of the same facts against a person whose trial has been finally disposed of in another Member State. Any period of deprivation of liberty served in the latter Member State arising from those facts must be deducted from any sanction imposed. Next to this, and to the extent permitted by national law, also sanctions not involving deprivation of liberty are to be taken into account in so far as they have been enforced. From the point of view of legal protection, it is positive to have this additional provision inserted in the Draft.

Dispute Settlement and Preliminary Rulings
The interpretation or application of both drafts, or at least some of their provisions, may give rise to disputes between Member States or between one or more Member States and the Commission of the EC.

As in the Convention on the protection of the EC's financial interests,[28] it has been proposed[29] that at an initial stage, disputes between Member States would be examined by the Council with a view to reaching a solution.[30] If no solution were found within six months, the matter might

[26] Except if – in respect of the same facts – the Member State concerned has requested the other Member State to bring the prosecution or has granted extradition of the person concerned.

[27] This exception would, however, not apply if those facts took place in the territory of the Member State where the judgment was rendered.

[28] Article 8.

[29] Article 8 Draft Protocol; Article 12 Draft Convention.

[30] In accordance with the procedure set out in Title VI TEU.

be referred to the Court of Justice of the EC by one of the Member States party to the dispute. Disputes between one or more Member States and the European Commission, which it has proved impossible to settle through negotiation, might be submitted to the Court as well.

As for the Draft Convention, initially both the French and United Kingdom delegations entered reservations. In their view, it would not be appropriate to provide for the Court to have jurisdiction in relation to the Convention, which – in their opinion – is not connected with the EU's first pillar like the Convention on the protection of the EC's financial interests. Later on – in a spirit of compromise – the French delegation changed its mind and could accept a competence for the Court.[31] The United Kingdom, however, has maintained its reservation.[32]

In the Draft Convention on the fight against corruption, it is also proposed to stipulate competence for the Court of Justice to deal with prejudicial questions on the interpretation of the Convention. Any judicial authority of a Member State might then request the Court to give a preliminary ruling on an issue raised in a proceeding pending before that authority, where it is of the opinion that a decision on this subject is necessary for it to render its judgment.

The Danish, Finnish, Irish and Swedish delegations have particular misgivings about this provision, and also the French delegation cannot accept it.[33]

Perhaps the idea to deal in the Protocol and the Convention itself with the questions concerning dispute settlement or preliminary rulings will need to be abandoned, as has also been the case for the Europol-Convention.[34]

As an alternative, one could think of an entirely optional system whereby the matter would be submitted to the Court only where the parties to the dispute agree and where the Commission is given no role other than the right to submit comments to the Court on disputes referred to it.[35] The drafting of a subsequent protocol to the Protocol and the Convention could be considered, both as regards dispute settlement and interpretation by way of preliminary rulings.[36]

---

[31] Doc.: 7751/96 JUSTPEN 75, 30 May 1996, 2, footnote 1.

[32] Doc.: 9042/96 JUSTPEN 103, 15 July 1996, 2.

[33] Doc.: 7751/96 JUSTPEN 75, 30 May 1996, 2; doc.: 9042/96 JUSTPEN 103, 15 July 1996, 2.

[34] *Official Journal of the European Communities*, No C 316/01, 27 November 1995. In contrast with earlier draft versions, and as a result of the repeated veto of the United Kingdom against a possible role of the Court of Justice with regard to dispute settlement, the present Article 40 of the Convention does not contain any provision about this.

[35] Doc.: 7391/96 JUSTPEN 69, 16, as referred to in doc.: 7751/96 JUSTPEN 75, 30 May 1996, 2, footnote 1.

[36] *See*, in this sense, a suggestion of the Italian delegation, doc.; 9042/96 JUSTPEN 103, 15 July 1996, 2–3.

CONCLUSION

The acceptance of European integration implies developing effective means in the Member States for combatting corruption in the EU context. At least it seems as if the Member States realize this.

According to the Draft Council Resolution for JHA cooperation for the period from 1 July 1996 to 30 June 1998,[37] which is about to be adopted, priority will be concentrated on – among other topics – the Draft Convention on corruption. It is, therefore, likely that a final agreement on the Draft Convention on the fight against corruption involving EC officials or officials of the EU Member States can be reached, under the Irish Presidency, before the end of the year, or at the latest under Dutch Presidency, at the beginning of 1997. It must be possible by that time to overcome the one question still outstanding, pertaining to possible jurisdiction for the Court of Justice.

Whether the Member States will be ready to ratify both the Draft Protocol to the Convention on the protection of the EC's financial interests and the more general Draft Convention on the fight against active and passive corruption within a reasonable period of time remains, however, unclear.

---

[37] Doc.: 9043/96 JAI 46, 18 July 1996.

PETER CSONKA

22. Corruption: The Council of Europe's Approach

INTRODUCTION – THE COUNCIL OF EUROPE

For those who are not familiar with the Council of Europe, it might be helpful to briefly introduce it: it was founded in 1949 as a European organization for intergovernmental and parliamentary cooperation. Its aim is to achieve a greater unity between its members for the purpose of safeguarding and realizing the ideals and principles which are their common heritage and facilitating their economic and social progress.[1] At present, the Council of Europe has 39 Member States.

Means of cooperation in the Council of Europe include discussion of questions of common concern in economic, social, cultural, scientific, legal and administrative matters and common action, notably through the conclusion of conventions and agreements. So far, more than 160 European instruments have been adopted under the auspices of the Council of Europe. These texts form a kind of *corpus juris* at the European level (published in the European Treaty Series) aiming at the harmonization of national law. They are binding for contracting parties, therefore governments have to sign and submit them to national Parliaments for ratification. Another type of legal document adopted by the Council of Europe is a recommendation addressed formally by the Committee of Ministers to Member States but having no binding legal effect. They represent, however, a common European consensus on a given matter and can be qualified as 'soft-law'. In certain cases, through their uniform application by Member States, they acquired quasi-binding effect as customary international law.

The most important achievements of the Council of Europe are in the area of the protection of human rights. The European Convention on Human Rights, through the jurisprudence of its control organs (the European Commission and the Court of Human Rights), gave rise to a very comprehensive case-law in respect of fundamental civil and political freedoms. Across Europe many important legislative reforms have been carried out in pursuit of the decisions delivered by the Convention's organs. Saturated by

---

[1] Article 1 of the Statute of the Council of Europe.

Barry A.K. Rider (ed.), Corruption: The Enemy Within, 343–353
© *Kluwer Law International. Printed in the Netherlands.*

the petitions, the current two-tier control mechanism of the Convention will soon undergo reforms to render it more efficient, particularly by reducing delays in court proceedings and providing remedies to its overburdening.

In the criminal law field, 20 conventions and more than 80 recommendations have been adopted, as well as a number of reports on various questions related to crime policy. Once signed and ratified by Member States, these conventions provide a multilateral framework of cooperation and replace several dozens of bilateral treaties between contracting parties. Their implementation is regularly controlled by expert committees which are responsible for identifying practical problems that might arise between parties and for interpreting and promoting the conventions. Amongst these conventions, the most well-known are probably the European Convention on Extradition (ETS No. 24) and the European Convention on Mutual Assistance in Criminal Matters (ETS No. 30). The most recent convention in the criminal law field is the Convention on Laundering, Search, Seizure and Confiscation of the Proceeds from Crime (ETS No. 141). Owing to its objective, the deprivation of criminals from their ill-gotten assets, and its innovative and comprehensive approach towards international cooperation, expanding from the first police investigations to trace and seize proceeds to enforcement of judicial orders of confiscation, this treaty is currently becoming one of the key international instruments in the fight against corruption.

CORRUPTION – THE PROBLEM

Corruption is contrary to everything that the Council of Europe stands for – democracy, human rights and the rule of law. Corruption may constitute a threat to the very existence of the state, if it deforms and decomposes its structure and organs and makes the citizens lose their trust in the credibility of the government. Corruption may create an uncontrollable political and social situation which can be easily exploited by antidemocratic forces. The problem is particularly acute in the newly emerging democracies, where the new values must find firm recognition and protection, and in any country in which corruption is widespread as to be met with forbearance by the people. Throughout Europe, however, the ever-increasing freedom of circulation of people and goods, a positive development in itself, increases also the risk of connections between organized crime and corruption. The response to the problem must therefore be international and a firm and joint action against corruption is required to maintain and strengthen democratic security in Europe.

At the 19th conference of the European Ministers of Justice in Malta in June 1994, which was at the origin of the work of the Council of Europe, the ministers dealt with the administrative, civil and penal law aspects of corruption.[2] At that Conference, the acting Secretary-General said: 'None of our countries is immune from the disease of corruption. This disease is spreading in countries which regard or regarded themselves as old and firmly established democracies; may of them are shaken by scandals. The disease is spreading in the new democracies and those countries of Central and Eastern Europe where democracy is still being built'. Does such a dark picture correspond to reality today in Europe?

Although corruption has always been present in the history of humanity, it might seem to the public at large, particularly when judging from press reports, that virtually all countries in the world, irrespective of their economic or political regime, are suffering from corruption more than ever before. This feeling is certainly reinforced by the overwhelming influence of the media, eager to attract, often in a sensational manner, the attention of an increasingly sensitive public, but factual evidence seems to support the view that corruption is spreading. The 'Mani Pulite' investigations in Italy, the 'Agusta' scandal in Belgium, Members of Parliament in the United Kingdom being accused of having accepted money for asking questions in Parliament, Spain being severely shaken by allegations involving large-scale corruption, well-known personalities of France's political and financial elite being brought to court for corruption and other white-collar offences, countries of Central and Eastern Europe saying that corruption represents the most serious threat to democratic reform and the privatization process, all these 'affairs' suddenly invading public life reveal something which is new: respectable politicians and influential businessmen no longer have immunity from public scrutiny (enhanced by the vigilance of the media) and are caught out by the criminal justice. One could make a long list of personalities having resigned, being prosecuted, convicted and even imprisoned in many countries. This list could include the names of Prime Ministers, ministers, mayors, Prosecutor-Generals, as well as of bankers and managers of large multinational companies, sometimes also performing as chairmen of football clubs. Their misbehaviour would include very diverse forms of 'corruption', a qualification which is supposed to cover everything that they have done dishonestly or fraudulently (and which did not expect to be treated as criminal).

'Corruption' in the above-mentioned examples is a term used, both by public opinion and the media, in different senses and with different meanings. Although no common definition has yet been found by the international community to describe corruption, everyone seems to agree that some political, social or commercial practices are corrupt. However, the qualification of certain practices as 'corrupt' and their eventual moral reprobation by the public opinion vary from country to country and do not necessarily

---

[2] *See* document GMC (95) 9, *Conclusions and Resolutions of the 19th Conference of European Ministers of Justice,* Valleta, Malta, 14–15 June 1994, Report by the Secretary-General of the Council of Europe.

imply that they are criminal offences under domestic criminal law. They may well be accepted or tolerated behaviour in certain parts of society, while in others they may be rejected, at least officially. Corruption is therefore primarily a moral issue and as such does not need a precise definition. But when the reprobation of society towards certain practices reaches the threshold beyond which the only possible repression is that by criminal law, the fundamental principles of criminal law require accurate description of the punishable behaviour. So far, it has not been possible for the international community to agree to a common definition of corruption. The examples referred to above include different qualifications under the criminal law of the countries concerned, such as bribery, the hard-core corruption offence, misuse of public funds, breach of trust, illegal taking of interest or *ingérence* and illicit funding of political parties.

CORRUPTION – A VARIETY OF APPROACHES

Notwithstanding the apparent spread of the phenomenon of corruption (or perhaps because of it), it seems difficult to arrive at a common definition, inasmuch as it has been held that 'no definition of corruption will be equally accepted in every nation'.[3] The definition has been discussed for a number of years in different fora and one single, commonly-accepted definition which would apply to all forms, types and degrees of corruption could not be found. The main reason is that the definition of corruption is closely connected with national or local cultures and habits, whereby various practices have at times and in certain circumstances been considered as manifestations of corruption, while those very same practices have at other times and in different circumstances been considered as licit if not also laudable.

Thee are, of course, very precise legal definitions in the Criminal Codes of what constitutes corruption, but one must consider first that those definitions are not harmonized in Europe and, second, that many people do not use the word 'corruption' in the strict, narrow sense of the criminal law. Moreover, in several – perhaps most – of the Criminal Codes of Europe, the word 'corruption' is not even mentioned. Instead, the Codes use a functional approach, that is, to define separate offences such as bribery, trafficking in influence or purchase of votes. The word 'corruption' is often used as a generic term to describe several of those offences in commentaries to the Criminal Codes or textbooks written by academics.

In view of the difficulty in finding agreement on a common definition, various international fora have preferred to concentrate on the definition of

---

[3] V.J. Gardiner, 'Defining Corruption' in *Coping with Corruption in a Borderless World*, proceedings of the conference held in Amsterdam in 1992, published by Kluwer, 33.

'illicit payment'[4] rather than on the wider notion of corruption, which embraces the former, but does not exclusively consist of this. There is no general agreement – with the exception of civil servants – on the question of who is liable to receive bribes in the passive corruption offence. As to persons other than civil servants, there is for the time being no stance on the question of extension of criminal law protection and responsibility. Does the law encompass elected representatives (also persons elected to international bodies, such as the European Parliament)? Should there be a difference between the local and national level? Should different rules apply to elected representatives and ministers? Are persons who, although not civil servants, perform functions which are of a public nature, included? Should bribery between totally private entities be included? Can lawyers or other members of the legal profession, such as notaries, be bribed, at least to the extent they may be said to perform public functions? In fact, the difficulty lies often in the definition of who is to be considered a 'public official'.

A study recently carried out by the Council of Europe[5] shows that if the bribery of a domestic public official, both in its active and passive form, that is, giving and taking bribes in public life, seems to be criminalized in all European countries, nonetheless great differences seem to subsist in the definition of the categories of persons within the public sector who may become perpetrators of the offence or, in the case of passive corruption, may become the target of the offence. There are also important variations concerning the bribery involving persons outside the public sector: some

---

[4] The Draft United Nations Convention contained the following provisions in Article 1:

'Each Contracting State undertakes to make the following acts punishable by appropriate criminal penalties under its national law:

(a)   The offering, promising or giving of any payment, gift or other advantage by any natural person, on his own behalf or on behalf of any enterprise or any person whether juridical or natural, to or for the benefit of a public official as undue consideration for performing or refraining from the performance of his duties in connection with an international commercial transaction.

(b)   The soliciting, demanding, accepting or receiving, directly or indirectly, by a public official of any payment, gift or other advantage, as undue consideration for performing or refraining from the performance of his duties in connection with an international commercial transaction.'

The Council of the OECD in the Recommendations on Bribery in International Business Transactions, on 27 May 1994, adopted the following definitions for the purposes of the Recommendation: 'bribery can involve the direct or indirect offer or provision of any undue pecuniary or other advantage to or for a foreign public official, in violation of the official's legal duties, in order to obtain or retain business.'

The Recommendation contains a footnote which states that '[t]he notion of bribery in some countries also includes advantages to or for members of a law-making body, candidates for a law-making body or public office and officials of political parties'. It should be noted that the provisions of the draft Convention and Recommendation are restricted to international commercial/business transactions.

[5] *See* document GMC (96) 28, Summary of the replies to the questionnaire on corruption.

countries also punish active and passive corruption committed in this sector, whereas this is unknown in several countries.[6]

When comparing national legislations in Europe concerning the hard-core corruption offence, active and passive bribery, it emerges that the two types of corruption are basically two sides of the same coin, one perpetrator offering or promising the advantage and the other perpetrator accepting the offer or the promise. Usually, however, it seems that the two perpetrators are not punished for complicity in the other one's offence. A relatively common feature of the offence in many countries is that it is usually already punishable at the stage of attempt – not only is it punishable to give or to accept an advantage (usually of an economic nature) but the offer or the promise or the acceptance is also punishable as a main offence. In practice, the difference is not so great, since the attempt is usually punished as severely as a main offence.

The advantages which are given are usually of an economic nature but may also be of a non-material nature, in accordance with the legislation and practice of the legislation of several countries. What is important is that the offender (or any other person, for instance, a relative) is placed in a better position than he was before the commission of the offence and that he is not entitled to the benefit. Such advantages may consist in, for instance, loans, food and drink (at least if it is of greater value), a case handled within a swifter time, better career prospects, etc. The act of corruption may be a positive one or may also consist in the omission of acting.

---

[6] The answers to the questionnaire suggest that the differences are much greater within the private sector than in the public sector. The bribery of an employee of a private domestic company is not contrary to criminal law at least of the following countries: Albania, Cyprus, Luxembourg, Malta, Poland, San Marino, Spain. In general, the criminalization of bribery of an employee of a private company requires additional conditions; for instance, in the Czech Republic bribery is a criminal offence only if it is related to a public interest matter, whereas in Liechtenstein only bribery of managerial employees is criminalized. In Norway, the criminalization is based on the notion of 'breach of trust'; in Bulgaria, only bribery of state employees is punishable.

Bribery of a foreign official is not (or not as such) contrary to criminal law in a majority of the replying countries (Albania, Cyprus, Finland, France, Liechtenstein, Luxembourg, Malta, Norway, Poland, Portugal, San Marino, Spain). Bribery of a foreign official is contrary to criminal law in the following countries: Austria, Bulgaria, Canada, the Czech Republic, Estonia, Slovakia, Slovenia, Sweden, the United Kingdom. Even though in many countries there is no specific offence of bribery of foreign officials, it may still be a criminal offence, e.g., under competition law (Austria) or if the conspiracy to bribe a foreign public official takes place in the country (Canada). Bribery of a foreign private company is not (or not yet or not as such) contrary to criminal law in the following countries: Albania, Cyprus, France, Japan, Luxembourg, Malta, Poland, Spain, the United Kingdom. In a majority of the replying countries, bribery of a foreign private company is contrary to criminal law (Austria, Bulgaria, Canada, the Czech Republic, Estonia, Finland, Liechtenstein, Norway, San Marino, Slovakia, Slovenia, Sweden).

The Criminal Codes of the Member States of the Council of Europe make some differences, usually in the degree of the offence (misdemeanour or felony), depending on who took the initiative of committing the offence. A distinction is also made depending on whether the act which is solicited is a part of the official's duty or whether he is going beyond his duties. For instance, corruption may be punishable if an official receives a benefit in return for dealing with a case more quickly, but could in such a case be limited to a misdemeanour, since it was still his duty to handle the case. If he should not have handled the case at all, for instance a licence should not have been given, the official would be liable to having committed a felony which would carry a heavier penalty. Several countries extend the scope of application to all public officials on the basis of the need to ensure fairness in the public service and the requirements of upholding confidence therein, whereas some countries limit it to certain categories of officials, for instance, elected officers such as judges, members of parliament, prosecutors, etc.

Some important considerations must therefore be taken into account when seeking the best approach to define corruption. If a wide definition is chosen, a number of offences which are not traditionally connected with a hard-core definition of corruption will be included in the definition. Such examples may include, for instance, fraud and offences connected with bankruptcy. If, on the other had, a too narrow definition is adopted, several offences which seem to belong to the hard core of corruption may be left out, for instance the offence of demanding an advantage in return for non-publication in the public press. One may even argue that it is questionable whether a definition is at all necessary. It could indeed be counterproductive to spend time in agreeing on a general definition when, in reality, it is more practical to adopt a functional approach. The discussion is well-known from other similar areas of international criminal law, where it has proved nearly impossible to arrive at common definitions in the matters of computer crime,[7] economic crime[8] or environmental crime.[9] A significant exception in this respect has been the definition of what constitutes a money laundering offence in several international instruments,[10] although it has been (rightly) contested that the 'laundering' definition is a 'real' definition

---

[7] *See* Recommendation No. R (89) 9 of the Committee of Ministers of the Council of Europe on Computer-Related Crime.

[8] *See* Recommendation No. R (81) 12 of the Committee of Ministers of the Council of Europe on Economic Crime.

[9] *See* Draft Convention on the Protection of the Environment through Criminal Law, declassified version, Directorate of Legal Affairs, Council of Europe, Strasbourg, June 1995.

[10] *See* the 1988 UN Convention against Illicit Trafficking in Narcotic Drugs, Article 3, and the 1990 Council of Europe Convention on Laundering, Search, Seizure and Confiscation of the Proceeds from Crime, Article 6.

because, as every definition provided by an international treaty, it would need adaptation when transformed into national criminal law.

It is equally important to keep in mind that corruption is not only a matter of criminal law. On the contrary, the corruption offence in itself is closely interlinked with civil and administrative law and must be seen in a wider context. The public official who is corrupt may be liable to administrative or labour law sanctions. Similarly, the company which seeks to gain advantage within the framework of public procurement may be liable to administrative or civil sanctions, for instance invalidation of the offer or the contract or punitive (exemplary) or treble damages. There is a close link between the laws on unfair competition and corruption, in that some countries have criminalized acts committed in this area, for instance, incitement to break contracts with a view to getting the contract for oneself, breaches of confidence or offences aiming at unlawful disclosure of trade secrecy. It is, therefore, not advisable to deal with the issue of corruption in the narrow context of criminal law but the matter must be dealt with more comprehensively, as the Council of Europe Draft Programme of Action against Corruption aims to do.

THE MANY FACETS OF CORRUPTION

Corruption is like a prism with many surfaces. It can be viewed from different angles, for example from the perspective of criminal law, civil law or organizational theory; or it can be seen as a social issue. If corruption is viewed too narrowly, only one side of the prism may be revealed, for example, corruption as criminal behaviour. Awareness of this problem sometimes also results in an unduly broad definition of the concept, as where a number of general offences committed by people in the course of their employment come to be treated as corruption, for example theft, embezzlement, fraud and other acts which prejudice the employer. This is incorrect. In essence, corruption is not about putting one's fingers in the till but about the abuse of power, or more accurately, improbity in the decision-making process. This definition can be refined still further, but it is in effect the lowest common denominator.

Corruption should not necessarily be equated with criminal corruption. Of course, corruption has always been a close companion of crime. This explains to a large extent the multiple forms it takes and the varied terminology used to describe it: bribery, graft, gift-taking, kick-backs, sharp business practices and so on. Likewise, both corruption and criminal corruption are expressions of the same attitude to morals, ethical principles and public function.

When one bribes a public officer, the primary concern of the law is not the corruption of the integrity of that officer, but the corruption of the system of proper government and proper administration. Indeed, the law in many countries views differently the situation of a self-employed tradesman being promised a heavy tip for doing a job well, and the analogous situation of the same tradesman employed with a public department who does the job well, after being promised the same substantial tip to perform so. In the latter case, such a payment would not be called 'a tip' but 'a bribe'. What the law considers in both cases is not the liberality of the giver or the enrichment or otherwise of the tradesman, but the fact that a tradesman employed by a public department should do a job well without the necessity of being offered extra remuneration by any person. The offering of bribes in such cases is deemed in itself a sufficient threat to the system, and consequently has been proscribed as the crime of corruption of a public officer.

The concept of corruption is therefore wider than that of criminal corruption. This differentiation is important for the simple reason that no comprehensive and all-embracing strategy in the fight against corruption can ever be formulated, if one were to limit such measures to criminal corruption alone. Putting it differently, a corrupt practice or system might not as yet be considered by law an offence, but such an omission would not render it less corrupt in its character. It would only mean that under the obtaining law or under a given system, no court action may as yet be taken to suppress it – it is not considered to be a crime and, of course, no punishment can ever be meted out.

Many judicial investigations initiated in recent years inside and outside Europe have revealed not only the extent of corruption but also the unsuitability of certain concepts of substantive criminal law (definition of an illicit advantage; definition of an official; taking account of intervention by third parties, particularly political groups; difficulties due to the distinction between passive corruption, active corruption and extortion; applicability of legislation prohibiting unfair competition; legal definition of periodic payments to political parties which are not connected to specific advantages for the company making the payments, etc.) and of certain mechanisms inherent in criminal procedure (rewards for denunciation; cooperation by accused persons with the judiciary, particularly those who return or permit the return of sums of money received illicitly; restrictions aimed at curtailing improper recourse to parliamentary immunity, etc.).

The Provisional Definition Adopted by the Council of Europe

The Council of Europe's Multidisciplinary Group on Corruption (GMC) adopted, for its part, the following provisional definition:

> Corruption as dealt with by the Council of Europe's GMC is bribery and any other behaviour in relation to persons entrusted with responsibilities in the public or private sector, which violates their duties that follow from

their status as a public official, private employee, independent agent or other relationship of that kind and is aimed at obtaining undue advantages of any kind for themselves or for others.

The purpose of this definition was to ensure that no matter would be excluded from the work of the Committee in the future. Obviously, such a definition will not necessarily match the legal definition offered in most of the member countries, in particular not the definition given by the criminal law, but it has the advantage of not prejudiciously restricting the discussion within excessively narrow confines.

However, the GMC realized, as its work progressed, that this definition was too wide for the purpose of discussing certain subjects. Within the context of drafting a convention or a recommendation, addressed to governments, the definition must necessarily be more precise and in the field of criminal law, it should even be narrower. Where prevention is discussed, a wider definition could be considered. The definition also is of importance to administrative law, for instance, in the context of drafting codes of conduct for public officials and to the civil law, for instance, in order to distinguish corruption from unfair competition. The GMC therefore requested its three working groups (criminal, administrative and civil) to keep under review the question of definition within their discussions, with a view to arriving at common solutions. To this end, the criminal working group drafted the 'Tentative List of Corruption Offences' found in the Appendix to the Draft Programme of Action against Corruption, thus adopting, for the moment, a functional approach instead of seeking to define corruption in generic terms.

As foreseen by the draft programme of action, the GMC has been and will keep considering, *inter alia*, two draft conventions on corruptions as from the beginning of 1996: a draft framework convention aiming to lay down the underlying principles of the whole Council of Europe action against bribery, including criminalization of corruption, denial of tax deductibility of bribes, corporate liability and a mechanism enabling the monitoring of the performance of future parties to the convention. This text seeks to provide a general basis for international action against corruption through political and legal commitments of the parties concerning the main principles referred to, thus ensuring that a dynamic move is created towards supplementary instruments. The question whether or not to elaborate a common definition has not yet been decided on. The current draft, which does not contain any definition of corruption but a list of corruption offences, which could be considered by the future parties as 'corrupt practices', is under discussion.

The other document examined by the GMC is a 'classical' criminal law convention, which may become a protocol to the framework convention but it may also remain a separate treaty. Drafting work is being carried out simultaneously on both instruments and the relationship between them shall be decided later.

The draft criminal law convention contains a list of offences, including – in the narrow sense – corruption (active, passive, domestic, foreign, private and public), trading in influence, money laundering of proceeds deriving from offences included in the convention, accounting offences and participatory acts. The natural persons who are concerned in the corruption offence are not only public officials but also private employees, international civil servants, and elected representatives of international bodies, as well as judges and officials of international courts. Not only natural persons but also corporations are concerned: the active and passive corruption of enterprises and associations, both domestic and foreign, is also foreseen by the draft.

CONCLUSIONS

Instead of drawing conclusions, it appears more suitable to draw attention to those factors which contribute, in a way, to generating corruption and which therefore must be addressed by governments sincerely willing to curb corruption. The main contributing factors of corruption seem to be in many cases the concentration of power, wealth and status, antidemocratic or autocratic regimes, a cumbersome bureaucracy, excessive administrative controls and trade restrictions, monopolies, patronage, governmental concessions for economic industrial and infrastructural development, a poorly organized and underpaid civil service, a weak judicial set-up and, as an overriding general ingredient, a materialistic concept of success where power, money, status and ostentation play a leading, if not primary, role. Unless effective remedies to fight and eradicate corruption are such as to encompass it in all its forms – and not just the criminal aspect – the undertaking may well be inadequate. The comprehensive programme of action elaborated by the Council of Europe seeks to promote this difficult undertaking.

Index